Towards a Comprehensive Therapy for Schizophrenia

Hans D. Brenner
Wolfgang Böker
Ruth Genner
(Editors)

Towards a Comprehensive Therapy for Schizophrenia

Hogrefe & Huber Publishers
Seattle · Toronto · Bern · Göttingen

Library of Congress Cataloging-in-Publication Data

is available via the Library of Congress Marc Database under the
LC Catalog Card Number 96-77690

Canadian Cataloguing in Publication Data

Main entry under title:
Towards a comprehensive therapy for schizophrenia
Translation of: Integrative Therapie der Schizophrenie. Papers presented at the IVth
International Schizophrenia Symposium held in Bern, Switzerland, Sept. 16–18, 1993.
Includes index.
ISBN 0-88937-175-X

1. Schizophrenia – Treatment – Congresses. I. Brenner, Hans D. 1943– . II. Böker, Wolfgang,
1933– . III. Genner, Ruth, 1951– . IV. International Schizophrenia Symposium
(4th : 1993 : Bern, Switzerland).
RC514.I5913   1996   616.89'8206   C96-931627-5

Cover illustration "Der Gross=Gott=Vater=Huth mit Skt. Adolf=Kuss, Riesen=Fonttaine" by
Adolf Wölfli (1864–1930) © Adolf-Wölfli-Stiftung, Art Museum, Bern, Switzerland

© Copyright 1997 by Hogrefe & Huber Publishers

USA: P.O. Box 2487, Kirkland, WA 98083-2487
                        Phone (206) 820-1500, Fax (206) 823-8324
CANADA: 12 Bruce Park Avenue, Toronto, Ontario M4P 2S3
                        Phone (416) 482-6339
SWITZERLAND: Länggass-Strasse 76, CH-3000 Bern 9
                        Phone (031) 300-4500, Fax (031) 300-4590
GERMANY: Rohnsweg 25, D-37085 Göttingen
                        Phone (0551) 49609-0, Fax (0551) 49609-88

Printed in Germany
ISBN 0-88937-175-X
Hogrefe & Huber Publishers, Seattle · Toronto · Bern · Göttingen

Contents

Hans D. Brenner and Wolfgang Böker
Preface IX

H. Freeman
Professor Wolfgang Böker, aet. 60 XI

List of Contributors XIII

Introduction: Unfolding of the Area

W. Böker and H.D. Brenner
Systemic Concepts of Schizophrenia and Their Implications for
Therapy Research 3

L. Ciompi
Non-Linear Dynamics of Complex Systems: The Chaos-Theoretical
Approach to Schizophrenia 18

W. Tschacher, C. Scheier and E. Aebi
Non-Linearity and Chaos in the Course of Psychoses –
An Empirically Based Classification of Dynamics 32

Focus on Influencing Biological Vulnerability

R.L. Borison and B.I. Diamond
Beyond the Dopamine Receptor: Clinical and Research Experience
with Risperidone 51

H.-J. Möller, T. Mager and H. Müller
Can the Negative Symptoms of Schizophrenia Be Influenced by
Neuroleptics? 63

Focus on Influencing Cognitive Vulnerability

M.F. Green, S. Hellman and R.S. Kern
Feasibility Studies of Cognitive Remediation in Schizophrenia:
Grasping the Little Picture 79

C. Perris
Schema-Focused Integrative Treatment of Patients with
Schizophrenic Disorder 94

W. Spaulding, D. Reed, D. Elting, M. Sullivan and D. Penn
Cognitive Changes in the Course of Rehabilitation 106

B. Hodel and H.D. Brenner
A New Development in Integrated Psychological Therapy
for Schizophrenic Patients (IPT): First Results of Emotional
Management Training 118

Focus on Weakening Stressors and/or Strengthening Protectors and Promoting Social Network and Social Support

A.S. Bellack
Social Skills Deficits and Social Skills Training: New Developments
and Trends 137

M.J. Goldstein, I. Rosenfarb, S.M. Woo and K.H. Nuechterlein
Transactional Processes which Can Function as Risk or Protective
Factors in the Family Treatment of Schizophrenia 147

H. Stierlin
Experiences with the Systemic Therapy of Psychoses 158

*M.A. Test, W.H. Knoedler, D.J. Allness, S. Senn Burke, S. Kameshima
and L. Rounds*
Comprehensive Community Care of Persons with Schizophrenia
Through the Programme of Assertive Community Treatment
(PACT) 167

D. Hell
The Implementation of Family Work in Everyday Practice 181

Focus on the Concept of Illness and on Coping Aimed at Episode Prevention

W. Gaebel
Early Pharmacotherapeutic Intervention in Relapse Prevention:
Fundamentals, Indication and Management 195

K.H. Wiedl
Coping-Orientated Therapy with Schizophrenic Patients:
General Guidelines, Starting Points and Issues of Evaluation 209

A. Schaub, K. Andres, H.D. Brenner and G. Donzel
Developing a Group Format Coping-Orientated Treatment
Programme for Schizophrenic Patients 228

J.S. Strauss
Processes of Healing and the Nature of Schizophrenia 252

G.J. Sarwer-Foner
The Humanity of the Schizophrenic Patient 262

Author Index 273
Subject Index 278

Preface

The search for more effective methods of influencing the acute symptoms, course and outcome of schizophrenia is as pressing a task as ever both for research and for clinical practice. Yet, although effective treatment is necessarily comprehensive and multidisciplinary, it involves more than merely combining various modes of intervention. Instead, it entails fine-tuning the kind, timing, intensity and duration of the interventions adopted based on clinical experience and on a sound underlying theoretical model of the disorder, and coordinating them in a carefully planned manner. In addition, it means determining the methods that are most effective for treating different symptoms and different patients.

In our opinion, the enormous advances which have recently been made in research on schizophrenia, especially in the areas of neurobiology and neuropsychology, provide a basis for designing efficacious treatment strategies. Most current theoretical models of schizophrenia seek to explain the aetiopathogenesis of this disorder in terms of genetic-environmental interaction. The individual's perceptual and cognitive (i. e., operations of information processing) dysfunctions, which correspond to genetically determined and environmentally acquired changes in the brain, interact with adverse environmental factors, transforming biological deviations into symptoms of schizophrenia. Schizophrenia is thus conceived as a pathogenetic process based on interacting biological and cognitive vulnerability factors, which reinforce each other's effects.

This understanding of schizophrenia provides a plausible starting point for therapeutic action. Neuroleptic medication aims at restabilising abnormal arousal in the brain and neurobiological regulatory systems. Cognitive training programmes serve to reduce or compensate for information-processing disturbances typical of schizophrenia. Social skills and problem-solving training is used to strengthen protective factors, e. g., social competence. Family work and family therapy focuses on reducing or alleviating the effects of stressors, and establishing or enhancing social support provided so as to, e. g., reduce high expressed emotion. Lastly, newer therapy approaches are directed at improving patient's coping competence by strengthening their ability to cope with psychosocial stressors and with illness-related strains, and by learning to recognise warning signs of relapse by using early intervention strategies.

We need to know more about the interactions between these various therapy approaches so as to be able to integrate them into optimal therapeutic action and to ultimately achieve a generally accepted standard of treatment. The IVth International Schizophrenia Symposium that took place at our Clinic in Bern from September 16–18, 1993 – "Towards a Comprehensive Therapy of Schizophrenia" – was expressly devoted to this purpose. The present book is a continuation of the reports on the 1985, 1987 and 1990 Bern Symposia. It contains the written versions of the papers presented at the 1993 Symposium.

We would thank all the authors for their contributions and for their great co-operation in writing their articles according to our suggestions and special requests. The German edition of this volume will be published by Hans Huber Publishers in Bern.

We express our special thanks to Frances Stirnemann-Lewis and Ruth Genner who took on the task of reading through and compiling the manuscripts with great care and circumspection. We are also deeply indebted to Professor Hugh Freeman for his guidance and advice, and for his final editing of all the contributions. We would also like to thank Christine Haas for her great commitment and patience in the extensive and labourious paperwork. Our thanks thus go to all those who have helped us in making this book come true.

We hope that the present Symposium volume will be just as widely read as the previous ones, and that it will help dispel the unfortunate myth that both those who work with individuals suffering from schizophrenia and the afflicted themselves are helpless in the face of the disorder. The Bernese teams which have to date been committed to conducting research on the treatment of schizophrenia will continue to be so in future.

Bern, Autumn 1995   Hans D. Brenner and Wolfgang Böker

Professor Wolfgang Böker, aet. 60

The publication of papers from the IVth International Symposium on Schizophrenia, Bern is a very appropriate occasion to commemorate the 60th birthday of Professor Wolfgang Böker. Together with Professor Hans Brenner, he was the originator of this important series of meetings, which have resulted in a unique sequence of monographs, containing contributions by many leading workers in this field. The Symposia have been highly successful, not only in the quality of their scientific presentations, but also in the opportunities they have provided for creative interactions between colleagues from several disciplines and many countries. All this has occurred in the impressive surroundings of the University of Bern Psychiatric Hospital, on the edge of a beautiful and historic city. They cannot fail to have been memorable occasions for everyone who has had the privilege of being able to attend. The bilingual arrangements of the Symposia have also been valuable in promoting communication between the anglophone and German-speaking psychiatric scientific communities.

Professor Böker was born in Jena – a city with an important academic tradition – and received his medical training at the University of Freiburg, receiving his Doctorate in 1960. During the next eight years, his postgraduate training was at the University of Freiburg, Bern, Zürich, and Heidelberg. In 1967, he had a Visiting Fellowship at Yale University, beginning a long and fruitful connection with the Department of Psychiatry there. In 1968, he became Oberarzt at the Social Psychiatric Clinic in Mannheim, and in the following year, Chief of the Psychiatric Outpatient Clinic. He was awarded Habilitation in Clinical Psychiatry by the University of Heidelberg in 1972 and two years later, the titles of Wissenschaftlicher Rat and Extraordinarius. Between 1975 and 1978, he was Vice-Director of University Psychiatric Clinic at the Central Institute for Mental Health, Mannheim, associated with the University of Heidelberg.

In 1978, Professor Böker returned to Bern, to the posts of Professor of Clinical Psychiatry and Director of the University Psychiatric Hospital. In 1972, he was honoured with the Hermann-Simon Prize (jointly with Professor Häfner) for work in social psychiatry on mentally disturbed violent offenders. He was Visiting Professor at the University of Washington, Seattle in 1987 and at the University of Gifu, Japan in 1992. His career therefore represents the importance of international and cross-cultural experience in psychiatry.

Professor Böker and his wife, Brigitte were married in 1966; they have a daughter and two sons. Frau Böker is well-known to those who have attended the Bern Symposia for her gracious hospitality and efficient organisation of the social events, which are always of outstanding quality.

Professor Böker's recent scientific work, in close association with Professor Brenner and other colleagues, has been primarily directed to investigating the cognitive aspects of schizophrenia and exploring self-healing attempts and other therapeutic approaches to these disturbances. Aspects of this pioneering work can be read in the four publications that have been based on the Symposia. Cognitive disorder represents one of the more difficult approaches to the management of schizophrenia, and the contribution to it already made by the Bern group has been outstanding. There is still much to be discovered, but the work accomplished at Bern represents the foundation of further progress that will undoubtedly come in subsequent years. This may eventually be a source of great hope and satisfaction to people who suffer from this terrible affliction.

Everyone who has had the privilege of participating in the Bern Symposia will join in greeting Professor Böker at his significant point in his career, and will wish him well for the years to come. The papers in this book are evidence of the contribution he has already made, both in his own scientific work and bringing together colleagues from many countries to share their ideas and experience.

Hugh Freeman

Contributors

E. AEBI, lic. phil., *Sozialpsychiatrische Universitätsklinik Bern, Laupenstrasse 49, CH-3010 Bern, Switzerland*

D. J. ALLNESS, MSSW, *Lecturer and Consultant, School of Social Work, University of Wisconsin, 1350 University Avenue, Madison, WI 53706, USA*

K. ANDRES, Dr. phil., *Universitäre Psychiatrische Dienste (UPD) Bern, Bolligenstrasse 111, CH-3072 Bern, Switzerland*

A. BELLACK, PhD, *Professor of Psychiatry, Medical College of Pennsylvania, Department of Psychiatry, 3200 Henry Avenue, Philadelphia, PA 19129, USA*

W. BÖKER, Prof. Dr. med., *Professor of Psychiatry, Universitäre Psychiatrische Dienste (UPD) Bern, Bolligenstrasse 111, CH-3072 Bern, Switzerland*

R. L. BORISON, MD, PhD, *Professor of Psychiatry, Department of Psychiatry, Medical College of Georgia, 1515 Pope Avenue, Augusta, GA 30912–3800, USA*

H. D. BRENNER, Prof. Dr. med. et phil., *Professor of Psychiatry, Universitäre Psychiatrische Dienste (UPD) Bern, Laupenstrasse 49, CH-3010 Bern, Switzerland*

L. CIOMPI, Prof. Dr. med., *Professor of Psychiatry, rte de la Cita 6, CH-1092 Belmont sur Lausanne, Switzerland*

B. I. DIAMOND, MD, *Professor of Psychiatry, Department of Psychiatry, Medical College of Georgia, 1515 Pope Avenue, Augusta, GA 30912–3800, USA*

G. DONZEL, lic. phil., *Universitäre Psychiatrische Dienste (UPD) Bern, Bolligenstrasse 111, CH-3072 Bern, Switzerland*

D. ELTING, MA, *Department of Psychology, University of Nebraska, Lincoln, NE 68588, USA*

W. GAEBEL, Prof. Dr. med., *Professor of Psychiatry, Psychiatrische Klinik der Heinrich-Heine Universität, Rheinische Landes- und Hochschulklinik, Bergische Landstrasse 2, D-40629 Düsseldorf, Germany*

M. J. GOLDSTEIN, PhD, *Professor of Psychology and Psychiatry, UCLA Family Project, University of California Los Angeles, Department of Psychology, Los Angeles, CA 90024–1563, USA*

M. F. GREEN, PhD, *Associate Professor, Department of Psychiatry and Biobehavioral Sciences, UCLA, Camarillo-Neuropsychiatric Institute Research Program, Box A, Camarillo, CA 93011, USA*

D. HELL, Prof. Dr. med., *Psychiatrische Universitätsklinik Zürich, Lenggstrasse 31, CH-3089 Zürich, Switzerland*

S. HELLMAN, MA, *Staff Research Associate, Department of Psychiatry and Biobehavioral Sciences, UCLA, Camarillo-Neuropsychiatric Institute Research Program, Box A, Camarillo, CA 93011, USA*

B. HODEL, Dr. phil., *Universitäre Psychiatrische Dienste (UPD) Bern, Bolligenstrasse 111, CH-3072 Bern, Switzerland*

S. KAMESHIMA, PhD, *Associate Professor, Japan College of Social Work, 3–1–30 Takeoka, Kiyose-City, Tokyo 204, Japan*

R. S. KERN, PhD, *Psychologist, Department of Psychiatry and Biobehavioral Sciences, UCLA, Camarillo-Neuropsychiatric Institute Research Program, Box A, Camarillo, CA 93011, USA*

W. H. KNOEDLER, MD, *Clinical Director, Program of Assertive Community Treatment, 108 S. Webster Street, Madison, WI 53703, USA*

T. MAGER, Dr. med., *Psychiatrische Klinik und Poliklinik der Universität Bonn, Sigmund Freud-Strasse 25, D-53105 Bonn, Germany*

H.-J. MÖLLER, Prof. Dr. med., *Psychiatrische Universitätsklinik, Nussbaumstrasse 7, D-80336 Munich, Germany*

H. MÜLLER, Dr. phil., *Psychiatrische Universitätsklinik, Nussbaumstrasse 7, D-80336 Munich, Germany*

K. NUECHTERLEIN, PhD, *Professor of Psychiatry and Biobehavioral Sciences, UCLA Neuropsychiatric Institute, Los Angeles, CA 90024, USA*

D. PENN, PhD, *Assistant Professor, Department of Psychology, Illinois Institute of Technology, Chicago, IL 60616–3793, USA*

C. PERRIS, MD, *Professor of Psychiatry, University of Umeå, Department of Psychiatry, S-90185 Umeå, Sweden*

D. REED, PhD, *Research Associate, Department of Psychology, University of Nebraska, Lincoln, NE 68588, USA*

I. ROSENFARB, PhD, *University of California Los Angeles, Department of Psychology, Los Angeles, CA 90024–1563, USA*

L. ROUNDS, MSSW, *Research Specialist, Department of Family Medicine, University of Wisconsin, 777 S. Mills Street, Madison, WI 53715, USA*

G. J. SARWER-FONER, MD, *Professor of Psychiatry, Wayne State University School of Medicine, 3220 Bloomfield Shores Drive, West Bloomfield, MI 48323, USA*

A. SCHAUB, Dr. phil., *Psychiatrische Universitätsklinik, Nussbaumstrasse 7, D-80336 Munich, Germany*

Ch. SCHEIER, lic. phil., *Universität Zürich, Institut für Informatik, Artificial Intelligence Laboratory, Winterthurerstrasse 190, CH-8052 Zürich, Switzerland*

S. SENN BURKE, BA, *Psychological Services Associate, Mendota Mental Health Institute, 301 Troy Drive, Madison, WI 53704, USA*

W. D. SPAULDING, PhD, *Professor of Psychiatry, University of Nebraska, 209 Burnett Hall, Lincoln, NE 68588–0308, USA*

H. D. STIERLIN, Prof. Dr. med et phil., *Ruprecht-Karls-Universität Heidelberg, Abteilung für Psychoanalytische Grundlagenforschung und Familientherapie, Mönchhofstrasse 15 a, D-69120 Heidelberg, Germany*

J. S. STRAUSS, MD, *Professor of Psychiatry, Yale University School of Medicine, 34 Park Street, New Haven, CT 06519, USA*

M. SULLIVAN, MSW, *Clinical Associate, Department of Psychology, University of Nebraska, Lincoln, NE 68588, USA*

M. A. TEST, PhD, *Professor of Psychology, School of Social Work, University of Wisconsin, 1350 University Avenue, Madison, WI 53706, USA*

W. TSCHACHER, Dr. phil., *Universitäre Psychiatrische Dienste (UPD) Bern, Laupenstrasse 49, CH-3010 Bern, Switzerland*

K. H. WIEDL, Prof. Dr. phil., *Universität Osnabrück, Abteilung Klinische Psychologie, Postfach 4469, D-49034 Osnabrück, Germany*

S. M. WOO, MA, *Research Associate, UCLA Family Project, Department of Psychology, University of California, Los Angeles, CA 90024, USA*

Introduction:
Unfolding of the Area

Systemic Concepts of Schizophrenia and Their Implications for Therapy Research

Wolfgang Böker and Hans Dieter Brenner

Summary

A systemic understanding of the complexity of relationships has reached out to many disciplines. In the last few years, research and therapy in schizophrenia has also followed this line of development. A psychosis such as schizophrenia calls for the development of what are virtually new perspectives, which would allow us to combine the findings and micro-theories about specific aspects, obtained at various levels of research, as a step towards an integrative general theory. This article reviews the present status of systems theories on the pathogenesis of schizophrenia and discusses its implications for both treatment and the organisation of service delivery systems. Maturana's theory of living systems, based on the concepts of structural determinism and autopoiesis, appears to bear particular relevance to the issues under discussion.

If systemic thinking is defined as a focus on patterns, relationships, and dynamics (Ropohl, 1978) – a recognition of the inter-relatedness of co-acting parts (components) of any living system – this perspective is applicable to many structurally organised processes which take place in schizophrenia. For example, it is a viable approach to the following subsystems and processes: neuronal networks which are the basis of interdependent brain processes; bio-chemical and bio-electric fluctuations of homeostasis; patterns of education and communication within the family; negative and positive feedback loops in the emergence of symptoms; long-term course trajectories; multi-personal forms of therapy; service delivery systems. Different systems theories such as cybernetics, synergetics, chaos theory, communication theory, and structural determinism deal with the problem of psychosis (overview e. g., in Böse & Schiepek, 1989; Reiter & Ahlers, 1991).

However, due to the breadth and heterogeneity of the terms used, divergent systemic concepts have emerged in such different disciplines as biology, physics, information theory, psychology, neurosciences, sociology, and epistemology. Further confusion also stems from both the various levels of abstraction in the terms elaborated, and the often unclarified question as to whether these concepts have been defined in scientific or metaphorical terms (Welter-Enderlin, 1988). Even though psychiatrists are accustomed to integrating and synthesising medical-scientific explanations with the hermeneutics of the arts, in the process of evolving their own approach to working with patients, they initially find it difficult to find their way through the labyrinth of systemic concepts.

Aetiopathogenetic Concepts and Systems Theory

Theories which emphasise the interactional nature of relationships – as opposed to static, descriptive, and reductionistic models – and which attempt to define the aetiological basis of illness, may in a broad sense be regarded as precursors of systemic concepts of schizophrenia. Eminent adherents of such concepts were stimulated by psychoanalysis and by other dynamic psychological theories such as Gestalt psychology, Lewin's field theory, the holistic school of psychology, and performance theory.

The New York psychiatrist Albert Scheflen was a pioneer in applying the systems paradigm to research on psychoses. In *Levels of Schizophrenia* (1981), he describes these illnesses on several levels of organisation, starting with the suprasystem of society and ending with the subsystem of the molecular structure of the brain. He shows how each level is cybernetically related to every other, and how processes at one level cause and maintain behaviour at every other. Disturbance of a function, e. g., in the mother-child relationship, can be corrected at the next level of social organisation, which is the family. Or neurosynaptic deficits are compensated for at the next level of organisation, which is the general level of neural activity and interaction.

Ciompi (1985) presented an overview of contemporary multi-dimensional models of schizophrenia. Those include:

- The stress-diathesis model (Falconer, 1965; Rosenthal, 1970; Gottesman & Shields, 1976)

- The stimulus-window model (Wing & Brown, 1970; Wing, 1975)

- The vulnerability hypothesis (Zubin & Spring, 1977; Zubin et al., 1983)

- The information-processing model (Venables, 1963; Chapman & Chapman, 1973; Nuechterlein & Dawson, 1984)

- The concept of basic disorders (Huber et al., 1979; Süllwold, 1981, 1983)

- The interactive developmental model (Strauss & Carpenter, 1981)

4

- The neural plasticity hypothesis (Haracz, 1984)

- The integrative psycho-biological model (Ciompi, 1981, 1982)

In a narrower sense, these multi-dimensional models may be regarded as predecessors of general systems concepts. This is due to the central importance of the homeostasis of psychological systems via negative feedback processes, in terms of first-order cybernetics, as well as the inter-relatedness of biological and psychosocial factors.

Newer systemic concepts such as those devised by Nuechterlein (1987), Brenner (1989), Ciompi (1989), and Koukkou-Lehmann et al. (1991, 1992) are based on the principle that schizophrenia is the result of complex psychological, biological, and social changes, which interact in a cyclical manner. Referred to as "bio-psychosocial theories," they integrate both negative and positive feedbacks, the latter being defined as mutually reinforcing loops. However, although a comprehensive theory of schizophrenia has yet to be developed, there is sound evidence that vulnerability, stress, coping, and competence are determining factors in the onset of illness, clinical remission and relapse, level of postmorbid social adjustment, and the magnitude of longer-term disability. On the other hand, very little is known about the ways biologically-based vulnerability, personality factors, environmental factors, symptoms of illness, the consequences of these symptoms, and the coping potential of individuals relate to the outcome of psychosis.

In Münster, a research group headed by Schiepek has been working on the systemic modelling of schizophrenia (Schiepek et al., 1992). Conceptualised in line with Mackey's and an der Heiden's model of "dynamic illness" (1982), psychosis is analysed in terms of self-organisational processes and "bifurcational phenomena." The latter are sudden modifications of the functional or structural state ("dissipative structures") due to adverse influences in the environment, particularly if these more or less random influences ("fluctuations") occur at critical points ("bifurcations"). Illness is thus explained as resulting from the process of being forced into a new and "rigid structure" or into "uncontrollable chaos." Schiepek et al. based their theory on Ciompi's model of schizophrenia (1988) and on concepts described in Böker and Brenner (1989). They undertook a computer simulation of retroactive interactions of five different variables: cognitive dysfunctions, stress, withdrawal, expressed emotion, and delusion. The following parameters mediated the interactions of these variables: diffuseness, affective-cognitive schemata, dopamine and serotonin metabolism, social competence, genetic risk, as well as five other "betaparameters," as indicators of the respective magnitude of feed-back interactions. It is of interest that the various courses of illness found in clinical longitudinal studies could be simulated in this

5

way, and that minor variations in the initial values might radically affect its outcome.

From a phenomenological perspective schizophrenic episodes are states of disorder, yet the mathematical model of synergetics depicts them as highly-structured patterns. In the computer model, psychotic states (processes) only occur when "random fluctuations" of stress or expressed emotions force variables beyond the range of stability. It is not that the biological, psychological and interactive systems are dysfunctional per se in schizophrenia, but rather that they are extremely vulnerable and hypersensitive. Psychotic behaviour is only brought about by abnormal parameter changes, even though they are basically reversible. Ciompi et al. have produced empirical evidence of chaotic processes and dissipative structures in the dynamic course of schizophrenia, using various mathematical procedures to analyse daily fluctuations of psychotic intensity – in one case observed for 751 days (Ciompi et al., 1992; see also Ciompi's contribution in this volume; Schmid, 1991).

The clinical value of computer simulation has yet to be clarified and empirically tested. Similarly, the hope that computerised monitoring of the long-term course of illness will be superior to clinical methods, such as in recognising early warning signs of relapse and that it will optimise therapeutic intervention, requires further validation. However, resolution of the question whether simulation of developing patterns of schizophrenia can serve to predict rather than merely describe the outcome of illness, might call for such a variety of individual data that the experienced clinician, with his powers of intuitive understanding and judgement, might be superior to this new methodological approach. The problem of integrating electrophysiological and chemical data with phenomenological findings has also to be resolved. As Schiepek (1993) self-critically put it, "Is it possible to decipher clear-cut patterns from all the 'white noise'?"

Treatment and Systems Theory

An impressive number of psychotherapists today engage in group therapy ("multipersonal systems") and call themselves "systemic therapists" or "systemic counsellors." The term "systemic therapy" primarily refers to various schools of family therapy – that field of psychiatry and psychology which has particularly been shaped by a systemic way of thinking. Detailed description of the various schools of family therapy – including those guided by a structural communication theory, or a systems-orientated approach – is not necessary here due to the extensive literature on this subject. Recently, efforts have been directed at integrating systemic and psycho-educational approaches in working with families with a psychotic member (e. g., Wynne, 1991). Yet the beneficial effects of systemic therapy that have been observed should not mask their lack of sound conceptual underpinnings.

Koukkou-Lehmann (1991, 1992), has devised an "integrative psychobiological functional model of the brain" based on her psychophysiological research, which has also stimulated developments in treatment methods and research in this area. In this model, "short-term fluctuations of the functional brain state reflect dynamic and selective adjustment of the contents of the working memory on the individual's current reality." The contents of the memory system, which are released by the functional state of the brain, determine and shape behaviour, resulting in the hypothesis that, "variations in a given store cause changes in behaviour and in psychological functioning" (Koukkou-Lehmann, 1992). This kind of concept is useful in the treatment of schizophrenic patients with poor cognitive functioning, in so far as psychopharmacological agents and various methods of psychotherapy affect different "states of the brain," which may, in turn, open up various memory systems and behavioural schemata.

Maturana's theory, postulating that all living systems are basically structurally determined and autopoietic (Maturana & Varela, 1987), might have an especially profound effect in reshaping therapeutic action along systemic lines. Based on insights gained in biology and neurophysiology, this theory amalgamates elements of general systems theory, the theory of evolution, Piaget's developmental theory, contextualism, and behaviourism into a carefully formulated organic theory of living systems. It is both a component part and an expression of the change that has taken place in epistemology since the 1980s, and can be considered paradigmatic for radical constructivism. As a cognitive-biological theory, it seems to be particularly suitable for advancing a new understanding of human beings, their transactions with the environment and with ensuing problems, thereby paving the way for conceptually-based and dynamic ways of behaving. This would, however, require that it is regarded as both a metatheory and the basis for therapeutic action. Although systemic therapy has been developing along these lines (with a shift of focus to various aspects of inner control, the meaning of symptoms, the course of therapy, etc.; cf. Reiter, 1992), similar efforts in the treatment of psychotic experience and behaviour in schizophrenia have not as yet been undertaken.

A brief description of the core elements of Maturana's theoretical concept is necessary at this point. According to this, all living systems are structurally determined, autopoietic systems which produce their own boundaries. This implies ongoing generative processes of self-renewal by which perturbations arising from exchanges with the world are transformed into more complex levels of self-identity. If equipped with a corresponding nervous system, self-observation leads to self-esteem. In autopoiesis, living systems have to change their structure if disruptive factors from the surrounding medium threaten the homeostasis. The cognitive process is thus closely related to the organisation and structure of a living system, cognition being secondary to the maintenance of autopoiesis. Consequently, perceptions must be assessed and selected for the sake of autopoiesis, whereby this selection can constitute exclusion of whatever might threaten the homeostasis of the system.

When systems interact with one another (communication), "structural coupling" occurs. Progressively retroactive processes of structural coupling ("recursive interaction") transform the living system. The autopoietic nature of all systems involved produces new cyclical deviations and compensatory structural changes. If the dynamics of self-organisation converge with allopoietic demands of collectives of organisms – which implies processes involved with the production rather than with the inner dynamics of the autonomy proper to living systems – then autopoietic systems can only be integrated once "consensual domains" (common domains of interest) emerge. "Consensuality" is, on the other hand, a basic prerequisite for the widening of these domains, since it facilitates two-way communication.

In the last few years, Maturana's line of radical constructivism has been criticised as being self-contradictory (Wendel, 1990), tautological and solopsistic (Tschacher, 1992), biological and antirealistic (Reiter, 1991). Although this theory is based on biological, physical and chemical findings, human beings are conceived as autopoietic systems that are not capable of recognising their own reality. We believe that these criticisms reflect an overemphasis and unconditional focus on such concepts as "structural determinism," with a neglect of such concepts as "structural coupling," "recursive interaction" and "consensuality." Both Maturana[1] himself and other radical constructivists like Luhmann (1990) define radical constructivism as a theory of knowledge based on empirical arguments, which takes into account the process of learning and communication, and does not deny the existence of a real external world.

Contrary to many critical opinions, this theory certainly allows therapy to be defined as a vehicle of change in both individuals and in social systems, which has more to do with what Böker called "therapeutic partnership" (1990) than with mere "active and normative pragmatism" (Knorr-Cetina, 1990). However, what certainly can be criticised is that neither the complexity of interaction between organism and surrounding medium (environment) nor the processes of development, learning and change have received due attention to date, and that its relevance as a clinical theory primarily depends on its further elaboration and refinement.

1 Personal communication

8

In addition, the fact that Maturana's theory is based on research in non-human organisms explains why his description of living systems requires some form of "translation" to make it relevant to the field of psychiatry in general and to schizophrenia in particular. It is certainly more difficult to apply than the empirically-based concept of self-organisation, which has been receiving ongoing attention in research on schizophrenia (cf. Ciompi et al.'s and Tschacher et al.'s contributions in this volume). Nevertheless, we believe that there is clinical evidence that the central elements of his theory can advance the treatment of those suffering from schizophrenia, and can also open out new vistas in understanding and working with them.

The notion that the human brain is a functionally-closed system of information processing, which only understands its own language, may have a very considerable impact on our ways of relating to individuals with schizophrenia. Cognition and perception are thus purely individual constructions, and their goodness-of-fit depends on the consensual domain in question. Function and fit, rather than right or wrong, thus become central issues. What is more, since there is no such thing as "instructive interactions" according to the principle of structural determinism, human beings cannot directly be changed or even controlled. This means that any kind of therapy always involves structural re-organisation, no matter how short-lived it might be, in the organism engaged in the therapy process. Maturana and Varela (1987) and Maturana (1982) maintain that human beings exist in a "network of structural couplings," which is constantly woven over our behaviour in an ongoing verbal communication process ("linguolaxis"). In other words, therapy can only work if new consensual domains are established by means of recursive structural coupling, which paves the way for the possibility of conceptual redefinitions and structural change. Merlo (1989) tried to integrate these ideas into a systemic concept of treatment for the acute and postacute phase of schizophrenic psychoses.

The training programmes we have devised for the rehabilitation of schizophrenia might be enhanced by structural determinism, thereby reviving insights obtained many years ago. These include the close connection between perception and action, as conceived by von Weizäcker in the *Gestaltkreis* (1947), von Foerster's (1981) aesthetic imperative, "If you want to understand, learn how to do things," and Lewin's summary of the holistic approach to psychology, "Tell me how he perceives the world, and I'll tell you what he'll do" (cited in Brunner, 1988). Thus, if psychotic patients with impaired cognitive, social and speech functioning can be motivated to do things and communicate about them in therapy, we can create "consensual domains" as a result of emerging patient-therapist coupling. In this manner, compensatory skills can be practised which will most likely have a beneficial effect both on the skill area targeted, e. g., manual skills, and on related areas of functioning such as perception and speech.

This approach is basically not new to the branch of psychology concerned with normal behaviour. For instance, in the field of education, comparable explanations for the effectiveness of comprehensive learning were formulated a long time ago. Gaining far-reaching understanding of the world we live in and acquiring functional and adaptive skills, involves practising a combination of intellectual, manual, athletic, musical, and social skills ("hand teaches head"). This insight encourages those engaged in psychiatric rehabilitation to believe in the promise that the individual parts of therapy packages have a pervasive effect (e. g., Integrated Psychological Therapy for Schizophrenic Patients (IPT) devised by Brenner et al., 1994, or the Social and Independent Living Skills Programmes (SILS) conceived by Liberman et al., 1990). Interestingly, there is evidence from studies on the mechanism of treatment effects of IPT that the nature of pervasiveness is more radial, i. e., between parallel subsystems of behavioural organisation, than it is vertical between elementary and more complex levels of functioning (see Hodel-Wainschtein, 1993).

New patient-therapist conceptual domains are the result of "consensuality" – a term Maturana coined to express "passion" or "love" as the inverse of indifference. This concept could enable therapy to become a process of far greater personal involvement than has so far been usual. By allowing for a "joint brainstorming," therapy becomes much more than a mere technical implementation of therapeutic procedures. Instead, therapist and patient proceed together over shorter or longer periods of life, neither being spared the structural changes caused by recursive interventions. Certain aspects of this conception can also be traced back to various theories of therapy: the psychoanalytical constructs of "transference" and "cross-transference"; Perris' "collaborative empiricism" (1989); the concept of empathy; the concept of "coevolution" as the "art of joint growth" (Willi, 1985), or our focus on the spirit of "partnership" in therapy (Böker, 1990, 1992).

However, the concepts of structural determinism and autopoiesis go well beyond the scope of any of these individual concepts, particularly when we consider their implications for the contents of therapy. The reflexive nature of autopoiesis, for example, which also operates in the development of schizophrenia, throws new light on the potential for change which might be inherent in a "functional concept of illness" and in a "functional concept of self." Both of these provide the patient with a consistent model for explaining the active part he/she plays in the illness and the options available for personal development (Süllwold & Herrlich, 1992). Maturana's theory could constitute a possible explanation for the improved treatment response of psychosocial approaches in therapy, which have increasingly incorporated psychoeducational components, as in various forms of family therapy, in "personal psychotherapy" developed by Hogarty et al. (1995), as well as in the "diagnostically specific psychotherapy" developed by Penick et al. (1991). The fact that therapy packages consisting of a combination of such new medical strategies as low-dosage maintenance therapy and of psychoeducational programmes for medication management and symptom management result in an improved treatment response can also be interpreted in the same vein (Marder et al., 1994).

However, from a structurally deterministic viewpoint, treatment response could be improved to an even greater extent if additional consensual domains were pursued, in addition to a functional concept of illness and a functional concept of the self. These might include such problem areas as coping with illness, general coping strategies, or a healthy style of life and leisure activity in those afflicted by schizophrenia. The principle of self-organisation via autopoiesis could become useful for a wide range of therapeutic purposes, particularly if it is initially based on the function and suitability of the patients own concepts and behaviour. Generating more functional and adaptive concepts for the individual patient would have to involve a joint endeavour on the part of patient and therapist to enhance self-referential changes. Current attempts to elaborate more comprehensive coping-orientated treatment programmes could thus greatly benefit from an increased emphasis on structural determinism and autopoiesis. This is because self-regulatory and self-organisational mechanisms are not only basic to these concepts and programmes, but are also their core therapeutic focus.

Service Delivery System and Systems Theory

The applicability of the systems perspective to the psychiatric service delivery system also deserves attention. The fact that an increasing number of caregivers and therapists who work with severely disabled people have the most divergent professional backgrounds means that, besides supplementing each other's efforts, they may also compete and interfere with each other. This, in turn, leads to new problems. Who defines the disorders to be targeted, and how are they to be defined? When and who is in charge? Up to what point should the learning and behavioural disorders evidenced by a young person genetically vulnerable to schizophrenia be viewed as a "developmental crisis" within an educational/psychiatric context, and from when should they rather be considered as a psychiatric problem requiring expert attention? When is family therapy called for? Who should provide it and how? Who is in charge of referral, treatment,

11

and long-term care? Who is to assume responsibility for a patient on the verge of losing control of himself?

Obviously, there are many crossroads, turn-offs and typical patterns down the path of diagnosis, referral, and treatment (Bergold, 1992) which are decisive in shaping the fate of many "institutionally-linked cases" (Steiner et al., 1988; Ahlers, 1991). Who can determine what happens in the increasingly enmeshed psychosocial network? Systemic considerations might be extremely useful in this difficult undertaking. They could help avoid overlapping and waste of time and services, and result in a more effective use of resources.

Influenced by Maturana's and Luhmann's theories of social systems, the psychologist Ludewig (1988) at Hamburg has been a pioneer in examining the core elements of a systemic understanding of psychosocial and clinical care, and in pointing out the recursive inter-relationships between the identified patient, communicative patterns, and the social system. "The patient's behaviour or the lack of it, is not the problem in itself. Rather, it becomes a problem through communication. If attempts are made to treat the problem in therapy – which means involving at least one therapist in the process – a 'problem system' is turned into a 'clinical' one, and in the worst of cases may result in negative interactions: Patients who repeatedly evidence the same pattern of problems in their individual and social worlds encounter therapists who respond to them in stereotyped ways so as to maintain inner and social coherence. Thus, problems in clinical practice are bound to occur such as annoyance, resistance, dropout, humiliation, power struggles, non-compliance, burn-out and clinical folie à deux or endless therapy" (Ludewig, 1988). The only way to avoid such intractable developments in the maze of institutional care involves repeated clarification of who is in charge of therapy and who defines the goals to be worked towards, which calls for a careful consideration of the various structural couplings involved in clinical practice.

Discussion

It would be useful to review critically the hitherto standard way of operating in therapy from a systemic perspective. First-order cybernetics, which is concerned with establishing or maintaining a stable state in psychological functions, have probably all too often shaped therapeutic action so far. In reality, restorative forces are frequently all the stronger, the more these present functions differ from the previous ones. The more imperative change becomes, the greater initial resistance there is. Resistance reaches a peak when significant structures of meaning (cf. "affect-logical schemata" according to Ciompi, 1982) are elicited, which are dependent on the accuracy of sensory data or on the representations of the self. Autopoietical systems can also become entrenched in circles of stagnation which are not progressive or may even be regressive, if the potential for self-organisation is either not given adequate support or is obstructed. Although this mechanism seems to be accounted for in various therapeutic techniques such as "paradoxical intervention" or "symptom prescription," it tends to be linked to the concern for restoring homeostasis.

On the other hand, second-order cybernetics involving not only negative but also positive feedback loops as well as feed forward processes teaches us that episodes of psychological instability can always stimulate neuronal restructuring, and that self-organisational processes are thus capable of providing potentially promising approaches to therapeutic intervention. The conclusion to be drawn is that the therapist should try and find out, with the help of his patient, what might occur if divergence from the norm was carried one step further. This does not mean merely letting the patient put his changed ways of experiencing and behaving into action, but rather that a joint effort should be made to define the original function and hidden progressive potential of a deviation from a previous state of homeostasis.

Future research on therapy in psychiatry will first have to transpose and accommodate the multitude of systemic terms including cybernetics, autopoiesis, synergetics, chaos, etc. to a single conceptual frame of reference, so as to reach consensus and clarification on various terms which have as yet been confusing or overly abstract. Nevertheless, systemic thinking is of indisputable heuristic value for theories of schizophrenia. Systemic concepts make us more aware of the most sensitive and easily influenced points of any system – whether it be a cerebral neuronal network, a family, or a service delivery system –, which interventions have an impact on the system as a whole, and conversely, how and when recursive processes affect the component parts of the system. Systems models may open out new vistas for a more comprehensive and plausible theory of schizophrenia, while systemic thinking could result in a new and beneficial alliance between caregivers and patients based on a joint effort to generate shared consensual domains in therapy.

References

Ahlers, C. (1991) Experten als Mitwirker im Problemsystem der Psychiatrie. Eine Fallgeschichte. In *Systemisches Denken und therapeutischer Prozess* (eds L. Reiter & C. Ahlers), pp. 160–183. Berlin: Springer-Verlag.

Bergold, J. B. (1992) The systemic character of the psychosocial and psychiatric health services. In *Self-Organization and Clinical Psychology* (eds W. Tschacher, G. Schiepek & E. J. Brunner), Springer Series in Synergetics, Vol. 58. Berlin: Springer-Verlag.

Böker, W. (1990) Patient, Angehörige und Arzt auf dem Weg zu einer Behandlungspartnerschaft. Kasuistik eines 19jährigen schizoaffektiven Krankheitsverlaufes. *Nervenarzt*, **61**, 565–568.

Böker, W. (1992) A call for partnership between schizophrenic patients, relatives and professionals. *British Journal of Psychiatry*, **161** (suppl. 18), 10–12.

Böker, W. & Brenner, H. D. (Eds.) (1989) Schizophrenia as a systems disorder. *British Journal of Psychiatry*, **155** (suppl. 5).

Böse, R. & Schiepek, G. (1989) *Systemische Theorie und Therapie. – Ein Handwörterbuch.* Heidelberg: Roland Asanger Verlag.

Brenner, H. D. (1989) The treatment of basic psychological dysfunctions from a systemic point of view. *British Journal of Psychiatry*, **155** (suppl. 5), 74–83.

Brenner, H. D., Hodel, B., Kube, G. & Roder, V. (1987) Kognitive Therapie bei Schizophrenen: Problemanalyse und empirische Ergebnisse. *Nervenarzt*, **58**, 72–83.

Brenner, H. D., Roder, V., Hodel, B., et al. (1994) *Integrated Psychological Therapy for Schizophrenic Patients.* Toronto: Hogrefe & Huber Publishers.

Brunner, E. J. (1988) Pioniere systemischen Denkens. In *Von der Familientherapie zur systemischen Perspektive* (eds L. Reiter, E. J. Brunner & S. Reiter-Theil), pp. 273–284. Berlin: Springer-Verlag.

Chapman, L. & Chapman, J. P. (1973) *Disordered Thought in Schizophrenia.* New York: Appleton-Century-Crofts.

Ciompi, L. (1981) Wie können wir die Schizophrenen besser behandeln? Ein neues Krankheits- und Therapiekonzept. *Nervenarzt*, **52**, 506–515.

Ciompi, L. (1982) *Affektlogik. Über die Struktur der Psyche und ihre Entwicklung. Ein Beitrag zur Schizophrenieforschung.* Stuttgart: Klett-Cotta.

Ciompi, L. (1985) Towards a coherent multidimensional understanding and therapy of schizophrenia: Converging new concepts. In *Psychosocial Treatment of Schizophrenia. Multidimensional Concepts, Psychological, Family and Self-Help Perspectives* (eds J. S. Strauss, W. Böker & H. D. Brenner), pp. 48–62. Toronto: Hans Huber Publishers.

Ciompi, L. (1988) *The Psyche and Schizophrenia. The Bond between Affect and Logic.* Cambridge, Mass.: Harvard University Press.

Ciompi, L. (1989) The dynamics of complex biological-psychosocial systems: four fundamental psycho-biological mediators in the long-term evolution of schizophrenia. *British Journal of Psychiatry*, **155** (suppl. 5), 15–21.

Ciompi, L., Ambühl, B. & Dünki, R. (1992) Schizophrenie und Chaostheorie. *System Familie*, **5**, 133–147.

Falconer, D. S. (1965) The inheritance of lability to certain diseases estimated from the incidence among relatives. *Annuals of Human Genetics*, **29**, 51–76.

Foerster, H. von (1981) Das Konstruieren einer Wirklichkeit. In *Die erfundene Wirklichkeit* (ed. P. Watzlawick). München: Piper-Verlag.

Gottesman, I. I. & Shields, J. (1976) A critical review of recent adoption, twin and genetics perspectives. *Schizophrenia Bulletin*, **2**, 360–398.

Haracz, J. L. (1984) A neural plasticity hypothesis of schizophrenia. *Neuroscience & Biobehavioral Reviews*, **8**, 55–71.

Hodel-Wainschtein, B. (1993) *Zur Frage der Pervasivität von Interventionseffekten bei schizophren Erkrankten. Eine Untersuchung über den Verlauf der Wirkungen von kognitiven und sozialen Therapieinterventionen sowie deren Kombinationen.* Doctoral thesis, Bern: University of Bern.

Hogarty, G. E., Kornblith, S. J., Greenwald, D., et al. (1995) A disorder-relevant psychotherapy for schizophrenia: description and preliminary findings. *Schizophrenia Bulletin,* in press.

Huber, G., Gross, G. & Schüttler, R. (1979) *Schizophrenie, eine Verlaufs- und sozialpsychiatrische Studie.* Berlin: Springer-Verlag.

Knorr-Cetina, K. (1989) Spielarten des Konstruktivismus. Einige Notizen und Anmerkungen. *Soziale Welt,* **40,** 86–96.

Koukkou-Lehmann, M. (1992) Hirnmechanismen der menschlichen Kommunikation und schizophrene Symptomatik. *Swiss Med,* **1-S/92,** 17–22.

Koukkou-Lehmann, M., Tremel, E. & Manske, W. (1991) A psychobiological model of the pathogenesis of schizophrenic symptoms. *International Journal of Psychophysiology,* **10,** 203–212.

Liberman, R. P., Mueser, K. T., Wallace, C. J., et al. (1990) Training skills in the psychiatrically disabled: learning, coping and competence. In *Schizophrenia. Concepts, Vulnerability and Intervention* (eds E. R. Straube & K. Hahlweg), pp. 193–216. Berlin: Springer-Verlag.

Ludewig, K. (1988) Problem – "Bindeglied" klinischer Systeme. Grundzüge eines systemischen Verständnisses psychosozialer und klinischer Probleme. In *Von der Familientherapie zur systemischen Perspektive* (eds L. Reiter & C. Ahlers), pp. 231–250. Berlin: Springer-Verlag.

Luhmann, N. (1990) Identität – was oder wie? In *Soziologische Aufklärung. 5. Konstruktivistische Perspektiven.* Opladen: Westdeutscher Verlag.

Mackey, M. C. & an der Heiden, U. (1982) Dynamical diseases and bifurcations: Understanding functional disorders in physiological systems. *Funktionelle Biologie & Medizin,* **1,** 156–164.

Marder, S. R., Wirshin., W. C., van Putten, T., et al. (1994) Fluphenazine versus placebo supplementation for prodromal signs of relapse in schizophrenia. *Archives of General Psychiatry,* **51,** 280–287.

Maturana, H. R. (1982) *Erkennen: Die Organisation und Verkörperung von Wirklichkeit.* Wiesbaden: Viehweg.

Maturana, H. R. & Varela, F. J. (1987) *Der Baum der Erkenntnis. Wie wir die Welt durch unsere Wahrnehmung erschaffen – Die biologischen Wurzeln des menschlichen Erkennens.* Bern: Scherz.

Merlo, M. C. G. (1989) Systemtheoretische Überlegungen zur Behandlung des akuten und postakuten Stadiums schizophrener Psychosen. *Psychiatrische Praxis,* **16,** 121–125.

Nuechterlein, K. H. (1987) Vulnerability model for schizophrenia: State of the art. In *Search for the Causes of Schizophrenia* (eds H. Häfner, W. F. Gattaz & W. Janzarik), pp. 297–316. Berlin: Springer-Verlag.

Nuechterlein, K. H. & Dawson, M. E. (1984) A heuristic vulnerability/stress model of schizophrenic episodes. *Schizophrenia Bulletin,* **10,** 300–312.

Penick, E. C., Read, M. R., Lauchland, J. C., et al. (1991) Diagnosis – specific psychotherapy. In *Integrating Pharmacotherapy and Psychotherapy* (eds B. D. Beitman & G. L. Klerman), pp. 45–68. Washington, DC: APA.

Perris, C. (1989) *Cognitive Therapy with Schizophrenic Patients*. London: Guilford Press.

Reiter, L. (1991) Wissenschaft als System. Über Reputation in der deutschsprachigen Familientherapie und systemischer Therapie. *Systeme*, **5**, 117–131.

Reiter, L. (1992) Systemisches Denken und Handeln – wohin? In *Systemische Theorie und Perspektiven der Praxis* (eds W. Schwerdt, E. Rathsfeld & G. Emlein). Frankfurt: Dietmar Klotz.

Reiter, L. & Ahlers, C. (1991) *Systemisches Denken und therapeutischer Prozeß*. Berlin: Springer-Verlag.

Ropohl, G. (1978) Einführung in die allgemeine Systemtheorie. In *Systemtheorie als Wissenschaftsprogramm* (eds H. Lenk & G. Ropohl). Königstein: Athenäum.

Rosenthal, D. (1970) *Genetic Theory and Abnormal Behavior*. New York: McGraw Hill.

Scheflen, A. (1981) *Levels of Schizophrenia*. New York: Brunner/Mazel.

Schiepek, G. (1993) *Nichtlineare Dynamik psychotischer Prozesse*. Paper held at the working conference entitled "Systemische Modellvorstellungen zur Schizophrenie" on September 15, 1993 in Bern.

Schiepek, G., Schoppek, W. & Tretter, F. (1992) Synergetics in psychiatry – simulation of evolutionary patterns of schizophrenia on the basis of nonlinear difference equations. In *Self-Organization and Clinical Psychology* (eds W. Tschacher, G. Schiepek & E. J. Brunner), Springer Series in Synergetics, Vol. **58**, pp. 163–194. Berlin: Springer-Verlag.

Schmid, G. B. (1991) Chaos theory and schizophrenia: elementary aspects. *Psychopathology*, **24**, 185–198.

Steiner, E., Hinsch, J., Reiter, L. & Wagner, H. (1988) Familientherapie als Etikett. Eine therapeutische Strategie bei institutionell verflochtenen Fällen? In *Von der Familientherapie zur systemischen Perspektive* (eds L. Reiter, E. J. Brunner & S. Reiter-Theil), pp. 137–158. Berlin: Springer-Verlag.

Strauss, J. S. & Carpenter, W. T. (1981) *Schizophrenia*. New York: Plenum.

Süllwold, L. (1981) Basisstörungen: Ergebnisse und offene Fragen. In *Schizophrenie. Stand und Entwicklungstendenzen der Forschung* (ed. G. Huber), pp. 269–275. Stuttgart: Huber.

Süllwold, L. (1983) *Schizophrenie*. Stuttgart: Kohlhammer.

Süllwold, L. & Herrlich, J. (1992) Vermittlung eines Krankheitskonzeptes als Therapiebestandteil bei schizophren Erkrankten. In *Verlaufsprozesse schizophrener Erkrankungen. Dynamische Wechselwirkungen relevanter Faktoren* (eds H. D. Brenner & W. Böker), pp. 274–279. Bern: Huber.

Tschacher, W., Schiepek, G. & Brunner, E. J. (1992) *Self-Organization and Clinical Psychology – Empirical Approaches to Synergetics in Psychology*. Berlin: Springer-Verlag.

Venables, P. H. (1963) Selectivity of attention, withdrawal and cortical activation. *Archives of General Psychiatry*, **9**, 92–96.

Weizsäcker, V. von (1947) *Der Gestaltkreis – Theorie der Einheit von Wahrnehmen und Bewegen* (3rd edn). Stuttgart: Thieme.

Welter-Enderlin, R. (1988) "Die Geister, die wir riefen . . ." – Von den Schwierigkeiten und möglichen Lösungen, den Systemansatz auf die Praxis zu übertragen. In *Von der Familientherapie zur systemischen Perspektive* (eds L. Reiter, E. J. Brunner & S. Reiter-Theil), pp. 175–188. Berlin: Springer-Verlag.

Wendel, H. J. (1990) *Moderner Relativismus*. Tübingen: Mohr.

Willi, J. (1985) *Koevolution. Die Kunst gemeinsamen Wachsens*. Reinbek: Rowohlt.

Wing, J. K. (1975) Impairments of schizophrenia. In *Life History Research in Psychopathology,* Vol. 4, (eds R. Wirt, G. Winokur & M. Roff). Minneapolis, University of Minnesota Press.

Wing, J. K. & Brown, G. W. (1970) *Institutionalism and Schizophrenia.* London: Cambridge University.

Wynne, L. C. (1991) System-Konsultation bei Psychosen: Eine bio-psycho-soziale Integration systemischer und psychoedukativer Ansätze. In *Die Behandlung psychotischen Verhaltens* (ed. A. Reiter). Heidelberg: Carl Auer.

Zubin, J. & Spring, B. (1977) Vulnerability: A new view of schizophrenia. *Journal of Abnormal Psychology,* **86**, 103–123.

Zubin, J., Magaziner, J. & Steinhauer, S. (1983) The metamorphosis of schizophrenia: From chronicity to vulnerability. *Psychosocial Medicine,* **13**, 551–571.

Non-Linear Dynamics of Complex Systems: The Chaos-Theoretical Approach to Schizophrenia

Luc Ciompi

Summary

The theory on non-linear dynamics of complex system ("chaos theory") has opened new approaches to many physical, chemical and biological phenomena. In psychiatry and schizophrenia, however, this new approach is still in its beginnings. In this paper, basic notions of chaos theory such as non-linear phase transitions, bifurcations, dissipative structures, deterministic chaos, and fractal dimensions are outlined. Their relevance for understanding short-term and long-term evolutionary dynamics of schizophrenia is demonstrated on clinical grounds and on the basis of empirical studies carried out by our own and other research groups. It is concluded that the chaos-theoretical approach has a considerable potential for deepening our understanding of schizophrenia understood as a typically "dynamic disease." In spite of the fact that the revolutionary paradigm of chaos theory, deriving from theoretical physics and winning at least one Nobel prize (Prigogine), has penetrated during the last 20–30 years nearly all other fields of science, psychiatry including schizophrenia, has still hardly been influenced by it. Presumably, this is not only due to a certain marginality of the discipline and to many popular misunderstandings around the concept of chaos, but also to the fact that there is still no general chaos theory, but only a multiplicity of partly overlapping and partly heterogeneous theoretical elements. These range from Thoms' (1975) catastrophe theory and Prigogine's dissipative structures to Mandelbrot's fractals and Haken's synergetics. The numerous popular books on this issue (e. g., Prigogine & Stengers, 1981; Gleick, 1987; Briggs & Peat, 1990; Cramer, 1989; Haken, 1991) are often very fascinating, but they scarcely offer any methodological tools. On the other hand, the professional publications (e. g., Shaw, 1981; Babloyantz, 1986; Degn et al., 1987; Schuster, 1989; Haken, 1990) tend to put off the reader with their complex mathematics. To find one's way through this jungle is therefore not easy for the psychiatrist. In the following, basic chaos-theoretical notions will be outlined and compared to relevant clinical observations and research evidence concerning schizophrenia.

Elementary Aspects of Current Chaos Theory

Since the many complexities of chaos theory can only be presented here with a few key words, it may be useful for the reader to consult introductory papers by Schmid (1991) and by Ciompi et al. (1992). Good introductions from the point of view of clinical psychology are also given by Kriz (1989) and an der Heiden (1992).

The first two key words (or phrases) are "non-linear phase transitions" and "dissipative structures." Chaos theory is in fact mainly concerned with non-linear, sudden "jumps" or phase transitions, appearing by self-organisation in systems of all kinds, when they are driven far from equilibrium by a continuous energy input. A classical example is the hexagonal convection cells – "Bénard-instability" – which appear suddenly, at a certain temperature, in a heated layer of a fluid (Fig. 1). Similar phenomena emerge also under natural conditions, in the sea or in the atmosphere. Other systems develop differently ordered patterns or behaviour when under an energy input; thus, disordered light combines to an ordered laser beam, termites aggregate to complex structures, and growing cities develop satellite-cities according to certain laws. Prigogine calls these patterns "dissipative structures" because they dissipate

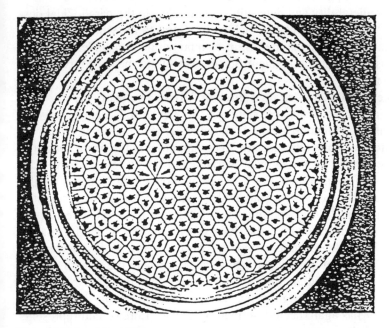

Figure 1. Bénard instability.

19

energy in a new way. Haken speaks of synergies which develop under the influence of certain control parameters and emerging order parameters; the latter will eventually "enslave" the whole system. In each case, repetitive positive feedback processes induce an escalation of the system's dynamics, until a point is reached at which transition in another overall pattern becomes inevitable.

The next key word is the "bifurcation" which takes place at the critical point referred above (Fig. 2). The system then "decides" which one of a number of different possible forms of behaviour to "choose." Beforehand, typical "fluctuations" are observed. Of particular interest is the fact that during this phase of lability, minimal causes can have an enormous effect: a good comparison is a labile rock on a ridge that may fall down, depending on a breath of wind, on one side or the other, causing either enormous damage or none at all (Fig. 3). The meteorologist Edward Lorenz (1963), one of the patriarchs of chaos theory, called this phenomenon the "butterfly effect," because theoretically, the flap of a butterfly's wing, intervening at a critical moment in Japan, can induce a hurricane in Hawaii, weeks or months later. The consequence of such minimal effects is that the behaviour of complex systems can, as a rule, be predicted only for a short time; this is particularly obvious for the weather. However, the dynamics of the system remain within certain limits, in spite of some possible extreme deviations. It is this interesting combination of unpredictability and determinism that leads to the paradoxical designation of a "deterministic chaos," which is central to the whole chaos theory. At the same time, this is the origin of innumerable misunderstandings, because chaos in this modern scientific sense is by no means equivalent to random disorder.

The next key word is the "strange attractor," for chaos-theory the most important individual case of a stable state towards which self-organisatory dynamic systems can obligatorily be driven under certain conditions. The most simple attractor is a point attractor, i. e., a certain point in the phase space (an abstract space formed by the relevant variables of the system), where a dynamic system can come to rest. For instance, without energy input, a pendulum will obligatorily come to a standstill, sooner or later. However, if it is activated by a spring, it will continuously go through identical states. In the phase space, such an attractor has the shape of a circle, and is therefore called a "limit cycle." One degree more complex is the torus (Fig. 4), and the highest complexity is shown by chaotic strange attractors, where the system will go unpredictably through slightly different trajectories that, however, remain located within a certain configuration. The first and probably best known strange attractor has again been described by Eduard Lorenz, and represents the evolution of the weather (Fig. 5). Another form is the Rössler-attractor

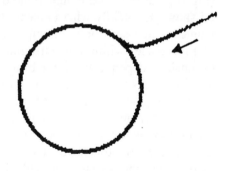

Figure 2. Point-attractor.

Figure 3. Limit circle.

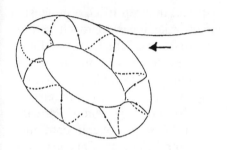

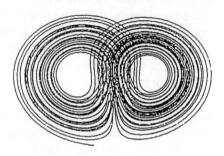

Figure 4. Torus.

Figure 5. Lorenz-attractor.

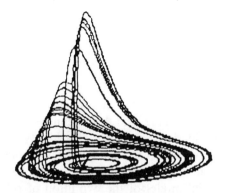

Figure 6. Rössler-attractor.

21

(Fig. 6), and there are innumerable other strange attractors (Figs. 2–6). They all show graphically what is meant by "deterministic chaos," particular dynamics which develop in an unpredictable sensitive dependency from minimal influences within a given frame. As a consequence of this combination of sensitive dependency and stability, strange (chaotic) attractors can function as highly sensitive "sensors" or "information processors" for environmental influences – a very important fact.

Two other qualities of strange attractors are of particular interest – their dimensionality and their fractal structure. The term "dimensionality" means that strange attractors have – like other geometrical figures – a certain dimension. Point, line, surface, and cube have integer dimensions, namely 0, 1, 2, and 3. In contrast, the dimensions of strange attractors can only be characterised by fractal numbers; they therefore have been termed "fractals" (Mandelbrot, 1983). Each strange attractor has a certain dimension which is a (relative) measure for the (often astonishingly) low number of variables that dominate the dynamics of the system. For instance, in sleep-EEG, a dimension near to 2 has been found, while in the state of wake, it can approach 9 (Rapp et al., 1989). Another important quality of these fractals is their self-similarity on great or small scales, as a consequence of the fact that the same fundamental laws are effective in each part of the system dynamics. Graphically, this is manifest in the phenomenon that the same fundamental forms are repeated in all forms of a complex system, e. g., a fern or a river system: Goethe had intuitively recognised this "essence," as in the *"gestalt"* (overall configuration) of plants, and for Husserl, it became a central element of his phenomenology. It is now known that nature is full of innumerable fractals, from the "gestalt" of certain clouds or crystals, to the form of plants and animals, to man and his/her individual habitus and style. Remarkably enough, the time series of one single arbitrary variable of the system can be a sufficient indicator for determining the dimension of the whole complex strange attractor.

The Relevance of Chaos Theory for Schizophrenia

Intuitively, it seems that most important aspects of chaos theory are relevant to the problem of schizophrenia, and this is confirmed by further consideration. Firstly, we are clearly in presence of a highly complex system, with numerous feedback loops and corresponding possibilities for non-linear transitions. This has already been demonstrated on the basis of my integrative psycho-socio-biological model of the evolution of schizophrenia in three phases (Fig. 7) (Ciompi, 1989). Such a model fulfils all theoretical conditions

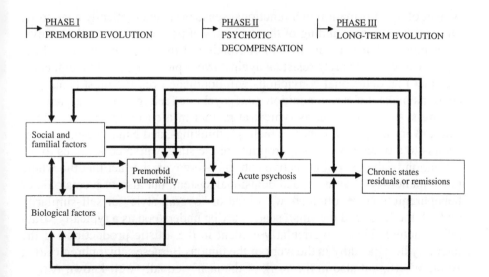

Figure 7. Evolutionary model of schizophrenia in three phases with feedback loops.

for chaotic processes with escalations, bifurcations, phase transitions, and attractor-like states of different kinds.

Clinically, there is first of all the transition from normal to a psychotic system of functioning – or "going crazy" – which seems to correspond to a non-linear "jump" in the chaos-theoretical sense. Conrad (1958), Bowers (1974), Scheflen (1978), Wing (1978) and other authors have all analysed this fascinating transformation, while Bateson (1979) compared the escalative interactions between patient and surroundings with a "runaway," and Bleuler (1984) spoke of a "point of no return" where the whole functional system suddenly switches into a psychotic state, in the sense of a typical bifurcation. The flickery instability of feeling and thinking preceding the outbreak of psychosis – the *trema* according to Conrad – appears to be analogous to the fluctuation preceding a bifurcation. Ambivalence as a cardinal symptom of schizophrenia thus appears in a new light. Furthermore, the sensitive dependency of psychotic behaviour to minimal environmental influences seems to correspond closely to the "butterfly effect" described above. In the state of *Wahnstimmung* (strong tendency for delusional misinterpretation), a word, a glimpse, or a spot of colour may serve as point of crystallisation around which a whole delirious system may be rapidly organised.

In *Affect Logic* (Ciompi, 1982; in English, 1988), I proposed the hypothesis that psychotic patterns of feeling, thinking, and behaving correspond to dissipative structures, as defined by Prigogine. In my view, the affective com-

23

ponent of all information in a functional sense plays energetically a key role. Only such an understanding of the dynamics of psychosis can explain why a delusional system – a new overall dissipation of the available emotional energy – can be so strongly resistant against every piece of cognitive evidence. The fact that delusional convictions will dominate even the most banal perceptions make it clear, in addition, that psychotic feeling-, thinking-, and behaving-systems function as typical attractors in a chaos-theoretical sense. Thus, every individual concrete feeling-, thinking-, and behaving-unit corresponds to a trajectory in an appropriate phase state, which contributes to the formation of the overall attractive pattern. Moreover, the fact that the whole phenomenology of an extended delusional system, but also of a catatonic or hebephrenic picture, often shows a kind of "overall style" or self-similarity on both the large and the small scale, may be understood as a typically "fractal" structure. This is particularly evident in the artistic productions of the mentally ill, especially in the work of the famous Bernese schizophrenic artist Adolf Wölfli, but also in the work of the nearly equally well-known Aloyse from Lausanne (cf. Steck, 1975).

Another important chaos-theoretical approach is the analysis of the time-structure of psychotic processes, with their characteristic unpredictability in the single case. This was not only found in our own investigations of the long-term evolution of clinical cases, but has been confirmed also in their short-term "micro-evolution" (see below). Chaos theory leads in fact to a new view of the problem of prognosis. For inherent reasons, prognostic possibilities in schizophrenia will always remain limited, because complex feedback loops will sooner or later induce unpredictable non-linear bifurcations with butterfly effects and chaotic attractors. Therefore, nearly identical initial states may lead to very different outcomes, and different initial states to very similar ones.

First Empirical Confirmations

Whilst it is both true and legitimate that the generation of chaos-theoretical hypotheses started with such clinical analogies, several research groups, among them our own, have made progress towards establishing an empirical basis for them.

For instance, King et al. (1983) were able to demonstrate the possibility that chaotic states occur in Dopamin metabolism. Huberman (1986) found a chaos-like dynamic in the eye movements of schizophrenics, Elkaim et al. (1987) constructed a model for escalating psychotic family processes, Hoffman (1987) simulated schizophrenia-like phenomena in neuronal networks

Figure 8. Empirical long-term courses according to Ciompi & Müller (1976) and computer-simulations according to Schiepek & Schoppek (1992).

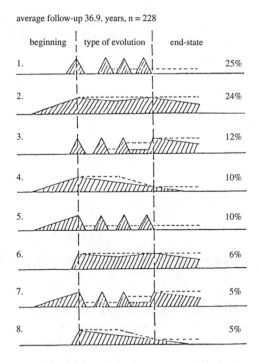

average follow-up 36.9. years, n = 228

beginning | type of evolution | end-state

1.   25%
2.   24%
3.   12%
4.   10%
5.   10%
6.   6%
7.   5%
8.   5%

dotted lines: variations of the same evolutionary type

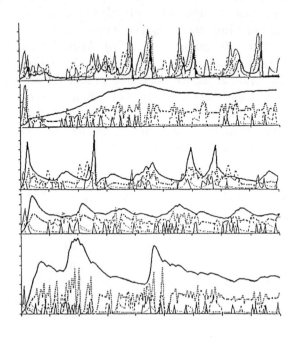

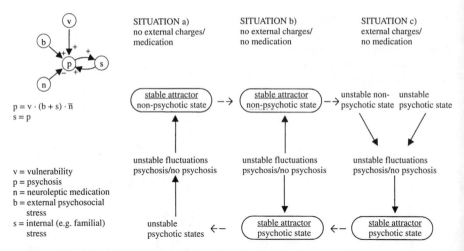

$p = v \cdot (b + s) \cdot \bar{n}$
$s = p$

v = vulnerability
p = psychosis
n = neuroleptic medication
b = external psychosocial
    stress
s = internal (e.g. familial)
    stress

Figure 9. Elementary dynamics in a simple vulnerability-stress-model.

("Hopfield systems"), and Simon (1989) explored schizophrenic language from a chaos-theoretical point of view. Probably the most promising approach is, however, the time series analysis of the dynamics of the course of schizophrenia, combined with the construction of mathematical models for computer simulation. By this approach, using a sophisticated model with five variables, Schiepek et al. (1992) succeeded in reproducing, quite accurately, the most important types of long-term evolution (Fig. 8) that we had found clinically (Ciompi et al., 1976). Also, the spectral electroencephalographic time series analyses by Koukkou et al. (1993) seem very promising; over several brain areas, they detected strange attractors, whose dimensionality was significantly higher in psychotic than in normal states.

The work by our own research group also illustrates the interest of combined modelling and time series analyses. Modelling began with a Boole-mathematical method which allows the inclusion also of variables that cannot be exactly measured (Thomas, 1973; Thomas & D'Ari, 1991). A first and deliberately very simple vulnerability-stress-model with a single feedback loop already showed possible bifurcations and attractor-like states (Fig. 9). A more refined modelling of the same dynamics with differential equations revealed, in addition, the chaos-theoretically interesting phenomenon of "hysteresis" or "bi-stationarity" (two different possible states of a system under the same external conditions, according to its history) (Ciompi et al., 1992). In a considerably more sophisticated model, Kupper et al. (1994) found clinically relevant attractor-like dynamisms during the process of rehabilitation (Fig. 10).

26

Figure 10. Result of kinetic logical analysis: chronicity as circular-stable process (Kupper et al., 1994).

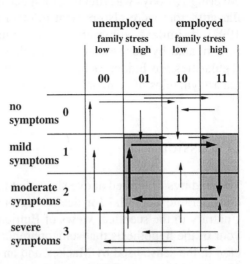

As a basis for time series analyses, precise observations were made of the daily micro-fluctuations of the intensity of psychotic symptoms, as registered on a seven-point scale, for patients from the therapeutic community *Soteria Berne*. First analyses with a conventional ARIMA-method by Aebi et al. (1993) were unable to detect any regularities, except a certain dependency on environmental influences. With the chaos-theoretical method of calculation described by Grassberger and Procaccia (1983), however, a strange attractor with a dimension of about 2:2 in the longest available time series (Fig. 11)

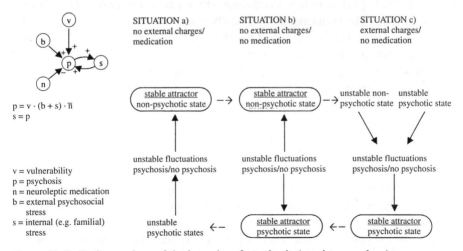

Figure 11. Daily fluctuations of the intensity of psychosis (maximum values).

27

covering 751 days was found (Ciompi et al., 1992; Ambühl et al., 1992). Similar attractors were also present in other individual cases (Tschacher et al., 1992). If similar findings are confirmed in long-term evolutions (as currently investigated by our research team), there no doubt will remain that fractal regularities are hidden behind the apparently irregular microdynamics and macrodynamics of schizophrenic courses.

Discussion

The findings described above show that the chaos-theoretical approach has a considerable potential for deepening our understanding of schizophrenia. Contrary to the sceptical views of Emrich et al. (1992), they all speak in favour of the hypothesis that schizophrenia is par excellence a "dynamic" disease in the sense used by Mackey and an der Heiden (1982). Non-linearities found in the course of illness by Strauss (1985) as well as self-healing mechanisms described by Böker (1987) point in the same direction. Moreover, the profile of a new general understanding of psyche and psychosis based on chaos theory is emerging. Also making use of my concept of affect logic (Ciompi, 1982, 1993), I would describe it in the following way: It is very likely that normal as well as psychotic patterns of feeling, thinking, and behaving correspond to hierarchically high-ranking attractor basins (zones of attraction within an appropriate phase space) – or dissipative structures – of a fractal chaotic structure. These basins function as highly sensitive state-dependent instruments for information processing which can jump, under the influence of modified control parameters and newly emerging order parameters, to new self-organising overall feeling-, thinking-, and behaving-systems. Examples of such systems are, in addition to the schizophrenic, manic or depressive psychoses, the "eigen-worlds" (idiosyncratic inner world) of people in love, in mourning, or in anger. Particular collective mentalities and ideologies of all kinds are also relevant. Specific states of consciousness and fundamental emotional moods thereby seem to function as typical control parameters in the sense of Haken, while dominating feelings or ideas may become typical "enslaving" order parameters.

It is evident that such a vision of the future generates many new questions and hypotheses for further research. Especially by influencing the control parameters described above, it may also lead – as in fact shown in our work at *Soteria Berne,* which demonstrated the therapeutic potential of an emotionally warm, supporting, and relaxed atmosphere for patients with schizophrenia (see Ciompi et al., 1992, 1993) – to new therapeutic intervention strategies. In spite of the fact that this whole new approach is just in its first beginnings, I continue to find it fascinating.

References

Aebi, E., Ackermann, K. & Revenstorf, D. (1993) Ein Konzept der sozialen Unterstützung für akut Schizophrene. Zeitreihenanalysen täglicher Fluktuationen psychotischer Merkmale. *Zeitschrift für Klinische Psychologie, Psychopathologie & Psychotherapie*, **41**, 18–30.

Ambühl, B., Dünki, R. M. & Ciompi, L. (1992) Dynamic systems and the development of schizophrenic symptoms. Springer, 1991. In *Self-Organization and Clinical Psychology, Series in Synergetics*, **58** (eds W. Tschacher, G. Schiepek & E. I. Brunner), pp. 195–203. Berlin: Springer

Babloyantz, A. (1986) *Molecules, Dynamics and Life. Introduction to Self-Organisation of Matter*. New York: John Wiley.

Bateson, G. (1979) *Mind and Nature. A Necessary Unit*. Toronto: Bantam Books.

Bleuler, M. (1984) Das alte und das neue Bild des Schizophrenen. *Schweizer Archiv für Neurologie, Neurochirurgie & Psychiatrie*, **135**, 143–149.

Böker, W. (1987) On self-help among schizophrenics: Problem analysis and empirical studies. In *Psychosocial Treatment of Schizophrenia* (eds J. S. Strauss, W. Böker & H. D. Brenner), pp. 167–179. Toronto: Huber.

Bowers, M. B. (1974) *Retrait from Sanity. The Structure of Emerging Psychosis*. New York: Human Science Press.

Briggs, J. F. & Peat, F. D. (1990) *Die Entdeckung des Chaos. Eine Reise durch die Chaostheorie*. München: Hauser.

Ciompi, L. (1982) *Affektlogik. Über die Struktur der Psyche und ihre Entwicklung. Ein Beitrag zur Schizophrenieforschung*. Stuttgart: Klett-Cotta. Translated into English: *The Psyche and Schizophrenia. The Bond between Affect and Logic* (1988). New Haven: Harvard University Press.

Ciompi, L. (1989) The dynamics of complex biological-psychosocial systems. Four fundamental psycho-biological mediators in the long-term evolution of schizophrenia. *British Journal of Psychiatry*, **155**, 15–21.

Ciompi, L. (1993) Die Hypothese der Affektlogik. *Spektrum der Wissenschaft (Vol. 2)*, pp. 76–82.

Ciompi, L. & Müller, C. (1976) *Lebensweg und Alter der Schizophrenen. Eine katamnestische Langzeitstudie*. Heidelberg: Springer-Verlag.

Ciompi, L. &. Müller, C. (1976) *Lebensweg und Alter der Schizophrenen. Eine katamnestische Langzeitstudie*. Heidelberg: Springer-Verlag.

Ciompi, L., Dauwalder, H. P., Maier, Ch., et al. (1992) The pilot-project "Soteria Berne." Clinical experiences and results. *British Journal of Psychiatry*, **161**, 145–153.

Ciompi, L., Ambühl, B. & Dünki, R. (1992) Schizophrenie und Chaostheorie. *System Familie*, **5**, 133–147.

Ciompi, L., Kupper, Z., Aebi, E., et al. (1993) Das Pilot-Projekt "Soteria Bern" zur Behandlung akut Schizophrener. II. Ergebnisse einer vergleichenden prospektiven Verlaufsstudie über 2 Jahre. *Nervenarzt*, **64**, 440–450.

29

Conrad, K. (1958) *Die beginnende Schizophrenie*. Stuttgart: Thieme.

Cramer, F. (1989) *Chaos und Ordnung. Die komplexe Struktur des Lebendigen*. Stuttgart: Deutsche Verlagsanstalt.

Degn, H., Holden, A. V. & Olson, L. F. (Eds.) (1987) *Chaos in Biological Systems*. New York: Plenum Press.

Emrich, H. & Hohenschutz, Ch. (1992) Psychiatric disorders: are they "dynamical diseases"? In *Self Organization and Clinical Psychology. Springer Series in Synergetics*, **58**, 204–212.

Elkaim, M., Goldbeter, A. & Goldbeter, E. (1987) Analysis of the dynamics of a family system in terms of bifurcations. *Journal of Social Biology & Structure*, **10**, 21–36.

Gleick, J. (1988) *Chaos – Die Ordnung des Universums*. München: Droemer Knaur.

Grassberger, P. & Procaccia, J. (1983) Characterization of strange attractors. *Physical Review Letter*, **50**, 346–349.

Haken, H. (1990) *Synergetics. An Introduction*. Berlin: Springer-Verlag.

Haken, H. (1991) *Erfolgsgeheimnisse der Natur. Synergetik: Die Lehre vom Zusammenwirken*. Stuttgart: Deutsche Verlagsanstalt.

an der Heiden, U. (1992) Chaos in health and disease – phenomenology and theory. In *Self-Organization and Clinical Psychology* (eds W. Tschacher, G. Schiepek & E. J. Brunner), pp. 55–87. Berlin: Springer-Verlag.

Hoffman, R. E. (1987) Computer simulations of neural information processing and the schizophrenia-mania dichotomy. *Archives of General Psychiatry*, **44**, 178–188.

Holden, A. V. (1987) *Chaos*. Manchester: University Press.

Huberman, B. A. (1986) *A Model for Dysfunctions in Smooth Pursuit and Eye Movement*. (Reprint. Xerox). Palo Alto, CA: Palo Alto Research Center.

King, R. & Barchas, J. D. (1983) An application of dynamic systems theory to human behavior. In *Synergetics of the Brain* (eds E. Basar et al.). Berlin: Springer-Verlag.

Koukkou, M., Lehmann, D., Wackermann, J., et al. (1993) Dimensional complexity of EEG brain mechanisms in untreated schizophrenia. *Biology & Psychiatry*, **33**, 397–407.

Kriz, J. (1989) *Synergetik in der klinischen Psychologie*. Research report, Department of Psychology. University of Osnabrück, December, 1989.

Kupper, Z., Hoffmann, H., Dauwalder, J. P. (1994) Das PASS-Programm: Modellierung dynamischer Zusammenhänge in der beruflichen Rehabilitation chronisch psychisch Kranker. In *Sozialpsychiatrie in der Praxis: Neue Projekte, empirische Untersuchungen und Analysen*. Münster: LIT.

Lorenz, E. N. (1963) Deterministic non-periodic flow. *Journal for Atmospheric Science*, **20**, 130–141.

Mackey, M. D. & an der Heiden, U. (1982) Dynamical diseases and bifurcations: understanding functional disorders in physiological systems. *Funktionelle Biologie & Medizin*, **1**, 156–164.

Mandelbrot, B. B. (1983) *The Fractal Geometry of Nature*. New York: Freeman.

Prigogine, I. & Stengers, I. (1981) *Dialog mit der Natur. Neue Wege naturwissenschaftlichen Denkens*. München: Piper.

Rapp, P. E., Bashore, T. R., Martinerie, J. M., et al. (1989) Dynamics of brain electrical activity. *Brain Topography*, **2**, 99–118.

Scheflen, A. E. (1978) Communicational concepts of schizophrenia. In *Beyond the Double-Bind* (ed. M. M. Berger), pp. 125ff. New York: Brunner & Mazel.

Schiepek, G. & Schoppek, W. (1992) Synergetik in der Psychiatrie: Simulation schizophrener Verläufe auf der Grundlage nicht-linearer Differenzengleichungen. *Systeme*, **6**, 22–57.

Schmid, G. B. (1991) Chaos theory and schizophrenia: Elementary aspects. *Psychopathology*, **24**, 185–198.

Schuster, H. G. (1989) *Deterministic Chaos*. Weinheim: VCH Verlagsgesellschaft GmbH.

Shaw, R. S. (1981) Strange attractors, chaotic behaviour and information flow. *Zeitschrift für Naturforschung*, **36 a**, 80.

Simon, F. B. (1989) Das deterministische Chaos schizophrenen Denkens. Ansätze zu einer Theorie der schizophrenen Denkstörung. *Familiendynamik*, **14**, 237–258.

Steck, H. (1975) *Aloyse. Psychopathology and Pictorial Expression. An International Iconographical Collection*. Vol. 22. Sandoz: Basel.

Strauss, J. S., Hafez, H., Liberman, R. P. & Harding, C.M. (1985) The course of psychiatric disorder, III: Longitudinal principles. *American Journal of Psychiatry*, **142**, 289–296.

Thoms, R. (1973) *Structural Stability and Morphogenesis*. London: Addison-Wesley.

Thomas, R. (1973) Boolean formalization of genetic control circuits. *Journal of Theoretical Biology*, **42**, 563–585.

Thomas, R. & D'Ari, R. (1991) *Biological Feedback*. Boca Raton, Florida: CRC Press

Tschacher, W., Schiepek, G. & Brunner, E. I. (1992) (Eds.) *Self-Organisation in Clinical Psychology*. Berlin: Springer-Verlag.

Wing, J. K. (Ed.) (1978) Clinical concepts of schizophrenia. In *Schizophrenia. Toward a New Synthesis*. New York: Brunner & Mazel.

Non-Linearity and Chaos in the Course of Psychoses – An Empirically Based Classification of Dynamics

Wolfgang Tschacher, Christian Scheier and Elisabeth Aebi

Summary

The paths of psychoses (mainly schizophrenic) were examined on the base of daily ratings of psychoticity in 14 long-term patients. Measures of non-linear dynamical properties of the disease process can be derived from these time series. We applied forecasting methods combined with statistical surrogate data tests and Lyapunov exponents. With this methodology, we assessed the class of dynamics expressed in the course of symptoms: eight out of fourteen patients present non-linear courses, of which 6 show signs of chaoticity; four time series can be modelled linearly as auto-regressive processes; two cases are classified as random. Thus, a considerable subset of our cases seem corroborative of Ciompi's "chaos theory of schizophrenia" which states that productive symptoms may be generated by a chaotic dynamical system of few non-linearly coupled variables. Yet, on the grounds of the present sample, no clear relation between phenomenological descriptors of patients and their dynamical classifications can be established.

Clinical observation gives ample evidence of how heterogeneous the courses of psychotic illnesses can be in the medium and long run. Classical descriptions of schizophrenia in psychiatry since Kraepelin and Bleuler therefore have commonly emphasised the processual character of this disorder. From this tradition a bundle of theories and models emerged which set out to classify the paths of psychosis (Ciompi, 1988; Strauss et al., 1985). But this tradition of studying the *psychotic process* is to a large extent either tied to qualitative-descriptive phenomenology or to cross-sectional empirical research. In their overview Häfner & Maurer (1991, p. 154) state that the field is still suffering from an "extreme shortcoming of longitudinal research."

In this paper we consider psychotic symptomatology from a longitudinal perspective by making use of empirical methods of time series analysis and modelling; this perspective is based on dynamical systems theory. Our starting point will be a discussion of psychoses as "dynamical disorders": we suggest that psychotic and non-psychotic behaviour can essentially be distinguished by the kind of dynamical regime or equilibrium realised. In the interdisciplinary field of dynamics two focal concepts are currently discussed (the phenomenon of self-organisation and the regime "deterministic chaos"); the relevance of either concept for psychiatric research will be highlighted. Finally, we will present the results of an investigation of empirical data on the paths of psychoses; this is accomplished by nonlinear techniques which have become available recently.

It seems inadequate to label psychosis *per se* as "chaotic," "nonlinear" or by any such attribute; even the narrower concept of schizophrenia probably represents different heterogeneous types of disorders (Andreasen & Olsen, 1982). Additionally, schizophrenia may manifest itself differently at each systems level. In the context of our study we see the option of statistically assessing the course of each single patient by the method of time series analysis; this makes it an idiographic study as claimed by phenomenology. We also restrict ourselves to statements about a specific systems level (i. e., the level of psychopathological time courses of 200 to 800 days); under these constraints we think it is possible to differentiate types of psychotic dynamics on an empirical basis. Finally we will compare this differentiation with phenomenological and diagnostic descriptions of our cases.

The Concept of Dynamical Diseases

The concept of dynamical diseases (Glass & Mackey, 1988) is based on the axiom that psyche, body, and social world may be subdivided into *systems*, which themselves consist of interacting components (cf. Bunge, 1979). In the respective basic disciplines psychology, biology and sociology this axiom has been elaborated especially by cybernetics. Recently the various attributes of *complex* systems (Nicolis & Prigogine, 1977) render the systems view a valuable heuristic principle especially in the field of psychiatry (Schiepek & Tschacher, 1995). In its application to psychosocial systems, however, the question of which components make up the system is far from trivial (Tschacher, 1990). Pragmatically we assume that researchers' biases (e. g., conventions of scientific disciplines) participate in determining the components. Thus, a system in psychiatry is never entirely the reflection of the objective world, but must also be viewed as the construction of an observer (Böker & Brenner, this book).

The interaction of components results in a dynamics characteristic of the system. In mental, social and biological systems this dynamics is often a state of equilibrium (in cybernetics: a loop with negative feedback). But the counterpart to homeostatic dynamics is also found: in random, turbulent or unpredictable behaviour (e.g., positive feedback amplifying small deviations). Whatever dynamics a concrete system may exhibit, the concept of dynamical diseases assumes it to be essential for any dysfunction that the interaction of system components is altered. Pathological behaviour evolves out of healthy behaviour by way of a bifurcation (a phase transition between two different dynamical regimes, cf. an der Heiden, 1992). A bifurcation is also found if an unordered complex system spontaneously evolves into an ordered state; this emergent phenomenon of pattern formation is studied in self-organisation theory and synergetics (Haken, 1983).

The dynamical concept of disorder prepares for no dichotomous judgement between "sick" and "healthy," but assesses "illness" to be merely a different way of functioning in the same system. Therefore, no ontological quality is ascribed to illness (disorder), rather, it is seen as a process deviating from normal. Additionally in complex systems there may exist a tendency to fixate recurring or enduring dynamics morphologically, which explains the increasing stability of chronic states (cf. Bischof, 1990). Insofar dynamical diseases may secondarily become "imprinted" into a substrate and manifest themselves in structural changes.

Put formally, we may start from *stochastic dynamical systems.* They can be symbolized by a differential equation with a stochastic term $F(t)$ describing external fluctuations that act on the system:

$$x'(t) = N(x(t), \mu) + F(t) \tag{1}$$

$x(t)$ is a vector of the state variables of the system dependent of time t (state variables are all m phenomenological descriptors of the system, thus spanning a state space of dimension m). N is the (linear or nonlinear) function that determines the temporal change of state variables. The function itself depends on the environment of the system expressed by a set of control parameters μ.

Equation (1) lends itself to the following simple classification of qualitatively distinguishable dynamical systems:

(a) $F(t) >> N(x(t),\mu)$: If the noise or random term is much larger than the deterministic part of the equation, system (1) becomes a more or less pure stochastic process. A special case is the temporally weighted noise of a moving average (MA) process.

(b) $F(t) << N(x(t),\mu)$: We get a deterministic system capable of producing equilibrium states ("attractors"). Examples of attractors are point attractors (the equilibrium is a constant, e.g., the mood of a well-balanced person); periodical attractors are oscillating equilibria: for instance the mood of some manic-depressive persons. Point attractors can be realised by systems with linear or nonlinear N, while all equilibria of higher complexity necessarily stem from nonlinear systems. The class of chaotic attractors has been widely discussed in recent years and seems relevant for many applications. Chaotic behaviour eludes long term forecasting by showing turbulent, mixing behaviour (Rössler, 1976; Abraham & Shaw, 1984), which is hardly captured by a common notion of homeostasis; it can nevertheless be shown that these attractors must be counted among those dynamical structures that – all in all – increase order.

(c) $N(x(t),\mu)/F(t) = R$: A combination of both former classes is predominant in empirical research, namely "noisy" deterministic systems (in our data with a signal-to-noise ratio of $9 > R > 0.6$). Here a further distinction is close at hand:

(c$_1$) N is nonlinear. Nonlinear dynamical systems are prerequisite for chaos and self-organisation.

(c$_2$) N is linear. The time series may then be modelled by an autoregressive (AR) process.

Dynamics and Psychodynamics

We have now reached a point where we can put forward our content hypothesis: psychotic episodes may be understood as manifestations of a chaotic system. Clues to this point are given in studies of Ciompi and coworkers (Ciompi et al., 1992). Schmid (1991) points to the consequences of scale invariance (an attribute of chaotic fractal attractors) for a multi-level approach to schizophrenia. The significance of the dynamical finding (chaotic process (c$_1$) vs. noise (a)) for the understanding of the underlying (psychobiosocial) system is outlined in Steitz et al. (1992); elaborating this former formulation we hold the following assignment to be useful:

Pure stochastic systems (a), whose time series do not show serial structure, possess high sensitivity for fluctuating environmental stimuli. In our study this poses a fundamental null hypothesis since environmental influences on psychoticity are not controlled for in our field data (rigorous control is possible only under experimental circumstances and as such incompatible with the acquisition of long and relevant time series). (a)-systems are suggested by behavioural theories (operant and classical conditioning) which take behaviour as largely under the control of external stimuli. In this case the dynamics of a system does not primarily result from its intrinsic properties.

35

Table 1. Patient population studied according to demographic and disorder-related criteria. Grouping was achieved by cluster analysis of the variables "vocational training", "attribution (of the cause of the disorder)", "high-EE" (expressed emotions in family), "social relations" (to persons outside the ward).

Patient (sex)	age	vocational training	diagnosis	extent of psychopath.	attribution	rehabili- tation	high-EE	social relations
56 (m)	18	drop-out	schizophrenia	large	intrinsic	good	yes	no
54 (f)	32	university	schizophrenia	very large	intrinsic	bad	yes	no
58 (f)	26	completed	borderline	large	extrinsic	bad	yes	no
51 (f)	23	completed	schizophrenia	large	extrinsic	bad	yes	no
13 (f)	23	drop-out	schizophrenia	large	extrinsic	good	yes	no
53 (m)	24	completed	schizophrenia	large	extrinsic	good	no	no
47 (f)	20	drop-out	schizophrenia	very large	extrinsic	bad	no	no
24 (m)	27	drop-out	borderline	large	extrinsic	good	yes	yes
41 (f)	18	none	adolesc. psychosis	small	extrinsic	good	yes	yes
62 (m)	20	completed	schizoaffective	moderate	extrinsic	good	no	yes
57 (f)	26	drop-out	schizophrenia	large	intrinsic	bad	no	no
34 (m)	25	drop-out	schizophrenia	large	extrinsic	bad	no	no
48 (f)	37	completed	schizophrenia	large	intrinsic	good	no	yes
19 (f)	29	completed	schizophrenia	large	intrinsic	good	no	yes

Table 2. Scale for daily ratings of psychotic derealisation (psychoticity).

1: relaxed, well-balanced, calm
2: unsteady, anxious, nervous, irritated
3: restless, tense, loaded, aggressive
   or
   depressive, cross, down-hearted, sad
   or
   ambivalent, irresolute
4: intimidated, agitated, confused, labile, loose associations
5: phenomena of derealisation and/or depersonalisation: surroundings or oneself appear unreal, strange, changed. Thought disturbance: absent-mindedness, pressure of thought, breaks of thought
6: ideas of reference, delusional projections, delusions: incorrigible convictions of oneself and the world contradict reality and experiences of others
7: hallucinations: perceptual experience without objective source of stimulation. Inexistent stimuli are heard, seen, felt, smelled. Catatonic phenomena: motor blockage, compulsive posture, stereotypy, mannerism, movement storm

Chaotic dynamics (c_1), on the other hand, point to the existence of a internally controlled, low-dimensional system unfolding relatively autonomously from environmental fluctuations. Empirical evidence of (c_1)-systems would be a validation of the dynamical disease concept for psychoses. In a complex network given by a person and all of his numerous cognitive, social, and biological interactions, we understand the emergence of a low-dimensional sys-

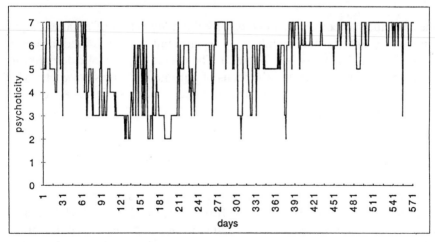

Figure 1. Plot of a time series (patient 47) of daily psychoticity ratings over a period of 572 days.

37

tem as a process of self-organisation. In the context of psychotherapy theories such systems seem compatible with psychoanalytical, cognitive, or systemic theories.

Methods

Subjects

We studied patients treated at the *Soteria Bern*; as a small therapeutic residential community, specialised for persons experiencing a first psychotic manifestation, this is based on ideas of milieu therapy and affect logic (Ciompi, 1991; Aebi et al., 1993 a). The prerequisite for inclusion in our sample was that a patient's daily manifestation of psychotic symptomatology could be observed almost completely for a long enough period of time (at least 200 days). Thus, the subjects did not constitute a random sample, but a population of long-stay Soteria patients.

Patients were assessed by two independent observers for their phenomenological characteristics, which were rated on the basis of detailed personal and interactional knowledge of the patients. The description of 14 patients is presented in Table 1.

Time Series Data

The longitudinal course was mapped by the daily rating of a patient's psychoticity by Soteria staff members. A seven-point scale was used, as described in Aebi et al. (1993 b, see Table 2). The course of psychotic derealisation measured with this scale was the focus of our interest. The state vector $\mathbf{x'}$ (t) after equation (1) therefore contains only one (global) variable. An example of a time series of a patient is depicted in Figure 1.

Forecasting Algorithm

The methodology of time series analysis has progressed considerably in recent years; linear (ARIMA-) models (Box & Jenkins, 1976), which have been in use for several decades, are more and more accompanied by nonlinear models (Tong, 1990). The rapid extension of nonlinear methods is important, especially in the context of innovative system theoretical approaches as self-organisation theory and chaos theory, which start out from nonlinear interactions within a system.

Our data sets are characterised by relatively short time series lengths, few steps of the scales, and probably high measurement error, which altogether is typical for psychosocial data acquisition. Therefore, methods that try to estimate the dimensionality of fractal attractors fail to be applicable (Steitz et al., 1992). For our study we decided to implement the nonlinear forecasting algorithm (NFA) proposed by Sugihara and May (1991). It can be shown that the NFA is robust concerning the restraints for data quality just mentioned (Scheier & Tschacher, 1994).

We continue with a short description of the NFA. First, the time series is divided into two halves; the first half is a "library" that can generate forecasts. In order to do that, the state space (or "phase space") of embedding dimension m is reconstructed using the method of Takens (1981). Each state of the system is described as one point in state space. Forecasting temporal development thus addresses the question of which point in state space is next approached by the system. On the grounds of axioms of dynamical systems theory (e. g., Rosen, 1970) it may be assumed that neighbouring points ("neighbours") in state space may change in a similar way if the system is deterministic.

For any time series measurement documented in our patients we may forecast the future development of any given state. The accuracy of this forecast may be defined as the correlation of expected development (extrapolated on the basis of next neighbours in the "library" data) with actual development (as realised in the second half of the time series). Figure 2 charts such correlations derived via NFA from the data set of Figure 1. As can be seen, the correlation value for time step 1 ("next day") is around 0.7. A forecasting period of five days, however, no longer yields a valid prognosis (the correlation has decreased to about 0.15 at an embedding dimension of $m = 3$).

The change of forecasting accuracy for increasing periods of time is characteristic for the kind of time series that has been mapped – we achieve some "fingerprint" of the system's dynamics. A linear autoregressive system, for instance, yields no decrease of correlations, but a constant positive value of forecasting accuracy; a random generator in a computer (or a noisy system, respectively) shows no correlations deviating from zero; a deterministic-chaotic system acts according to sensitive dependence on initial conditions (the definition of chaos: Bergé et al., 1984) by giving a trajectory of prognoses that resembles the one depicted in Figure 3: short-term predictability with non-predictability in the longer run is a basic sign of deterministic chaos.

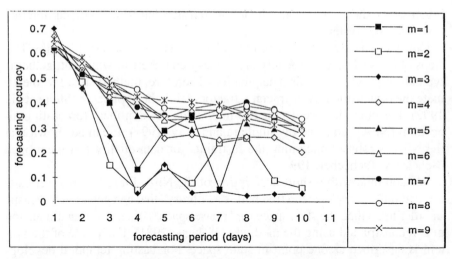

Figure 2. Courses of forecasting accuracies computed with the Sugihara-May algorithm (NFA), embedding dimensions from 1 to 10, based on the data of Figure 1.

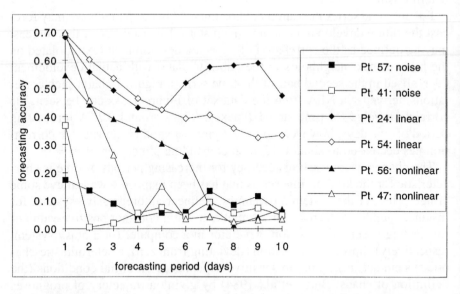

Figure 3. (c_1)-systems, (a)-systems, (c_2)-systems: courses of forecasting accuracies for six exemplary psychosis time series.

Surrogate Data Method

We use the method of surrogate data in order to evaluate the statistical significance or our time series classification with the NFA. The method is described at length in Theiler et al. (1992) and Scheier and Tschacher (1994), so that we may introduce it here by a short example: first we compute a discriminating statistic with the forecasting method NFA, say the forecasting accuracy for the period "one day." This value in the times series of Figure 2 is about $r = 0.70$ (see Fig. 3). Then we determine the respective values for a number of surrogate data (i. e., artificially generated "time series," that are identical with the measured data according to mean, variance and length); in this way we gain a *distribution* of discriminating statistics. Thus we can test if the empirical time series can be discriminated from a population of surrogate data.

Tests were employed in two ways: first, we tested if empirical time series can be predicted better than random; secondly, we fit autoregressive models to the original data, used the various realisations of models as surrogate data sets and examined if empirical data can be forecast better than their linear models. Thus, the surrogate data method allows us to test two null hypotheses:

Null hypothesis (1): The time series behaves like a string of random numbers as far as forecastability is concerned, i. e., is an (a)-system according to the classification given above. Here surrogates can be generated by scrambling the original data: time series length, mean, and standard deviation remain the same, but serial dependency is eliminated.

Null hypothesis (2): The time series to be examined behaves like a linear autoregressive process, is a (c_2)-system. Surrogate data in this test are different realisations of an AR(1) model of the time series.

The rejection of both null hypotheses indicates that a certain time series contains nonrandom serial structure and is nonlinear.

Lyapunov Exponents

These "characteristic exponents" count among the ergodic measures of a dynamical system (Eckmann & Ruelle, 1985), i. e., signify invariants of systems dynamics. The largest Lyapunov exponent is an indicator for divergence of neighbouring trajectories in state space. Divergence (> 0) points to entropy production and sensitive dependence from initial conditions, in other words, deterministic chaos. Calculating is sensible if the testing of null hypotheses (1) and (2) shows that the course of a psychosis can be understood as a non-

41

linear (c_1)-system. then gives an indication of whether there is nonlinearity in the sense of deterministic chaos. We used the algorithm after Wolf et al. (1985).

Cluster Analyses

Finally we clustered the various descriptors of 14 empirical time series in order to find out about the subgroups in these cases. We used hierarchical cluster analyses with appropriate correlation coefficients (Pearson-r for the NFA- and surrogate data; Goodman-Kruskal-Gamma as the distance metric for phenomenological data) (Wilkinson, 1989). For analysing the latter data the ratings had to be quantified – we therefore "translated" the ordinal scales (e. g., the scale "attribution" was quantified in this way: intrinsic = 1; extrinsic = –1).

Results

Different groups of psychotic courses can already be seen in visual inspection as soon as the 14 data sets are assessed by the NFA. Two courses in each group, respectively, are presented in Figure 4. The first group of courses yields forecasting curves that resemble those of chaotic-deterministic systems (denoted as "nonlinear" in the legend of Figure 4). The discussion of the population dynamical time series in Sugihara and May (1991) corresponds to our finding of a variable amount of noise in our nonlinear time series, which reduces one-day forecasts to values of between 0.92 (approx. 10% noise) and 0.4 (approx. 60% noise). These time series are probably (c_1)-systems. Further time series can be characterised as random data sets ((a)-systems, "noise" in Fig. 4) or autoregressive processes ((c_2)-systems, "linear"). This last group of psychoses shows no significant change in forecasting accuracy over time.

These results are supported by the significance tests on the null hypotheses of the surrogate data method. In Table 2 we listed the forecasting accuracies after Sugihara and May for the psychoses time series and the effect measures for null hypotheses (1) and (2). The table shows that eight out of fourteen patients (57%) have nonlinear dynamics. Four time series are best modelled as autoregressive linear processes. Two cases are classified as random. The results of significance tests are summarised under the heading "model" in Table 2.

Table 3. Results of the non-linear forecasting method NFA and related significance tests. "Forecasting accuracy": the degree of predictability of a time series (maximum NFA correlation between forecast one day ahead and actual data); "forecasting decline": mean forecasting accuracy one day ahead *minus* mean forecasting accuracy five days ahead; "l": value of the largest Lyapunov exponent; "$H_O(1)$": noise effect measure from test of the first null hypothesis; "$H_O(2)$": linearity effect measure (effect measures are values under a standard normal distribution; e. g., 1.96 (*) is significant at a 5 % error level (both sides), 2.58 at the 1 % level (**). This table is grouped according to cluster analysis of the data included in the table.

62	0.790	0.422	0.024	12.22**	0.98	AR
54	0.696	0.229	0.014	17.13**	1.23	AR
24	0.852	0.408	0.002	11.97**	0.87	AR
51	0.920	0.288	0.142	11.28**	1.90	nl
13	0.661	0.269	0.104	10.84**	1.72	AR (nl?)
47	0.698	0.344	0.27	15.27**	2.18*	nl
34	0.479	0.325	0.004	11.64**	2.28*	nl (AR?)
48	0.472	0.364	0.02	4.70**	2.18*	nl (AR?)
56	0.578	0.206	0.372	9.26**	6.66**	nl
19	0.671	0.326	0.243	5.13**	2.33**	nl
53	0.757	0.45	0.214	4.59**	3.42**	nl
58	0.358	0.123	0.117	2.72**	8.16**	nl
41	0.477	0.113	0.002	1.66	4.91**	noise (nl?)
57	0.174	0.005	0.021	0.80	5.26**	noise

The largest Lyapunov exponents are also given in Table 2; they support our classification made on the basis of significances since nonlinear courses show the highest values. Thus, at least in six cases we may assume that clear signs of chaotic dynamics are present.

The values listed in Table 2 were analysed for internal structure by cluster analysis. This resulted in three subgroups or clusters, which are graphically indicated in the table by spaces. The three qualitatively distinguished types of courses differentiated by the tests of the surrogate data method are suggested by cluster analysis as well. The transitions between the groups of linear, nonlinear, and noisy systems are not clear-cut, though.

Phenomenological descriptors were quantified and then clustered in the same manner. The result of this analysis is again illustrated by graphical groupings in Table 1. We find that the three dynamical clusters are not congruent with phenomenological clusters. This incompatibility also turns up in correlational analyses (which cannot be detailed here): no significant correlations are found to exist between phenomenological and quantitative-dynamical variables in our 14 cases.

Discussion

In our opinion a number of central questions concerning schizophrenia and psychosis research can only be answered by longitudinal studies. In this paper we treated the basic question of which kind of dynamics reigns psychotic courses: Is the unpredictable and seemingly turbulent sequence of daily symptomatology the expression of a nonlinear system or does it simply reflect environmental fluctuations? In the former case we might approach schizophrenia and similar psychoses on a new foundation, i. e., by interpreting them as dynamical diseases. A palette of methods and phenomena would then be accessible to psychiatry, especially those developed and refined in the field of dynamical science, of synergetics and chaos theory (Tschacher et al., 1992). The validity of such an approach has recently been questioned for different reasons in the case of schizophrenic psychoses (as opposing bipolar depression) (Emrich & Hohenschutz, 1992).

Our investigation actually presents clear evidence to the point that a larger proportion of the psychoses we studied show *nonlinear time courses*. This is the (to our knowledge) first time that the validity of the concept of dynamical diseases could be established on statistical grounds in this important area of psychopathology. Additionally, we succeeded in showing by the estimation of Lyapunov exponents that most of the nonlinear courses may be interpreted as expressions of low-dimensional chaos. This applies to at least six out of eight nonlinear cases. Reversely, this interpretation is supported by the fact that in linear and noisy data sets of our population exponents do not deviate significantly from zero.

The context of the paths of psychopathology measured under field conditions is influenced by many factors, i. e., is high-dimensional. We therefore may assume that nonlinear dynamics is a reflection of the eigen-activity of the psychobiological system "psychosis" which is embedded in the social milieu "Soteria." We see this as an example of *self-organisation*, by which a nonlinear chaotic system is contrasted against a complex environment by an emergent process of pattern formation.

Phenomenology

Our studies have so far not resulted in a congruence between dynamical clustering and groups gained by clinical phenomenological descriptions. The most interesting chaotic courses (i. e., the (c_1)-systems with positive) are mainly schizophrenic psychoses (in one case – Pt. 58 – a borderline disorder).

But we find among these courses favourable and unfavourable paths of the disorder as well; in respect to social interaction and insight into the illness (attribution) the 58 "chaotic" patients are heterogeneous, too.

The same applies to a prognosis we held to be plausible a priori: the less severe a psychosis (as in a borderline disorder), the noisier should be its course. In other words, (a)-systems indicate environmentally contingent behaviour. Our results do not readily support this idea: one of the (a)-systems is generated by a schizophrenic disorder (see Pt. 57 in Table 1). Altogether we think that hypotheses on the connection of dynamics and phenomenology are yet to be generated by correlative-heuristic methods. General statements about this issue must remain vague also due to the small number of cases available at the present time.

We might infer different conclusions from the fact that diagnoses of single patients do not correspond well with dynamical parameters. On the one hand, it is certainly desirable to accommodate diagnoses to path characteristics more than is done in standard taxonomies. A more valid diagnostic system should evolve in this way. On the other hand, our preliminary results encourage idiography which we see not as a method of hermeneutics alone. Each person develops his/her own dynamics; psychoses are private and "creative" phenomena, too, and therefore cannot be subsumed under a category completely (Scharfetter, 1990).

Outview

Time series data of the length reported here, especially with regular daily ratings, are probably rare; they were acquired through observations under special conditions in the course of years. Nevertheless, a number of optimisations are desirable: if scales were more differentiated the course of psychoses could be investigated more thoroughly and reliably (our research group has therefore advanced to data acquisition with multiple time series in the meantime). The topic of the interaction of different symptoms (say, positive and negative symptoms) in schizophrenic disorders has stimulated various incompatible theories which equally draw upon cross-sectional correlational studies (Maurer & Häfner, 1989). We think it is evident that these theories can be further discussed only by applying finer temporal resolution in the sense of multiple time series analysis.

If – as now seems justified – we may count a considerable proportion of psychoses among the dynamical disorders, cross-sectional research approaches even in large samples must in principle leave the essence of these psychoses in the dark. We adopt the opinion of Strauss et al. (1985, p. 295): ". . . the issues of sequence and patterns cannot be neglected indefinitely: they potentially hold answers for too many crucial questions." Beyond this, we think it is time to advocate the theory of dynamical systems as a methodology to be used within psychiatry and psychology. The consequences of a dynamical view will be far-reaching; they not only concern the theory but also the therapy of these disorders.

Chaos does not mean total uncontrollability (as is suggested by colloquial language), but increasing unpredictability combined with short-term determination. Thus, therapeutic intervention can contain a moment of "chaos control": the time span between intervention and evaluation (which guides new interventions) should be chosen accordingly (Mayer-Kress, 1992). The question of dealing with complex systems may be approached also in the context of synergetics; applications to clinical psychology are already being discussed (Kruse & Stadler, 1990; Schiepek et al., 1992; Tschacher, 1990). Psychosis is then understood as a dynamical pattern generated by a self-organising system (i. e., as the attractor of a dynamical disease); theoretically, there are different ways of restituting the dynamics to non-psychotic regions of state space. First, with gradual variation of the environment ("control parameters") the attributes of attractors change in an often discontinuous manner. Second, if other "non-pathological" attractors continue to exist there is an opportunity to drive the system into the bassins of these attractors by single interventions or perturbations, i. e., even without changing control parameters. Functioning in these attractors then has to be stabilised structurally in the sense of relapse prevention.

In the future a more systematic and fundamental elaboration of a dynamical intervention theory will have to be developed. We hope to have stimulated such an endeavour with the present article.

Acknowledgements

We are grateful for the labourious documentations done by Soteria team members. Data acquisition was made possible by the pilot project Soteria (grant of the Swiss National Fund) headed by Luc Ciompi.

References

Abraham, R., & Shaw, C. (1984) *Chaotic Behavior . Dynamics – the Geometry of Behavior* (Vol.2) Santa Cruz: Aerial Press.
Aebi, E., Ciompi, L. & Hansen, H. (1993 a) *Soteria im Gespräch – über eine alternative Schizophreniebehandlung*. Bonn: Psychiatrie-Verlag.

Aebi, E., Ackermann, K. & Revenstorf, D. (1993 b) Ein Konzept der sozialen Unterstützung für akut Schizophrene – Zeitreihenanalysen täglicher Fluktuationen psychotischer Merkmale. *Zeitschrift für Klinische Psychologie, Psychopathologie & Psychotherapie*, **41**, 18–30.

Andreasen, N. C. & Olsen, S. (1982) Negative versus positive schizophrenia. *Archives of General Psychiatry*, **39**, 789–794.

Bergé, P., Pomeau, Y. & Vidal, C. (1984) *Order Within Chaos. Towards a Deterministic Approach to Turbulence*. New York: Wiley.

Bischof, N. (1990) Ordnung und Organisation als heuristische Prinzipien des reduktiven Denkens. *Nova Acta Leopoldina*, **63**, 285–312.

Box, G. E. P. & Jenkins, G. (1976) *Time Series Analysis: Forecasting and Control*. San Francisco: Holden-Day.

Bunge, M. (1979) *Treatise on Basic Philosophy. Ontology II: A World of Systems (Vol. 4)*. Dordrecht: Reidel.

Ciompi, L. (1991) Affects as central organising and integrating factors. *British Journal of Psychiatry*, **159**, 97–105.

Ciompi, L. (1988) Learning from outcome studies. Towards a comprehensive biological-psychological understanding of schizophrenia. *Schizophrenia Research*, **1**, 373–384.

Ciompi, L., Ambühl, B. & Dünki, R. (1992) Schizophrenie und Chaostheorie. *System Familie*, **5**, 133–147.

Eckmann, J. & Ruelle, D. (1985) Ergodic theory of chaos and strange attractors. *Reviews of Modern Physics*, **57**, 617–656.

Emrich, H. & Hohenschutz, C. (1992) Psychiatric disorders: Are they "dynamical diseases"? In *Self-Organization and Clinical Psychology* (eds W. Tschacher, G. Schiepek & E. J. Brunner), pp. 204–212. Berlin: Springer-Verlag.

Glass, L. & Mackey, M. (1988) *From Clocks to Chaos. The Rhythms of Life*. Princeton: University Press.

Gleick, J. (1987) *Chaos – Making a New Science*. New York: Viking.

Häfner, H. & Maurer, K. (1991) Are there two types of schizophrenia? In *Negative versus Positive Schizophrenia* (eds A. Marneros, N. C. Andreasen & M. T. Tsuang), pp. 134–159. Berlin: Springer-Verlag.

Haken, H. (1983) *Synergetics – an Introduction* (3rd edn.). Berlin: Springer-Verlag.

an der Heiden, U. (1992) Chaos in health and disease – phenomenology and theory. In *Self-Organization and Clinical Psychology* (eds W. Tschacher, G. Schiepek & E. J. Brunner), pp. 55–87. Berlin: Springer-Verlag.

Kruse, P. & Stadler, M. (1990) Stability and instability in cognitive systems: Multi-stability, suggestion and psychosomatic interaction. In *Synergetics of Cognition* (eds H. Haken & M. Stadler), pp. 201–215. Berlin: Springer-Verlag.

Maurer, K. & Häfner, H. (1991) Dependence, independence or interdependece of positive and negative symptoms. In *Negative versus Positive Schizophrenia* (eds A. Marneros, N. C. Andreasen & M. T. Tsuang), pp. 160–182. Berlin: Springer-Verlag.

Mayer-Kress, G. (1992) *Chaos and Crises in International Systems*. Talk presented at SHAPE Technology Symposium on crisis management, Mons, Belgium (3/19– 3/20/92).

Nicolis, G. & Prigogine, I. (1977) *Self-Organization in Nonequilibrium Systems*. New York: Wiley.

Rosen, R. (1970) *Dynamical Systems Theory in Biology (Vol. I)*. New York: Wiley.

Rössler, O. (1976) An equation for continuous chaos. *Physical Letters*, **57A**, 397–398.

Scharfetter, C. (1990) *Schizophrene Menschen*. München: Psychologie-Verlags-Union.

Scheier, C. & Tschacher, W. (1994) Nichtlineare Analyse dynamischer psychologischer Systeme I: Konzepte und Methoden. *System Familie*, **7**, 133–144.

Schiepek, G. & Tschacher, W. (Eds.) (1995) *Synergetik in Psychologie und Psychiatrie*. Berlin: Springer (in preparation).

Schiepek, G., Fricke, B. & Kaimer, P. (1992) Synergetics of psychotherapy. In *Self-Organization and Clinical Psychology* (eds W. Tschacher, G. Schiepek & E. J. Brunner), pp. 239–267. Berlin: Springer-Verlag.

Schmid, G. (1991) Chaos theory and schizophrenia: Elementary aspects. *Psychopathology*, **24**, 185–198.

Steitz, A., Tschacher, W., Ackermann, K. & Revenstorf, D. (1992) Applicability of dimension analysis to data in psychology. In *Self-Organization and Clinical Psychology* (eds W. Tschacher, G. Schiepek & E. J. Brunner), pp. 367–384. Berlin: Springer-Verlag.

Strauss, J. S., Hafez, H., Lieberman, P. & Harding, C. M. (1985) The course of psychiatric disorder, III: Longitudinal principles. *American Journal of Psychiatry*, **142**, 289–296.

Sugihara, G. & May, R. (1990) Nonlinear forecasting as a way of distinguishing chaos from measurement error in time series. *Nature*, **344**, 734–741.

Takens, F. (1981) Detecting strange attractors in turbulence. In *Lecture Notes in Mathematics* (eds D. A. Rand & L. Ss Young), p. 898. Berlin: Springer-Verlag.

Theiler, J., Galdrikian, B., Longtin, A., et al. (1992). Using surrogate data to detect nonlinearity in time series. In *Nonlinear Modeling and Forecasting* (eds M. Casdagli & S. Eubank). Redwood City: Addison-Wesley.

Tong, H. (1990) *Non-Linear Time Series*. Oxford: Oxford University Press.

Tschacher, W. (1990) *Interaktion in selbstorganisierten Systemen. (Grundlegung eines dynamisch-synergetischen Forschungsprogramms in der Psychologie)*. Heidelberg: Asanger.

Tschacher, W., Schiepek, G., & Brunner, E. J. (Eds.) (1992) *Self-Organization and Clinical Psychology. Empirical Approaches to Synergetics in Psychology*. Berlin: Springer-Verlag.

Wilkinson, L. (1989) *SYSTAT: The System for Statistics*. Evanston, IL.: SYSTAT Inc.

Wolf, A., Swift, J. B., Swinney, H. L. & Vastano, J. (1985) Determining Lyapounov exponents from a time series. *Physica*, **16D**, 285–317.

Focus on Influencing Biological Vulnerability

Beyond the Dopamine Receptor: Clinical and Research Experience with Risperidone

Richard L. Borison and Bruce I. Diamond

Summary

Risperidone represents a new class of antipsychotic drugs which are potent antagonists at both serotonin and dopamine receptors. The efficacy and safety of risperidone in controlled and uncontrolled trials in schizophrenic patients indicate that it is effective for both positive and negative symptoms, whilst producing a very low rate of extrapyramidal side effects. Although there is only limited data directly comparing risperidone with conventional antipsychotics, it appears that it is at least as efficacious and probably produces less neurological side effects than these traditional treatments. Given its pharmacology as a serotonin-dopamine antagonist, risperidone may have therapeutic applications in other neuropsychiatric disorders.

Although the antipsychotics have proved to be "wonder drugs" in the sense that they have allowed many schizophrenic patients who otherwise would have been institutionalised for long periods to rejoin their communities and often lead productive and fulfilling lives, there still remains a need to seek more effective treatments. This is because conventional antipsychotic medication, while generally treating the positive symptoms of schizophrenia (e. g., delusions, hallucinations, thought disorder) to a satisfactory extent, generally does poorly in treating the negative symptoms (e. g., poverty of speech, withdrawn behaviour, poor social relationships, anhedonia). Furthermore, conventional antipsychotic compounds have the propensity for producing disabling neurological side-effects, whether reversible (dystonia, pseudoparkinsonism, akathisia) or mostly irreversible (tardive dyskinesia). In addition to these extrapyramidal side-effects (EPS), the antipsychotics also have the potential to induce clinically significant hypotension, anticholinergic effects, cardiac arrhythmias, sedation, convulsions, and agranulocytosis. Therefore, even when such an agent is producing a maximal therapeutic action, its multiple side-effects may in some cases lead to poor satisfaction and compliance with treatment on the part of patients.

51

Although the first true antipsychotic, chlorpromazine, was pharmacologically diverse in its neurotransmitter-blocking properties (on norepinephrine, dopamine, and serotonin receptors), the "dopamine hypothesis" suggested that dopaminergic dysfunction was the underlying pathophysiology of schizophrenia, and that blockade of these receptors was the essential component of antipsychotic activity (Meltzer & Stahl, 1976). This led to a search for more specific and potent antidopaminergic drugs. Ironically, though the development of such drugs has not improved the treatment of schizophrenia over the last 40 years, it has rather changed the side-effect profile of antipsychotics, increasing the incidence of neurological side-effects, while decreasing the autonomic ones.

However, the status quo in the treatment of schizophrenia was challenged with the development of clozapine. Although this drug can produce serious toxicity (particularly agranulocytosis), in selected samples of schizophrenics unresponsive to conventional antipsychotics, it is an efficacious antipsychotic compound for the positive symptoms of schizophrenia, and possibly for the negative ones (Kane et al., 1988). This activity occurs despite clozapine being the weakest dopamine-D_2 blocker among the antipsychotic drugs; however it is more potent as a serotonin 5-HT_2 antagonist. These surprising data have led to a re-evaluation of the pharmacology of antipsychotic action, and have suggested that potent 5-HT_2 blockade may increase the efficacy of D_2 blockers (particularly in regard to negative symptoms) and decrease the occurrence of EPS (Meltzer, 1989).

The role of serotonin in schizophrenia still remains somewhat enigmatic, with studies of postmortem schizophrenic brain tissue indicating decreased 5-HT_{1A} binding, whereas 5-HT_2 binding has been described in different studies as decreased, normal, or elevated (Whitacker et al., 1981; Reynolds et al., 1983; Arora & Meltzer, 1991; Hashimoto et al., 1991). Likewise, both cerebrospinal fluid levels of metabolites and platelet reuptake studies of serotonin have yielded conflicting results (Modai et al., 1979; Wood et al., 1983; Nyback et al., 1983; Bleich et al., 1988). The use of direct agonists, such as lysergic acid diethylamide (LSD) had indicated either an increase in psychotic symptoms in schizophrenics or alternatively a blunted response to LSD's psychedelic effects (Bozormenyi & Szara, 1958; Itil et al., 1969), while the partial 5-HT agonist m-chlorophenylpiperazine (mCPP) has been reported to exacerbate or improve the positive symptoms of schizophrenia (Kahn et al., 1992; Krystal et al., 1993). Although these disparate data may seem somewhat discouraging in arguing for a role of serotonin in schizophrenia, there are no better clinical data in support of a direct role. Therefore, serotonin does appear to play a role, although a complex one, in the pathophysiology, and therefore the pharmacology of schizophrenia.

This reformulation of thinking on the pharmacology of antipsychotic action has led to the development of new antipsychotic agents, which have been designed to balance antidopaminergic and antiserotonergic actions (Janssen et al., 1988; Leysen et al., 1992). The first of these new agents to become widely available is risperidone (Bersani et al., 1990). The review here of the clinical pharmacology of risperidone, indicates that this compound may help to rewrite our understanding of both the pathophysiology and therapeutics of schizophrenia.

The role of serotonin in schizophrenic psychopathology could not be adequately tested until specific serotonergic blocking agents became available. Among the first of these was ritanserin, which potently blocks 5-HT_2 and 5-HT_{1C} receptors; initial clinical trials in schizophrenic subjects suggested that it had, at best, a moderate antipsychotic effect (Gerlach, 1991). The clinical results of adding ritanserin to fixed doses of haloperidol were most interesting (Bersani et al., 1986); not only did ritanserin improve haloperidol's therapeutic action, but this was particularly pronounced for the negative symptoms of schizophrenia; the EPS that were being produced by haloperidol were also decreased.

Whilst the interaction of serotonergic and dopaminergic systems in the brain is complex, it appears that serotonin plays an inhibitory modulatory role on dopaminergic function (Jones et al., 1980; Korsgaard et al., 1985). Studies of haloperidol in schizophrenic subjects have indicated that the therapeutic effect of this drug on positive symptoms is not correlated with absolute changes in the levels of cerebrospinal fluid homovanillic acid or 5-hydroxyindoleacetic acid. Rather, its therapeutic action correlates with the ratio of these two metabolites – in other words, with the relative changes in dopamine and serotonin turnover (Kahn et al., 1993). However, this neurochemical observation has not yet been systematically studied in the therapeutics of the negative symptoms of schizophrenia. These data suggest that the efficacy of an antipsychotic drug is not dependent on either dopamine or serotonin alone, but rather on the interaction between (at least) these two systems.

Risperidone is extensively metabolised in man, with one metabolite, 9-hydroxy-risperidone (9-OH-RIS), being as active pharmacologically as the parent compound. It would therefore appear that the antipsychotic action of risperidone is mediated both by the parent compound and the 9-hydroxy metabolite (Mannens et al., 1990), and that the sums of these two compounds are equivalent in either slow or fast metabolisers (Huang et al., 1991). The plasma level of risperidone does not change with food (Vanden-Bussche et al., 1988), and increases in a linear manner in relationship to dosage. Risperidone is a substrate for cytochrome P-450IID6, and its metabolism may be slowed by other drugs that are substrates for this enzyme; however, this is very unlikely to have any clinical significance, as the combined total of risperidone and 9-OH-RIS will stay approximately the same, whereas only the ratios of these two compounds may be changed.

Single-dose pharmacokinetic trials (Borison et al., 1994) in 24 schizophrenic subjects receiving 4 mg of risperidone indicated that peak plasma levels for risperiodone and 9-OH-RIS both occur at approximately 1.5 hours after ingestion. The half-life for risperidone is approximately 3.5 hours and that for 9-OH-RIS approximately 23 hours. Although it is recommended that treatment with risperidone be initiated at 1 mg twice-daily, a single 4 mg dosage was well tolerated by patients in this study. Postural hypotension, the major concern if treatment is begun at higher doses, was seen in only one out of 24 subjects, whereas sedation was the major complaint, occurring in 83%. Although 9-OH-RIS blood levels are between 33–67% of risperidone blood levels, it is possible that the longer half-life of this metabolite contributes to the pharmacodynamic profile of risperidone, in which a twice-daily dose is adequate for antipsychotic control. This longer half-life for the metabolite would also suggest that a once-daily schedule may produce therapeutic benefits, and future studies will be needed to test this hypothesis. Furthermore, considering how well tolerated a 4 mg dose of risperidone was in this group of schizophrenics, it would suggest that in patients with normal cardiovascular systems, a higher initial dose of risperidone may be well tolerated, thereby offering the advantage of immediate sedation that may be of benefit in the treatment of acutely agitated patients.

There have been several large double-blind, multi-centre controlled studies of risperidone. In a subset of one study, Chouinard et al. (1993) reported on the efficacy of risperidone (2 mg, 6 mg, 10 mg, 16 mg/day) versus haloperidol (20 mg/day) or placebo treatment. After a seven-day placebo washout period, 135 schizophrenic subjects were randomised to double-blind medication. Therapeutic efficacy was determined using the Positive and Negative Symptom Scale (PANSS) (Kay et al., 1987). Using the criterion for improvement as a 20% or greater decrease in PANSS score, the 6 mg risperidone treatment group was significantly improved, compared with placebo ($p < 0.001$), with a trend towards its being superior to haloperidol treatment. The other three doses of risperidone also achieved statistical significance compared to placebo ($p < 0.01$). All treatments were significantly better than placebo on the positive symptom subscale of the PANSS, though only the 6 mg dose was statistically superior to placebo ($p < 0.009$) on the negative symptom subscale. In comparing the onset of efficacy, this dose of risperidone produced significant efficacy compared to placebo by the end of the first week of treatment, whereas haloperidol did not statistically differentiate itself from placebo until the second week of treatment.

In this study, extrapyramidal side-effects were measured using the Extra-pyramidal Side-Effect Rating Scale (ESRS) (Chouinard et al., 1980), and revealed that no dose of risperidone was significantly different from placebo in producing parkinsonian symptoms; however, haloperidol treatment produced significantly (p < 0.05) more parkinsonism than either placebo or risperidone (2 mg, 6 mg, 16 mg daily doses). Whilst the use of antiparkinsonian agents during treatment was no different comparing placebo to any dose of risperidone, subjects receiving haloperidol required significantly (p < 0.005) more such medication. Risperidone was observed also to have a significant anti-dyskinetic action in those patients meeting Research Diagnosis Criteria for tardive dyskinesia (Schooler & Kane, 1982), whereas haloperidol did not. Previous studies with risperidone have also demonstrated an antidyskinetic action (Borison et al., 1991). The most common adverse events, other than EPS recorded during this study were agitation, anxiety, and insomnia, with haloperidol producing the highest incidence of all three of these side-effects.

In a larger study of 388 patients using the same study design, the 6 mg and 16 mg doses of risperidone were statistically superior to placebo (p < 0.001) and haloperidol (p < 0.05) on the total PANSS (Marder & Meibach, 1994). These same two doses were the only treatments that produced a significant reduction (p < 0.01) in negative symptoms when compared to placebo. Doses of risperidone at 10 mg showed no statistical difference from placebo in the occurrence of EPS, though the 16 mg dose and haloperidol did produce significantly more EPS (p = 0.01).

In addition to these well controlled clinical trials, approximately ten open trials with risperidone (Borison et al., 1992; Grant & Fitton, 1994) have been published. There has been a remarkable consistency in the findings of these studies, indicating that 4–8 mg/day was the optimal dosage of risperidone, that both positive and negative symptoms of schizophrenia improved at these dosages, and that EPS were relatively uncommon in this dose-range. Of particular interest was one long-term study of risperidone for one year or more, in over 100 schizophrenic subjects (Mertens, 1991). This demonstrated both the long-term efficacy and safety of risperidone, but of greatest interest was the fact that even though a definite therapeutic action was observed after the first one or two weeks, this effect continued to increase for up to seven months, prior to a plateauing of benefits. Thus, the controlled trials which were conducted over a 6–8 week period may have underestimated the full therapeutic action of risperidone, which is likely to continue to develop over a number of months.

There have been smaller therapeutic trials comparing risperidone with haloperidol (DeCuyper, 1989; Svestka et al., 1990; Borison et al., 1991; Claus et al., 1992; Borison et al., 1993), perphenazine (Høyberg et al., 1993), and clozapine (Heinrich et al., 1991). In the studies versus haloperidol (2–

20 mg/day), which totalled 159 patients, treatment with risperidone (2–20 mg/day) was either therapeutically equivalent or superior to haloperidol in schizophrenic subjects, with many fewer EPS being produced. In one (Claus et al., 1992), the population studied was of chronic treatment-resistant schizophrenics, who had failed to show any response to haloperidol; risperidone resulted in a rapid and statistically significant improvement, particularly in the negative symptoms of schizophrenia. In the first published double-blind, placebo-controlled trial of risperidone versus haloperidol, while both drugs were statistically superior to placebo in lessening schizophrenic psychosis, risperidone was therapeutically superior, and produced significantly fewer EPS (Borison et al., 1991). A study of risperidone (4 mg or 8 mg/day) versus clozapine (400 mg/day) over four weeks (Heinrich et al., 1991) showed that the 4 mg dose of risperidone was equally efficacious to clozapine, and that there was no difference in the incidence of EPS. Although efficacious, the 8 mg dose of risperidone was not as effective as either the 4 mg dose of risperidone or clozapine treatment. In comparison with perphenazine, risperidone was more effective in reducing the negative symptoms, though both drugs produced equal numbers of EPS (Høyberg et al., 1993).

Its unique pharmacology of balanced serotonergic-dopaminergic blockades suggests many future clinical applications for risperidone; among the areas to be explored is a potential role in mood and anxiety disorders. Currently, it is common to use neuroleptics in the management of patients with either psychotic depression or bipolar disorder. Serotonin is believed to play a very significant role in affective disorders, and risperidone would be expected to produce an antimanic action in bipolar disorder, as do other neuroleptics. However, it may also be less likely to produce depression as a side-effect (its antiserotonergic actions are similar to the mechanism of antidepressant medication, such as mianserin or trazodone), and if so, risperidone might be a particularly helpful adjunct to the mood stabilising actions of lithium, carbamazepine, etc. The efficacy of neuroleptics in the treatment of psychotic depression is relatively poor (approximately 33% of subjects respond), whereas combined antidepressant/antipsychotic drug treatment has much greater efficacy (approximately 67%) (Anton et al., 1985). If risperidone's antiserotonergic properties confer on it mood-elevating actions similar to those of ritanserin (Gelders, 1989), risperidone might be a single agent that could adequately treat psychotic depression and perhaps schizo-affective disorder. Uncontrolled clinical observations have suggested that clozapine may be of particular use in treating schizo-affective illness (McElroy et al., 1991), most likely due to its antiserotonergic actions and therefore risperidone, which is a more potent antiserotonergic agent, should be of even greater potential efficacy.

It has long been known that, as major tranquillizers, antipsychotic agents have an anxiolytic action in low doses. It is also recognised that serotonergic dysfunction is among the major neurochemical abnormalities in anxious patients (Eison, 1989). In the treatment of anxiety, antipsychotic drugs have no potential for dependence or withdrawal, unlike benzodiazepines, and unlike the azapirones, such as buspirone, they are effective when used on a PRN basis, with a relatively rapid onset of anxiolytic action. The major disadvantages of using antipsychotics in this way are anticholinergic side-effects, cardiovascular side-effects, sedation, and EPS, but in low doses, risperidone is virtually free of these side-effects. The other major concern with antipsychotic treatment though, is the potential for causing tardive dyskinesia, but it can be inferred from risperidone's pharmacology that, when given at low, anxiolytic doses, it would have a very low liability for producing tardive dyskinesia, and it may also be a particularly effective anxiolytic due to its antiserotonergic action.

It is difficult to ascertain with any certainty whether risperidone will, like other antipsychotic agents, eventually produce tardive dyskinesia (TD) and if so, whether this will be a rate lower than with other drugs. It has been suggested that the antiserotonergic action of clozapine gives it a lower liability for producing TD than that of conventional antipsychotics (Meltzer et al., 1989; Meltzer, 1991). If this is true, the greater antiserotonergic action of risperidone would also make this compound less likely to produce TD, although it is significantly more antidopaminergic than clozapine. Prospective studies have indicated that the production of EPS is significantly associated with the appearance of TD (Kane et al., 1982) and therefore, the low incidence of EPS with risperidone suggests that TD would also be less frequent with this drug. However, only long-term prospective studies with risperidone will provide a final answer as to its potential for producing TD.

Another area of antipsychotic drug use has been in the treatment of behavioural disorders, such as aggressive/hostile acts, paranoid thoughts, wandering, pacing, etc. associated with elderly, usually demented patients. Although a number of new cognitive enhancing agents are being developed, their ability to increase intellectual capacity does not necessarily result in improved behaviour. Antipsychotic medication, although commonly used to treat behavioural disorders in the elderly, has potentially severe limitations in this population. Not only can their anticholinergic side-effects affect memory and worsen dementia, but the autonomic side-effects of blurred vision, tachycardia, urinary retention, and constipation may produce toxic side-effects in organ systems already compromised through senescence. Among the signs of antipsychotic drug-induced parkinsonism is a loss of postural reflexes, which, coupled with the potential for hypotension and sedation, places geriatric patients at a high risk for falling and injuring themselves. In contrast, the extremely low liability of risperidone at therapeutic doses for cardiovascular side-effects, autonomic effects, EPS, or sedation would seem to make it a very suitable agent for treating the geriatric patient. Although small doses of risperidone (2 mg/day) are likely to be therapeutic in this age-group, our own experience indicates that many elderly patients can safely be titrated to 6 mg within the first three days of treatment.

Antipsychotic agents have also been used in the treatment of behavioural disorders associated with the mentally retarded. Studies have indicated that serotonin may play an important role in impulsive, aggressive behaviour in people with learning disabilities (Brown et al., 1982), as well as in relation to autism (Schain & Freedman, 1961; Campbell et al., 1988). As the mentally retarded appear to be at greater risk for developing EPS, a drug such as risperidone has the potential for not only being better tolerated than other neuroleptics, due to its low propensity for producing EPS, but also possibly for being therapeutically superior, as a result of its strong antiserotonergic action. Although antipsychotics are of limited value in autism (Anderson et al., 1984), the antiserotonergic action of risperidone may prove to be particularly effective in this group of patients.

The potent and balanced serotonin-dopamine antagonist properties of risperidone have resulted in a compound which appears to treat the broad range of positive and negative symptoms in schizophrenia more successfully when compared to conventional antipsychotic drugs. Furthermore, when used at appropriate therapeutic doses, these beneficial actions of risperidone are associated with the development of minimal or no EPS. Risperidone appears to have a potent antidyskinetic action, and although its risk for producing tardive dyskinesia is not yet determined, at lower doses this risk should theoretically be minimal. This pharmacological and clinical profile indicates that risperidone is a very promising agent for the first-line treatment of both acute and chronic schizophrenic illness, and of geriatric behavioural disorders. Furthermore, given its efficacy and safety profile, its action on the serotonergic system, and the large role that serotonin plays in affective disorders, anxiety, aggression, impulsivity, and possibly autism, risperidone may have potential therapeutic applications across a broad spectrum of psychiatric and behavioural disorders.

References

Anderson, L. T., Campbell, M., Grega, D. M. et al. (1984) Haloperidol in the treatment of infantile autism: Effects on learning and behavioral symptoms. *American Journal of Psychiatry*, **141**, 1195–1202.

Anton, R. F., Ressner, E. L., Hitri, A. et al. (1985) Efficacy of amoxapine in psychotic depression: Relationship to serum prolactin and neuroleptic activity. *Journal of Clinical Psychiatry Monograph Series*, **3**, 8–13.

Arora, R. C. & Meltzer, H. Y. (1991) Serotonin (5-HT2) receptor binding in the frontal cortex of schizophrenic patients. *Journal of Neural Transmission, General Section*, **85**, 19–29.

Bersani, G., Grispini, A., Marini, A. et al. (1986) Neuroleptic-induced extrapyramidal side-effects: Clinical perspectives with ritanserin (R 55667), a new selective 5-HT2 receptor blocking agent. *Current Therapeutic Research*, **40**, 492–499.

Bersani, G., Bresa, G. M., Meco, G. et al. (1990) Combined serotonin-5HT2 and dopamine-D2 antagonism in schizophrenia: Clinical, extrapyramidal and neuroendocrine response in a preliminary study with risperidone (R 64 766). *Human Psychopharmacology*, **5**, 225–231.

Bleich, A., Brown, S.-L., Kahn, R. et al. (1988) The role of serotonin in schizophrenia. *Schizophrenia Bulletin*, **14**, 297–315.

Borison, R. L., Diamond, B. I., Pathiraja, A. et al. (1991) Clinical profile of risperidone in chronic schizophrenia. In *Risperidone: Major Progress in Antipsychotic Treatment* (ed. J. M. Kane), pp. 31–36. Oxford: Oxford Clinical Communications.

Borison, R. L., Diamond, B. I., Pathiraja, A. et al. (1992) Clinical overview of risperidone. In *Novel Antipsychotic Drugs* (ed. H. Y. Meltzer), pp. 233–239. New York: Raven Press.

Borison, R. L., Pathiraja, A. P., Diamond, B. I. et al. (1993) Risperidone: Clinical safety and efficacy in schizophrenia. *Psychopharmacology Bulletin*, **29**, 95–100.

Borison, R. L., Diamond, B. I., Pathiraja, A. et al. (1994) Pharmacokinetics of risperidone in chronic schizophrenic patients. *Psychopharmacology Bulletin*, **30**, 193–197.

Bozormenyi, Z. & Szara, D. T. (1958) Dimethyltryptamine experiments with psychotics. *Journal of Mental Science*, **104**, 445–453.

Brown, G. L., Ebert, M. H., Goyer, P. F. et al. (1982) Aggression, suicide and serotonin: Relationships to CSF amine metabolites. *American Journal of Psychiatry*, **139**, 741–746.

Campbell, M., Adams, P., Small, A. M. et al. (1988) Efficacy and safety of fenfluramine in autistic children. *Journal of the American Academy of Child & Adolescent Psychiatry*, **27**, 434–439.

Chouinard, G., Ross-Chouinard, A., Annable, L. et al. (1980) The extrapyramidal symtom rating scale. *Canadian Journal of Neurological Sciences*, **7**, 233.

Chouinard, G., Jones, B., Remington, G. et al. (1993) A Canadian multicenter placebo-controlled study of fixed doses of risperidone and haloperidol in the treatment of chronic schizophrenic patients. *Journal of Clinical Psychopharmacology*, **13**, 25–40.

Claus, A., Bollen, J., DeCuyper, H. et al. (1992) Risperidone versus haloperidol in the treatment of chronic schizophrenic inpatients. A multicenter double-blind comparative study. *Acta Psychiatrica Scandinavica*, **85**, 295–305.

DeCuyper, H. J. A. (1989) Risperidone in the treatment of chronic psychotic patients. An overview of the double-blind comparative trials. In *30 Years of Janssen Research in Psychiatry* (ed. F. J. Ayd), pp. 116–122. Baltimore: Ayd Medical Communications.

Eison, M. S. (1989) The new generation of serotonergic anxiolytics: Possible clinical roles. *Psychopathology,* (suppl. 1), **22**, 13–20.

Gelders, Y. G. (1989) Thymosthenic agents, a novel approach in the treatment of schizophrenia. *British Journal of Psychiatry* (suppl. 5), **155**, 33–36.

Gerlach, J. (1991) New antipsychotics: Classification, efficacy and adverse events. *Schizophrenia Bulletin*, **17**, 289–309.

Grant, S. & Fitton, A. (1994) Risperidone: A review of its pharmacological properties and therapeutic potential in schizophrenia. *Drugs*, in press.

Hashimoto, T., Nishino, N., Nakai, H. et al. (1991) Increase in serotonin 5-HT$_{1A}$ receptors in prefrontal and temporal cortices of brains from patients with chronic schizophrenia. *Life Sciences*, **48**, 355–363.

Heinrich, K., Klieser, E., Lehmann, E. et al. (1991) Experimental comparison of the efficacy and compatability of risperidone and clozapine in acute schizophrenia. In *Risperidone: Major Progress in Antipsychotic Treatment* (ed. J. M. Kane), pp. 37–39. Oxford: Oxford Clinical Communications.

Høyberg, O. J., Fensbo, C., Remvig, J. et al. (1993) Risperidone versus perphenazine in the treatment of chronic schizophrenic patients with acute exacerbations. *Acta Psychiatrica Scandinavica*, **88**, 395–402.

Huang, M.-L., Van Peer, A., Woestenborghs, R. et al. (1991) *Steady-state tolerance and pharmacokinetics of orally administered risperidone (R 64766) in healthy male volunteers. A pharmacokinetic report based on revised assay procedures.* (Clinical Research Report RIS-FRG-9002). Beerse: Janssen Research Foundation.

Itil, T. M., Keskiner, A., Holden, J. M. C. et al. (1969) The use of LSD and ditran in the treatment of therapy-resistant schizophrenics: Symptom provocation approach. *Disease of the Nervous System* (suppl. 2), **30**, 93–103.

Janssen, P. A. J., Niemegeers, C. J. E., Awouters, F. et al. (1988) Pharmacology of risperidone (R 64766), a new antipsychotic with serotonin-S2 und dopamine-D2 antagonistic properties. *Journal of Pharmacology & Experimental Therapeutics*, **244**, 685–693.

Jones, D. L., Mogenson, G. J. & Wu, M. (1980) Injections of dopaminergic, cholinergic, serotonergic and Gabergic drugs into the nucleus accumbens: Effects on locomotor activity in the rat. *Neuropharmacology*, **20**, 29–37.

Kahn, R. S., Siever, L. J., Gabriel, S. et al. (1992) Serotonin function in schizophrenia: Effects of metachlorophenylpiperazine in schizophrenic patients and healthy subjects. *Psychiatry Research*, **43**, 1–12.

Kahn, R. S., Davidson, M., Knott, P. et al. (1993) Effect of neuroleptic medication on cerebrospinal fluid monoamine metabolite concentrations in schizophrenia. *Archives of General Psychiatry*, **50**, 599–605.

Kane, J. M., Woerner, M., Weinhold, P. et al. (1982) A prospective study of tardive dyskinesia development: Preliminary results. *Journal of Clinical Psychopharmacology*, **2**, 345–349.

Kane, J. M., Honigfeld, G., Singer, J. et al. (1988) Clozapine for the treatment-resistant schizophrenic: A double-blind comparison versus chlorpromazine/benztropine. *Archives of General Psychiatry*, **45**, 789–796.

Kay, S. R., Fiszbein, A. & Opler, L. A. (1987) The Positive and Negative Syndrome Scale (PANSS) for schizophrenia. *Schizophrenia Bulletin*, **13**, 261–276.

Korsgaard, S., Geralch, J. & Christenson, E. (1985) Behavioral aspects of serotonin-dopamine interaction in the monkey. *European Journal of Pharmacology*, **118**, 245–252.

Krystal, J. H., Seibyl, J. P., Price, L. H. et al. (1993) m-Chlorophenylpiperazine effects in neuroleptic-free schizophrenic patients. *Archives of General Psychiatry*, **50**, 624–635.

Leysen, J. E., Janssen, P. M. F., Gommeren, W. et al. (1992) In vitro and in vivo receptor binding and effects on monoamine turnover in rat brain regions of the novel antipsychotics risperidone and ocaperidone. *Molecular Pharmacology*, **41**, 494–508.

Mannens, G., Huang, M.-L., Meuldermans, W. et al. (1990) *Absorption, excretion and metabolism of risperidone in volunteers after a single dose of 1 mg.* (Clinical Research Report R 64766/25). Beerse, Belgium: Janssen Research Foundation.

Marder, S. R. & Meibach, R. C. (1994) Risperidone in the treatment of schizophrenia. *American Journal of Psychiatry*, **151**, 825–835.

McElroy, S. L., Dessain, E. C., Pope, H. G. et al. (1991) Clozapine in the treatment of psychotic mood disorders, schizoaffective disorder, and schizophrenia. *Journal of Clinical Psychiatry*, **52**, 411–414.

Meltzer, H. Y. (1989) Clinical studies on the mechanism of action of clozapine: The dopamine-serotonin hypothesis of schizophrenia. *Psychopharmacology*, **99**, 18–27.

Meltzer, H. Y. (1991) The mechanism of action of novel antipsychotic drugs. *Schizophrenia Bulletin*, **17**, 263–288.

Meltzer, H. Y. & Stahl, S. M. (1976) The dopamine hypothesis of schizophrenia: A review. *Schizophrenia Bulletin*, **2**, 19–76.

Meltzer, H. Y., Matsubara, S. & Lee, J.-C. (1989) Classification of typical and atypical antipsychotic drugs on the basis of dopamine D-1, D-2 and serotonin-2 pKi values. *Journal of Pharmacology & Experimental Therapeutics*, **251**, 238–246.

Mertens, C. (1991) Long-term treatment of chronic schizophrenic patients with risperidone. In *Risperidone: Major Progress in Antipsychotic Treatment* (ed. J. M. Kane), pp. 44–48. Oxford: Oxford Clinical Communications.

Modai, I., Rotman, A., Munitz, H. et al. (1979) Serotonin uptake by blood platelets of acute schizophrenic patients. *Psychopharmacology*, **64**, 193–195.

Nyback, H., Berggren, B. M., Hindmarsh, T. et al. (1983) Cerebroventricular size and cerebrospinal fluid monoamine metabolites in schizophrenic patients and healthy volunteers. *Psychiatry Research*, **9**, 301–308.

Reynolds, G. P., Rossor, M. N. & Iverson, L. L. (1983) Preliminary studies of human cortical 5-HT2 receptors and their involvement in schizophrenia and neuroleptic drug action. *Journal of Neural Transmission* (suppl.), **18**, 273–277.

Schain, R. J. & Freedman, D. X. (1961) Studies on 5-hydroxyindole metabolism in autistic and other mentally retarded children. *Journal of Pediatrics*, **58**, 315–318.

Schooler, N. R. & Kane, J. M. (1982) Research diagnoses for tardive dyskinesia: *Archives of General Psychiatry*, **39**, 486–487.

Svestka, J., Ceskova, E., Rysánek, R. et al. (1990) Double-blind clinical comparison of risperidone and haloperidol in acute schizophrenic and schizoaffective psychoses. *Acta Nervica Superior*, **32**, 237–238.

Vanden-Bussche, E., Heykants, J. & De Coster, R. (1988) Pharmacokinetic profile and neuroendocrine effects of the new antipsychotic risperidone. *Psychopharmacology*, (suppl.) **96**, 334.

Whitaker, P. M., Crow, T. J. & Ferrier, I. N. (1981) Tritiated LSD binding in frontal cortex in schizophrenia. *Archives of General Psychiatry*, **38**, 279–280.

Wood, P. L., Suranyi-Cadotte, B. E., Nair, N. P. V. et al. (1983) Lack of association between (3H)imipramine binding sites and uptake of serotonin in control, depressed and schizophrenic patients. *Neuropharmacology*, **22**, 1211–1214.

Can the Negative Symptoms of Schizophrenia Be Influenced by Neuroleptics?

Hans-Jürgen Möller, Torsten Mager and Horst Müller

Summary

Severe methodological problems – the differentiation between negative symptoms, extrapyramidal symptoms, and depression, as well as the differentiation between primary and secondary negative symptoms – can lead to misleading conclusions in the evaluation of drug effects on negative symptoms. A review of published studies in this field provides no clear conclusion as to whether neuroleptics in general have an effect on primary negative symptoms, or whether certain neuroleptics, e. g., the atypical ones, are superior to others in this respect. Path-analytical statistics are able to differentiate between a drug's "direct" effect on negative symptoms and its indirect one (via productive symptoms, extrapyramidal symptoms, etc.). When such an approach was applied to the data of the North-American risperidone study, the superiority in the "direct" effect (not explainable by differences in the effect on productive symptoms and extrapyramidal symptoms) of risperidone over haloperidol could be demonstrated in patients suffering from an acute schizophrenic episode. Whether this result can be transferred to the chronic deficit forms of schizophrenia should be tested in a study of such patients.

A primary goal in the development of new drugs to treat schizophrenia is the alleviation of negative symptoms, but there are major methodological problems in assessing the efficacy of antipsychotic agents from this point of view. In the first part of this paper we will summarise the main problems of this kind. In the second part, an approach to differentiate direct effects on negative symptoms from indirect effects (caused via effects on positive symptoms, extrapyramidal symptoms, etc.) will be described, using the data from one of the large trials on risperidone.

Methodological Problems

Several different concepts of the negative syndrome have been proposed (e. g., Helmchen, 1988; Rösler & Hengesch, 1990). According to Sommers' review (1985), the main negative symptoms involve affect, arousal, cognition, and social functioning and are reflected, for example, by blunted affect, apathy, attentional deficit, poverty of thought or speech, and social withdrawal. Whereas some authors support a broad concept of negative symptoms (Gibbons et al., 1985; Meltzer & Zureick, 1989), others prefer a narrower view (Strauss et al., 1974; Wing, 1978). The discrepancies between them involve symptoms such as incoherence, loosening of associations, and thought blocking, which may be interpreted as either negative or positive. The development of special instruments like the Scale for the Assessment of Negative Symptoms (SANS – Andreasen, 1981) or the Positive & Negative Syndrome Scale (PANSS – Kay et al., 1987) was an important advance in the measurement of negative symptoms, but there are several differences between these scales (Zinner et al., 1990; Möller, 1991). The lack of homogeneity in the definition and measurement of negative symptoms has important clinical implications. Different types of negative symptoms may appear at different stages of schizophrenia or may respond differentially to pharmacological or psychosocial treatments (Meltzer & Zureick, 1989).

Another problem in the interpretation of rating scale data is that negative symptom scores correlate positively with the severity of the drug-induced Parkinson syndrome (Hoffman et al., 1987; Prosser et al., 1987; Bandelow et al., 1990; Gaebel, 1990). Furthermore, there is a correlation between negative symptoms and hyperkinetic features such as akathisia and dyskinesia (Barnes & Braude, 1985; Waddington et al., 1985). Similarly, the psychometric differentiation between depression and negative symptoms is difficult (Maier et al., 1990).

The pathogenetic differentiation between primary and secondary negative symptoms, as proposed by Carpenter et al. (1985), appears of great relevance in this context. Whereas primary negative symptoms are the direct consequence of a deficit state, the secondary symptoms are either: (a) consequences of the positive ones (e. g., social withdrawal because of paranoid ideas); (b) extrapyramidal side-effects (EPS) (e. g., motor retardation as an indicator of akinesia); (c) depressive symptoms (e. g., post-psychotic or pharmacogenic depression); or (d) social understimulation (e. g., hospitalisation). On the basis of this differentiation, the treatment of negative symptoms should depend upon their causes.

In chronic cases, negative symptoms tend to be more stable (Kay & Opler, 1987; Carpenter et al., 1988) and this increases the possibility of finding clear results in evaluative studies. In the acute stage of schizophrenia, investigation of the treatment of negative symptoms is complicated by the instability of the syndrome and the heterogeneity of its causes. In particular, the fluctuation of negative symptoms with the strength of positive symptoms is a great problem in interpreting the results of treatment.

Following the primary/secondary distinction, the overlapping of primary and secondary negative symptoms with EPS, especially akinesia and depression, must be taken into account. Therefore, the varying profiles of different neuroleptics in causing EPS need to be considered carefully, as well as any concomitant treatment with anticholinergics.

In the light of these difficulties and the fact that earlier clinical studies of conventional neuroleptics focussed mainly on positive symptoms, it is not surprising that our knowledge of neuroleptic effects in this field is both limited and controversial. For example, Crow (1980) proposed that negative symptoms are largely unresponsive to neuroleptic treatment because they are manifestations of irreversible structural changes in the central nervous system. Meltzer & Zureick (1989), however, came to the conclusion that there is considerable empirical evidence for the proposition that negative symptoms do diminish during the course of treatment with neuroleptic drugs.

Controlled Studies on Negative Symptoms

In his review on classical neuroleptics, Goldberg (1985) cited five large placebo-controlled studies to demonstrate that negative and/or deficit symptoms in schizophrenia do indeed respond to neuroleptic treatment. For example, in the NIMH collaborative studies on phenothiazines, highly significant drug-placebo differences were shown in connection with a variety of "positive, negative and deficit schizophrenic symptoms." The latter two categories included: indifference to environment or apathy, hebephrenic symptoms or inappropriate affect, slowed speech and movements, poor social participation, poor self-care and confusion. Greater drug effects were said to be shown on "negative" symptoms like hebephrenic symptoms, poor social participation, confusion, and poor self-care rather than on positive symptoms. However, without subtraction of the placebo effect, the negative or deficit symptoms did not change as much as the positive symptoms.

Goldberg also quoted the review by Cole et al. (1966) of other controlled studies on phenothiazines, in which similar results were found. Two studies demonstrated a reduction in blunted affect and indifference, four showed an effect on withdrawal/retardation, and four a drug effect on autistic behaviour and mannerisms. However, problems of interpreting such data have to be taken into account: all these studies were performed in acute schizophrenic patients, and the definition of negative symptoms seems to have been very broad, since hebephrenic symptoms, confusion, and mannerisms were included.

Meltzer et al. (1986) also expressed the view that negative symptoms respond to conventional neuroleptics. Meltzer (1985) had studied schizophrenic inpatients treated for an average of 10 weeks with neuroleptics (and other agents), using an 11-item negative symptom scale. Significant improvement was found between admission and discharge in both positive and negative symptoms, which was more significant in women. This improvement was substantial in 21 of the 55 patients with extensive negative scores. Consistent with this result, we found in a similar investigation of a large sample of schizophrenic inpatients treated under routine care conditions – mostly with haloperidol as treatment of first choice – that not only productive symptoms, but also symptoms of the depressive-apathetic spectrum were reduced between admission and discharge (Möller & von Zerssen, 1981, 1982, 1986). The IMPS factor "retardation and apathy" was interpreted as a specially useful indicator of negative symptoms.

Comparing perazine and haloperidol, Gaebel (1993) reported differential effects on the spectrum of negative symptoms. While no difference was found between the two neuroleptics with respect to productive symptoms and most SANS dimensions, parazine was found to be therapeutically superior with respect to flat affect.

It has been proposed that diphenylbutylpiperidines are more effective than other neuroleptics in the treatment of negative symptoms (Pinder et al., 1976; Gould et al., 1983). Pinder et al. reviewed 22 double-blind studies – most of them not specifically designed to investigate the therapeutic effect on negative symptoms – comparing pimozide with other neuroleptics. Individual BPRS items were clearly specified in only ten of these and in most, both pimozide and the standard neuroleptics were effective in decreasing emotional withdrawal, blunted affect and motor retardation. Only in two studies (Andersen et al., 1974; Kolivakis et al., 1974) did pimozide have comparatively better results with regards to emotional withdrawal or psychomotor retardation items. Nevertheless, the general conclusion of Pinder et al. was that pimozide may be superior to other neuroleptics in improving psychomotor retardation and emotional withdrawal. De Leon and Simpson (1991) summarised the results on nine more recently published double-blind studies comparing pimozide with other neuroleptics. Six studies in chronic schizophrenics with a prolonged treatment period are perhaps more important in relation to the stability of negative symptoms, but in general, these studies gave no evidence for an advantage of pimozide. In only one (Abuzzahab & Zimmermann, 1980) was pimozide shown to be superior to fluphenazine with respect to the withdrawal/retardation factor. In two of the three studies which used pimozide in higher dosages in acute schizophrenia, there was a tendency for pimozide to be more effective for psychomotor retardation or anergia (Chouinard & Annable, 1982; Haas & Beckmann, 1982).

For the other diphenylbutylpiperidines – penfluridol and fluspirilene – the situation is quite similar to that with pimozide (De Leon & Simpson, 1991). In these studies, there was no overall difference between penfluridol or fluspirilene and the comparators with respect to negative symptoms. However, in one double-blind study, penfluridol was reported to be more effective in reducing the anergia factor (Gallant et al., 1974), and in one comparing fluspirilene with fluphenazine decanoate (Malm et al., 1974), an advantage was found with respect to negative symptoms.

Whilst the benzamides have also been described as advantageous with respect to negative symptoms, most published data have been collected for sulpiride (De Leon & Simpson, 1991). The evidence for a specific anti-autistic activity of sulpiride comes fundamentally from open trials (Peselow & Stanley, 1982). Although earlier double-blind trials seemed to support this hypothesis, their results have to be questioned because of severe methodological problems (Edwards et al., 1980). More recent and better designed double-blind trials, reviewed by De Leon & Simpson (1991), mostly did not show any specific effect for sulpiride on negative symptoms. Only one study out of four suggested a specific anti-autistic activity on one scale, and this was probably due to there being fewer extrapyramidal symptoms. More recently, amisulpride and remoxipride have been developed. In a double-blind study in acute schizophrenics, remoxipride was more effective than haloperidol in reducing negative symptoms (Laux et al., 1990), and favourable data have also been reported for amisulpride (Petit et al., 1984; Lecrubier et al., 1989).

The strongest body of evidence supporting the ability of atypical antipsychotic drugs to improve negative symptoms is available from studies of clozapine (Müller-Spahn, 1990; Meltzer, 1991). Kane et al. (1988) examined the efficacy of clozapine in treatment-resistant schizophrenic patients: 305 subjects with a history of failure to respond to at least three neuroleptics of two different classes were treated with high doses of haloperidol for 6 weeks. Less than 2% responded; the non-responders plus a small group of haloperidol-intolerant patients were then randomly assigned to clozapine or chlorpromazine plus an anticholinergic drug for 6 weeks. Clozapine was superior to chlorpromazine in decreasing BPRS positive symptoms from weeks 1 to 6, and BPRS anergia/withdrawal showed greater improvement in the clozapine than the chlorpromazine group between weeks 2 and 6. Similarly positive results were reported by Claghorn et al. (1987) and Meltzer et al. (1989). However, in their metaanalysis of controlled studies comparing clozapine and haloperidol in acute schizophrenic patients, Angst et al. (1989) did not find any special advantage for clozapine: the improvement of negative symptoms was similar with the two drugs.

The recently developed and more potent D_2–S_2 receptor antagonist, risperidone appears to have demonstrated advantages in treating negative symptoms (Niemegeers et al., 1990); Gelders, 1990), especially in the North American risperidone study (Marder & Meibach, 1994).

Statistical Differentiation of Direct and Indirect Drug Effects on Negative Symptoms

Review of the literature (Möller, 1993) leads to the conclusion that neuroleptics, especially some atypical neuroleptics, can in fact reduce negative symptoms. However, as most of these trials were carried out in patients with both negative and productive symptoms, during acute exacerbations of schizophrenic psychoses, the question arises whether these negative symptoms were predominantly secondary to the productive symptoms. Only one study demonstrated that the improvement of negative symptoms did not depend on the reduction of positive symptoms (Meltzer & Zureick, 1989). In the interpretation of such data, the overlap between negative symptoms of schizophrenia, EPS, and depression has to be taken seriously into account. An alternative hypothesis to the direct effect of drugs on negative symptoms is that one drug induces or reduces depression, akinesia, or sedation more than the other, and that negative symptoms are influenced more by one drug than the other in this way (Tab. 1).

Many methodological issues must be solved, if the information given by drug trials on negative symptoms is to be increased (Tab. 2) (Möller et al., 1994).

One of these problems is the differentiation between direct and indirect drug effects on negative symptoms. As a possible statistical approach to this, we applied a path-analysis to the data of the large North American trial on risperidone (Marder & Meibach, 1994). In this study different doses of risperidone (2, 6, 10, 16 mg p. d.) were compared to 20 mg haloperidol p.d. and to placebo in about 500 patients suffering from an acute schizophrenic episode. The date demonstrated both drugs improved positive and negative symptoms markedly and significantly. In the North American study, the in-

Table 1. Possible mistakes in interpreting data of studies on negative symptoms.

1.	Different antidepressant effect a) type of neuroleptic b) co-medication
2.	Different Parkinsonian side effects a) type of neuroleptic b) anticholinergic co-medication
3.	Different efficacy on positive symptoms in consequence different efficacy on negative symptoms secondary to positive symptoms

Table 2. Suggestion of the working group on negative symptoms in schizophrenia (Möller et al., 1994).

Aim: Evaluation of treatment effects on negative symptoms in schizophrenia

1.	Patient selection: a) positive symptoms not dominating the actual clinical picture, e. g., PANSS negative type b) duration of negative symptoms > 6 months c) stable condition of the schizophrenic illness > 6 months d) flat affect and poverty of speech as core symptoms of negative symptoms e) no/low depression score
2.	Design: double-blind comparison to placebo or active drug strategy
3.	Efficacy parameters: BPRS, SANS or PANSS
4.	Other scales: depression scales, EPS scales
5.	Statistical analyses: a) end-point comparison b) interaction with productive symptoms, depression, EPS

tent-to-treat-analysis had shown for the most appropriate dose of risperidone – 6 mg – a significantly higher reduction (Fig. 1) of positive and negative symptoms than with haloperidol 20 mg (t-Test, p < 0.05) (Janssen Research Foundation, 1991; Marder & Meibach, 1994). Risperidone induced fewer extrapyramidal side effects than haloperidol (Möller, in press).

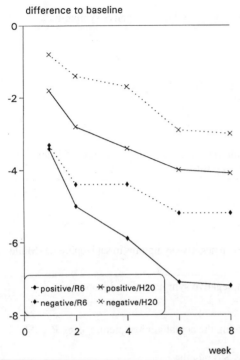

Figure 1. Mean shift in positive and negative symptoms with 6 mg risperidone (R6) versus 20 mg haloperidol (H20) (North American study).

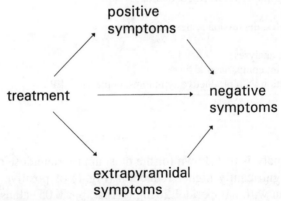

Figure 2. Relationships between treatment effects on positive, extrapyramidal, and negative symptoms.

The question arises whether this efficacy of risperidone on negative symptoms can be interpreted as a direct effect, or whether it may have to be explained as secondary to a more potent effect on positive symptoms, compared to haloperidol, and/or to fewer Parkinsonian side effects.

We tried to answer this question by a path-analysis of the relevant data. Figure 2 shows a simplified model of the most important variables and their relationships.

It is assumed that the neuroleptic treatment affects positive symptoms (positive symptoms score of the PANSS), extrapyramidal symptoms (score of the Extrapyramidal Symptom Rating Scale – ESRS; Chouinard et al., 1980), and negative symptoms (negative symptoms score of the PANSS). A "direct effect" of the treatment on (primary) negative symptoms is assumed, if the treatment effect on negative symptoms cannot be "explained" (statistically) by changes in positive and/or extrapyramidal symptoms. There is a fundamental similarity between this statistical approach and the proposal by Carpenter et al. (1985): The conclusion on primary negative symptoms is based on the exclusion of secondary negative symptoms. The way of exclusion, however, is different. Carpenter et al. assume primary negative symptoms, if treatments of causes of secondary negative symptoms fail to improve negative symptoms. We assume direct effects, if changes in causes of secondary negative symptoms fail to predict observed changes in negative symptoms. Not all arrows in Figure 2 should be interpreted as causal influences: the arrow from "extrapyramidal symptoms" to "negative symptoms" marks a confounding of concepts which results from diagnostic difficulties. To not overload the model, we ignored the confoundation between depressive and negative symptoms which seems according to our analyses of the data of less importance.

Our analyses aimed at the question whether the apparent superiority of risperidone in negative symptoms can be explained by effects on secondary negative symptoms alone. It could be demonstrated by the pathway-analysis that even after statistical control of indirect effects on secondary negative symptoms, risperidone was superior to haloperidol in negative symptoms. The estimated difference which cannot be explained by baseline values and changes in positive or extrapyramidal symptoms amounts to 1.7 points at the negative subscale of the PANSS.

Conclusion

Severe methodological problems – the differentiation between negative symptoms, extrapyramidal symptoms, and depression, as well as the differentiation between primary and secondary negative symptoms – can lead to misleading conclusions in the evaluation of drug effects on negative symptoms. Because of these methodological pitfalls a clear conclusion as to whether neuroleptics in general or certain neuroleptics have an effect on primary negative symptoms cannot be drawn. Path-analytical statistics are able to differentiate between a direct effect and an indirect one (via productive symptoms, extrapyramidal symptoms etc.) on negative symptoms. Therefore, this method should be applied to the data evaluating the efficacy of drugs in negative symptoms of schizophrenia.

References

Abuzzahab, F. S. & Zimmermann, R. L. (1980) Factors determining patient tenure on a 3-year double-blind investigation of primozide versus fluphenazine HCI. *Advances in Biochemical Psychopharmacology*, **24**, 547–550.

Andersen, K., D'Elia, G., Hallberg, B., et al. (1974) A controlled trial of pimozide and trifluoperazine and chronic schizophrenic syndromes. *Acta Psychiatrica Scandinavica*, **50** (suppl. 240), 43–46.

Andreasen, N. C. (1981) *Scale for the Assessment of Negative Symptoms (SANS)*. Iowa City/IA: University of Iowa City.

Angst, J., Stassen, H. H. & Woggon, B. (1989) Effect of neuroleptics on positive and negative symptoms and the deficit state. *Psychopharmacology*, **99**, 41–46.

Bandelow, B., Müller, P., Gaebel, W., et al. (1990) Depressive syndromes in schizophrenic patients after discharge from hospital. *European Archives of Psychiatry & Clinical Neurosciences*, **240**, 113–120.

Barnes, T. R. & Braude, W. M. (1985) Akathisia and tardive dyskinesia. *Archives of General Psychiatry*, **42**, 874–878.

Carpenter, W. T., Jr., Heinrichs, D. W. & Alphs, L. D. (1985) Treatment of negative symptoms. *Schizophrenia Bulletin*, **11**, 440–452.

Carpenter, W. T., Jr., Heinrichs, D. W. & Wagman, A. M. I. (1988) Deficit and nondeficit forms of schizophrenia: the concept. *American Journal of Psychiatry*, **145**, 578–583.

Chouinard, G. & Annable, L. (1982) Pimozide in the treatment of newly admitted schizophrenic patients. *Psychopharmacology*, **76**, 13–19.

Chouinard, G., Ross-Chouinard, A., Annable, L. & Jones, B. D. (1980) The Extrapyramidal Symptom Rating Scale. *Canadian Journal of Neurological Sciences*, **7**, 233.

Claghorn, J., Honigfeld, G., Abuzzahab, P. S., et al. (1987) The risks and benefits of clozapine versus chlorpromazine. *Journal of Clinical Psychopharmacology*, **7**, 377–384.

Cole, J. O., Goldberg, S. C. & Davis, J. M. (1966) Drugs in the treatment of psychosis: controlled studies. In *Psychiatric Drugs* (ed. P. Solomon), pp. 153–180. New York: Grune & Stratton.

Crow, T. J. (1980) Molecular pathology of schizophrenia. More than one disease process? *British Medical Journal*, **280**, 66–68.

De Leon, J. & Simpson, G. M. (1991) Do schizophrenic negative symptoms respond to neuroleptics? *Integrative Psychiatry*, **7**, 39–47.

Edwards, J. G., Alexander, J. R., Alexander, M. S., et al. (1980) Controlled trial of sulpiride in chronic schizophrenic patients. *British Journal of Psychiatry*, **137**, 522–529.

Gaebel, W. (1990) Erfassung und Differenzierung schizophrener Minussymptomatik mit objektiven verhaltensanalytischen Methoden. In *Neuere Ansätze zur Diagnostik und Therapie schizophrener Minussymptomatik* (eds H.-J. Möller & E. Pelzer), pp. 79–90. Berlin: Springer-Verlag.

Gaebel, W. (1993) Parkinsonoid, Akinese, negative und depressive Symptomatik bei schizophrenen Erkrankungen. In *Therapie im Grenzgebiet von Psychiatrie und Neurologie* (eds H.-J. Möller & H. Przuntek), pp. 54–74. Berlin: Springer-Verlag.

Gallant, D. M., Mielke, D. H., Spirtes, M. A., et al. (1974) Penfluridol: an efficacious long-acting oral antipsychotic compound. *American Journal of Psychiatry*, **131**, 699–702.

Gelders, Y. G. (1990) Die Bedeutung des 5-HT2-Rezeptor-Antagonismus für die Behandlung der Schizophrenie unter spezieller Berücksichtigung der Minussymptomatik. In *Neuere Ansätze zur Diagnostik und Therapie schizophrener Minussymptomatik* (eds H.-J. Möller & E. Pelzer), pp. 225–230. Berlin: Springer-Verlag.

Gibbons, R. D., Lewine, R. R. J., Davis, J., et al. (1985) An empirical test of a Kraepelinian versus a Bleulerian view of negative symptoms. *Schizophrenia Bulletin*, **11**, 390–396.

Goldberg, S. C. (1985) Negative and deficit symptoms in schizophrenia do respond to neuroleptics. *Schizophrenia Bulletin*, **11**, 453–456.

Gould, R. J., Murray, K. M. M., Reynolds, J. J. & Snyder, S. H. (1983) Antischizophrenic drugs of the diphenylbutylpiperidine type act as calcium channel antagonists. *Proceedings of the National Academy of Sciences of the United States of America*, **80**, 5122–5125.

Haas, S. & Beckmann, H. (1982) Pimozide versus haloperidol in acute schizophrenia. A double blind controlled study. *Pharmacopsychiatria*, **15**, 70–74.

Helmchen, H. (1988) Methodologische und strategische Erwägungen in der Schizophrenie-Forschung. *Fortschritte der Neurologie & Psychiatrie*, **56**, 379–389.

Hoffman, W. F., Labs, S. M. & Casey, D. E. (1987) Neuroleptic-induced parkinsonism in older schizophrenics. *Biological Psychiatry*, **22**, 427–439.

Janssen Research Foundation (Ed.) (1991) *Clinical Research Report RIS-INT-3*, November 1991 (N 87562). Beerse: Janssen.

Kane, J. M., Honigfeld, G., Singer, J. & Meltzer, H. Y. (1988) Clozapine for the treatment-resistant schizophrenic: A double-blind comparison versus chlorpromazine/benztropine. *Archives of General Psychiatry*, **48**, 789–796.

Kay, S. R. & Opler, L. A. (1987) The positive-negative dimension in schizophrenia: its validity and significance. *Psychiatric Developments*, **5**, 79–103.

Kay, S. R., Opler, L. A. & Fiszbein, A. (1987) *Positive and Negative Syndrome Scale (PANSS). Rating Manual*. San Rafael/CA: Social and Behavioral Documents.

Kolivakis, T., Azim, H. & Kingstone, E. (1974) A double-blind comparison of pimozide and chlorpromazine in the maintenance care of chronic outpatients. *Current Therapeutic Research*, **16**, 998–1004.

Laux, G., Klieser, E., Schröder, H. G., et al. (1990) A double-blind multicentre study comparing remoxipride, two and three times daily, with haloperidol. *Acta Psychiatrica Scandinavica*, **82** (Suppl. 358), 125–129.

Lecrubier, Y., Puech, A. J., Boyer, P., et al. (1989) Comparative double-blind study of two doses of amisulpride (25 and 50 mg) and placebo in the treatment of the negative syndrome of non-psychotic subjects. In *Amisulpride* (eds P. Borenstein, P. Boyer, A. Braconnier, *et al*), pp. 167–181. Paris: Expansion Scientifique Française.

Maier, W., Schlegel, S., Klinger, T., et al. (1990) Die Negativsymptomatik im Verhältnis zur Positivsymptomatik und zur depressiven Symptomatik der Schizophrenie: Eine psychiatrische Untersuchung. In *Neuere Ansätze zur Diagnostik und Therapie schizophrener Minussymptomatik* (eds H.-J. Möller & E. Pelzer), pp. 69–78. Berlin: Springer-Verlag.

Malm, U., Perris, C., Rapp, W. & Wedren, G. (1974) A multicenter controlled trial of fluspirilene and fluphenazine enanthate in chronic schizophrenic syndromes. *Acta Psychiatrica Scandinavica*, Suppl. **249**, 94–116.

Marder, S. R. & Meibach, R. C. (1994) Risperidone in the treatment of schizophrenia. *American Journal of Psychiatry*, **151**, 825–835.

Meltzer, H. Y. (1985) Dopamine and negative symptoms in schizophrenia: critique of the type I–II hypothesis. In *Controversies in Schizophrenia* (ed. M. Alpert), pp. 110–136. New York: Guilford.

Meltzer, H. Y. (1991) The effect of clozapine and other atypical antipsychotic drugs on negative symptoms. In *Negative Versus Positive Schizophrenia* (eds A. Marneros, N. C. Andreasen & M. T. Tsuang), pp. 365–376. Berlin: Springer-Verlag.

Meltzer, H. Y. & Zureick, J. (1989) Negative symptoms in schizophrenia: a target for new drug development. In *Clinical Pharmacology in Psychiatry* (eds S. G. Dahl & L. F. Gram), pp. 68–77. Berlin: Springer-Verlag.

Meltzer, H. Y., Sommers, A. A. & Luchins, D. J. (1986) The effect of neuroleptics and other psychotropic drugs on negative symptoms in schizophrenia. *Journal of Clinical Psychopharmacology*, **6**, 329–338.

Meltzer, H. Y., Bastani, B., Kwon, K. Y., et al. (1989) A prospective study of clozapine in treatment-resistant patients. I: Preliminary report. *Psychopharmacology*, **99** (suppl.), 68–72.

Möller, H.-J. (1991) Typical neuroleptics in the treatment of positive and negative symptoms. In *Negative Versus Positive Schizophrenia* (eds A. Marneros, N. C. Andreasen & M. T. Tsuang), pp. 341–364. Berlin: Springer-Verlag.

Möller, H.-J. (1993) Neuroleptic treatment of negative symptoms in schizophrenic patients. Efficacy problems and methodological difficulties. *European Neuropsychopharmacology*, **3**, 1–11.

Möller, H.-J. (in press) Extrapyramidal side effects of neuroleptic medication: focus on risperidone. In *Serotonergic Mechanisms in Antipsychotic Treatment* (eds J. Kane, H.-J. Möller & F. Awouters). New York: Dekker.

Möller, H.-J. & von Zerssen, D. (1981) Depressive Symptomatik im stationären Behandlungsverlauf von 280 schizophrenen Patienten. *Pharmacopsychiatria*, **14**, 172–179.

Möller, H.-J. & von Zerssen, D. (1982) Depressive states occurring during the neuroleptic treatment of schizophrenia. *Schizophrenia Bulletin*, **8**, 109–117.

Möller, H.-J. & von Zerssen, D. (1986) *Der Verlauf schizophrener Psychosen unter den gegenwärtigen Behandlungsbedingungen*. Berlin: Springer-Verlag.

Möller, H.-J., van Praag, H. M., Aufdembrinke, B., et al. (1994) Negative symptoms in schizophrenia: considerations for clinical trials. *Psychopharmacology*, **115**, 221–228.

Müller-Spahn, F. (1990) Die Bedeutung von Neuroleptika der neueren Generation in der Therapie schizophrener Patienten mit Minus-Symptomatik. In *Neuere Ansätze zur Diagnostik und Therapie schizophrener Minussymptomatik* (eds H.-J. Möller & E. Pelzer), pp. 207–215. Berlin: Springer-Verlag.

Niemegeers, C. J., Awouters, F. & Janssen, P. A. J. (1990) Pharmakologie der Neuroleptika und relevante Mechanismen zur Behandlung von Minussymptomatik. In *Neuere Ansätze zur Diagnostik und Therapie schizophrener Minussymptomatik* (eds H.-J. Möller & E. Pelzer), pp. 185–197. Berlin: Springer-Verlag.

Peselow, E. D. & Stanley, M. (1982) Clinical trials of benzamides in psychiatry. *Advances in Biochemical Psychopharmacology*, **35**, 163–194.

Petit, M., Zann, M. & Colonna, L. (1984) Etude contrôlée de l'effet désinhibiteur de faibles doses de sulpiride dans les psychoses schizophréniques déficitaires. *Encéphale*, **10**, 25–28.

Pinder, R. M., Brogden, R. N., Sawyer, P. R., et al. (1976) Primozide: A review of its pharmacological properties and therapeutic uses in psychiatry. *Drugs*, **12**, 1–40.

Prosser, E. S., Csernansky, J. G., Kaplan, H., et al. (1987) Depression, Parkinsonian symptoms, and negative symptoms in schizophrenics treated with neuroleptics. *Journal of Nervous & Mental Disease*, **175**, 100–105.

Rösler, M. & Hengesch, G. (1990) "Negative" Symptome im AMDP-System. In *Veränderungsmessung in Psychiatrie und Klinischer Psychologie* (eds U. Baumann, E. Fähndrich, R. D. Stieglitz & B. Woggon), pp. 329–339. München: Profil.

Sommers, A. A. (1985) "Negative symptoms": conceptual and methodological problems. *Schizophrenia Bulletin*, **11**, 364–379.

Strauss, J. S., Carpenter, W. T., Jr. & Bartko, J. J. (1974) The diagnosis and understanding of schizophrenia. III. Speculations on the processes that underlie schizophrenic symtoms and signs. *Schizophrenia Bulletin*, **1**, 61–69.

Waddington, J. L., Youssef, H. A., Molloy, A. G., et al. (1985) Association of intellectual impairment, negative symptoms, and aging with tardive dyskinesia: Clinical and animal studies. *Journal of Clinical Psychiatry*, **46**, 29–33.

Wing, J. K. (1978) Clinical concepts of schizophrenia. In *Schizophrenia: Toward a New Synthesis* (ed. J. K. Wing), pp. 1–30. London: Academic Press.

Zinner, H. J., Kraemer, S. & Möller, H.-J. (1990) Empirische Untersuchungen zur Konkordanz verschiedener Minussymptomatik-Skalen sowie zur Korrelation mit testpsychologischen Befunden. In *Neuere Ansätze zur Diagnostik und Therapie schizophrener Minussymptomatik* (eds H.-J. Möller & E. Pelzer), pp. 59–68. Berlin: Springer-Verlag.

Focus on Influencing Cognitive Vulnerability

Feasibility Studies of Cognitive Remediation in Schizophrenia: Grasping the Little Picture

Michael Foster Green, Susan Hellman and Robert S. Kern

Summary

Recently, investigators have wondered whether neurocognitive deficits in schizophrenia can be modified with cognitive/behavioural interventions. Feasibility studies of cognitive remediation have tried to modify performance under particular conditions, such as with enhanced instructions and organisational strategies. In contrast, generalisation studies determine whether the effects of intervention influence other types of tasks, or other functional and clinical domains. We argue that there are advantages to using a stepwise approach in which studies of feasibility can guide generalisation studies with the selection of intervention methods.

This paper will survey recent feasibility studies in our lab. Detailed instructions produced a dramatic short-term improvement in one measure of concept formation (The Wisconsin Card Sorting Test), but contingent reinforcement did not influence performance, either alone or in combination with the instructions. For a measure of early visual processing (The Span of Apprehension), performance was improved by a combination of contingent reinforcement and instructions. By using controlled trials, we can determine which forms of intervention modify specific cognitive components. Such information provides direction for studies of generalisation.

Considerable progress has been made in identifying and describing cognitive deficits in schizophrenia ranging from simple sensory components to highly complex social problem-solving. Recently, however, investigators have considered whether we can move beyond identifying these deficits to modifying them through cognitive and behavioural means. This endeavour, which focuses on relatively specific cognitive components, is referred to as *cognitive remediation*, as opposed to the broader term of cognitive therapy which generally refers to the modification of beliefs and attitudes.

Studies of cognitive remediation have been of three types, displayed in Figure 1: feasibility studies, studies of rate limiting factors, and generalisation studies (Green, 1993).

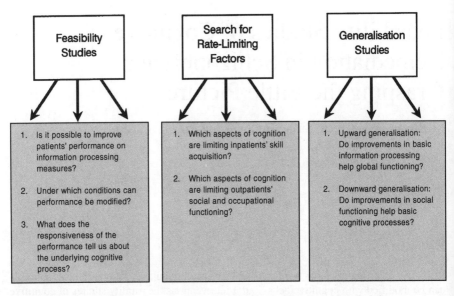

Figure 1. Types of designs for cognitive remediation studies in schizophrenia.

Feasibility studies are designed to determine whether performance deficits can be modified under any conditions. If they can, the question shifts to which types of intervention seem most effective in the short run, and which interventions show most durability over time. Interventions have included enhanced instructions, organisational strategies, and contingent reinforcement. In addition to these largely clinical goals, feasibility studies provide basic information about the nature of the cognitive processes underlying poor performance. For example, if contingent reinforcement affects performance on a certain measure, but enhanced instructions do not, the processes limiting performance may include motivation or alertness.

Studies of *rate-limiting factors* have typically examined the correlations between information-processing variables and an outcome measure that is relevant to functioning in the real-world functioning. In our clinical research lab, we have selected outcome measures which indicate the degree of success with skills training activities (Bowen et al., 1994; Corrigan et al., 1994; Kern et al., 1992). The patients in our studies have been chronic inpatients, and skills training activities represent the most obvious demand in their daily lives. Other investigators who have worked with outpatients have considered social and occupational functioning as outcome measures (Buchanon et al., 1993; Goldberg et al., 1993).

80

The goal of *generalisation* studies is to determine whether the effects of intervention are limited to the training task, or if they extend to other types of tasks. In generalisation studies, the intervention is directed at one cognitive level (ranging from basic cognition to complex social functioning), but the effects of the intervention are assessed at another level. *Upward* generalisation is the notion that training in basic information processing will influence outcome measures such as skills acquisition or occupational functioning. The upward generalisation could also include studies of the impact of cognitive training on psychiatric symptoms. *Downward* generalisation refers to the possibility that improvements due to psychosocial intervention will affect basic cognition.

In general, American and Japanese researchers have been more concerned with studies of feasibility and, to a lesser extent, rate-limiting factors (e. g., Bellack et al., 1990; Fukuda et al., 1990; Green et al., 1992; Kern et al., 1992; Mueser et al., 1991). In contrast, central Europeans have emphasised studies of generalisation (e. g., Brenner et al., 1990; Kraemer et al., 1991; Olbrich & Mussgay, 1990). This separation of approaches is not optimal because studies of generalisation require an *a priori* selection of cognitive processes and interventions. Schizophrenic patients show deficits on a wide range of cognitive tasks; so which deficits, among many, should be targeted? Likewise, which interventions should be applied? Basic information from studies of feasibility and rate-limiting factors can guide these decisions and provide a foundation for generalisation studies.

This paper will survey recent data from a series of feasibility studies in our lab that have used two information processing measures: The Wisconsin Card Sorting Test and The Span of Apprehension. In addition, we will discuss how findings from these feasibility studies can serve to guide studies of generalisation.

Studies of the Wisconsin Card Sorting Test

The Wisconsin Card Sorting Test (WCST) has recently received considerable attention in the psychopathology literature (e. g., Berman et al., 1986; Braff et al., 1991; Weinberger et al., 1986). Interest in its use with schizophrenic patients stemmed from the belief that it was highly sensitive to the functioning of the dorsolateral prefrontal cortex (Milner, 1963). Given the long-standing interest in prefrontal functioning in schizophrenia, it seemed natural to apply the WCST to schizophrenic patients. Though support for the linkage between the WCST and the prefrontal cortex is far from compelling (Anderson et al., 1991), this test does assess patients' ability to establish and shift cognitive sets. These are considered key cognitive deficits in schizophrenia, regardless of the specific neuroanatomical underpinnings.

In the WCST, the subject is required to match cards to one of four target cards, on the basis of three rules (colour, shape, or number). Subjects are not told how to match the cards; simply if they are right or wrong; from this feedback alone, they are to work out the correct sorting rule. If a subject makes ten consecutive correct responses, the sorting rule changes without warning. Subjects then need to determine the new sorting rule, again based only on feedback from the experimenter. Successful completion of the WCST requires subjects to *attain* a concept (sorting rule), *maintain* this concept for ten consecutive responses, and *switch* the concept when the rule changes.

Schizophrenic patients typically perform poorly on this test, and it has been argued that it is generally not possible for them to learn it. This notion came from a study in which schizophrenic patients showed improved performance while they were receiving detailed instruction, but their performance dropped down to baseline levels, once the instructions were withdrawn (Goldberg et al., 1987).

Instructions and Reinforcement on the WCST

In our first study of this series (Green et al., 1992), we administered a computerised version of the WCST four times to a group of 46 schizophrenic patients. This version of the WCST is comparable to the manual card version for this population (Hellman et al., 1992 a). Each administration was 64 trials, half of the standard administration. The conditions were given in the following order:

1) Patients first received the standard version of the WCST, in which no information is provided about the specific matching strategy.

2) Subjects then received contingent reinforcement (two cents) for every correct response.

3) Subjects continued to receive reinforcement and also received detailed trial by trial instructions that were similar to those used by Goldberg et al. (1987). Subjects were informed about the sorting procedures, and if they made ten consecutive correct responses, were informed about the change in sorting rules. After each correct response, subjects were told why it was correct, and after each wrong response, were given alternative sorting rules.

4) Lastly, the subjects received contingent reinforcement alone, as in the second condition.

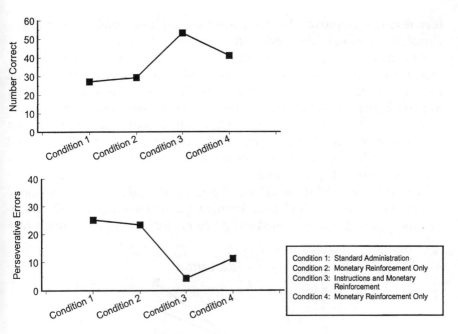

Figure 2. Wisconsin Card Sorting Test Performance.

The addition of contingent reinforcement alone did not change the patients' performance, suggesting that the poor performance was not due simply to motivational/alertness factors (see Fig. 2). When detailed instructions were given, their performance improved dramatically; this is not surprising, because the instructions were detailed and highly structured. When the instructions were withdrawn and the reinforcement maintained, patients still showed substantial gains at an immediate post-test.

These results suggest that patients can learn the WCST with a brief, single session of training, at least so far as an immediate post-test is concerned. Contingent reinforcement alone did not appear to be helpful. However, we wondered what would have happened if we had used a higher amount of reinforcement or a more salient reinforcer.

Level of Reinforcement and WCST Performance

Our negative results, using two cents/correct response as a contingent reinforcement, were consistent with Bellack et al. (1990), who used five cents for each correct response. However, another study reported that ten cents per correct response improved WCST performance (Summerfelt et al., 1991). Hence, the amount of the reinforcement might be critical.

To examine this question, we carried out a study in which patients were assigned to receive either low or high levels of reinforcement (two vs. ten cents per correct response). To ensure that the reinforcement was as salient as possible, we also set up a mini-store in the laboratory with items from the hospital store (e. g., sodas, granola bars, cigarettes, decaffeinated coffee, fruit etc.). All subjects had had experience with purchasing items from the hospital store, and understood that they could use money earned during testing to purchase items from this mini-store.

We were interested in the effects of contingent reinforcement, both alone and in combination with detailed instructions. A new sample of 32 schizophrenic inpatients was recruited and randomly assigned to four groups (n =

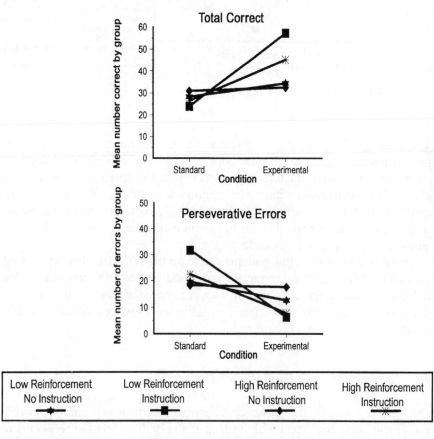

Figure 3. High versus low levels of reinforcement on the Wisconsin Card Sorting Test.

84

8 per group) in a 2 × 2 design (presence vs. absence of instruction × high vs. low reinforcement). First, all groups received identical administrations of the computerised WCST under standard conditions (no instructions, no reinforcement). During the second administration, two groups received low and two groups received high levels of reinforcement. One group within each reinforcement level also received detailed instructions; the other did not.

The results (see Fig. 3) indicated that instructions had a large impact on WCST performance, but that the level of reinforcement had no effect, either when given alone or in combination with instructions. Furthermore, the results were in the opposite direction to that predicted: groups receiving high levels of reinforcement showed a slight and non-significant tendency to perform worse than the groups receiving low levels of reinforcement (Hellman et al., 1992b). We concluded that WCST performance of chronic schizophrenic inpatients is responsive to detailed instructions, but not to contingent reinforcement.

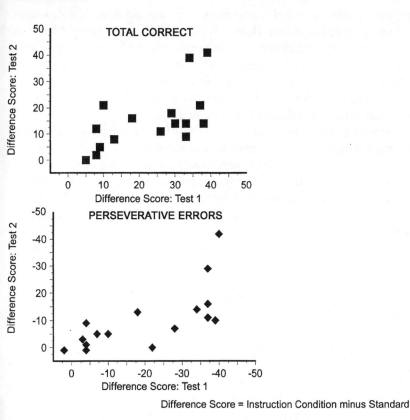

Difference Score = Instruction Condition minus Standard

Figure 4. Stability of improvement on the Wisconsin Card Sorting Test.

Stability of Individual Differences

Although the patients, as a group, responded to the detailed instructions in both of the studies described above, a closer look at the data revealed a puzzling situation. It was not surprising that the patients showed improvements while receiving detailed instructions, because a substantial amount of structure was provided. It was surprising that some of the patients still had difficulty with the WCST, even while receiving detailed instructions. Some patients were clearly better able to benefit from the presence of structure than others. The variability across subjects could be due to state-related (perhaps symptom-related) factors such as momentary fluctuations in attention. On the other hand, the variability may reflect rather stable differences in the patients' ability to profit from structure. To test this possibility, we determined the effects of instruction at two different times and assessed the strength of the test-retest stability.

Sixteen schizophrenic subjects (those who had received detailed instructions) from the study described above (Hellman et al., 1992b) were brought back one week later to receive two additional administrations of the WCST. We examined the stability of rank order over time by correlating the amount of improvement on the first day (subtracting uninstructed from instructed administration) with the amount of improvement one week later. We used the Spearman Correlation Coefficient to reduce the effects of outliers on the statistic.

It can be seen from the two scatterplots (Fig. 4) that the correlation between improvement at the two testing sessions was substantial (Spearman $r = 0.68$ for the total correct and 0.80 for the perseverative errors). We next considered whether using the "dynamic" change scores provided information beyond that contained in the "static" scores from the uninstructed conditions. The Spearman correlations were recalculated after partialing out the performance from the uninstructed administrations at both sessions. The resulting correlations remained large and significant ($r = 0.73$ for number correct and 0.63 for perseverative errors), suggesting strong test-retest stability of the change score that is not merely the result of initial performance.

Of course, documenting the stability of improvement over time represents only the first step. We wish to raise the possibility that "dynamic" indices (i. e., those that reflect change over time) may provide valid indicators of social and occupational functioning (Wiedl & Schottke, in press). Perhaps a "dynamic probe" could help us select subjects who are most likely to benefit from settings in which external structure is provided, such as skills training groups and sheltered occupational placements.

Modifying Performance on the Span of Apprehension

Although the WCST assesses key cognitive deficits of schizophrenia, it is not known whether it is an indicator of vulnerability to schizophrenia (Zubin & Spring, 1977). Vulnerability indicators are cognitive deficits that are apparent across clinical state, when patients are in remission as well as when they are in episode. Additionally, vulnerability indicators are found in populations who carry increased risk for schizophrenia such as first-degree relatives of patients. Some studies (e. g., Franke et al., 1992; Pogue-Geile et al., 1991) have found WCST deficits in first-degree relatives of schizophrenic patients, suggesting that WCST performance fits the pattern of a vulnerability indicator. However, another group failed to find deficits in first-degree relatives (Scarone et al., 1993). In addition, Penn et al. (1993) found that after clinical improvement, the performance of schizophrenic patients on a modified version of the WCST did not differ from normal controls. The results from these last two studies suggest that the WCST is not a vulnerability indicator.

Compared with the WCST, the status of The Span of Apprehension (Span) as a vulnerability indicator is more secure. Since deficits on the Span have been found both in the offspring of schizophrenic patients (Asarnow et al., 1977) and in patients during states of remission (Nuechterlein et al., 1992), the version of the Span that is used in these studies (Asarnow & Nuechterlein, 1987) is likely to be an indicator of vulnerability to schizophrenia.

The Span is a measure of early visual processing. In the version of the Span that has been developed at UCLA, subjects are told that letters will be flashed on a screen, and that either the letter T or F will be in each array; either two or 11 nontarget letters are presented in other positions. The letters are presented briefly (usually less than 100 ms), so most of the cognitive processing occurs after the display has disappeared from the screen. This is done by scanning an internal representation (called the icon) of the visual display. Subjects indicate (usually by pressing a response button) whether they saw a T or an F. Dependent measures include accuracy and reaction time, although accuracy was the only measure of interest for our remediation study.

We wanted to determine if the performance of schizophrenic patients could be modified on this measure either through instructions alone, reinforcement alone, or the combination of the two (Kern et al., 1995). This study used 40 schizophrenic inpatients in a 4-group by 4-test design. Subjects were first given the Span under standard conditions for 64 trials (half of the total administration). Next, during the intervention condition, three groups received an intervention and a control group received a repeat of the standard administration. The Span was given twice more (immediately and one-week post-test) with standard administration for all groups.

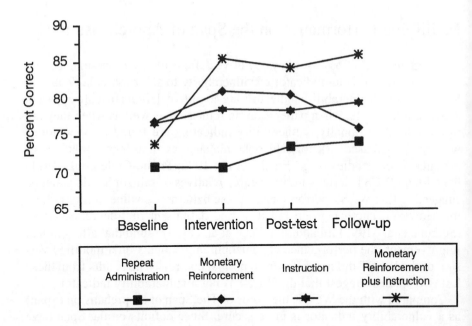

Figure 5. Span of Apprehension Test Performance.

Interventions were given only during the second administration; all other administrations were identical for all groups. Patients were divided into four groups of ten each that differed on type of intervention: 1) One group received reinforcement only (two cents for each correct response). 2) One group received instructions. These instructions differed from those used with the WCST in that they were designed to alert subjects and remind them of the task demands. Enhanced instructions were administered twice: before practice trials and before experimental trials. 3) One group received both reinforcement and enhanced instructions. 4) A control croup received repeat administrations of the Span without any interventions.

The results shown in Figure 5 demonstrate a rather substantial effect of the interventions. We used the score from the first test of each subjects as a covariate to control initial differences. The results indicated that a combination of instructions and reinforcement resulted in a large improvement in performance. This improvement remained significant after intervention was withdrawn, even at a one-week post-test.

The group that received both instructions and reinforcement performed at a level similar to normal controls who received the Span without intervention in another study from our lab (both groups performed at approximately 85%

accuracy). This is not to say that the combination of interventions normalised performance on the Span because it is not known how normal controls would have performed if they had received the interventions.

It initially might appear inconsistent that a putative vulnerability indicator like the Span can be modified by rather simple interventions. However, there is nothing logically inconsistent about a vulnerability indicator that is responsive to modification. By analogy, increased dopaminergic activity might be seen as part of the vulnerability to schizophrenia, yet that activity is modified every time the patient takes neuroleptic medication (K. Nuechterlein, personal communication, 1993).

Discussion

This overview of feasibility studies illustrates differences between two information processing measures that were not apparent until we tried to modify performance. In the case of the WCST, detailed instructions produced dramatic improvement, at least for a short time. Contingent reinforcement (both money and tangible reinforcers) did not influence performance, either by itself or in combination with the instructions. In contrast, Span performance was influenced by a combination of contingent reinforcement and instructions. The enhanced instructions for the two measures were quite different, and we do not assume that they necessarily operated through the same mechanism. Given the negative results for reinforcement across several studies, we can conclude that processes influenced by contingent reinforcement (e. g., allocation of attentional resources, or general motivation) were not restricting the performance of the schizophrenic patients on the WCST. Our data were collected from chronic schizophrenic patients and the conclusions may not apply to schizophrenia in general. The success of monetary reinforcement alone in one study (Summerfelt et al., 1991) with less symptomatic patients serves as a reminder to consider sample characteristics.

At a conceptual level, it is easy to confuse performance on an indicator with the construct of interest. For example, we might wish to improve early visual processing (the construct), but we do so by influencing performance on the Span (the indicator). Interventions are targeted and monitored at the behavioural level, but the construct of interest lies at a deeper, cognitive level. In general, feasibility studies like those described above assume that improvement in the behavioural indicator is paralleled by improvement in the underlying construct. The validity of this assumption can be tested if multiple indicators of the same construct are used in the same study because improvement in the construct should be reflected in multiple indicators. Such studies deserve high priority.

Feasibility studies are only one aspect of the broader area of cognitive remediation. The findings from feasibility studies can be combined with results from the studies of rate-limiting factors to establish well-grounded generalisation studies. For example, we saw that a combination of enhanced instructions and monetary reinforcement can improve Span performance, at least for a one-week period. From studies of rate-limiting factors in our laboratory, we also know that the Span correlates highly with a particular aspect of social function, namely social cue perception. Span performance predicted social cue recognition which was assessed by having patients identify social cues from videotaped segments of interpersonal situations (Corrigan et al., 1994 a). To the extent that early visual processing limitations are constraining social cue recognition, we could generate a reasonable hypothesis that remediation of early visual processes (those assessed by the Span) might yield improvements on social cue perception. Although admittedly speculative, this type of hypothesis provides a testable starting point for generalisation studies.

Generalisation studies require *a priori* selection of cognitive indicators and forms of intervention. However, the empirical justification for making such selections has been slow in emerging. There are advantages to using a stepwise approach in which studies of feasibility and rate-limiting factors are conducted prior to generalisation studies. By identifying specific cognitive components that underlie both laboratory performance and social functioning, we gain insight into the cognitive limitations that restrict patients' functioning in the real world. By using controlled trials, we can determine which forms of intervention modify these cognitive components. Such information provides clear direction and powerful justification for studies of generalisation.

Acknowledgements

The authors thank Cynthia Christenson and Mary Jane Arruda, MS, for their help with the preparation of this manuscript. The projects described in this paper could not have been done without the co-operation of the staff and administration of Camarillo State Hospital. Funding for the recruitment and diagnostic assessment of the patient samples came from NIMH Grant MH-43292 to Dr. Green. Data analyses and statistical consultation were provided by Sun Hwang, MS, MPH and Jim Mintz, PhD. Data analyses, diagnostic training, and symptom assessment were supported through the UCLA Clinical Research Center for the Study of Schizophrenia (MH-30911; R. P. Liberman, P.I.)

References

Anderson, S. W., Damasio, H., Jones, R. D., et al. (1991) Wisconsin Card Sorting Test performance as a measure of frontal lobe damage. *Journal of Clinical & Experimental Neuropsychology*, **13**, 909–922.

Asarnow, R. F., Steffy, R. A., MacCrimmon, D. J. & Cleghorn, J. M. (1977) An attentional assessment of foster children at risk for schizophrenia. *Journal of Abnormal Psychology*, **86**, 267–275.

Asarnow, R. F. & Nuechterlein, K. H. (1987) Manual and computer program for forced-choice, partial report span of apprehension test: Version 1. Unpublished manual and program.

Bellack, A. S., Mueser, K. T., Morrison, R. L., et al. (1990) Remediation of cognitive deficits in schizophrenia. *American Journal of Psychiatry*, **147**, 1650–1655.

Berman, K. F., Zec, R. F. & Weinberger, D. R. (1986) Physiologic dysfunction of dorso-lateral prefrontal cortex in schizophrenia II: Role of neuroleptic treatment, attention, and mental effort. *Archives of General Psychiatry*, **43**, 126–135.

Bowen, L., Wallace, C. J., Glynn, S. M., et al. (1994) Schizophrenics' cognitive functioning and performance in interpersonal interactions and skills training procedures. *Journal of Psychiatric Research,* **28**, 289–301.

Braff, D. L., Heaton, R., Kuck, J., et al. (1991) The generalized pattern of neuropsychological deficits in chronic schizophrenic outpatients with heterogeneous Wisconsin Card Sorting results. *Archives of General Psychiatry*, **48**, 891–898.

Brenner, H. D., Kraemer, S., Hermantz, M., et al. (1990) Cognitive treatment in schizophrenia. In *Schizophrenia: Concepts, Vulnerability, and Interventions* (eds E. R. Straube & K. Hahlweg), pp. 161–191. New York: Springer-Verlag.

Buchanon, R., Breier, A. & Carpenter, W. (1993) *Treatment of negative symptoms and cognitive impairments.* Presented at the annual conference for the American Psychiatric Association, San Francisco, CA.

Corrigan, P. W., Green, M. F. & Toomey, R. (1994 a) Cognitive correlates to social cue perception in schizophrenia. *Psychiatry Research*, **53**, 141–151.

Corrigan, P. W., Wallace, C. J., Schade, M. L. & Green, M. F. (1994) Learning medication self-management skills in schizophrenia: relationships with cognitive deficits and psychiatric symptoms. *Behavior Therapy*, **25**, 5–15.

Franke, P., Maier, W., Hain, C. & Klingler, T. (1992) Wisconsin Card Sorting Test: an indicator of vulnerability to schizophrenia? *Schizophrenia Research*, **6**, 243–249.

Fukuda, M., Niwa, S., Hiramatsu, K., et al. (1990) Differential effects of psychological intervention on P300 amplitudes between schizophrenics and normal subjects (abstract). *Japanese Journal of Psychiatry & Neurology*, **44**, 768.

Goldberg, T. E., Weinberger, D. R., Berman, K. F., et al. (1987) Further evidence for dementia of the prefrontal type in schizophrenia? A controlled study of teaching the Wisconsin Card Sorting Test. *Archives of General Psychiatry*, **44**, 1008–1014.

Goldberg, T. E., Greenberg, R. D., Griffin, S. J., et al. (1993) The effect of clozapine on cognition and psychiatric symptoms in patients with schizophrenia. *British Journal of Psychiatry*, **162**, 43–48.

Green, M. F. (1993) Cognitive remediation in schizophrenia: Is it time yet? (Special Article). *American Journal of Psychiatry*, **150**, 178–187.

Green, M. F., Ganzell, S., Satz, P. & Vaclav, J. (1992) The Wisconsin Card Sort Test: Remediation of a stubborn deficit. *American Journal of Psychiatry*, **149**, 62–67.

Hellman, S. G., Green, M. F., Kern, R. S. & Christenson, C. D. (1992 a) Comparison of the card and computer versions of the Wisconsin Card Sorting Test with psychotic patients. *International Journal of Methods in Psychiatric Research*, **2**, 151–155.

Hellman, S. G., Green, M. F., Kern, R. S. & Christenson, C. (1992 b) The effects of instruction versus reinforcement on the Wisconsin Card Sorting Test. *Journal of Clinical & Experimental Neuropsychology*, **14**, 63.

Kern, R. S., Green, M. F. & Goldstein, M. J. (1995) Modification of performance on the Soan of Apprehension, a putative marker of vulnerability to schizophrenia? *Journal of Abnormal Psychology*, **104**, 385–389.

Kern, R. S., Green, M. F. & Satz, P. (1992) Neuropsychological predictors of skills training for chronic psychiatric patients. *Psychiatry Research*, **43**, 223–230.

Kraemer, S., Zinner, H. J. & Moller, H. J. (1991) Cognitive training and social skills training in relation to basic disturbances in chronic schizophrenic patients. In *Proceedings of the World Congress of Psychiatry: 1989*. Amsterdam: Elsevier.

Milner, B. (1963) Effects of different brain lesions on card sorting. *Archives of Neurology*, **9**, 90–100.

Mueser, K. T., Bellack, A. S., Douglas, M. S. & Wade, J. H. (1991) Prediction of social skill acquisition in schizophrenic and major affective disorder patients from memory and symptomatology. *Psychiatry Research*, **37**, 281–296.

Nuechterlein, K. H., Dawson, M. E., Gitlin, M., et al. (1992) Development processes in schizophrenic disorders: Longitudinal studies of vulnerability and stress. *Schizophrenia Bulletin*, **18**, 387–424.

Olbrich, R. & Mussgay, L. (1990) Reduction of schizophrenic deficits by cognitive training: An evaluative study. *European Archives of Psychiatry & Neurological Sciences*, **239**, 366–369.

Penn, D. L., Willem Van Der Does, A. J., Spaulding, W. D., et al. (1993) Information processing and social cognitive problem solving in schizophrenia: Assessment of interrelationships and changes over time. *The Journal of Nervous & Mental Disease*, **181**, 13–20.

Pogue-Geile, M. F., Garret, A. H., Brunke, J. J. & Hall, J. H. (1991) Neuropsychological impairments are increased in siblings of schizophrenic patients. *Schizophrenia Research*, **4**, 381–397.

Scarone, S., Abbruzzese, M. & Gambini, O. (1993) The Wisconsin Card Sorting Test discriminates schizophrenic patients and their siblings. *Schizophrenia Research,* **10**, 103–107.

Summerfelt, A. T., Alps, L. D., Wagman, A. M. I. et al. (1991) Reduction of perseverative errors in patients with schizophrenia using monetary feedback. *Journal of Abnormal Psychology*, **100**, 613–616.

Weinberger, D. R., Berman, K. F. & Zec, R. Z. (1986) Physiologic dysfunction of dorsolateral prefrontal cortex in schizophrenia: I. Regional cerebral blood flow evidence. *Archives of General Psychiatry*, **43**, 114–124.

Wiedl, K. H. & Schottke, H. (in press) Dynamic assessment of selective attention in schizophrenic subjects: The analysis of intraindividual variability of performance. In *European Contributions to Dynamic Assessment* (ed. J. S. Carlson). London: JAI Press Ltd.

Zubin, J. & Spring, B. (1977) Vulnerability – a new view of schizophrenia. *Journal of Abnormal Psychology*, **86**, 103–126.

Schema-Focused Integrative Treatment of Patients with Schizophrenic Disorder

Carlo Perris

Summary

Cognitive therapy with schizophrenic patients can be used at various levels and with different goals in mind. Such levels range from attempts at correcting basic cognitive deficits assumed to occur in most of the patients, to attempts aimed at a restructuration of dysfunctional schemata which are assumed to determine how the patient gathers and processes information. In the present article a comprehensive and integrated treatment programme is highlighted. The aim of the treatment is the identification and restructuration of dysfunctional working models of self and environment.

Cognitive therapy with schizophrenic patients can be carried out at various levels and with different goals in mind. One way to differentiate among the different modalities which have been proposed so far, is to distinguish between a "molecular" and a "molar" approach. Within the molecular approaches, a number of methods can be included. Firstly, there is the correction of basic cognitive deficits as used by Spaulding, Liberman, and others in the USA (Liberman et al., 1986; Spaulding et al., 1986; McGlashan et al., 1990), by Brenner et al. in Bern (Brenner et al., 1980, 1987; Stramke & Brenner, 1983), and by several other German authors (Buchkremer & Fiedler, 1987; Hermanutz & Gestrich, 1987; Kraemer et al., 1987; Peter et al., 1989; Olbrich & Mussgay, 1990). Secondly, there are the self-instructional training originally proposed by Meichenbaum (Meichenbaum & Cameron, 1973; Meyers et al., 1976), and methods of intervention aimed at a modification/reduction of abnormal beliefs and of hallucinatory experiences that have been reported in the literature (Watts et al., 1973; Johnson et al., 1977; Greene, 1978; Milton et al., 1978; Hole et al., 1979; Alford et al., 1982; Hartman & Cashman, 1983; Fowler & Morley, 1989; Chadwick & Lowe, 1990).

The molar approach includes those forms of intervention which are aimed at the identification and eventual modification/restructuring of more basic dysfunctional cognitive/emotive schemata, or "working models" of self and

94

environment which the patient can be assumed to have developed in the on-going transactions with the environment during their upbringing. Recent investigations suggest that this latter approach, originally conceived by Beck (1976) for the treatment of emotional disorders, might also be as feasible and effective for patients suffering from more severe psychopathological disorders, e. g., those with a severe axis 2 personality disorder (Beck & Freeman, 1990) or schizophrenic disorders (Perris, 1989; Kingdon & Turkington, 1991; Perris et al., 1992; Fowler, 1992; Chambon & Marie-Cardine, 1993; Chambon et al., 1993).

This paper will discuss one such molar approach, as it was originally conceived at Umeå in 1986 for the treatment of severely disturbed patients, and successively implemented in several other places in Sweden.

The term "integrative" included in the title of this article requires a few comments. Firstly, it should be understood both in the sense that the treatment programme integrates therapeutic components based on different principles from those of individual cognitive therapy (e. g., milieu and group therapy, nonverbal therapeutic strategies, medication). Secondly, in the sense that such an integration of therapeutic strategies is not meant as haphazard eclecticism, but as a purposeful combination of different therapeutic principles, which are expected to interact in a meaningful way to promote a successive integration at a higher level of the patient's personality structure. For example, strictly individualised medication at a low dosage is regarded as a useful and some-times necessary component of treatment to influence those neurohumoral processes which are involved in the very cognitive processes which are among the targets of therapeutic interventions in order to facilitate the use of various therapeutic strategies, rather than merely keep symptoms under control. On the other hand, access to a tolerant, family-style therapeutic milieu permits keeping dosages of psychotropic drugs at the lowest effective level.

Since understandable space-limits do not permit a complete description of all the components of the treatment programme which also comprises milieu and group therapy (a full description is available elsewhere, Perris 1989), I will restrict myself at this juncture to a few remarks on the rationale behind the use of a schema-focused treatment approach to patients with a schizophrenic disorder, and on the main steps of the assumed therapeutic process. Before concluding, however, I would like to briefly report also on a few preliminary results of a naturalistic two-year follow-up of a small series of patients who have completed treatment.

The Rationale of a Schema-Focused Treatment and the Main Characteristics of the Therapeutic Approach

The premises which the integrated schema-focused approach is based on include:

a) Awareness of the heterogeneity of the disorders subsumed under the label "schizophrenia";

b) Rejection of simplistic causal explanations of those disorders in favour of more complex aetiopathogenetic models based on the concept of "individual vulnerability";

c) Awareness of the multifactorial nature of the global disability of patients suffering from a schizophrenic disorder.

Among these, particular importance is obviously given to the concept of individual vulnerability. However, it should be emphasised that whereas most of the models focused on vulnerability proposed since the original suggestion by Zubin and Spring (1977) have regarded vulnerability mostly in biological terms and as a stable, enduring trait of the individual, in our model we take into account not only the relatively invariant biological characteristics of an individual's personality – in its broadest sense – but also the development of dysfunctional meaning structures (Lundh, 1988). For these, the determining

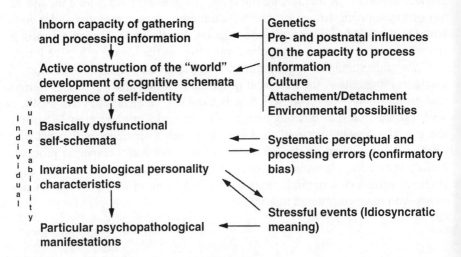

Figure 1. A theoretical framework to define individual vulnerability.

influence of both biological factors and early interactional experiences is crucial (Perris, 1988). The structures which are relevant in the present context are those encompassing the individual's self-schema, in which those schemata are also embedded, which are related to the individual's working models (Bowlby, 1969–1980) of his/her relationship (past, present, and future) to the environment, i. e., his/her interpersonal schemata (Safran & Segal, 1990).

The framework guiding our research and treatment programme, akin to that suggested by Ciompi (1982), is shown in Figure 1. Although the arrows in the figure are depicted only unidirectionally in order to avoid overload, it should be emphasised, however, that the importance of interactive processes in the determination of individual vulnerability is not limited to the interplay between biological factors and early emotional experiences. It also encompasses the continuing dialectical transactions between the (vulnerable) person on the one hand and the (immediate and large) environment on the other.

The main characteristics of the "working models" of self and environment include:

a)   They have both a cognitive and an affective component;

b)   They are the result of a generalised representation;

c)   They are most stable and out of awareness; and

d)   They can change as a consequence of concrete experiences.

Of particular importance is that despite the fact that working models are assumed to be relatively invariant, they are assumed to be modifiable through appropriate interventions.

The main assumption behind a schema-focused approach to schizophrenic patients is that the individual who will develop a schizophrenic syndrome has, for reasons related to his/her particular predicament, developed a fundamentally dysfunctional self-schema. This comprises both a dysfunctional self-image, and dysfunctional basic assumptions concerning his/her relationships (past, present, and future) to the environment. Those dysfunctional assumptions, in turn, are continuously sustained and reinforced by a variety of cognitive distortions in the comprehension and processing of information (e. g., arbitrary inference, selective attention/inattention, overgeneralisation, dichotomous thinking), which, obviously, are not pathological per se but become pathogenic when acting as a self-confirmatory bias. A few examples of dysfunctional working models which can be identified in schizophrenic patients comprise: "I must avoid unpleasant situations at all costs," "To show one's own feelings is dangerous," "Other people are too intrusive and demanding." Table 1 shows some of the cognitive distortions which occur more frequently in schizophrenics than in other kind of patients.

Table 1. Some cognitive distortions (*) which can be observed in patients suffering from a schizophrenic disorder.

– Use of symbolic logic (includes "predicative thinking" as described by Arieti)
– Desymbolisation
– Lack of awareness of the asymmetry which usually characterises human relationships
– Concretisation of concepts and their transformation into perceptions

(*) Most of these distortions might be understood in terms of primary process thinking. We prefer to understand them in terms of egocentrism.

The practice of therapy based on the premises reported so far does not substantially differ from that originally described by Beck et al. (1979) for the treatment of emotional disorders. However, a few distinguishing characteristics can be summarised as follows:

a) Necessity to develop a therapeutic relationship based on mutual trust and on collaborative empiricism;

b) A focus on the healthy part of the patient's personality;

c) A focus on problems to be solved rather than on symptoms to be eliminated;

d) A working through of those problems, moving from less threatening ones toward those which are more emotionally loaded;

e) Promoting reality testing (e. g., by means of homework assignments).

Of particular importance with this type of patients is the development of a therapeutic relationship based on collaborative empiricism (Beck et al., 1979). To conceptualise such a relationship, we have borrowed the metaphor of a secure base suggested by Bowlby (1973). According to his attachment theory (Bowlby, 1969, 1980), access to a secure base is an indispensable prerequisite for the growing child to be able to feel safe to explore profitably the surrounding world, i. e., to learn. Transferred into the practice of therapy, the concept of attachment and secure base implies that the therapist in charge of each individual patient has to behave in a way apt to promote attachment. This includes assuming the role of a secure base, in order to facilitate and to sustain the patient's exploration of painful experiences, and successively, the development of autonomy and competence.

The main steps of the therapeutic process are summarised in Table 2. It is expected that more basic cognitive deficits (e. g., attention) are positively in-

Table 2. Main components of the therapeutic process.

Distancing

Reattribution

Development of metathinking

Decentering

Neutralisation of automatic thoughts

Correction of cognitive distortions

Training in interpersonal skills

Modification of basic meaning structures
(Restructuring)

---

fluenced by treatment as a whole. Preliminary findings supporting this hypothesis have been presented elsewhere (Perris et al., 1990). It should be observed that the sequence shown in Table 2 should always be regarded as flexible, and the use of various strategies to promote change must be strictly individualised. One particular obstacle to the progress of therapy, and especially to the use of cognitive techniques can be the patients' lack of ability to think about their own thoughts, i.e., a deficit in metathinking. When this occurs, it can be necessary to start the exploration, moving from feelings experienced by the patient in various given situations before being able to map the occurrence of self-defeating automatic thoughts.

At the end of treatment, which in our experience lasts about two years on average, the patient is expected to have become able to:

a) Gain and maintain a positive self-image;

b) Make and sustain social contacts;

c) Apply skills and knowledge to new situations;

d) Accept limitations and inadequacies searching at the same time for possible improvements of the situation;

e) Develop a realistic outlook on the future.

Preliminary results of a Naturalistic Two-Year Follow-Up of Patients Who Have Completed Treatment

Coming to a close, I would like to briefly summarise some preliminary results of a currently ongoing evaluation that is being carried out at the various treatment centres which we have implemented. Table 3 shows the basic characteristics of a small series of 21 patients with a schizophrenic disorder, who have completed treatment and been followed-up for at least two years after discharge from the unit.

Table 3. The evaluation group (discharged Jan '87, May '91) (N = 28).

Age ($\bar{x}$) diagnosis	Sex	N	Onset	First contact with psychiatric services	Admission
Psychotic	Men	12	18	19.5	25.5
disorder	Women	9	16	18	27
Personality	Men	3	21	22	26.5
disorder	Women	4	15	21	23

The duration of treatment is shown in Table 4. It can be seen that only a minority of patients remained at a treatment unit for two years. Twenty-one patients did not utilise psychiatric services during the follow-up. Three patients were admitted to a psychiatric ward for less than ten days (mostly for a check-up of ongoing medication), whereas four were admitted for more than ten days. No suicides occurred. At the end of the follow-up, 25 patients were living on their own whereas three were still living with their parents.

Changes in symptomatology, measured by means of a schizophrenia subscale of the Comprehensive Psychopathological Rating Scale (CPRS; Asberg

Table 4. Duration of treatment at a centre (months) and years of follow-up (no. of patients).

Duration of treatment at a centre (months)	Duration of follow-up (yrs.) (no. of patients)							
	1.5	2	2.5	3	3.5	4	4.5	5
6		1						
12		4		3		4		1
18		6	1		1	1	1	1
24	1	1	2					

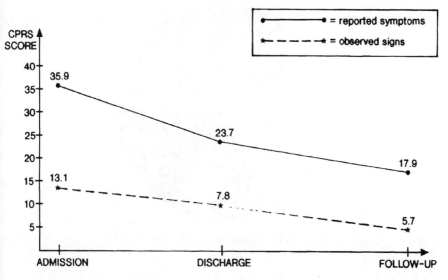

Figure 2. Changes in symptomatology (CPRS-subscale for schizophrenia) in patients with a schizophrenic disorder (N = 21).

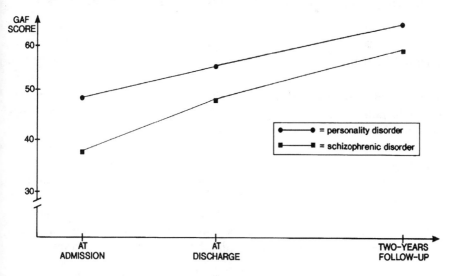

Figure 3. Global adjustment, GAF-score, mean values.

Figure 4. Type of occupation at follow-up (no. of patients) (N = 28).

et al., 1978) are shown in Figure 2, whereas changes in the GAF scale are shown in Figure 3. Important to notice as concerns these two measures is that gains made at discharge have not only been maintained but also have continued to increase at the end of the follow-up. Figure 4 shows the level of occupation at the end of the observation period. It must be pointed out that the label "occupational training" includes those governmental initiatives taken to limit unemployment, and does not exclusively refer to sheltered work.

Conclusions

The integrated treatment approach that has been developed and implemented in small, family-style residences, of which only one major component has been mentioned in this presentation, appears to be easily feasible in practice and well suited for young patients suffering from a schizophrenic disorder. The emphasis on structure and activity which characterises cognitive therapy promotes order and counteracts passivity and withdrawal. The goals of therapy are made explicit and the process to reach such goals well defined. In particular, it appears that changes which involve a restructuring of a patient's self-schema can be achieved within an acceptable span of time, which seems to be shorter than what is the case with other types of psychotherapy.

References

Alford, G. S., Fleece, L. & Rothblum, E. (1982) Hallucinatory-delusional verbalizations. Modification in a chronic schizophrenic by self-control and cognitive restructuring. *Behavior Modification*, **6**, 421–435.

Asberg, M., Perris, C., Schalling, D. & Sedvall, G. (1978) The CPRS-Development and applications of a psychiatric rating scale. *Acta Psychiatrica Scandinavica*, Supp. **271**.

Beck, A. T. (1976) *Cognitive Therapy and the Emotional Disorders.* New York: International Universities Press.

Beck, A. T. & Freeman, A. (1990) *Cognitive Therapy of Personality Disorders.* New York: Guilford Press.

Beck, A. T., Rush, A. J., Shaw, B. F. & Emery, G. (1979) *Cognitive Therapy of Depression.* New York: Guilford.

Bowlby, J. (1988) *A Secure Base.* New York: Basic Books.

Bowlby, J. (1969–1980) *Attachment and Loss, Vols. 1–3.* London: Hogarth Press.

Brenner, H. D., Hodel, B., Kube, G. & Roder, V. (1987) Kognitive Therapie bei Schizophrenen: Problemanalyse und empirische Ergebnisse. *Nervenarzt,* **58**, 72–83.

Brenner, H. D., Stramke, W. G., Meves, J., et al. (1980) Erfahrungen mit einem spezifischen Therapieprogramm zum Training kognitiver und kommunikativer Fähigkeiten in der Rehabilitation chronisch schizophrener Patienten. *Nervenarzt,* **51**, 106–112.

Buchkremer, G. & Fiedler, P. (1987) Kognitive versus handlungsorientierte Therapie. *Nervenarzt,* **58**, 481–488.

Chadwick, P.D.J. & Lowe, C.F. (1990) Measurement and modification of delusional beliefs. *Journal of Consulting & Clinical Psychology*, **58**, 225–232.

Chambon, O. & Marie-Cardine, M. (in press) *La Psychothérapie Cognitive des Psychoses.* Paris: Masson.

Chambon, O., Rouviere, S., Favrod, J. & Marie-Cardine, M. (1993) La psychothérapie cognitive des délires chroniques. *Thérapie Comportementale et Cognitive*, **3**, 4–15.

Ciompi, L. (1982) *Affektlogik.* Stuttgart: Klett-Cotta.

Fowler, D. (1992) Cognitive behaviour therapy in the management of patients with schizophrenia: Preliminary studies. In *Psychotherapy of Schizophrenia; Facilitating and Obstructive Factors* (eds A. Werbart & J. Cullberg) Oslo: Scandinavian University Press.

Fowler, D. & Morley, S. (1989) The cognitive-behavioural treatment of hallucinations and delusions: a preliminary study. *Behavioural Psychotherapy*, **17**, 267–282.

Greene, R. J. (1978) Auditory hallucination reduction: First person singular. *Journal of Contemporary Psychotherapy,* **9**, 167–170.

Hartman, L. M. & Casham, F. E. (1983) Cognitive-behavioral and psychopharmacological treatment of delusional symptoms. A preliminary report. *Behavioural Psychotherapy*, **11**, 50–61.

Hermanutz, M. & Gestrich, J. (1987) Kognitives Training mit Schizophrenen. *Nervenarzt,* **58**, 91–96.

Hole, R. W., Rush, A. J. & Beck, A. T. (1979) A cognitive investigation of schizophrenic delusions. *Psychiatry*, **42**, 312–318.

Johnson, W. G., Ross, J. M. & Mastria, M. A. (1977) Delusional behavior: An attributional analysis of development and modification. *Journal of Abnormal Psychology,* **86**, 421–426.

Kingdon, D. J. & Turkington, D. (1991) The use of cognitive behavior therapy with a normalizing rationale in schizophrenia. *Journal of Nervous & Mental Disease*, **179**, 207–211.

Kraemer, S., Sulz, K. H. D., Schmid, R. & Lässle, R. (1987) Kognitive Therapie bei standardversorgten schizophrenen Patienten. *Nervenarzt*, **58**, 84–90.

Liberman, R. P., Mueser, K. T., Wallace, C. J., et al. (1986) Training skills in the psychiatrically disabled: learning coping and competence. *Schizophrenia Bulletin*, **12**, 631–647.

Lundh, L.-G. (1988) Cognitive therapy and the analysis of meaning structures. In *Cognitive Psychotherapy: Theory and Practice* (eds C. Perris, I. M. Blackburn & H. Perris), pp. 44–61. Heidelberg: Springer-Verlag.

McGlashan, T. H., Heinssen, R. K. & Fenton, W. S. (1990) Psychosocial treatment of negative symptoms in schizophrenia. In *Schizophrenia: Positive and Negative Symptoms and Syndromes. Modern Problems of Pharmacopsychiatry* (ed. N. C. Andreasen), pp. 175–200. Basel: Karger.

Meichenbaum, D. & Cameron, R. (1973) Training schizophrenics to talk to themselves. A means of developing attentional controls. *Behavior Therapy*, **4**, 515–534.

Meyers, A., Mercatoris, M. & Sirota, A. (1976) Use of covert self-instruction for the elimination of psychotic speech. *Journal of Consulting & Clinical Psychology*, **44**, 480–482.

Milton, F., Patwa, V. K. & Hafner, R. J. (1978) Confrontation vs. belief modification in persistently deluded patients. *British Journal of Medical Psychology*, **51**, 127–130.

Olbrich, R. & Mussgay, L. (1990) Reduction of schizophrenic deficits by cognitive training: An evaluative study. *European Archives of Psychiatry & Neurological Sciences*, **239**, 366–369.

Perris, C. (1989) *Cognitive Therapy with Schizophrenic Patients*. New York: Guilford Press.

Perris, C. (1988) Intensive cognitive-behavioural psychotherapy with patients suffering from schizophrenic psychotic or post-psychotic syndromes: Theoretical and practical aspects. In *Cognitive Psychotherapy. Theory and Practice* (eds C. Perris, I. M. Blackburn & H. Perris), pp. 324–375. Heidelberg: Springer-Verlag.

Perris, C., Nordström, G., Troeng, L. (1992) Schizophrenic disorders. In *Comprehensive Casebook of Cognitive Therapy* (eds A. Freeman & F.M. Dattilio) New York: Plenum.

Perris, C., Toresson, P., Skagerlind, L. et al. (1990) Integrating components in a comprehensive cognitive treatment program for patients with a schizophrenic disorders. In *Psychiatry: A World Perspective, Vol. 3* (eds C. N. Stefanis, A. D. Rabavilas & C. R. Saldatos), pp. 724–729. Amsterdam: Elsevier.

Peter, K., Glaser, A. & Kühne, G.-E. (1989) Erste Erfahrungen mit der kognitiven Therapie Schizophrener. *Psychiatrie, Neurologie & Psychologie*, **41**, 485–491.

Safran, J. D. & Segal, Z. V. (1990) *Interpersonal Processes in Cognitive Therapy*. New York: Basic Books.

Spaulding, W. D., Storms, L., Goodrich, V. & Sullivan, M. (1986) Applications of experimental psychopathology in psychiatric rehabilitation. *Schizophrenia Bulletin*, **12**, 560–577.

Stramke, W. G. & Brenner, H. D. (1983) Psychologische Trainingsprogramme zur Minderung kognitiver Störungen in der Rehabilitation chronisch schizophrener Patienten. In *Empirische Schizophrenieforschung: Experimentalpsychologische Ergebnisse und Beispiele ihrer Anwendung in Behandlung und Rehabilitation* (eds H. D. Brenner, E.-R. Rey & W. G. Stramke), pp. 182–201. Bern: Huber.

Watts, F. N., Powell, G. E. & Austin, S. V. (1973) The modification of abnormal beliefs. *British Journal of Medical Psychology*, **46**, 359–363.

Zubin, J. & Spring, B. (1977) Vulnerability: A new view of schizophrenia. *Journal of Abnormal Psychology*, **86**, 103–123.

Cognitive Changes in the Course of Rehabilitation

Will Spaulding, Dorie Reed, Dirk Elting, Mary Sullivan and David Penn

Summary

This paper summarises a series of studies intended to sort out the relationships between cognitive impairments and those failures in personal and social functioning that make schizophrenia a behaviourally disabling condition. The data suggest the following relationships: (1) Cognitive and macrosocial levels of functioning are moderately related, while cognitive and microsocial levels of functioning are moderately related, while cognitive and microsocial levels of functioning are more modestly related, and social skill measures, symptom measures and observational measures of ambient social behaviour are only very weakly related; (2) Both cognitive functioning and social skills measured at pre-treatment predict macrosocial changes.

Today, most psychopathologists understand schizophrenia as more than simply an illness; it is seen rather as a system of interacting processes of disease and organismic compensation, changing developmentally over many years. Our understanding of the roles of cognitive impairment and vulnerability in the aetiology of schizophrenia has gradually grown along with that realisation. We have begun to organise our understanding of schizophrenic cognition in the new light of systemic, developmental, and biopsychosocial models of the disorder. Most recently, we have begun to identify the relationships between cognitive impairment and those failures in personal and social functioning that make schizophrenia a behaviourally disabling condition. As Brenner (1987) has demonstrated, we can now construct credible biosystemic models of schizophrenia which conceptually integrate our understanding of neurophysiological, cognitive, and sociobehavioural factors.

These developments have created a climate of excitement and enthusiasm among both researchers and clinicians; part of this comes from the prospect of adding to our comprehensive theoretical understanding of schizophrenia as a systems disorder. A less dramatic but nonetheless important part of the scientific/technological development process is exploration of the "practical particulars" of using cognitive theory and technology in the rehabilitation of schizophrenia. In order to use this technology to optimise assessment and treatment, we need an empirically validated *nomological net* of measures; these describe the relationships between cognitive impairments and other characteristics of schizophrenia at the levels of neurophysiological, psychological, and social functioning.

One set of practical particulars concerns impairments in cognitive, micro-social, and macro-social functioning as they are found in schizophrenia's chronic residual phase, in severely and persistently disabled patients who are undergoing rehabilitation. The issues can be stated as a series of four research problems:

1. What are the correlational relationships, in chronological cross-section, between cognitive, micro-social, and macro-social functioning?

2. Do pre-treatment levels of cognitive and micro-social functioning predict treatment response in macro-social functioning?

3. Are treatment-related changes in cognitive and micro-social functioning associated with treatment-related changes in macro-social functioning?

4. Are cognitive changes produced by non-specific rehabilitation processes, or by specific modalities with target cognitive impairments?

These questions are addressed here with data collected over a period of ten years, in three separate studies. All three studies were conducted in a 40-bed comprehensive psychiatric rehabilitation programme in the Lincoln Regional Center, a state hospital in Nebraska.

Figure 1 shows a schematic of the first study, hereafter called Cohort 1. After a stabilisation period to ensure the patients were optimally medicated

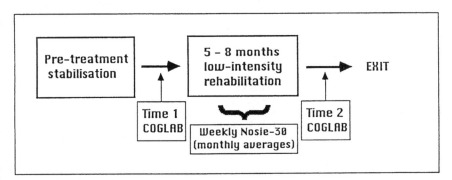

Figure 1. Cohort 2 (N = 112).

and not in an exacerbated episode, they were assessed with COGLAB, a computerised cognitive/neuropsychological test battery developed in our laboratory. They then entered a low-intensity rehabilitation phase, consisting of treatment in a structured inpatient therapeutic milieu, a few hours per week of intensive social skills training, and 10–15 hours per week of structured recreational and occupational activities. Rehabilitation at this intensity is not much different from the low-demand, highly-structured milieu preferred for restabilisation after an exacerbated episode, except that activities are directed at improving functioning enough for discharge to a sheltered community setting. Five to eight months later, the subjects were assessed again with CO-GLAB. In the interim, their social behavioural functioning was measured with the NOSIE-30, a widely used observational instrument that uses weekly staff ratings of patients' behaviour. The NOSIE-30 was administered weekly, and condensed into monthly averages.

Figure 2 shows the second study, Cohort 2, which is currently underway. Their medium-intensity rehabilitation programme includes up to 20 hours per week of intensive social and living skills training, a contingency-management-based approach to milieu treatment, and up to 20 additional hours of structured leisure and occupational activities. While this programme is of much higher intensity than that of Cohort 1, it does not approach high-inten-

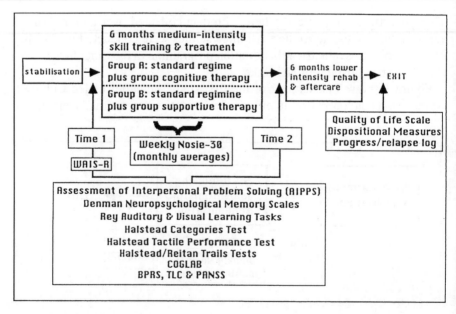

Figure 2. Cohort 2 (N = 44).

sity programmes such as those described by Paul and Lentz (1977), which include up to 70 hours per week of skill training and structured activities, with a token economy-based therapeutic milieu. The pre- and post-testing for this group includes a number of additional neuropsychological measures, skill performance measures and interview-based symptom measures, as well as the COGLAB. Weekly NOSIE-30 collection continues, and there will be a one-year follow-up assessment of overall progress and quality of life.

The subjects in Cohort 2 are quasi-randomly assigned to one of two experimental conditions. Subjects in the first condition receive about 80 hours of group cognitive therapy, which is essentially an American version of the cognitive portions of Brenner's Integrated Therapy Programme for Schizophrenic Patients (Brenner et al., 1983). Those in the second condition receive the same amount of a group supportive therapy that was developed for this study and based on standard descriptions of such measures for chronic psychiatric inpatients. The two treatments were designed to have a number of general characteristics of group therapy in common, so that differences in effects would be attributable solely to specific procedures of the cognitive therapy condition. Observational analyses of therapy sessions in our laboratory have confirmed that the two techniques have specifiable features in common, as well as features that are distinct (Terryberry-Spohr et al., 1991, 1992).

The third study (Penn et al., 1993) was smaller in scale; it was ad hoc and cross-sectional, using psychiatric interview, NOSIE-30, and social skills assessment data collected at the same site as Cohorts 1 and 2. Data from these three studies are examined in turn, as the four research questions are considered.

The first question, "What are the cross-sectional relationships between cognition and other levels of functioning?" was examined with a series of multiple regression analyses of Cohort 1. For these analyses, a selection of COGLAB measures was used to construct multiple regression formulae to "predict" (only in the statistical sense) the values of the NOSIE-30 subscales during the month in which the COGLAB was administered. Separate formulae were computed for Time 1 and Time 2, about six months apart. Table 1 shows the results of the analyses: the key results are the squared multiple correlations, or R squares, which express the predictive power of their respective formula as the proportion of NOSIE-30 variance which is accounted for by COGLAB measures. Thus, an R square of .20 means that 20% of the variance is accounted for. All the non-zero correlation values in this and the subsequent tables are statistically significant. Table 1 shows the multiple correlations after they have been mathematically adjusted downward to correct for the analysis procedure's tendency to capitalise on chance correlations. The adjusted R square is thus a fairly conservative estimate of the true relationship between these measures.

109

Table 1. Relationships between cognitive and social functioning during six months of comprehensive psychiatric rehabilitation; NOSIE-30 and COGLAB, Cohort 1, N = 112 (adapted from Spaulding et al., in press).

NOSIE subscale	Adjusted R square	
	Time 1	Time 2
COM	0.16	0.36
INT	0	0.04
NEA	0.19	0.28
IRR	0.12	0.08
PSY	0.25	0.30
RET	0.09	0.10
Total Assets	0.17	0.22

As Table 1 shows, cognition as measured by COGLAB is more closely associated with some NOSIE subscales than with others. At Time 1, CO-GLAB accounts for 17% of Total Assets (Tot), a NOSIE summary scale which incorporates all the subscales. At Time 2, it rises to 22%, with most of the increase due to the Social Competence (COM) subscale, which measures the patients' ability to adhere to a personal daily schedule and participate in rehabilitation activities, and to the Neatness (NEA) subscale, which measures the patients' physical appearance, grooming and hygiene.

A detailed description of the various cognitive measures which produce these correlations is beyond the scope of this paper (see Spaulding et al., in press), but a broad array of different measures across the COGLAB's entire spectrum are involved in the various formulae. Further study will be required to conclude confidently which specific cognitive measures are most strongly associated with which NOSIE subscales, but at this point it can be said that cognitive functioning is generally associated with patients' response to the rehabilitation milieu. Cognitive functioning is reflected in these data in the patients' ability to respond to the programme's demands for following a daily schedule of rehabilitation activities, for appropriate hygiene and grooming, and to avoid psychotic behaviour in the ward milieu. The difference between Time 1 and Time 2 probably reflects a gradual increase in demands, as rehabilitation progresses: when demands are lesser, cognitive impairment is less disabling, and so the association between COGLAB and NOSIE is weaker.

Table 2 summarises analyses from the Penn et al. (1993) study. This time, regression formulae were constructed which used COGLAB measures to predict concurrent performance in a social skills assessment procedure. The latter is a role-play assessment of patients' performance in casual conversation (Penn et al., 1994). It is briefer and less comprehensive than the Assessment of Interpersonal Problem Solving Skills (AIPSS) (Donahoe, unpublished),

Table 2. Relationships between cognitive functioning and performance on a social skills assessment task, N = 38 (adapted from Penn et al., 1993).

Role playing measure	Backward stepwise solution	
	COGLAB measure	Adjusted R square
Overall skill	CPT false alarms	0.27
Nonverbal	Card sort random errors	0.11
Paralinguistic	reaction time	0.13

which is now being used in the Cohort 2 study, but it does yield three measures of basic socialisation ability. The three subscales of the skill assessment were predicted by COGLAB, accounting for 11% to 27% of common variance. Several COGLAB measures are involved in each prediction, but in this case, we used stepwise analyses to identify the single most powerful predictor set. In each case, this was found to be a single COGLAB variable, but a different one for each skill assessment subscale. This continues to suggest that different cognitive impairments are associated with different skill impairments, but we cannot confidently conclude that this is not an artefact of psychometric properties of COGLAB. Nevertheless, it is evident that there are at least general relationships between cognition and social skill performance.

Table 3 also summarises results from the Penn et al. (1993) study, showing the correlations between the skill assessment and concurrent NOSIE-30 subscales. These correlations are small and isolated. The figure in parentheses is only marginally statistically significant, before a correction for multiple measures. In view of the previous findings on the COGLAB and the NOSIE, the most parsimonious inference is that the COGLAB is predicting performance in two rather different and minimally related domains – the micro-social functioning measured by the skill assessment, and the more macro-social functioning measured by the NOSIE.

Table 3. Relationships between social skills performance and a milieu-based observation measure, N = 38 (adapted from Penn et al., 1993).

NOSIE Subscale	Pearson r		
	Overall Skill	Non-verbal	Paralinguistic
COM	0	0	0
INT	0	0	0.35
NEA	0.33	0	0.39
IRR	0	0	0
PSY	0	0	0
RET	0	0	((0.26))

Table 4. Relationships between social skills performance and an interview-based assessment of symptomatology, N = 38 (adapted from Penn et al., 1993).

Role play measure	Pearson r PANSS positive	negative
Overall skills	0	0
Nonverbal	0	0
Paralinguistic	0	0.33

Table 4 also summarises results from the Penn et al. study, showing the correlations between the skill assessment and the Positive & Negative Syndrome Scales (PANSS; Kay et al., 1987), an interview-based measure of schizophrenic symptoms. Again, the relationships are small and limited in scope; social skills performance impairments are not simply a reflection of positive or negative symptoms.

Thus, in response to the first key question, it may be concluded that the cognitive functions measured by COGLAB are significantly related to macrosocial functioning in the treatment milieu, as measured by the NOSIE-30. This relationship becomes stronger as low-intensity rehabilitation progresses, probably because of gradually increasing demands on patients' social behaviour. Further, cognitive functioning is related to performance in social skills assessment tasks, which is a microsocial level of functioning. There is as yet no evidence in these data for relationships between social skills and the more macrosocial functioning measured by the NOSIE-30. However, the analyses of Cohort 1 indicate that while these relationships may be robust, they are not large. Sample sizes larger than that of the Penn et al. (1992) study will be necessary to investigate relationships between microsocial and macrosocial functioning further.

Table 5 shows analyses of Cohort 1 data which refer to the second key question, concerning the true clinical predictive power of the cognitive measures. The data have been statistically corrected to compensate for artifactual correlations produced by initial values effects. This is done by computing a *residualised change score*, from which the variance attributable to the initial value has been removed. Table 5 shows the ability of COGLAB measures at Time 1 to predict the change in NOSIE-30 scores from Time 1 to Time 2. When the entire patient sample is analysed together, the prediction is statistically significant but weak, accounting for only 4% of Total Assets variance. However, when the sample is subdivided, based on whether each subject's Time 1 NOSIE is above or below the sample median, there is a striking difference. For patients who begin with a low NOSIE, the prediction of change is not above chance. For patients who begin with a high NOSIE, there is con-

Table 5. Predicting change in social functioning by initial cognitive functioning (Time 1 COGLAB and NOSIE-30 change scores; Cohort 1, N = 112) (adapted from Spaulding et al., in press).

| NOSIE subscale | Full Sample | Adjusted R square | |
		LO NOSIE grp	HI NOSIE grp
COM	0.05		
INT	0.12		
NEA	0		
IRR	0		
PSY	0.05		
RET	0.06		
Total Assets	0.04	0	0.27

siderable predictive power. Case-by-case examination of these data suggests that this relationship is produced by a specific group of patients who have high NOSIE's but poor COGLAB performance at Time 1. These patients tend to show a significant drop in NOSIE functioning in the course of low-intensity rehabilitation. This finding converges with the previous one in suggesting that patients with initially poor cognitive functioning have more difficulty in responding to the rehabilitation milieu.

Preliminary analyses of Cohort 2 suggest that with additional neuropsychological measures, the predictive power of initial cognitive assessment is greatly increased, accounting for as much as 44% of NOSIE change. This is consistent with findings from other laboratories that suggest that impairments in perception, attention, short-term memory, and conceptual processing all contribute to schizophrenic patients' social dysfunction, and are possibly limiting factors in response to psychosocial treatment (Bowen, 1988; Corrigan, 1993; Toomey et al., 1993; Mueser et al., 1993). Also, assessment of microsocial functioning appears to have predictive power, with initial AIPSS scores predicting as much as 47% of NOSIE change. One cannot be confident of elaborate conclusions with

Table 6. Concomitant changes in cognitive and social functioning NOSIE-30 change scores and COGLAB change scores; Cohort 1, N = 11 (adapted from Spaulding et al., in press).

NOSIE subscale	Adjusted R square
COM	0.13
INT	0.12
NEA	0.15
IRR	0
PSY	0.05
RET	0.16

the incomplete Cohort 2 sample size, but so far, analyses of Cohort 2 also continue to suggest that the predictive power of initial cognitive assessment is quite different for different subgroups of patients.

To proceed to the third key question, Table 6 shows analyses of relationships between changes in COGLAB measures and changes in NOSIE scores in the Cohort 1 study. As before, the data were corrected to remove the effects of initial values for both the COGLAB and the NOSIE change scores. Change in Total Assets shares 11% common variance with COGLAB changes, with up to 16% common variance between COGLAB and specific NOSIE subscales. This may be the first empirical demonstration that changes in cognitive functioning are related to changes in macrosocial functioning in a low-intensity rehabilitation environment. It is interesting that the NOSIE subscales involved in these relationships are different form those involved in cross-sectional correlations. Most notable in this regard is the Psychoticism (PSY) subscale, which measures psychotic-like behaviour in the ambient social milieu. PSY is "predicted" (in the statistical sense) quite strongly in the cross-sectional analyses, but changes in PSY are not strongly associated with changes in cognitive functioning.

Analyses of Cohort 2 have not revealed relationships between concurrent change in cognitive and macrosocial functioning, but before, the size of these changes are such that a larger sample size is probably required to observe them.

Finally comes the question of most direct relevance to treatment: Do rehabilitation activities produce improvements in cognitive functioning? Our analyses of Cohort 1 suggest that low-intensity rehabilitation does not reliably produce any changes in COGLAB performance. The relationships between COGLAB and NOSIE summarised in Table 6 were produced by both improvement and deterioration within the sample. Neither NOSIE nor COGLAB showed significant group changes from Time 1 to Time 2. However, in Cohort 2, there was significant improvement in three neuropsychological measures, the COGLAB card sorting task, the Halstead Categories Test, and the Halstead-Reitan Tactile Performance Test. The absence of changes in Cohort 1, at least on card sorting performance, is evidence that the change in Cohort 2 was not simply a practice effect. Practice effects on the other tasks cannot be definitively ruled out yet, but are improbable, in view of the lack of previous reports of practice effects in this population, and the six-month period between testings. These findings are similar to those of van der Gaag (1992), in that he found differential change on the COGLAB card sorting task associated with different treatment conditions. However, the two treatment conditions are not easily comparable.

The most interesting aspect of this finding is that all three of these tests measure executive and response-organisation abilities which have been associated

114

with frontal lobe dysfunction in schizophrenia. They are distinct from all the other measures in the Cohort 2 assessment battery in that regard. In view of the accumulating studies which show that performance on the Wisconsin Card Sorting Test can be improved by treatment-like experimental procedures (Green et al., 1990; Summerfelt et al., 1991; see also Green's, this volume) it is tempting to hypothesise that recovery of frontal executive and response-organisation functioning is an important mediator of the benefits of psychiatric rehabilitation. Caution is indicated, however, in making such a deduction. Functioning in this domain also improves in the course of hospitalisation and drug treatment following an acute exacerbation, in depressive as well as schizophrenic patients (Penn et al., 1993). The improvement in Cohort 2 could possibly be attributable to aspects of the medium-intensity rehabilitation milieu other than psychosocial treatment which optimise neurophysiological functioning. For example, the richness of the cognitive and behavioural data generated by the rehabilitation programme may stimulate the prescribing psychiatrist to titrate drug dosages more accurately to optimal levels. Further research is required to pinpoint the origins of the Cohort 2 treatment effect.

Cohort 2 has not yet produced evidence that these cognitive changes are specific to the most explicitly "cognitive" components of standard rehabilitation methods. It is important to note in this regard that the "non-cognitive" modalities in the Standard Regimen of Cohort 2 were nevertheless "cognitively sensitive", in that the skill training procedures included various manoeuvres explicitly designed to compensate for patients' cognitive impairments. So far, our data suggest that cognitively sensitive skill training may do more than simply minimise the effects of impairments on skill acquisition – it may actually produce improvements in the impaired processes themselves.

Thus, the results of these three studies are collectively relevant to the four key research problems by stimulating the following tentative conclusions:

1. In cross-section, cognitive and macrosocial levels of functioning in stable chronic schizophrenic patients undergoing rehabilitation are moderately related, with measures sharing up to 35% common variance. Cognitive and microsocial levels of functioning are more modestly related, with measures sharing up to 27% common variance. Social skill measures, symptom measures, and observational measures of ambient social behaviour are only very weakly related.

2. Both cognitive functioning and social skills, measured at pre-treatment, appear to predict macrosocial changes in the context of psychiatric rehabilitation, possibly even more strongly than they "predict" (in the statistical sense) concurrent macrosocial behaviour, at least for some subgroups.

3. There is some concomitant improvement in cognitive and microsocial functioning in a low-intensity rehabilitation milieu, sharing about 11% common variance.

4. Improvement in cognitive functioning associated with psychiatric rehabilitation appears to be distributed across both molar and molecular cognitive processes, although the molar levels, associated with concept manipulation and executive processing, show the most robust effects. So far, there is little evidence that these improvements are associated with specific modalities within the psychiatric rehabilitation armamentarium.

References

Bowen, L. (1988) *Prediction of schizophrenic patients' response to skill training with laboratory assessment of attentional deficits.* Doctoral dissertation, California School of Professional Psychology, Los Angeles.

Brenner, H. (1987) On the importance of cognitive disorders in treatment and rehabilitation. In *Psychosocial Treatment of Schizophrenia* (eds J. Strauss, W. Böker & H. Brenner). Toronto: Huber.

Brenner, H., Stramke, W., Hodel, B. & Rui, C. (1983) *A treatment program for impaired cognitive functions aimed at preventing chronic disability among schizophrenic patients.* Paper presented at World Psychiatric Association Symposium, Baltimore.

Corrigan, P. (1993) *Recognition of situational cues in schizophrenia: A limited capacity model.* Paper presented at Association for Advancement of Behavior Therapy, Atlanta.

Donahoe, C. P. (unpublished) *Assessment instruments for problem-solving skills.* Available from author at Audie L. Murphy Memorial Veterans Hospital, San Antonio, TX.

Green, M. F, Ganzell, S., Satz, P. & Vaclav, J. F. (1990) Teaching the Wisconsin Card Sorting test to schizophrenic patients (letter to the editor). *Archives of General Psychiatry*, **47**, 91–92.

Kay, S., Fizbein, A. & Opler, L. (1987) The Positive and Negative Syndrome Scale (PANSS) for schizophrenia. *Schizophrenia Bulletin*, **13**, 261–276.

Mueser, K., Doonan, R., Penn, D. et al. (1993) Affect perception, social functioning and social skills in chronic schizophrenia. Paper presented at Association for Advancement of Behavior Therapy, Atlanta.

Paul, G. L. & Lentz, R. J. (1977) *Psychosocial Treatment of Chronic Mental Patients: Milieu versus Social Learning Programs.* Cambridge: Harvard University Press.

Penn, D., Hope, D., Spaulding, W. & Kucera, J. (1994) Social anxiety in schizophrenia. *Schizophrenia Research*, **11**, 277–284.

Penn, D., Mueser, K., Spaulding, W. et al. (1993) *Information processing and social competence in chronic schizophrenia.* Paper presented at Association for Advancement of Behavior Therapy, Atlanta.

Penn, D., van der Does, J., Spaulding, W. et al. (1993) Information processing and social-cognitive problem solving in schizophrenia. *Journal of Nervous & Mental Disease*, **181**, 13–20.

Spaulding, W., Penn, D. & Garbin, C. (in press) Cognitive changes in the course of psychiatric rehabilitation. In *Cognitive Rehabilitation of Schizophrenia* (eds M. Merlo, C. Perris & H. D. Brenner) Toronto: Hogrefe & Huber.

Summerfelt, A. T., Alphs, L. D., Wagman, A. M. I. et al. (1991) Reduction of perseverative errors in patients with schizophrenia using monetary feedback. *Journal of Abnormal Psychology*, **100**, 613–616.

Terryberry-Spohr, L., Elting, D., Hope, D. & Spaulding, W. (1991) *Treatment of chronic inpatients: Differentiating group therapies using a psychotherapy process q-sort*. Paper presented at Association for Advancement of Behavior Therapy, New York.

Terryberry-Spohr, L., Elting, D., Mohamed, S. et al. (1992) *Differentiating group therapies for chronic inpatients using a psychotherapy process q-sort*. Paper presented at Association for Advancement of Behavior Therapy, Boston.

Toomey, R., Schuldberg, D., Green, M. & Corrigan, P. (1993) *Social perception of nonverbal cues in schizophrenia: Relationship with deficits in cognition and social problem solving*. Paper presented at Association for Advancement of Behavior Therapy, Atlanta.

van der Gaag, M. (1992) *The Results of Cogntitive Training in Schizophrenic Patients*. Delft, Netherlands: Eburon.

A New Development in Integrated Psychological Therapy for Schizophrenic Patients (IPT): First Results of Emotional Management Training

Bettina Hodel and Hans Dieter Brenner

Summary

The relationship between disordered cognitive and emotional processing are considered to be a prominent feature of schizophrenia. Rigid information processing results in withdrawal from reality and a fragmentary relationship to the environment. Yet only a few methods have been developed for modifying emotional coping. Integrated Psychological Therapy for Schizophrenic Patients (IPT) improves disordered cognitive and social skills, indirectly taking into consideration emotional processing in a highly structured therapeutic proceeding. We recently devised an additional IPT subprogramme (Emotional Management Training) which directly aims at reducing the negative influences of disruptive emotions in cognitive and social functioning. It is an eight-step training programme which starts off with patients' description of depicted emotions and advances from analyses of patients' spontaneous coping strategies to acquirement of individualised coping behaviour. Results from first evaluations carried out on 31 schizophrenic patients indicated that the new procedure has a more significant impact on cognitive mastery than either relaxation therapy or focused cognitive training.

Information-processing disorders, which are considered to be a "core psychological deficit" in schizophrenia (cf. Lang & Buss, 1965; Gjerde, 1983; Nuechterlein & Dawson, 1984; Braff, 1991; Corrigan et al., 1992; Cornblatt, in press), are increasingly being analysed in terms of their interaction with disordered emotional processing (cf. Hemsley, 1990; Berenbaum & Oltmanns, 1992; Dworkin, 1992). This, in turn, is also considered to be a prominent feature of schizophrenia (cf. Morrison & Bellack, 1981; Jackson et al., 1989; Bellack, 1990; Heimberg et al., 1992; Bellack, this volume).

Several assumptions have been made on the mechanisms underlying the relationships between information-processing disorders and emotional processing. Gjerde (1983) postulated that emotions can aggravate information-processing disorders via heightened arousal, while Brenner (1987) specified that emotions may increase the pervasive effects of cognitive disorders on behavioural functioning. Hemsley (1990, 1994) suggested that the cognitive disorders in schizophrenia are due to structural deficits, i. e., an impaired neural substrate of the cognitive capacity, and that they can be reinforced by emotional stress, which overtaxes the individual's available coping skills and leaves him/her incapable of dealing with situations in a well-adjusted manner.

Brenner (1989) has recently developed a heuristic model which outlines the interactions between the neural, cognitive, and emotional processes involved in the control of behaviour. Based on the distinction between episodic and participatory processes elaborated by Pribram (1981), it links participatory processes to positive emotions, and episodic processes to negative emotions. Participatory processes tolerate incongruities between one's own expectations and a current situation, for the purpose of perceiving new external stimuli considered to be relevant. Therefore, they are linked to perceptual information-processing, which, in turn corresponds to the arousal system and to external control. This is due to the fact that the neurochemical substrate of the arousal system consists of reciprocal norepinephrinergic and serotonergic pathways which, coming from the brain stem, reach widespread brain areas and thus support responsivity to external stimuli. By comparing new external stimuli to previous experiences, the current situation may seem to be more controllable, so that optimistic feelings, e. g., interest and hope, are likely to arise.

On the other hand, the model postulates that episodic processes tend to block those external stimuli which are incongruent with one's own expectations. Such stimuli which are not blocked are transformed by conceptual information-processing; this corresponds to the activation system and to internal control, since the activation system is regulated through nigrostriatal and mesolimbic-mesocortical dopamine pathways, partly in combination with cholinergic neuronal systems, where internal control is predominant. The failure to compare new external stimuli to previous experiences results in an inability to react adequately to current situations, and in pessimistic feelings such as fear and social alienation. Due to the activation system's inherent bias towards a predominance of internal control, connected with rigid planning of behaviour, schizophrenic patients are easily "frozen" into a state of negative outcome expectancy. At the same time, negative emotions corresponding to episodic processes increase rigid information processing. The schizophrenic patient withdraws more and more from reality and his/her relationship to the environment become fragmentary and irregular.

119

In addition to the elaboration of theoretical concepts, several experimental studies have been carried out on the mechanisms of the relationship between cognitive and emotional processing in schizophrenia: earlier investigations focused on the perception and appraisal of emotion: there is evidence that schizophrenic patients are less capable of adequately perceiving emotions than depressive patients, and that both groups perform more poorly than normals (Cutting, 1981; Walker et al., 1984; Feinberg et al., 1986; Gessler et al., 1989). Under emotional stress schizophrenics react rigidly with perceptual withdrawal (Käsermann, 1986; Berenbaum et al., 1987; Mandal & Gewali, 1989). Additionally, they perform more poorly in emotion-perception tasks than other groups of psychiatric patients, but under structured "laboratory-conditions," show relatively adequate performance in emotional appraisal (Dougherty et al., 1974; Walker et al., 1984; Feinberg et al., 1986). However, both the reproduction and the appraisal of stressful and adverse situations may be impaired in schizophrenia (Russel & Fehr, 1987), and negative emotions in particular can be misconceived or even ignored (Muzekari & Bates, 1977; Novic et al., 1984). The overall appraisal of another person's emotions – which can be estimated by skills of miming – has been found to be impaired in non-paranoid schizophrenics, suggesting weak cognitive schemata for emotional information. However, paranoid patients were found to be more accurate at appraising negative facial affects, suggesting better developed negative emotional aspects in their cognitive schema (Kline et al., 1992).

Current investigations focus on schizophrenic patients' ability to differentiate between and within emotions, as well as on their emotion-miming skills. It seems that impaired emotional discrimination does not depend on the nature of the emotions depicted. Instead, on the one hand, impairment can be significantly associated with the severity of negative symptoms like social withdrawal or mental retardation (Heimberg et al., 1992). On the other hand, it can be a result of an incapability to discriminate cues representing different qualities of a single emotion (Bellack, this book). Pitman et al. (1987) rated skills of facial expression in both non-paranoid and paranoid schizophrenic patients, as well as in a control group. While non-paranoid subjects were found to have significantly less eye contact compared to the others, the paranoid patients displayed significantly fewer facial movements. Schneider et al. (1990) showed that both emotional information-processing and responsiveness might be impaired in schizophrenia: schizophrenic patients were found to exhibit reduced facial activity in social interaction more often than depressive patients. Berenbaum & Oltmanns (1992) showed that schizophrenics differed significantly from both depressive and normal subjects in their facial expressions of emotions, but not in any self-reported emotional experiences, except for positive ones.

120

Interventions for Disordered Processing of Emotion

One of the earliest procedures for restoring disordered emotional processing in schizophrenia was Meichenbaum's and Cameron's (1973) self-instruction training, which involves four steps for the management of emotional stress in schizophrenia. First, self-instructions are used to reduce emotional arousal (e. g., "Don't worry. Worrying won't help"). Second, self-instructions are used in the form of self-guidance in carrying out tasks (e. g., "One step at a time. You can handle the situation"). Third, self-instructions are initiated to handle failure and frustration (e. g., "It will be over shortly"). In the last step, self-reinforcement is practised (e. g., "It worked. You did it"). Within the framework of personal-effectiveness training, Liberman et al. (1975) demonstrated how schizophrenic patients can learn adequate behaviour for expressing emotions, if modeling, shaping, and prompting are used in short role-plays, devised by the patients themselves. Learning to identify and express emotions is particularly emphasised in friendship and dating skill training (Liberman et al., 1989). Falloon (1987) developed a method of thought-stopping with schizophrenic patients, which involved instructing them to shout "Stop" to reduce arousal, when overwhelmed by emotion. Kraemer et al. (1990, 1994) devised a four-step training intervention to introduce patients to emotionally-loaded situations: First, the problematic situations are defined ("What is the problem?"). Second, alternative solutions are generated. Third, strategies for controlling heightened arousal are specified ("How can I reduce my panic?"). In a final step, the consequences of behaviour are anticipated (cf. Kraemer et al., 1990).

Brenner et al. (1987, 1994) have developed a special training programme – Integrated Psychological Therapy for Schizophrenic Patients (IPT) – to improve both cognitive and behavioural functioning. It consists of five subprogrammes for groups of five to seven patients (see also Roder et al., 1988, 1992). Although training is focused on the remediation of disordered cognitive and behavioural functions, patients are also introduced to emotionally-loaded stimuli. In the first subprogramme (Cognitive Differentiation), elementary cognitive skills like concentration, attention, and concept-formation are trained by introducing both neutral and emotionally-loaded verbal stimuli. In the subsequent subprogramme (Social Perception), patients proceed from recognising and interpreting single social stimuli to entire social interactions of a more complex and subtle nature, which are depicted on visuals. The next subprogramme (Verbal Communication) aims at improving communication skills such as listening, understanding, and responding, and offers training in neutral and emotionally-loaded conversation. The last two subprogrammes

(Social Skills and Interpersonal Problem Solving) focus on role plays and cognitive components e. g., behavioural planning and problem-solving skills, as means of acquiring affiliative and instrumental skills needed for increasing social competence (cf. Bellack, 1989; Bellack et al., 1990; Liberman et al., 1986, 1987, 1993).

Emotional Management Training

Results of studies on the mechanisms of treatment effects, as well as practical experience, have demonstrated that patients could show "cracks" within their improvement under IPT (see Hodel, 1993 a). Analyses of patients' outcomes showed on the one hand that under emotional taxing, their cognitive disorders could re-emerge, and on the other, that emotional influences could block or reduce their cognitive improvement obtained under IPT training (Brenner et al., 1990, 1992; Hodel, 1993 a). These results caused the recent development of an additional IPT subprogramme for reducing the negative influences of maladaptive emotions on cognitive functioning in schizophrenia. The aim of the additional subprogramme (Emotional Management Training) is to improve the ability to cope with emotions by means of both cognitive and behavioural intervention (Sandner et al., 1991; Konen et al., 1993; Hodel, 1993 b). This subprogramme involves a sequence of eight steps (see Fig. 1). A main therapist and a co-therapist are responsible for the training-group of five to seven schizophrenic patients.

In the first step, both the emotions and the context stimuli depicted on a visual display are defined and described in detail (e. g., quality, intensity, duration and cause of the emotions). In the second step, the patients' own experiences of similar emotions are described in the same manner to reflect about one's own emotions. In the third step patients report on their own experiences and on the consequences of their cognitions and behaviour in cop-

---

1. Description and analysis of depicted emotions
2. Description of the patient's emotions
3. Description of patient's coping
4. Elaboration of alternative coping strategies
5. Analysis of adequacy of coping strategies
6. Individualisation of coping strategies
7. Role-plays
8. Habituation to individual coping strategies

Figure 1. Therapeutic steps of Emotional Management Training.

ing with these emotions (e. g., "How was the emotion – cognitively and/or behaviourally – reduced or prolonged?"). This step should allow patients to understand linkages between emotion, behaviour, and cognition. In the fourth step, alternative strategies are added to the reported coping strategies by means of "brain-storming." This step should help patients to elaborate new options for coping. In the fifth step, coping strategies are analysed, based on the criteria of "constructiveness" and "practicability." This step should prompt thinking about the adequacy of possible emotional coping strategies. In the sixth step, the adequate strategies are listed, and the ones that are considered to be alternatives to past strategies, yet neither overly frightening nor inconsistent with prevalent interests and behaviour-patterns, are selected. This step should elicit highly concrete individualised strategies for coping with specific emotionally-loaded situations. In the seventh step, the individually selected strategies are role-played in a setting with defined situations, and are subsequently evaluated both by the patients and the therapists. This step can be considered a "warming-up" process with new coping strategies. In the eighth and final step, each patient practises individual coping strategies in additional role-plays for habituation purposes. To promote generalisation of the strategies that have been acquired, the patients are advised to record both the individual coping strategies and the situations in which they are enacted. At follow-up sessions, patients are questioned as to if and how the strategies acquired in therapy were actually used in everyday life, and as to their outcome. In the case of failure, alternative coping strategies are chosen, which are then tested and rehearsed in role-plays.

Evaluation of Emotional Management Training

Emotional Management Training was evaluated in two studies. In the first one, an effect-comparison was carried out between Emotional Management Training and relaxation therapy (distress training); the latter consists of muscle relaxation, coordination of breathing and motor behaviour etc., (cf. Andres et al., 1992). In the second one, an effect comparison was conducted between Emotional Management Training and the IPT subprogramme Cognitive Differentiation. The visual displays used in Emotional Management Training were initially rated by 64 normal subjects according to their emotional content and the stress they caused, and were then incorporated into the IPT subprogramme on Social Perception (cf. Roder et al., 1988, 1992).

Method

Subjects

The present report involves 31 of 33 DSM-III-R first admission schizophrenic patients who were recruited at our clinic. They had a mean age of 31 years ($\bar{x}$ = 31.2, s. d. = 6.8) and were of average intelligence (IQ: $\bar{x}$ = 104.2, s. d. = 12.6). Their mean length of hospital stay was about two years ($\bar{x}$ = 2.5, s. d. = 3.9) and their mean length of illness about six years ($\bar{x}$ = 5.9, s. d. = 2.2). Using the parallelisation criteria of age, sex, hospitalisation and illness duration, the patients were assigned to one of four groups. Finally, two groups (one with seven and one with nine patients) participated in the first comparison (Emotional Management Training and Relaxation Therapy) and two others (one with eight and one with seven patients) in the second comparison (Emotional Management Training and Cognitive Differentiation). All groups received two sessions weekly, each of 45 minutes, over a seven-week study period. Training was carried out in both groups jointly by a main therapist and a co-therapist. In addition, a psychologist was in charge of the measurements.

Measures

For rating and assessing treatment effects, the following measures were administered prior to and after each of the training procedures: (1) the PE[1] (Pictures with Emotions; Hodel, 1992) and the FCS (Frankfurt Subjective Condition Scale; Süllwold & Herrlich, 1990) to assess emotional information processing; (2) three subtests of the RPM (Repeated Psychological Measurement; Fahrenberg et al., 1977) Syllable Memorising, Word Recognition and Crossing-out Numbers, as well as the FCQ (Frankfurt Complaint Questionnaire; Süllwold & Huber, 1986) to assess cognitive information processing; (3) the NOSIE (Honigfeld et al., 1976) to assess social adjustment.

---

1 The "Pictures with Emotions" was developed at our clinic. It consists of two series of 15 photos for repeated measurement, each of which should be rated as either "agreeable," "disagreeable" or "don't know." Before being used in this study, they had undergone preliminary tests for validity and reliability with 15 normal subjects (Zehnder, 1992).

Results

Before analysing the effects of each comparison, the prior measurements of the groups were compared by means of a Mann Whitney U-Test. There were no significant differences in the initial measurements. Table 1 shows the results of Wilcoxon Tests used for analysing within-group changes of the first comparison "Emotional Management Training and Relaxation Therapy."

In Emotional Management Training significant improvements were found in the following measures: Pictures with Emotions, FCS, Syllable Memorising, FCQ, and NOSIE. In contrast, the group receiving Relaxation Therapy only demonstrated significant improvement in the FCS and in Crossing-out Numbers. Additionally, the efficiency increases of the groups were compared for each measure by means of a Mann Whitney U-Test as shown in Table 2.

Syllable Memorising, FCQ, and NOSIE significantly differentiated both groups. The Emotional Management Training group showed superior results

Table 1. Pre-post comparison of the groups "Emotional Management Training" and "Relaxation Therapy" by Wilcoxon Tests.

(a) Group "Emotional Management Training" (n = 7)

Measures/Groups	$\bar{x}$		SD		Wilcoxon Tests	
	pre	post	pre	post	z	p
Pictures with Emotions	6.75	14.63	7.94	10.34	−2.52	0.01
FCS	31.88	18.13	19.98	12.28	−2.52	0.01
Syllable M.	4.00	8.75	2.67	2.05	−2.52	0.01
Word R.	18.00	17.36	6.74	6.52	−1.60	n.s.
Crossing N.	4.88	5.38	1.36	1.30	−1.83	n.s.
FCQ	27.50	19.00	4.24	4.57	−2.52	0.01
NOSIE	6.13	10.75	1.89	3.69	−2.52	0.01

(b) Group "Relaxation Therapy" (n = 9)

Measures /Groups	$\bar{x}$		SD		Wilcoxon Tests	
	pre	post	pre	post	z	p
Pictures with Emotions	7.89	10.67	7.34	8.22	−1.19	n.s.
FCS	32.11	20.33	16.65	11.48	−2.66	0.01
Syllable M.	3.44	4.00	2.24	2.59	−1.83	n.s.
Word R.	17.56	16.56	7.21	5.70	−1.26	n.s.
Crossing N.	6.11	7.56	1.17	1.74	−2.20	0.05
FCQ	27.00	25.78	4.21	4.30	−1.47	n.s.
NOSIE	4.22	4.78	1.86	1.56	−1.48	n.s.

Table 2. Comparison of the efficiency-increases of the groups "Emotional Management Training" and "Relaxation Therapy" by Mann Whitney U-Test.

Measures/Groups	Emotional Management Training (n = 7)		Relaxation Therapy (n = 9)		Mann Whitney U-Test	
	x̄ pre-post	sd pre-post	x̄ pre-post	sd pre-post	z	p
Pictures with Emotions	7.88	6.18	2.78	5.69	−1.12	n.s.
FCS	−13.75	13.92	−11.78	7.53	−1.30	n.s.
Syllable M.	4.75	2.37	0.56	0.72	−3.42	0.01
Word R.	−0.64	0.92	−1.00	2.08	−1.76	n.s.
Crossing N.	0.50	0.54	1.45	1.41	−1.39	n.s.
FCQ	−8.50	5.50	−1.22	2.28	−2.95	0.01
NOSIE	4.63	2.56	0.56	1.01	−3.12	0.01

in these three measures, compared with the group receiving Relaxation Therapy (cf. averages in Tab. 2). In addition, the pre-post differences in both groups were adjusted according to the variances of the pre-measurements of all 16 patients (cf. Smith et al., 1980), yielding the "effect size" (cf. Grawe et al., 1990), as shown in Figure 2: Emotional Management Training led to greater effect sizes than Relaxation Therapy.

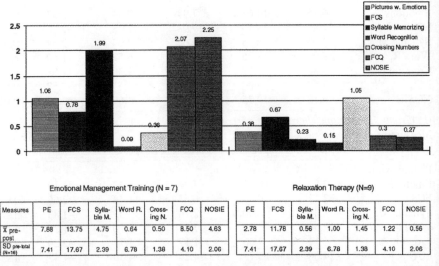

Figure 2. Effect sizes of the groups "Emotional Management Training" and "Relaxation Therapy".

Table 3. Pre-post comparison of the groups "Emotional Management Training" and "Cognitive Differentiation" by Wilcoxon Tests.

Group "Emotional Management Training" (n = 8)

Measures/Groups	x̄		SD		Wilcoxon Tests	
	pre	post	pre	post	z	p
Pictures with						
Emotions	12.63	19.00	6.78	7.31	−2.52	0.05
FCS	27.25	19.00	19.49	14.51	−2.31	0.05
Syllable M.	6.63	10.38	0.52	3.07	−2.38	0.05
Word R.	20.25	13.13	6.52	1.96	−2.20	0.05
Crossing N.	5.00	9.25	1.51	1.17	−2.52	0.05
FCQ	31.25	18.00	3.88	4.54	−2.52	0.05
NOSIE	8.50	9.13	1.20	1.13	−1.83	n.s.

Group "Cognitive Differentiation" (n = 7)

Measures/Groups	x̄		SD		Wilcoxon Tests	
	pre	post	pre	post	z	p
Pictures with						
Emotions	11.57	12.71	6.43	1.99	−1.47	n.s.
FCS	29.00	28.43	17.66	17.31	−1.83	n.s.
Syllable M.	6.86	7.14	0.38	0.69	−0.91	n.s.
Word R.	19.14	17.71	7.38	5.90	−1.83	n.s.
Crossing N.	5.71	7.57	2.49	1.51	−2.20	0.05
FCQ	31.00	19.00	4.58	4.44	−2.37	0.05
NOSIE	8.43	8.57	1.39	1.27	−1.00	n.s.

Table 3 shows the results of Wilcoxon Tests used for analysing within-group changes in the second comparison (Emotional Management Training and Cognitive Differentiation) The within-group changes were found to result in different courses: significant improvement was evident for the Emotional Management Training-group in all measures except the NOSIE. In contrast to this, the Cognitive Differentiation group only improved significantly in Crossing-out Numbers and in the FCQ.

The results of the subsequent comparison between the groups' efficiency increases by means of a Mann Whitney U-Test are depicted in Table 4. The Pictures with Emotions, FCS, Syllable Memorising, and Crossing-out Numbers significantly differentiated both groups. The Emotional Management Training group performed significantly better in these four measures, compared with the Cognitive Differentiation group (cf. averages in Tab. 4).

Subsequently, the pre-post differences in both groups were adjusted according to the variances of the pre-measurements of all 15 patients (cf. Smith et al., 1980). The outcome of the groups' effect sizes is shown in Figure 3. In

Table 4. Comparison of the efficiency-increases of the groups"Emotional Management Training" and "Cognitive Differentiation" by Mann Whitney U-Test.

Measures/Groups	Emotional Management Training (n = 8)		Cognitive Differentation (n = 7)		Mann Whitney U-Test	
	x̄ pre-post	sd pre-post	x̄ pre-post	sd pre-post	z	p
Pictures with Emotions	6.37	4.53	1.14	1.67	−3.11	0.01
FCS	−8.25	7.72	−0.57	0.54	−2.25	0.05
Syllable M.	3.75	2.71	0.28	0.76	−2.51	0.05
Word R.	−7.12	5.61	−1.43	1.61	−1.54	n.s.
Crossing N.	4.25	1.58	1.87	1.34	−2.51	0.05
FCQ	−13.25	1.98	−12.00	4.40	−1.57	n.s.
NOSIE	0.63	0.74	0.14	0.37	−0.77	n.s.

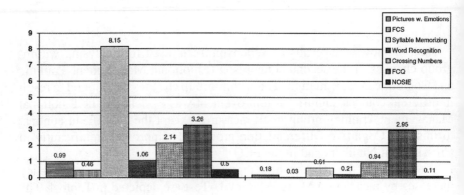

Figure 3. Effect sizes of the groups "Emotional Management" and "Cognitive Differentia-tion."

128

all measures, Emotional Management Training led generally to greater effect sizes than Cognitive Differentiation.

Discussion

Although disorders of emotional processing have been considered a hallmark of schizophrenia since Bleuler's (1911) pioneering work, there has been a paucity of experimental research on techniques for modifying them. This might have been due to the problem of operationalising both the emotions per se and the individual style of coping with emotions. For instance, Nuechterlein et al. (1992) showed that the concept of Expressed Emotion (EE) is based either on critical or benign comments, or on hostile or overprotective behaviour evidenced by significant others towards the patient. On the other hand, the subjective level of experience and the patient's manner of coping with EE have generally not been assessed at all, and if they are, are based either on global measures, e. g., number of relapses, or on isolated behavioural patterns e. g., number of eye movements.

As long as individual ways of coping with emotions cannot be adequately rated, the effects of emotion training cannot be properly assessed either. Nevertheless, several procedures for modifying emotional coping have been developed over the past two decades. They can be divided into two groups: (a) direct training procedures which help patients to deal with and control emotions by means of behaviour therapy techniques (see Meichenbaum & Cameron, 1973; Kraemer et al., 1990, 1994; Falloon, 1987), and (b) indirect training procedures, which rely on modeling or on working with emotionally-loaded therapy material for habituation effects and for raising the emotional threshold (see Liberman et al., 1975, 1989; Brenner et al., 1987, 1994).

The emotion training procedure that we devised attempts to incorporate both direct and indirect procedures. In the first step, visual displays depicting emotions foster habituation to emotional stressors (indirect procedure), whereas in subsequent steps, alternative ways of appraising emotions and their behavioural consequences are generated and behavioural coping strategies are rehearsed (direct procedure).

This combination of indirect and direct training procedures is based on the heuristic model conceived by Brenner (1989) and described above. In Emotional Management Training, habituation may lead to a lowering of the arousal level, thereby enabling stressful stimuli to be processed. Emotional appraisal and rehearsal of behavioural coping strategies may activate both participatory processes and relevant perceptual information-processing, so that stressful situations may seem to be more controllable. The results of our studies are in line with these assumptions: The "combined" Emotional Management Training procedure yielded greater therapeutic effects than either a relaxation therapy or a focused cognitive training procedure. Assessment of the validity of the results might be based on two methodological aspects of the studies' outcome: in comparison with the relaxation therapy or the IPT sub-programme for Cognitive Differentiation, only the effect sizes of Emotional Management Training are comparable with those of the overall evaluation of IPT (see Brenner et al., 1994). Additionally, the effect sizes of the measurement of Syllable Memorising are strikingly evident after Emotional Management Training. Results such as this should be highlighted, as verbal memory can directly be linked with the acquirement of new social skills (Kern et al., 1992; Corrigan et al., 1992).

Considering the subjective experiences of the patients who took part in Emotional Management Training, nearly all the patients reported that they had actually made use of the coping skills acquired in therapy in real-life situations, and experienced them as having a particularly emotionally stabilising effect (Zehnder, 1992). Therefore, Emotional Management Training might serve as protection against emotionally-loaded situations (see Holzman & Bivens, 1988), as the capacity to deal with one's social environment seems to have improved (cf. Brenner, 1989; Verres, 1990). Such *in vivo* transfer can be facilitated by the intervention-techniques of Emotional Management Training: (1) new coping strategies are acquired by cognitive as well as by behavioural processes; (2) new coping strategies are acquired in accordance with the patients' individual interests and behavioural patterns; (3) new coping strategies are acquired until habituation has taken place.

However, these results should be considered as preliminary due to the limited sample sizes, even though the samples showed no significant differences in terms of socio-demographic variables, and due to the measures used, which could be criticised for their lack of specificity to emotional functioning in general and to individual ways of coping in particular. In addition, a reduction might occur in the number of significant improvements if validity or reliability analyses were undertaken (e. g., Alpha-Adjustment by Kaehler, 1990) to test for any overlap between the dependent variables which might bias the results.

The growing weight of empirical evidence for the interrelationship between disordered emotional processing, information processing disorders, and social performance in schizophrenia suggests the necessity of addressing disordered emotional processing (see Bellack in this book). This might indicate that the Emotional Management Training devised by the authors of this article could be a promising new aspect in the rehabilitation of schizophrenic patients.

References

Andres, K., Brenner, H. D. & Bellwald, L. (1992) Körperzentrierte Arbeit mit schizophrenen Patienten. *Swiss Med,* **1-S/92,** 40–42.

Bellack, A. S. (1994) *Psychosocial Treatment in Schizophrenia.* Paper presented at the XIth International Symposium for Psychotherapy of Schizophrenia, June 12–16, Washington D.C.

Bellack, A. S. (1989) A comprehensive model for treatment of schizophrenia. In *A Clinical Guide for the Treatment of Schizophrenia* (ed. A. S. Bellack). New York: Plenum Press.

Bellack, A. S., Morrison, R. L., Wixted, J. T. et al. (1990) An analysis of social competence in schizophrenia. *British Journal of Psychiatry,* **156,** 809–818.

Berenbaum, H. & Oltmanns, T. F. (1992) Emotional experience in schizophrenia and depression. *Journal of Abnormal Psychology,* **101,** 37–44.

Berenbaum, H., Snowhite, R. & Oltmanns, T. F. (1987) Anhedonia and emotional responses to affect evoking stimuli. *Psychological Medicine,* **17,** 677–684.

Bleuler, E. (1911) *Dementia Präcox oder die Gruppe der Schizophrenien.* Leipzig: Deuticke.

Braff, D. L. (1991) Information processing and attentional abnormalities in the schizophrenic disorders. In *Cognitive Bases of Mental Disorders* (ed. P.A. Magaro). Newbury Park, CA: Sage Publications.

Brenner, H. D. (1989) The treatment of basic psychological dysfunctions from a systemic point of view. In *Schizophrenia as a Systems Disorder: The Relevance of Mediating Processes for Theory and Therapy)* (eds H. D. Brenner & W. Böker). *British Journal of Psychiatry,* **155** (suppl. 5), 74–83.

Brenner, H. D., Hodel, B., Kube, G. & Roder, V. (1987) Kognitive Therapie bei Schizophrenen: Problemanalyse und empirische Ergebnisse. *Nervenarzt,* **58,** 72–83.

Brenner, H. D., Hodel, B., Roder, V. & Corrigan, P. (1992) Treatment of cognitive dysfunctions and behavioral deficits in schizophrenia: Integrated Psychological Therapy. *Schizophrenia Bulletin,* **18,** 21–26.

Brenner, H. D., Kraemer, S., Hermanutz, M. & Hodel, B. (1990) Cognitive treatment in schizophrenia. In *Schizophrenia: Concepts, Vulnerability and Intervention* (eds E.R. Straube & K. Hahlweg). Berlin: Springer-Verlag.

Brenner, H. D., Roder, V., Hodel, B., & Kienzle, N. (1994) *Integrated Psychological Therapy for Schizophrenic Patients (IPT)* Seattle: Hogrefe & Huber.

Cornblatt, B. A., Lenzenweger, M. F., Dworkin et al. (in press) Childhood attentional deficits predict social isolation in adults at risk for schizophrenia. *British Journal of Psychiatry.*

Corrigan, P. W., Wallace, C. J. & Green, M. F. (1992) Deficits in social schemata in schizophrenia. *Schizophrenia Research,* **8,** 129–135.

Cutting, J. (1981) Judgement of emotional expression in schizophrenia. *British Journal of Psychiatry,* **139,** 1–6.

Dougherty, F. E., Bartlett, E. S. & Izard, C. E. (1974) Responses of schizophrenics to expressions of fundamental emotions. *Journal of Clinical Psychology,* **30,** 243–246.

Dworkin, R. H. (1992) Affective deficits and social deficits in schizophrenia: What's what? *Schizophrenia Bulletin,* **18,** 59–64.

Fahrenberg, J., Kuhn, M., Kulick, B. et al. (1977) Repeated Psychological Measurement. *Diagnostica,* **23,** 15–36.

Falloon, I. R. H. (1987) Cognitive and behavioral interventions in the self-control of schizophrenia. In *Psychosocial Treatment of Schizophrenia* (eds J. S. Strauss, W. Böker & H. D. Brenner). Toronto: Huber.

Feinberg, T. E., Rifkin, A., Schaffer, C. et al. (1986) Facial discrimination and emotional recognition in schizophrenia and affective disorders. *Archives of General Psychiatry*, **43**, 276–279.

Gessler, S., Cutting, J., Frith, C. D. et al. (1989) Schizophrenic inability to judge facial emotion: a controlled study. *British Journal of Clinical Psychology*, **28**, 19–29.

Gjerde, P. F. (1983) Attention capacity dysfunction and arousal in schizophrenia. *Psychological Bulletin*, **93**, 57–72.

Grawe, K., Caspar, F. & Ambühl, H. (1990) Die Berner Therapievergleichstudie: Wirkungsvergleich und differentielle Indikation. *Zeitschrift für Klinische Psychologie*, **19**, 338–361.

Heimberg, C., Gur, R., Erwin, R. J. et al. (1992) Facial emotion discrimination: III. Behavioral findings in schizophrenia. *Psychiatry Research*, **42**, 253–265.

Hemsley, D. R. (1994) A cognitive model for schizophrenia and its possible neural basis. *Acta Psychiatrica Scandinavica*, **90** (suppl. 384), 80–86.

Hemsley, D. R. (1990) What have cognitive deficits to do with schizophrenia? *British Journal of Psychiatry*, **130**, 167–173.

Hodel, B. (1993 a) *Zur Frage der Pervasivität von Interventionseffekten bei schizophren Erkrankten*. Visp: Mengis Druck & Verlag.

Hodel, B. (1993 b) Weiterentwicklungen des IPT: Das Training "Umgang mit Emotionen" im Vergleich mit dem Training "Kognitive Differenzierung" (Abstract). *Schizophrenie Sonderheft*, 1, 18.

Hodel, B. (1992) *Bilder mit Emotionen: Ein Test zur Erfassung von Emotionswahrnehmungen*. Unpublished paper, Psychiatrische Universitätsklinik Bern.

Holzman, P. S. & Bivens, L. W. (1988) Basic behavioral sciences. *Schizophrenia Bulletin*, **14**, 423–456.

Honigfeld, G., Gilles, R. D. & Klett, L. L. (1976) Nurses' Observation Scale for Inpatient Evaluation. In *ECDEU Assessment Manual for Psychopharmacology* (ed. W. Guy) Rockville; MD: USGPO.

Jackson, H. J., Minas, I. H., & Burgess, P. M. (1989) Negative symptoms and social skills performance in schizophrenia. *Schizophrenia Research*, **2**, 457–463.

Kaehler, W. M. (1990) *SpssxPC*. Braunschweig: Vieweg.

Käsermann, M. L. (1986) Dialoge zwischen Psychiatriepatient und Arzt: Missverständnisse verstehen lernen ? *Uni Press (Universität Bern)*, **49**, 12–15.

Kern, R. S., Green, M. F. & Satz, P. (1992) Neurophysiological predictors of skills training for chronic schizophrenic patients. *Journal of Psychiatric Research*, **4**. 223–230.

Kline, J. S., Smith, J. E. & Ellis, H. C. (1992) Paranoid and nonparannoid schizophrenic processing of facially displayed affect. *Journal of Psychiatric Research*, **26**, 169–182.

Konen, A., Neis, L., Hodel, B., & Brenner, H. D. (1993) A propos des thérapies cognitivo-comportementales de la schizophrénie: Le programme intégratif de thérapies psychologiques (IPT). *L'Encéphale*, **19**, 47–55.

Kraemer, S., Dinkhoff-Awiszus, G. & Möller, H. J. (1994) Modification of Integrated Psychological Therapy for Schizophrenic Patients (IPT). In *Integrated Psychological Therapy for Schizophrenic Patients (IPT)* (eds H. D. Brenner, V. Roder, B. Hodel et al). Seattle: Hogrefe & Huber.

Kraemer, S., Zinner, H. T. & Möller, H. J. (1990) Kognitive Therapie und Sozialtraining: Vergleich zweier verhaltenstherapeutischer Behandlungskonzepte für chronisch schizophrene Patienten. In *Theorie und Praxis kognitiver Therapieverfahren bei schizophrenen Patienten* (ed. R. Schüttler). München: Zuckschwerdt.

Lang, P. J. & Buss, A. H. (1965) Psychological deficit in schizophrenia: II. Interference and activation. *Journal of Abnormal Psychology*, **70**, 77–106.

Liberman, R. P., Delisi, W. J. & McCann, M. (1975) *Personal Effectiveness*. Champaign: Research Press.

Liberman, R. P., Delisi, W. J., Mueser, K. M. et al. (1989) *Social Skills Training for Psychiatric Patients*. New York: Pergamon Press.

Liberman, R. P., Jacobs, H., Boone, S. E. et al. (1987) Skills training for the community adaption of schizophrenia. In *Psychosocial Treatment of Schizophrenia* (eds J. S. Strauss, W. Böker & H.D. Brenner). Toronto: Huber.

Liberman, R. P., Mueser, K. T. & Wallace, C. J. (1986) Training skills in the psychiatrically disabled: Learning coping and competence. *Schizophrenia Bulletin*, **12**, 631–647.

Liberman, R. P., Wallace, C. J., Blackwell, G. et al. (1993) Innovations in skills training for the seriously mentally ill: the UCLA Social and Independent Living Skills Modules. *Innovations & Research*, **2**, 43–60.

Mandal, M. K. & Gewali, H. (1989) Identifying the components of facial emotion and schizophrenia. *Psychopathology*, **22**, 295–302.

Meichenbaum, D. & Cameron, R. (1973) Training schizophrenics to talk to themselves. A means of developing attentional controls. *Behavior Therapy*, **4**, 515–534.

Morrison, R. L. & Bellack, A. S. (1981) The role of social perception in social skill. *Behavior Therapy*, **12**, 69–79.

Muzekari, L. H. & Bates, M. E. (1977) Judgement of emotion among chronic schizophrenics. *Journal of Clinical Psychology*, **33**, 662–666.

Novic, J., Luchins, D. J. & Perline, R. (1984) Facial affect recognition in schizophrenia: Is there a differential deficit? *British Journal of Psychiatry*, **144**, 533–537.

Nuechterlein, K. H. & Dawson, M. E. (1984) Information processing and attentional functioning in the developmental course of schizophrenic disorders. *Schizophrenia Bulletin*, **10**, 160–203.

Nuechterlein, K. H., Snyders, S. & Mintz, J. (1992) Paths to relapse: Possible transactional processes connecting patient illness onset, expressed emotion, and psychotic relapse. In *Onset and Course of Schizophrenic Disorders* (eds W. Böker & H. D. Brenner). *British Journal of Psychiatry*, **161** (suppl. 18), 88–96.

Pitman, R. K., Kolb, B., Orr, S. P. et al. (1987) Ethological study of facial behavior in nonparanoid and paranoid schizophrenic patients. *American Journal of Psychiatry*, **144**, 99–102.

Pribram, K. H. (1981) Emotions. In *Handbook of Clinical Neuropsychology* (eds S. B. Filskov & T. J. Boll). New York: Wiley.

Roder, V., Brenner, H. D., Kienzle, N. et al. (1988) *Integriertes Psychologisches Therapieprogramm (IPT) für schizophrene Patienten*. München: Psychologie Verlags Union.

Roder, V., Brenner, H. D., Kienzle, N. et al. (1992) *Integriertes Psychologisches Therapieprogramm (IPT) für schizophrene Patienten* (2nd edn.). Weinheim: Psychologie Verlags Union.

Russel, J. A. & Fehr, B. (1987) Relativity in the perception of emotion in facial expressions. *Journal of Experimental Psychology*, **116**, 223–237.

133

Sandner, M., Hodel, B. & Brenner, H. D. (1991) *Treatment of Emotional and Cognitive Vulnerability of Schizophrenic Patients.* Abstract of the International Congress on Schizophrenia and Affective Psychoses, September 14–16, 1991, Geneva.

Schneider, F., Heimann, H., Himer, W. et al. (1990) Computer-based analysis of facial action in schizophrenic and depressed patients. *European Archives of Psychiatry & Clinical Neuroscience*, **240**, 67–76.

Smith, M., Glass, G. V. & Miller, T. I. (1980) *The Benefits of Psychotherapy.* Baltimore: John Hopkins University Press.

Süllwold, L. & Herrlich, J. (1990) *Frankfurter Befindlichkeitsskala (FBS) für schizophren Erkrankte.* Berlin: Springer-Verlag.

Süllwold, L. & Huber, G. (1986) *Schizophrene Basisstörungen.* Berlin: Springer-Verlag.

Verres, R. (1990) Wirkfaktoren in der Verhaltenstherapie. In *Wirkfaktoren der Psychotherapie* (ed. H. Lang). Berlin: Springer-Verlag.

Walker, E., McGuire, M. & Bettes, B. (1984) Recognition and identification of facial stimuli by schizophrenics and patients with affective disorders. *British Journal of Clinical Psychology*, **23**, 37–44.

Zehnder, D. (1992) *Bilder mit Emotionen. Eine Untersuchung zur Erfassung der Emotionswahrnehmung bei schizophren Erkrankten.* Unpublished paper, Psychiatrische Universitätsklinik Bern.

Focus on Weakening Stressors and/or Stengthening Protectors and Promoting Social Network and Social Support

Social Skills Deficits and Social Skills Training: New Developments and Trends

Alan S. Bellack

Summary

Social skills training is widely regarded as one of the most effective psychosocial strategies for the treatment of schizophrenia. While its effectiveness in teaching social behaviour has been well documented, its impact on role functioning in the community is unclear. This paper identifies several aspects of schizophrenia that are not adequately covered by current skills training techniques, and that may limit the generalisability of training. Issues discussed include individual differences between patients and within patients over time, the effects of anxiety and avoidance behaviour, and the uncertain role of deficits in social perception.

Schizophrenia is marked by a number of severe and handicapping symptoms. It would be arbitrary to label any one as the "worst", but none has a more pernicious effect than the profound impairment in social functioning that characterises this disorder. Poor social competence contributes to the impoverished quality of life and social isolation experienced by many patients; it interferes with functioning in the work place, within the family, and in residential facilities. Social disability is a primary source of stress, and prevents patients from developing the supportive relationships that could provide a buffering effect; thus, it is a potent predictor of symptom exacerbations and rehospitalisation.

The panoply of interpersonal dysfunctions is not simply a by-product of both positive and negative symptoms. Schizophrenic patients either with or without prominent negative symptoms exhibit marked social impairments, even when positive symptoms are pharmacologically controlled. The persistent nature of social impairments is reflected in the list of prodromal and residual symptoms described in DSM-III-R (APA, 1987), including: marked social isolation, marked impairment in role functioning, and markedly peculiar behaviour. Social competence is now understood to depend on the smooth integration of a variety of forms of verbal, paralinguistic, and non-verbal behaviour that are cumulatively referred to as "social skills" (Hersen & Bellack, 1976 a; Morrison & Bellack, 1987). Research conducted in my laboratory over the last decade has demonstrated that schizophrenic patients have profound and persistent deficits in social skills. Acute psychosis and severe negative symptoms necessarily decrease social competence, but social skills are only moderately correlated with either positive or negative symptoms, once the acute phase of illness has begun to remit (Mueser et al., 1990). We have demonstrated that patients without pronounced negative symptoms also exhibit significant social skills deficits (Bellack et al., 1990), that these deficits are relatively stable over time (Mueser et al., 1990), and that they have a substantial impact on quality of life and ability to fulfil social roles (Mueser et al., 1990).

Issues in Social Skills Training

In the light of the prevalence and profound impact of social dysfunction, social behaviour has been a frequent target of intervention. The most thoroughly investigated and promising strategy for alleviating social disability and enhancing competence is social skills training (SST) (Bellack & Mueser, 1993). SST is a highly structured educational procedure in which patients are taught to perform specific forms of behaviour, such as maintaining eye contact and providing social reinforcers during conversations. Some approaches have also included training in social problem-solving, in an effort to enhance generalisation (Liberman et al., 1986).

The basic skills training technology was developed in the 1970s, and remains substantially unchanged. A series of single-case and small group studies have demonstrated its effectiveness in teaching patients basic social niceties, conversational skills, assertiveness, heterosocial skills, medication management, etc. (Hersen & Bellack, 1976 b). Six larger comparative trials have been conducted in the last decade, and each has replicated the findings of these smaller demonstration studies (see Tab. 1). Moreover, the data indicate that skills training has a beneficial effect on both psychotic symptoms and relapse rate, and that the effects of training are maintained over (at least) a 6–12 month follow-up.

It is clear that SST is an effective teaching strategy, but many questions remain about the clinical utility of the intervention (Benton & Schroeder, 1990; Halford & Hayes, 1991). The efficacy of psychosocial treatment for schizophrenia should be judged on the basis of its impact on relevant domains of community functioning and quality of life. In regard to SST, the essential

Table 1. Controlled trials of social skills training.

1. Brown & Munford (1983)
2. Spencer, Gillespie & Ekisa (1983)
3. Bellack, Turner, Hersen & Luber (1984)
4. Wallace & Liberman (1985)
5. Hogarty et al. (1986; 1991)
6. Eckman et al. (1992)

questions concern the impact of treatment on social behaviour and role functioning in the community, but this issue has not been adequately assessed in any controlled trial. It is unclear if the training effects demonstrated in the clinic and laboratory generalise to the natural environment, or if they increase patients' ability to fulfill essential social roles (e. g., worker, student, spouse). The beneficial effects of SST on symptoms and outcome could result from factors totally unrelated to the skills training per se.

One factor that may limit our ability to produce generalisable and durable results is our relative lack of knowledge about precisely why patients fail in social encounters. We know that patients have deficits in diverse aspects of behaviour that are important components of social competence, but we do not know *why* they have deficits (e. g., inadequate learning history, learned avoidance, cognitive impairments), or if these deficits are central to poor role performance. For example, illustrating gestures might be useful for emphasis, but might not be essential if other aspects of behaviour were employed at adequate levels. Consequently, we do not know what should be the most appropriate treatment targets. Skills training strategies have been developed substantially on the basis of clinical observation, analogue studies of limited social encounters (e. g., assertiveness), and the trial-and-error application of social learning principles, rather than on the basis of systematic, empirical study of social behaviour in the types of naturalistic situations most relevant to patients. The following sections highlight several issues that have not been adequately examined, and suggest some directions for future research.

Individual Differences in Treatment Needs

An increasing body of evidence suggests that different patients have substantially different handicaps and liabilities, and require interventions that differ in form and/or substance. For example, Mueser et al. (1991) found that 50% of schizophrenic patients had persistent deficits in social skills over a one-year period, while 11% did not differ from non-patient controls during that period, and the remainder showed variable performance over time. In another study, social skill deficits were found to be associated with memory impairments, but not with positive or negative symptomatology (Mueser et al., 1991). Patients with more pronounced memory impairments did not learn as well during social skills training, and did not retain what they were able to learn over a three-month follow-up interval.

Another example of individual differences in treatment needs and learning capacity is provided by a study we conducted on the Wisconsin Card Sorting Test (WCST: Heaton, 1981), which is thought to tap the higher level cognitive functions controlled by the prefrontal cortex. It is not directly related to social functioning, but is a measure of the type of problem-solving capacity needed in social situations. Schizophrenic patients have been shown to have marked impairments on the WCST (Van der Does & Van den Bosch, 1992). We attempted to improve WCST performance with a brief training regime that closely paralleled the techniques employed in social skills training (Bellack et al., 1990). Overall, the results were very positive, demonstrating that, as a group, schizophrenic patients can learn to perform at normative levels. However, 18% of subjects performed adequately at baseline, and thus required no training, while a small number of others could not learn the relatively simple task. These results suggest that some patients may have profound cognitive impairments that would impede learning in skills training programmes that focus on social problem-solving. If this conclusion is valid, brief training on the WCST or other information-processing tests might be useful as a predictor of performance in skills training and/or point to the need for different types of training.

The data described above indicate that there is considerable between-subject variance; there also is substantial within-subject variability over time. Schizophrenic patients change and develop over the course of adulthood, and have different treatment needs at different points in their lives. Adolescent and young adult patients often have the same desires for separation from family and independence as do their non-affected peers. They are equally rebellious and disinclined to take advice from adults, including the message that they have a chronic illness that requires treatment, even during periods of remission (Wing, 1987). Young patients must gradually come to grips with their disability and their inability to achieve goals and aspirations, as well as the continuing torment of symptoms and readmissions.

The data are not clear, but it appears as if many patients reach some accommodation to their difficulties in middle and late adulthood, whether by developing secondary negative symptoms and withdrawing or by more adaptive strategies. Many older patients seem more receptive to treatment, and have more modest goals and more pragmatic concerns (e. g., managing welfare cheques, finding accommodation) (Strauss, 1989). Further research is needed to determine if these gradual changes necessitate different forms of intervention, as well as different content and emphases. The traditional practice of assigning all patients to the same treatment groups in lock-step fashion is fundamentally flawed.

Anxiety and Avoidance

Historically, the schizophrenic patient has been viewed as lacking an adequate sense of self and being a more or less passive participant in treatment. Current conceptions of negative symptoms, including anergia and anhedonia, reflect this heritage; most patients certainly seem to be unmotivated and uncooperative at some times during their illness. However, both empirical data and clinical experience suggest that it is a critical error to accept withdrawal, passivity, or even active resistance as inflexible characteristics.

Strauss (1989) has lucidly argued that it is essential to consider schizophrenic patients as goal-directed, having an active will, and attempting to cope with the illness as best they can. Two implications of this hypothesis warrant particular attention. Persistent psychotic symptoms are among the most terrifying and disruptive aspects of the illness, leading to depression, withdrawal, and (possibly) negative symptoms. It may be impossible to stimulate patients to be concerned about the social environment and interpersonal goals when they are besieged by hallucinations, confused by delusions, and overwhelmed by minor stresses. In fact, withdrawal might be the most effective adaptive strategy in the face of these problems. It may be possible to teach social skills while patients are actively psychotic, but it might not be possible to get them to use the skills in the community until these symptoms are substantially controlled.

The inclination to avoid or escape from anxiety and stress may affect the use of social skills in other areas as well. One of the most popular components of social skills training programmes has been assertion skills. Ample data indicated that schizophrenic patients are deficient in these skills, and it has been hypothesised that they would experience decreased stress and achieve more satisfaction if they could be taught to stand up for their rights. While patients can learn appropriate assertive behaviour, anecdotal evidence suggests they rarely use these in the community. There are four likely reasons for this lack of generalisation: (1) they do not retain what they learn during treatment sessions; (2) they have deficits in social perception and consequently do not know when to use the skills they have learned; (3) they experience high levels of anxiety in conflict situations which inhibits assertive behaviour, and 4) they lack the motivation to perform the behaviour, due to expectations of failure or negative symptoms.

My colleagues and I carried out a study that examined two of these possibilities: social perception deficits and behavioural inhibition (Bellack et al., 1992). Thirty-four schizophrenic patients in an acute inpatient hospital were compared with 24 inpatients with major affective disorder and 19 non-patient controls on tests of role-play and affect perception. The roleplay consisted of 12 simulated conversations in which the subject was questioned about some error or had to resolve some disagreement. The items were empirically selected to be relevant to the population and to provide moderate difficulty. In half of the role plays, the subject was to imagine interacting with a friend, and half were to represent interactions with a parent. In one half of each subset, the confederate confronted the subject with high-EE type criticism and hostility; in the remaining scenes, the confederate asked non-critical questions or made non-hostile suggestions. Schizophrenic patients were less assertive than patients in the other two groups, regardless of the confederate role or the level of criticism/hostility directed at them. When questioned or challenged, they tended to be submissive, and failed to suggest solutions to problems or request the partner to change his/her behaviour. However, their difficulty was not so much passivity as an inability or unwillingness to admit mistakes. Rather than offer appropriate apologies or explanations, they tended to deny making errors and made up child-like lies. Notably, this tendency to avoid or escape was equally apparent in both the benign and highly critical conditions. They were just as likely to lie and unlikely to apologise to a benign partner as to a high-EE partner. This avoidant style appears to be a relatively reflexive, self-protective response which serves to avoid further discussion of unpleasant issues.

Social Perception

The second half of the Bellack et al. (1992) study described above involved a social perception test in which subjects were asked to judge the feelings of people involved in interactions similar to those employed for the role-play test. As with that test, the actors in the scenes expressed either high-EE criticism and hostility or mild questioning and disagreement. Pilot testing indicated that the two types of scenes were highly discriminable to a non-patient sample. Schizophrenic patients exhibited marked impairments in social perception: they were fairly accurate in their appraisal of benign or neutral affect, but consistently underestimated the intensity of highly negative affect. There are two likely explanations for these results: schizophrenic patients may be unable to detect or decode the cues which distinguish very different levels of criticism and hostility or alternatively, they may find conflict to be highly distressing, and try to minimise or ignore it. Interestingly, poor social perception was inversely correlated with the frequency of lies. This finding is consistent with the hypothesis that lying might be a coping response to control for confusing or anxiety-producing input.

The hypothesis that schizophrenic patients have a deficit in the ability to decode negative affect is supported by a number of other studies that have found deficits of affect perception in schizophrenic cohorts. However, a number of questions remain about the precise nature of the deficits. In particular, the problem could be more a function of attentional impairment than perception deficits per se. Consequently, we conducted a second study that examined the parameters of social perception more extensively (Bellack et al., 1993). Specifically, the purpose of this study was to examine affect perception under a variety of stimulus formats, and determine if schizophrenic patients have a specific and consistent deficit, or if the accuracy of their judgements varies as a function of the amount of information provided and the difficulty of the task. Subjects were 25 schizophrenic patients, 10 patients with schizo-affective disorder, 11 with bipolar disorder, and 19 matched non-patient controls. All patients were medicated and in the latter stages of an acute hospital admission.

Subjects were assessed on an empirically developed measure that consisted of 30 brief (15-sec) videotaped segments, derived from movies and television shows: eight scenes depicted highly negative affect, 14 were mildly negative, and eight involved positive affect. The test was administered first without sound, and then readministered 30-min later with the soundtrack, in order to determine if performance was improved when the additional information provided by the auditory cues was available. Two measures of facial affect perception based on photographs and two measures of non-affect perception were also administered.

Surprisingly, the schizophrenic and schizo-affective groups did not differ from either the bipolar or the non-patient groups on any of the measures of affect perception. Notably, they were able to make accurate judgements on both versions of the videotaped measure. In addition, affect perception in schizophrenic and schizo-affective patients was not correlated with symptoms or history of illness, and there were no differences between male and female subjects. These findings challenge the hypothesis that schizophrenia is marked by a specific deficit in affect perception.

A careful re-examination of the literature indicates that support for the deficit hypothesis is quite tenuous. Table 2 provides an overview of the recent literature on this topic.

Table 2. Recent research on affect perception.

	Pts.	Stim.	Neg. Affect	Differential Deficit
Feinberg et al. (1986)	A	S		Gen
Morrison et al. (1988)	A	V	✓	?
Gessler et al. (1989)	A	S		Gen
	C	S		no diff
	Rem	S		no diff
Heimberg et al. (1991)	A	S	=	✓
Archer et al. (1992)	C	S	=	Gen
Cramer et al. (1992)	?	V	✓	?
Joseph et al. (1992)	Rem	V		no diff
Kline et al. (1992)	A (non-par)	S	✓	✓
	paranoid	S	=	no diff
Kerr & Neale (1993)	C	S		Gen

Most studies that have reported deficits in perception have used very brief stimulus presentation formats, increasing the attentional demands on subjects, or have tested highly impaired, chronic patients. With the exception of the study by Heimberg et al. (1991), all studies that included non-affect perception control tasks found that schizophrenic patients have a generalised performance deficit, rather than a specific deficit in affect perception. Overall, the data indicate that schizophrenic patients who do not have significant generalised cognitive deficits can make accurate judgements about affect, when they are given adequate time and information.

This conclusion raises questions about the most appropriate content and focus for SST. Is it necessary to teach facial affect perception skills? It remains to be determined if schizophrenic patients have a functional impairment in real social situations. For example, they may have difficulties when they are under stress or overstimulated, or when they are presented with inconsistent cues. However, that is an empirical question which should be answered before perception skills are incorporated into training programmes. Teaching the identification and discrimination of more complex and subtle affect displays also may not be necessary, as social conflicts typically extend over time and provide consistent and redundant cues. We previously hypothesised that poor discrimination between highly critical/hostile and benign disagreements might reflect a learned avoidance response (i. e., patients have learned to deny or avoid conflictual situations). If so, it may be more appropriate to focus on the differential consequences of the two levels of affective arousal, rather than simply teaching fundamental stimulus discrimination. That is, patients might no longer feel compelled to deny and avoid situations involving disagreements, if they learned to cope with conflict more effectively and experienced less distress.

Despite the questions raised above, the view that social skills training is the most effective psychosocial intervention available for work with schizophrenic patients remains convincing. It is a very flexible strategy that can be tailored to the needs of individual patients. It focuses on practical skills and teaches patients at a rate and in a way in which they can experience success. Consequently, patients tend to like it. Many patients who refuse to participate in other treatments will attend skills training programmes, because they experience success and see the training as relevant to their life situations. Conversely, as previously indicated, there are many unanswered questions about the generalisability of the effects of current programmes and the most relevant content for training, as well as which patients can profit from training and when during the course of the illness training should be implemented (e. g., during acute episodes or only after substantial remission). These questions can only be resolved through careful empirical study. It may be expected that future training programmes will be much more effective, as we learn more about the illness and apply that knowledge to tailor the training carefully to the needs and capacities of individual patients.

Acknowledgements

Preparation of this manuscript was supported by USPHS grants MH-38636, MH-39998, and MH-41577 from the National Institute of Mental Health.

References

American Psychiatric Association (1987) *Diagnostic & Statistical Manual of Mental Disorders* (3rd edn., revised). Washington, DC: APA.

Bellack, A. S., Morrison, R. L., Wixted, J. T. & Mueser, K. T. (1990 a) An analysis of social competence in schizophrenia. *British Journal of Psychiatry*, **156**, 809–818.

Bellack, A. S. & Mueser, K. M. (1993) Psychological treatment for schizophrenia. *Schizophrenia Bulletin*, **19**, 317–336. (NIMH Special Report: Schizophrenia 1993).

Bellack, A. S., Mueser, K. M., Morrison, R. L, et al. (1990) Remediation of cognitive deficits in schizophrenia. *American Journal of Psychiatry*, **147**, 1650–1655.

Bellack, A. S., Mueser, K. M., Wade, J. & Sayers, S. (1992) The ability of schizophrenics to perceive and cope with negative affect. *British Journal of Psychiatry*, **160**, 473–480.

Benton, M. K. & Schroeder, H. E. (1990) Social skills training with schizophrenics: A meta-analytic evaluation. *Journal of Consulting & Clinical Psychology*, **58**, 741–747.

Halford, W. K. & Hayes, R. (1991) Psychological rehabilitation of chronic schizophrenic patients: Recent findings on social skills training and family psychoeducation. *Clinical Psychology Review*, **11**, 22–44.

Heaton, R. K. (1981) *Wisconsin Card Sorting Test Manual*. Odessa, F.G.: Psychological Assessment Resources.

Hersen, M. & Bellack, A. S. (1976 a) A multiple baseline analysis of social skills training in chronic schizophrenics. *Journal of Applied Behavior Analysis*, **9**, 239–245.

Hersen, M. & Bellack, A. S. (1976 b) Social skills training for chronic psychiatric patients: Rationale, research findings and future directions. *Comprehensive Psychiatry*, **17**, 559–580.

Liberman, R. P., Mueser, K. T., Wallace, C. J. et al. (1986) Trainings skills in the psychiatrically disabled: Learning coping and competence. *Schizophrenia Bulletin*, **12**, 631–647.

Morrison, R. L. & Bellack, A. S. (1987) The social functioning of schizophrenic patients: Clinical and research issues. *Schizophrenia Bulletin*, **13**, 715–726.

Mueser, K. T., Bellack, A. S., Douglas, M. S. & Morrison, R. L. (1991) Prevalence and stability of social skill deficits in schizophrenia. *Schizophrenia Research*, **5**, 167–176.

Mueser, K. T., Bellack, A. S., Douglas, M. S. & Wade, J.H. (1991) Prediction of social skills acquisition in schizophrenic and major affective disorder patients from memory and symptomatology. *Psychiatry Research*, **37**, 281–296.

Mueser, K. T., Bellack, A. S., Morrison, R. L. & Wade, J. H. (1990) Gender, social competence and symptomatology in schizophrenia: A longitudinal analysis. *Journal of Abnormal Psychology*, **99**, 138–147.

Mueser, K. T., Bellack, A. S., Morrison, R. L. & Wixted, J. T. (1990) Social competence in schizophrenia: Premorbid adjustment, social skills, and domains of functioning. *Journal of Psychiatric Research*, **24**, 51–63.

Strauss, J. S. (1989) Subjective experiences of schizophrenia: Toward a new dynamic psychiatry-II. *Schizophrenia Bulletin*, **15**, 179–187.

Van der Does, A. J. W. & Van den Bosch, R. J. (1992) What determines Wisconsin Card Sorting performance in schizophrenia. *Clinical Psychology Review*, **12**, 567–584.

Wing, J. K. (1987) Psychosocial factors affecting the long-term course of schizophrenia. In *Psychosocial Treatment of Schizophrenia* (eds J. S. Strauss, W. Böker & H. D. Brenner), pp. 13–29. Toronto: Hans Huber.

Transactional Processes Which Can Function as Risk or Protective Factors in the Family Treatment of Schizophrenia

Michael J. Goldstein, Irwin Rosenfarb, Stephanie Woo and Keith Nuechterlein

Summary

Previous work on expressed emotion (EE) has focused primarily on the attitudes and behaviours of relatives and have neglected the patient's contribution to the affective climate of the family. The present paper reports analyses of direct interactional data collected from a sample of recent onset schizophrenics and their relatives, mostly parents which quantified expressions of sub-clinical psychopathology in patients. The data revealed distinctive differences in the level and type of sub-clinical psychopathology between patients from high and low EE homes in both verbal and nonverbal channels of communication. These differences were most pronounced in behaviours which appeared to be sub-clinical forms of positive rather than negative symptoms. Indications of these findings for the development of the next generation of psychoeducational family programs are discussed.

There is now a preponderance of evidence that transactions between a schizophrenic patient and his or her close relatives are related to the risk of recurrence of the patient's disorder within one year after hospital discharge (Goldstein et al., in press). Specifically, certain levels of criticism and/or emotional overinvolvement expressed by relatives during an index episode of the patient-relative's disorder, have been found to be risk factors for relapse (Kavanagh, 1992). Previous work by our research group has found that these affective attitudes, extracted from an interview and termed high expressed emotion (EE), are correlated moderately with the probability that they will be expressed overtly in actual transactions with a schizophrenic patient-relative during the post-discharge period (Miklowitz et al., 1984; Miklowitz et al., 1989).

Following the epidemiological model, numerous family intervention programmes have been developed, designed to reduce the likelihood that relatives will express critical attitudes and/or engage in emotionally-overinvolved behaviours, in order to improve the course of a patient's short-term course. The results of a number of clinical trials, in which some type of what has been termed "psychoeducational family therapy" was added to standard medication management, have revealed very positive effects for family involvement (see Lam, 1991 and Goldstein, 1992 for a review of these programmes).

The design of these psychoeducational family programmes have been driven largely by attempts to modify those risk factors observable in relatives. There has been little attention to the patient's contribution to the family environment or how recurrent patient-relative transactions may influence the response to psychoeducational family treatment. One reason for the relative neglect of the patient's contribution to the family environment is that numerous studies, with a few exceptions, have failed to find a correlation between the severity or form of the patients' symptomatology and the relatives' EE attitudes or interactive behaviours. In fact, in a recent review, Vaughn concluded that "one consistent finding over the years is that schizophrenic patients from high EE and low EE households are not significantly different in a clinical sense ... they cannot be distinguished on measures of pre-morbid adjustment, severity of psychopathology on admission or residual symptomatology after discharge" (Vaughn, 1989, pp. 16–17).

This conclusion was drawn from numerous studies in which the form or severity of patient behaviour was evaluated in the context of interactions between the patient and clinicians. However, relatives' attitudes and behaviours do not grow out of how their patient-relative behaves with clinicians, but rather in their own day to day interactions with them. Also, it may not be gross signs or symptoms of psychopathology that trigger high EE attitudes or negative affective interactions, but more subtle, sub-clinical signs of psychopathology that occur repeatedly over time. In a recent study, we have focused on this issue to determine whether a more fine-grained analysis of patient-relative transactions, obtained in two ten-minute interactions collected shortly after patients were discharged from the hospital following an index episode of schizophrenia, might reveal a more precise picture of the schizophrenic patient's contribution to the affective climate of the family.

Method

Subjects

This paper is based on a sample of 61 recent-onset schizophrenic patients and key relatives, who participated in the Developmental Processes in Schizophrenia Disorders Project (Nuechterlein et al., 1992). Patients met the following inclusionary criteria: age between 16 and 45; living with or in significant contact with parent(s) or spouse; and no evidence of mental retardation, organic central nervous system disease or significant or habitual substance abuse. All patients received a study diagnosis of schizophrenic disorder or schizoaffective disorder, mainly schizophrenic type, by Research Diagnostic Criteria (RDC; Spitzer et al., 1978). All patients also satisfied DSM III-R criteria for schizophrenia. Details of the screening and diagnostic procedures are described in detail elsewhere (Nuechterlein et al., 1992).

Procedure

Relatives of the patients were administered the Camberwell Family Interview (CFI; Vaughn & Leff, 1976) for rating expressed emotion (EE) as soon as possible after the patient was admitted into the hospital, almost always within one month. Approximately 5½ weeks (M = 37.6 days, SD = 20.2) after the patient had been discharged from the hospital which was approximately six weeks (M = 40 days, SD = 25.4) after administration of the CFI, patients and their parents participated in a direct interaction procedure. This procedure has also been described in detail elsewhere (Miklowitz et al., 1989) and it involved two ten-minute discussions based on problems previously identified by family members in individual interviews. The discussions were stimulated by tape-recorded vignettes composed of comments from a relative or patient to one another, obtained during the same interviews, which had been responded to a few minutes later by the other family member in the absence of the original speaker. Half of the ten-minute discussions began with a previously tape-recorded vignette which originated from a relative, and the other half from the patient, in a counterbalanced order across family groups. Following the playing of the audio-taped vignettes, the family group, typically composed of one or two parents and the patient, were left alone to discuss the issue represented on the tape, with the instructions to "tell each other why you said what you did on the tape, how you feel about the issue and try to reach some solution to the problem." Each problem discussion was allocated ten minutes and at the end of the first discussion, the experimenter entered the room and presented the vignette for the second discussion.

Measures

The CFI yielded a measure of expressed emotion, either high or low EE, based on 6 critical comments (high EE-critical) or a rating of 4 on the emotional overinvolvement (EOI) rating scale (high EE-EOI). Scores or ratings below these cut-off points were rated low EE.

As indicated in previous reports, the direct interaction data were reduced to verbatim transcripts and coded for the relative's affective style (AS; Doane et al., 1981; Miklowitz et al., 1989). The AS system represents interpersonal analogues of EE attitudes and consists of (1) support statements, (2) harsh criticisms – statements which criticise the character or motives of the patient, (3) benign criticisms – statements which criticise specific behavioural actions of the patient, and (4) intrusive statements, which reflect comments about the motives or intentions of the patient, not apparent in the patient's statements.

The present report deals with two ways of examining the direct interaction data for signs of sub-clinical psychopathology manifested by the patient towards his/her relatives. In these analyses, both the verbal behaviour of patients, as revealed in the verbal transcripts, and their nonverbal and paraverbal behaviour, as seen on the videotapes of the interactions, were utilised. The verbal behaviour of patients was analysed with a system developed by Irwin Rosenfarb, a post-doctoral fellow on our project, and the videotaped verbal and paraverbal behaviour by Stephanie Woo, a graduate student on our project.

Both Rosenfarb and Woo based their coding systems for sub-clinical psychopathology manifested in direct interaction with relatives, on the dimensions of Expanded Version of the Brief Psychiatric Rating Scale (Lukoff et al., 1986). Each investigator used these dimensions to identify sub-clinical manifestations of such things as anxiety, depression, unusual thought content, etc. For the analyses of these same dimensions in nonverbal and paraverbal behaviour, criteria were developed which utilised only movement, facial expression, vocal intensity, and unusual social behaviours (turning one's back to another, moving too close into someone's personal space, etc.).

The coding system for verbal behaviour was termed the Patient Symptom Profile (PSP; Rosenfarb, 1993) and the coding system for non- and paraverbal behaviour was termed the Behavioural Symptom Rating System (BSRS; Woo, 1993).

150

Results

Patient Symptom Profile Data (PSP)

The data from this coding system focused solely on verbal behaviour of patients, and were factor analysed to reduce the number of categories for subsequent analysis. Two clearly defined factors emerged, as seen in Table 1, one termed odd or disruptive behaviour and the other negative mood. There is a temptation to view these as clusters of sub-clinical positive and negative symptoms, but since they do not overlap exactly with the usual definitions of those terms, we used the above factor names. Analyses of variance revealed no differences in the negative mood cluster as a function of relatives EE sta-

Table 1. Patient sub-clinical profile factors (Rosenfarb, 1993).

Odd or disruptive behaviour	Factor loading	Negative mood	Factor loading
Unusual thinking	0.83	Depression	0.47
Suspiciousness	0.93	Anxiety	0.72
Irritability/Anger	0.74	Somatic concerns	0.80
Socially inappropriate		Lack of energy	0.48
behaviour	0.74	Boredom	0.30
		Seeing oneself as	
		schizophrenic	0.58

Percent variance accounted for 27.7%   Percent variance accounted for 22.3%

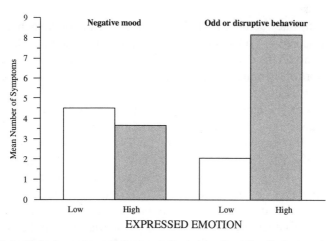

Figure 1. Sub-clinical psychopathology manifested in direct family interaction evaluated from verbatim transcripts (from Rosenfarb et al., 1993).

tus. However, there was a highly significant effect for EE for the odd and disruptive cluster (F(1.39) = 8.01, p = .007). In particular, the schizophrenics from high EE homes expressed more unusual thoughts and hostile verbalisations in direct transaction with their relatives than those from low EE homes.

Behaviour Symptom Rating System (BSRS)

The nonverbal and paraverbal data were coded by a different team of researchers from those who code from transcripts using the PSP. The BSRS data were also factor analysed and they yielded a three-factor solution as seen in Table 2.

Table 2. BSRS Factors – Nonverbal and Paraverbal Behaviours (from Woo et al., 1993).

Flattened affect		Hostile/unusual behaviour		Depressed/withdrawn behaviour	
	Factor loading		Factor loading		Factor loading
Blunted affect	0.61	Hostility	0.87	Depression	0.79
Motor retardation	0.82	Unusual behaviour	0.72	Emotional withdrawal	0.82
Anxiety	−0.84				
% Variance[a]	0.28	% Variance	0.21	% Variance	0.20

[a] Percent variance accounted for

Once again, one factor captured more overt behaviours such as unusual behaviour (instead of unusual thought) and hostility. The other factors were termed Flattened Affect and Depressed-Withdrawn Behaviour. Scores on two of these factors discriminated patients from high vs. low EE families. As with the PSP data, patients from high EE, as contrasted with low EE homes showed higher ratings on the Hostile-Unusual Behaviour factor (F = 8.80, p < .004). Both component items paralleled the trend factor (F = 5.83, p < .02 and F = 5.69, p < .02, respectively). The score for Flattened Affect factor also revealed high-low EE differences (F = 4.42, p < .04), with high EE patients showing higher ratings. However, this result required some interpretation, as a major component on this factor was the *anxiety* item, which coded *negatively* in it. So, the lowest score on this factor was due to the much higher rating on nonverbal signs of anxiety in *low* as contrasted with the high EE for patient-relatives (F = 4.94, p < .03 for anxiety). No significant EE differences were found for the other components of this factor.

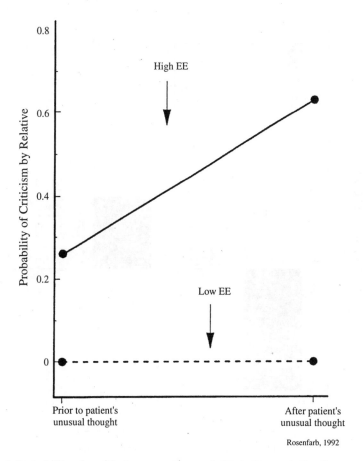

0.8

High EE

↓

Probability of Criticism by Relative

0.6

0.4

0.2

Low EE

↓

0

Prior to patient's
unusual thought

After patient's
unusual thought

Rosenfarb, 1992

Figure 2. Probability of a critical comment by a relative before and after the expression of an unusual thought by the patient, by EE level of the relative.

Relationship of Sub-Clinical Psychopathology to AS Behaviour of Relatives

The next issue addressed was the linkage between manifestation of sub-clinical psychopathology and the affective behaviour expressed by relatives. Rosenfarb addressed this issue by analysing the sequences of one component of his PSP system, unusual thoughts expressed by a patient and the expression of criticism by a relative coded by the AS system. He found that in high EE families, unusual thoughts occurred early in the ten-minute interaction, and once expressed, increased the likelihood that another critical remark would be expressed by a relative. Thus, the cycle observed was unusual thought – criticism – another un-

153

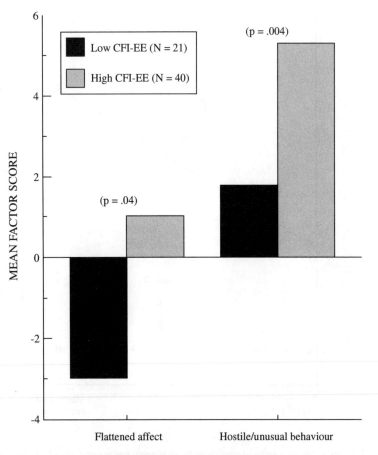

Figure 3. BSRS factor scores: Patients from high and low EE families (from Woo et al., 1993).

usual thought, suggesting a transactional process in which a sign of sub-clinical psychopathology triggers a major affective response which in turn increases the likelihood of more sub-clinical psychopathology.

Woo approached this issue in another way by examining the rates of non-verbal indices of unusual and hostile behaviour as a function of the pattern of affective style across the two ten-minute interactions. She found that the more negative the AS behaviours of the relatives, the higher the rate of un-usual behaviour and hostile behaviour by the patient (see Fig. 4). However, unlike the pattern found by Rosenfarb, Woo found the rate of *nonverbal* in-dices of sub-clinical psychopathology did not vary widely across a ten-minute

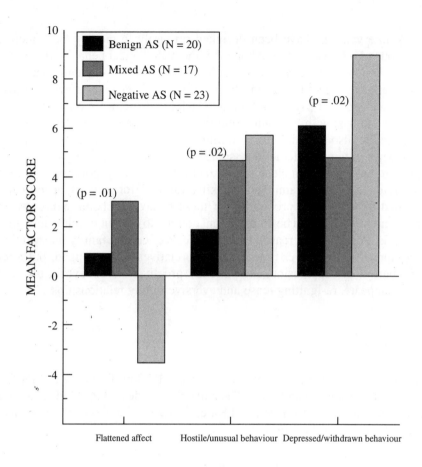

BSRS SYMPTOM FACTOR

Figure 4. BSRS factor scores: Patients from benign, mixed, and negative Affective Style (AS) pattern families (from Woo et al., 1993).

interaction, but remained high when negative AS statements recurred periodically during the family discussion.

Discussion

The analysis of sub-clinical psychopathology manifested by schizophrenic patients when interacting with close relatives indicates highly intimate connections to the type and intensity of affect expressed by these relatives. Most family interventions have been designed primarily to modify the affective behaviour of relatives with the hope that the pathological behaviours of patients will gradually fade as affect tone improves. Yet, the sequential analyses by Rosenfarb suggest that a significant trigger for negative affect are those sub-clinical signs of psychopathology which are difficult for relatives to understand and deal with. It would seem that our therapeutical model should be broadened to also include efforts to train patients to respond in more appropriate ways in family interactions, so as to reduce the probability of negative affective responses from close family members. The incorporation of a type of individually-based "family social skills training" for patients, specifically designed to reduce the probability of these behaviours being expressed in family interaction, could be an important adjunct to current psychoeducational models. Possibly, one reason why the effects of current family intervention programmes weaken over time is that the relatives have changed, but after some period of suppression, the patient's proclivity to behave in difficult ways reappears, re-igniting tense and aversive family relationships.

Acknowledgements

This research was supported by NIMH grant MH 30911, and by NIMH fellowships to Rosenfarb and Woo. The authors are indebted to Sibyl Zaden for coding the interactions for AS, and Karen Snyder for supervising the collection and scoring of the CFI data.

References

Doane, J. A., West, K. L., Goldstein, M. J. et al. (1981) Parental communication deviance and affective style. *Archives of General Psychiatry,* **38**, 679–685.

Goldstein, M. J. (1992) The family and schizophrenia: Some current issues. In *Psychotherapy of Schizophrenia: Facilitating and Obstructive Factors* (eds A. Werbart & J. Cullberg). Oslo: Scandinavian University Press.

Goldstein, M. J., Strachan, A. M. & Wynne, L. (in press) DSM-IV literature review: Relational problems with high expressed emotion. *DSM-IV Sourcebook.*

Kavanagh, D. J. (1992) Recent developments in expressed emotion and schizophrenia. *British Journal of Psychiatry,* **160**, 601–620.

Lam, D. H. (1991) Psychosocial family interventions in schizophrenia: A review of empirical studies. *Psychological Review*, **21**, 423–441.

Lukoff, D., Nuechterlein, K. H. & Ventura, J. (1986) Manual for the expanded Brief Psychiatric Rating Scale (BPRS) *Schizophrenia Bulletin,* **12**, 594–602.

Miklowitz, D. J., Goldstein, M. J., Falloon, I. R. H. & Doane, J. A. (1984) Interactional correlates of expressed emotion in the families of schizophrenics. *British Journal of Psychiatry,* **144**, 482–487.

Miklowitz, D. J., Goldstein, M. J., Doane, J. A. et al. (1989) Is expressed emotion an index of a transactional process? I. Relative's affective style. *Family Process,* **28**, 153–167.

Nuechterlein, K. H., Dawson, M. E., Gitlin, M. et al. (1992) Developmental processes in schizophrenia disorders: Longitudinal studies of vulnerability and stress. *Schizophrenia Bulletin,* **18**, 387–425.

Rosenfarb, I. (1992) *Coding manual for the Patient Symptom Profile.* Unpublished Manuscript, University of California, Los Angeles.

Spitzer, R. L., Endicott, J. & Robins, E. (1978) Research diagnostic criteria: Rationale and reliability. *Archives of General Psychiatry,* **357**, 773–782.

Vaughn, C. E. (1989) Expressed emotion in family relationships. *Journal of Child Psychology & Psychiatry,* **30**, 13–22.

Vaughn, C. E. & Leff, J. P. (1976) The influence of family and social factors on the course of psychiatric illness: A comparison of schizophrenic and depressed neurotic patients. *British Journal of Psychiatry,* **129**, 125–137.

Woo, S. (1993) *Coding manual for the Behavioral Symptom Rating System.* Unpublished manuscript, University of California, Los Angeles.

Experiences with the Systemic Therapy of Psychoses

Helm Stierlin

Summary

The paper reports on experience that our Heidelberg team has made with the systemic therapy of schizophrenic, schizo-affective and bipolar psychoses during the past nine years. Insights gained from two follow-up studies, each with an average three-year interval between the end of therapy and the follow-up, proved useful. The goal of systemic therapy is the reversal of the psychotic client's excommunication; a number of strategies suitable for this purpose are described.

The diagnosis of a psychosis frequently amounts to a person's excommunication by the dominant community. Depending on the observer's orientation, the psychotic individual is either seen as perpetrator or victim of the excommunication, but in either case, he or she is now considered to be mad, no longer accountable and – according to Karl Jaspers (1953) – no longer accessible to empathic understanding.

However, the dominant excommunicating community is no monolithic block. It consists of various interacting systems or sub-systems – the psychiatric, the occupational and the family, which is the one in which there is the greatest emotional investment. The processes in these systems that finally lead to an excommunication are often long-lasting and complex. The English psychiatrist R. Dennis Scott described them in a study in 1967, though he did not speak of excommunication, but of "closure." This study comprised 40 schizophrenics and their families. Trying to understand the processes that eventually result in a person's excommunication, he observed the following (more or less typical) course of events: A child, adolescent, or young adult elicits negative attention; he often gazes vacuously, is easily excitable, fails in his studies, and becomes conspicuous in one way or another. Thus, he attracts the worrisome interest of other family members and, in particular, the parents. As a rule, this involvement has an amplifying effect on the behaviour in question. This in turn evokes what Scott called the "shadow of the ancestors": Family members think of an uncle, a grandfather, a cousin, or other relative who was, or still is mad. They question themselves: Is the madness that runs in the family breaking out again? Then follow anxious conversations with employers and teachers, with the family doctor and, thereafter, with a neurologist or psychiatrist. Finally, it is openly and officially confirmed what one so long has suspected: one is dealing with a psychosis, an illness. Thus, closure or excommunication is effected.

After such closure, other recursive processes come into play: the excommunicated individual appears haunted by inner perceptions and thought processes reminding one of a "home movie" that has got out of control. Outside observers interpret its productions – hearing voices, strange body sensations, bizarre behaviour, abrupt emotional outbursts, etc. – as symptoms of a psychosis. We could also – following a suggestion made by Gunther Schmidt – talk of an "inner parliament" which descends into chaos, and is paralysed, or usurped by a dictator, makes the psychotic individual look peculiar, and this individual is then likely to further isolate himself from others and let his "home movie" run unchecked. A young unemployed female patient of mine, for example, secludes herself up to 24 hours a day in a small apartment, not daring to step out into the street. However, in her apartment, she suffers from hellish visions – productions of her home movie – which cause her to move restlessly around until she finally collapses. Another patient, a school teacher who has retired early, also leads a lonely existence, letting herself be tortured for many hours at a time by the thought of the many mice which are invading her apartment and which, she is firmly convinced, have been let loose by her former head teacher.

Once the excommunicated person is admitted to hospital as a psychiatric patient, we can often speak of his or her "expulsion" – by the family, spouse, social network, or society. But such an expulsion often amounts to increased involvement, though at a distance: expellers and expellees remain massively involved in each other. The expellee feels humiliated and unjustly treated and possibly plans revenge. The expellers appear paralysed by guilt feelings and/or feel righteous indignation. In one way or another, further recursive processes unfold which sustain if the patient's excommunication is not institutionalised: as a "mental patient," he or she remains stigmatised. The longer that rehabilitative measures take, the more complicated the way back into the normal world becomes. And the more he or she adjusts to a career as a handicapped and mentally ill patient, the more difficult a new beginning appears to be.

When sealed by the diagnosis of a psychosis, closure reduces complexity and clarifies matters: this can relieve the patient as well as his family. What is at issue now is an illness for which nobody can be held responsible and whose treatment can be left to medical experts. But such reduction of complexity and release from guilt feelings have their price. As long as one accepts the notion of an illness and behaves correspondingly, the possibilities for influencing psychotic behaviour will decrease. As long as the course of the illness is unknown, one can at best learn to live with the illness – just as a diabetic patient has to learn to live with his.

However, the question as to how and whether the patient as well as his family members can influence psychotic behaviour remains central, as our experiences in Heidelberg show (Retzer et al., 1991). The psychotic individual and his family – but not only these – tend towards an either/or type of thinking: either one exerts influence or is influenced, is the controller or the controllee. In an exaggerated form, this may also be reflected in a schizophrenic's symptom picture: either he experiences himself as all-powerful, the centre of the universe or – as is more frequently the case – as totally powerless and as influenced by forces which inject voices into his brain, extract his thoughts, or inflict bodily torture.

Psychic well-being, though, like adaptation to the dominant society, seems to go together with a middle position between omnipotence and powerlessness. This implies that autonomy and dependence, the ability to exert influence as well as to experience oneself as being influenced, do not exclude but require each other. In other words: autonomy together with the capacity and readiness to influence symptomatic behaviour, and even within limits to take responsibility for it, also imply an awareness of our dependencies. This includes our dependence on a functioning body and central nervous system, on clean air and healthy food, on a functioning eco-system and social network, and even on a lawful democratic society.

When applying the metaphor of an "inner parliament," one may describe a position in the middle between omnipotence and powerlessness as one whereby conflicting interests and inner drives or needs can negotiate compromises in a democratic discourse. In this way, neither will executive action be blocked nor will important "parliamentary" fractions be suppressed or remain dissociated. This will then show up in more tolerance for ambivalence, as well as in an increasing confidence in one's self-regulation.

Within the view presented here, the functional psychoses provide evidence of a failure in conflict management – both within the individual who is diagnosed as psychotic and within the problem system. Here, the organisation of time, as described by Simon et al. (1989) will play a central role. In this, the concepts of "synchronous dissociation and diachronous dissociation" denote ideal types of extreme forms of avoidance of ambivalence and conflict. These can be avoided when conflicting positions are presented and/or perceived either almost simultaneously so that there is no longer an experience of intrapsychic or interpersonal conflict; or as being so separated from each other in time – i.e., as diachronously dissociated – that an experience of conflict is also missing. We can speak of synchronous dissociation when, as in many systems diagnosed as schizophrenic, the relational reality appears greatly "softened-up," so that an outside observer will be inclined to speak of "crazy-talk," of the members not sharing a common focus of attention, of a handing out of false receipts, of mystification, disconfirmation, etc. Experiences of conflict and suffering then seem to have been wiped away. Since conflicting positions and statements arrive at an observer almost simultaneously, he or she is prevented from feeling the conflict "internally." If, on the other hand, diachronous dissociation prevails, conflicting positions appear chronologically drawn so far apart from each other that one no longer perceives them as belonging to one and the same person. This happens with manic-depressive individuals, in whom contradictory and potentially conflicting value systems remain chronologically isolated from each other, and hence dissociated. However, during transitional phases between manic and depressive episodes, if isolated and dissociated value and drive systems collide, we can expect more open conflict – again both within the index patient and within the problem system. This would help explain the increased suicidal risk of some bipolar patients during such transitional periods, if we view the suicide as evincing aggression, that is now being turned against one's own self and/or against members of the problem system.

Within the view presented here, the schizo-affective psychoses merit our special interest. In them, there is typically a mixture of synchronous and diachronous dissociation, of a softening of reality and communicational fogginess on the one hand and a hardening of reality and clarity of communication on the other. Certain members of the problem system may, at different times, either actively contribute to a hardening or to a softening of the relational reality. Such a mixture of synchronous and diachronous dissociation can be dangerous and explosive. Intense conflict, mutual devaluation, destructive – and in particular self-destructive – behaviour may then be observed in some or all members. But in such dangers there may also lie that which can save us, as the German poet Hölderlin put it in his poem "Patmos." As therapists of these families we face an openly conflictual situation. That poses problems, but we are, as a rule, also more vitalised and challenged to intervene creatively than with families with a more clear-cut schizophrenic or manic-depressive symptom picture where conflicts remain more covert.

Implications for the Practice of Systemic Therapy

The term systemic therapy denotes a form of psychotherapy which approaches clients as members of a human system – mostly a family or couple system – in which shared rules, shared basic assumptions and typical interactional patterns prevail. In the field of family therapy it represents one of the major therapeutic orientations. It follows from the above that the primary goal of systemic therapy should be the reversal of the psychotic's excommunication. For this purpose, therapeutic intervention should be carried out with a dual focus in mind: one should be the psychotic client and the other the problem system. The participation of the members of this system in the therapeutic sessions is desirable, but not absolutely necessary. There exists also the possibility of systemic individual therapy, as described by Weber and Simon (1987).

When we focus on the individual psychotic client, we should, from the very beginning, try to treat him or her as a fully respected and fully accountable member of their particular communicational community which is typically the family. This often requires added efforts to engage the client as a partner in a dialogue. These conversations should, amongst other things, aim at reversing the excommunication and provide the participating family members with a model of how this can best be done. At the same time, they should point to ways in which the psychotic client may influence his or her own psychotic behaviour. However, this rarely seems possible without questioning or widening the meanings attributed to the illness concept. This was also suggested by follow-up studies carried out by our team with a sample of schizophrenic, schizo-affective and bipolar patients who had been treated by us (Retzer et al., 1991; Retzer, 1994). The average follow-up time after the end of the systemic therapy was approximately three years. At follow-up, there was a mean reduction of the relapse rate of approximately 76%, as compared with the period before systemic therapy, that was subsequently correlated with seven variables measuring the interactional style and reality construction. However, only one variable correlated significantly with the decrease in the relapse rate: this was concerned with the changes in the patient's and the family members' thinking about the patient's "illness" and his or her ability to influence symptomatic behaviour (Retzer et al., 1991; Retzer, 1994).

A possible way of implanting the notion that the psychotic client can influence his psychotic behaviour is to ask what he or she could do to increase this behaviour. Through such indirect means, the client and participating family members may get the implicit message: that which one can increase one can also decrease or even stop doing altogether. When exploring possibilities for influencing psychotic behaviour, one should let oneself be guided by the descriptions and metaphors which the client and his family offer or accept. An example is a chronic schizophrenic client whom John Strauss observed over a long period of time. Her return into the non-psychotic community began on the day when she realised she could turn off the radio with the voices that harassed her (Davidson & Strauss, 1992). If the client accepts the metaphor of a home movie, one can ask what he or she could do in order to let it run full speed or, in other words, what could be done to amplify his or her psychotic productions – fantasies, delusions, visions of hell, etc. In this situation, one may speak of self-hypnosis that is bound to become ever more terrifying, or point out how the "home movie" may get out of control to the extent that the client is warding off stimulations and hence also corrections coming from outside. It may also be useful to suggest to the psychotic patient that he asks himself whether that which he and the members of the family view negatively as an expression or consequence of the illness – hearing voices, having delusional ideas, engaging in bizarre behaviour, etc. – could not perhaps be seen in a more positive light, e. g., as helping to abstain from rash decisions with respect to one's choice of a partner or profession. In this way, one may possibly counteract splitting and dissociative processes, and perhaps foster self-regulation and tolerance of ambivalence.

With the problem system in focus – usually consisting of the family and couple system – the therapist should ask how interventions might help to improve the management of conflicts between the members of the system, the assumption being that the psychotic symptomatology is an expression and consequence of conflict avoidance or, perhaps more correctly: conflict mismanagement. Typically, intrasystemic conflict mismanagement and individual intrapsychic mismanagement appear intertwined (Stierlin, 1994). At the systems level, such mismanagement of conflicts appears to be a consequence of relational games whose rules and patterns operate in such a way as to resolve conflicts only by one member's final excommunication. In order that this could be reversed by the system, the therapist should counteract either a synchronous dissociation (as is the case with many schizophrenic patients) or a diachronous dissociation (as is the case with many manic-depressive systems). In practice, this means that from the extreme poles of either a diachronous or a synchronous dissociation, i. e., from the extremes of an unduly hardened or unduly softened-up relational reality, the patient should be helped to move into the schizo-affective spectrum which, within the perspective presented here, is midway between schizophrenia on the one hand and manic-depressive psychosis on the other. This means the patient and the family should be helped to face conflicts more squarely. However, conflicts may now easily escalate, but there is also that which may save the client and his family, e. g., the discovery of third ways, the construction of creative solutions, the move from a rigid either-or way of thinking to a more flexible both-and attitude, the recognition of one's own contribution to the dysfunctional patterns and learning more effective management of crises and conflicts.

In order to foster such developments, the therapist should guard his neutrality in several domains. Firstly, by staying neutral with regard to the attempts of individual members to define and impose their reality constructions as the only true and objective ones. Secondly, by staying neutral with respect to the desirability of certain value positions versus others (e. g., orderliness of change versus disorderliness) and thirdly, with respect to the desirability and possibility of change versus non-change. Such multi-levelled neutrality of the therapist perhaps represents the most important contribution to reversing the client's excommunication, and hence moving toward more effective intrapsychic as well as intersystemic conflict management.

However, neutrality is not enough: Certain active strategies are also needed. In the work at Heidelberg, some of these have proved particularly useful and promising. Among these is "therapeutic splitting": therapists show themselves as "split" with respect to the existence or desirability of a certain state of affairs or option for action. Such splitting can be performed most effectively when co-therapists voice different positions: e. g., one therapist shows himself as sceptical regarding the possibility or desirability of changes in certain behaviours that are considered "psychotic." As a reason he may point out that too many adjustments might be required from the family in too short a time. The other therapist doubts this, he conveys that the symptomatic behaviour could soon be given up, because the family appears to have provided evidence of resources and possible solutions that could make this behaviour superfluous. If there is only one therapist, he or she may split himself or herself, allowing the client to participate in the battle of the opposing forces within his or her breast. In this way, the client understands that ambivalence is a normal experience and that it is also normal to wrestle with ambivalence. At the same time, one can be confident that finally the ambivalence will balance out, that goal-directed and solution-orientated action in the individual will become possible again and the family as a whole will function better than before.

A further useful strategy is "externalisation," described by the Australian therapist Michael White (White & Epston, 1990). This means that the difficulties for all concerned persons, resulting from the psychosis, are reified in a convenient manner. At the same time, they are defined as a problem that is located neither in the inner life of the psychotic client nor in the relationships between the members of the system, but rather projected onto the outside – "externalised." Once they are located there, they can be fought as an enemy against whom the client and the members of his family can now unite in joint action. White applied this strategy with particular success in treating chronic psychotic patients; with its help, he counteracts the demoralisation and torturous search for causes and culprits which had so far mired the client and members of the family in a morass of hopelessness.

In Heidelberg, we have worked similarly for some time, often making use of the reified concept of "psychosis" when this was offered to us by the client and/or his family. We have acknowledged that the psychosis was a force by which the client and his family felt overpowered, but also asked how far its realm extended, and whether changes in the quality or amount of its power had been observed in different temporal, spatial, or interpersonal contexts. If such changes had been noticed, one could then ask how these could be explained, and how the power of the psychosis might possibly be influenced in one way or another. The reified and externalised psychosis can be further constructed as a partner in relationships – a partner who could also enter into alliances with different members. In the same way, psychotic behaviour could be shown to depend on certain contexts and liable to be influenced by what the psychotic patient did. One can see this as another way of facilitating and acknowledging ambivalence, as well as a more constructive management of conflicts.

When we apply this externalising and reifying strategy, we use a "hard" concept of psychosis as a means of entering the psychotic game. But we may enter the game also from the opposite side, by using soft metaphors, such as "walking in a fog," "getting down to earth," or "being on a merry-go-around," as these are offered to us by the client and family members. With the help of such metaphors, we enter the semantic and communicational world of the patient and family "by the backdoor," in order to focus then, step-by-step, on more specific contexts and behaviour. In this way, we may also make use of the earlier mentioned possibilities of influencing psychotic behaviour and hence of arriving at a better management of conflict and perhaps a reversal of the excommunication.

References

Davidson, L. & Strauss, J. S. (1992) Sense of self in recovery from severe mental illness. *British Journal of Medical Psychology*, **65**, 131–145.

Jaspers, K. (1953) *Allgemeine Psychopathologie*. Heidelberg: Springer-Verlag.

Retzer, A. (1994) *Familie und Psychose*. Stuttgart: G. Fischer.

Retzer, A., Simon, F. B., Weber, G., et al. (1991) A follow-up study of manic-depressive and schizo-affective psychoses after systemic family therapy. *Family Process*, **30**, 139–153.

Schmidt, G. *Personal communication*.

Scott, R. D. & Ashworth, P. L. (1967) Closure at the first schizophrenic breakdown. A family study. *British Journal of Medical Psychology*, **42**, 13–32.

Simon, F., Weber, G., Stierlin, et al. (1989) Schizo-affektive Muster. Eine systemische Beschreibung. *Familiendynamik*, **14**, 190–213.

Stierlin, H. (1994) *Ich und die anderen. Psychotherapie in einer sich wandelnden Gesellschaft.* Stuttgart: Klett-Cotta.

Weber, G. & Simon, F. (1987) Systemische Einzeltherapie. *Zeitschrift für systemische Therapie*, **3**, 192–206.

White, M. & Epston, D. (1990) *Literate Means to Therapeutic Ends.* New York: W. W. Norton.

Comprehensive Community Care of Persons with Schizophrenia Through the Programme of Assertive Community Treatment (PACT)

Mary Ann Test, William H. Knoedler, Deborah J. Allness,
Suzanne Senn Burke, Shinya Kameshima and Laura Rounds

Summary

While most research on the treatment of persons with schizophrenia has investigated interventions only singly or in combinations, and for relatively brief periods of time, both theory and findings from empirical research suggest that comprehensive and long-term intervention might yield significantly greater and more lasting impacts. However, research on intervention of this kind is difficult, partly because of the sheer problems of implementing truly comprehensive, integrated treatment in community settings, which is the current arena for long-term care. We describe here the Programme of Assertive Community Treatment (PACT), one means by which comprehensive, integrated bio-psycho-social treatment can be delivered in the community to persons with schizophrenia. We summarise the considerable research supporting the efficacy of this approach in the short run, and then describe the design of an in-progress, long-term study and summarise its early results. Finally, we offer speculation regarding the "critical ingredients" responsible for the effectiveness of the PACT model. The overall findings suggest that long-term, comprehensive care of persons with schizophrenia may provide the necessary biological and psychosocial buffers from stress to allow these individuals to live in a sustained fashion in the community, with a decent quality of life, despite what are often chronic, severe mental illnesses.

In a recent review of the status of the psychosocial treatment of schizophrenia, Bellack & Mueser (1993) stated, "Although the importance of comprehensive and longitudinal intervention programmes is widely recognised (Ciompi, 1987; Wing, 1987), the empirical literature has focused on relatively short term, compartmentalised strategies." The current paper will respond to this gap in the literature by describing the implementation and research findings of a comprehensive model for the treatment of schizophrenia called the Programme of Assertive Community Treatment, or PACT. In earlier publications, this model was named Training in Community Living, or TCL.

The need for comprehensive treatment of persons with schizophrenia is suggested by both theory and findings from treatment research. The vulnerability-stress framework for understanding schizophrenia, for instance, suggests that positive impacts on the course and outcome of the disorder, as well as on quality of life will be optimised if treatment programmes simultaneously contain interventions with several different objectives. These are: (a) to decrease biological vulnerability (e. g., provision of psychotropic medication); (b) to help the client strengthen protective factors (e. g., through social skills, work rehabilitation, and social supports), and (c) to help weaken environmental stressors (e. g., through assistance to clients in meeting basic needs and securing supportive work and living environments) (Liberman, 1988). The empirical treatment literature, meanwhile, supports the efficacy of a number of these interventions when they are delivered singly, but at the same time draws attention to their limitations in terms of effect, size, scope, and duration. These results suggest that more comprehensive and longer-term strategies might have a more powerful and lasting impact on the course and outcome of illness (Bellack & Mueser, 1993).

The paucity of research into the impact of long-term comprehensive treatment on persons with schizophrenia is perhaps largely a result of the sheer difficulty of implementing integrated, yet individualised comprehensive programmes of care. This task is particularly challenging now that the community, rather than the hospital, has become the main arena of long-term care.

Since the 1970s, we have implemented a research programme in Madison, Wisconsin to develop and evaluate comprehensive community care for persons with severe mental illness. This effort has resulted in a comprehensive, integrated care model called the "Programme of Assertive Community Treatment" or PACT. A number of controlled studies by ourselves and others (in the United States, Australia, and Great Britain) demonstrate the efficacy of this model when it is administered in the short run (i. e., for approximately one year). Based on these findings, the model is now being quite widely disseminated, both in the United States and elsewhere (Allness et al., 1985). Further, we are undertaking a study of the long-term implementation of this model with young adults who have schizophrenic disorders (Test, 1992; Test et al., 1985). In this controlled study, young adults with schizophrenia are receiving this comprehensive treatment intervention in a continuous fashion for at least seven years.

A major aim of this paper is to describe the PACT treatment model in order to convey a picture of one means by which comprehensive, integrated bio-psycho-social treatment can be delivered in the community to persons with

168

schizophrenia. We also briefly review the research supporting the efficacy of this approach in the short run. Finally, we describe the design of our current long-term study and summarise its early results.

The PACT model evolved out of our earlier work on the research ward of Mendota State Hospital in Madison, Wisconsin in the 1960s (Marx et al., 1973). We observed that the comprehensive and 24-hour supports of the hospital were often needed, though in a less intensive way, when our clients reached the community. Indeed, over time we came to believe that hospitalisation could be avoided altogether by many clients, if they received comprehensive community care instead. As many others have noted, however, it is much more difficult to provide comprehensive care in the community than in the hospital. In this respect, three areas are particularly problematic (Test, 1992). Firstly, community service systems are usually fragmented and complex: often, the needed bio-psycho-social services are provided in different agencies, under different roofs, and by an array of personnel. For instance, a community "system" might contain a medication clinic, a day treatment centre, a sheltered workshop, and a halfway house. Often, there is little integration of care, and additionally, the deficits of schizophrenia prevent many of these clients from being able to negotiate such a complex system. Secondly, most agencies expect the client to come into their office to receive services: again, the symptoms of schizophrenia often make this impossible, resulting in drop-out from services and subsequent relapse. Finally, services in the community are rarely individualised, but often involve plugging clients into a limited number of "programmes." Seldom do clients receive exactly the mix and amount of services that they need, when they need them.

In the development of the PACT model, a major part of our response to these problems was to create a "core services team" or "continuous treatment team" (Torrey, 1986). A core services team is a community-based, multidisciplinary team of mental health staff who serve as a fixed point of responsibility for a defined group of clients. The team is responsible for assisting the client to meet needs in all areas of life. In our current long-term study, this interdisciplinary team consists of 14 staff, who are responsible for 120 young adults with schizophrenia. The team provides coverage seven days a week, 24 hours a day, and operates out of an office in the community.

Three things are especially important about how the PACT core services team operates. Firstly, the team itself provides the majority of bio-psycho-social services to its clients, rather than referring the client out to an array of other providers.

The Madison PACT core team, for instance, provides clients with medication, supportive and problem-solving therapy, housing, occupational rehabilitation, crisis intervention, and an array of other intervention. Even if the core team refers the client to another provider, it still maintains responsibility for seeing that the client's needs are successfully addressed. This fixed point of responsibility, "one team does all" approach avoids the complex, fragmented service system that so often exists in the community. Further, by using the same team to provide both what are often called "treatment" and "rehabilitation" services, the complex interaction of symptoms and psychosocial functioning can be efficiently and effectively dealt with. Finally, use of a core services team results not only in continuity of care across functional areas and across time, but also continuity of caregiver, since the client needs to relate to only a single set of staff.

The second critical aspect of how the team operates is that it is mobile. Specifically, team members use assertive outreach to provide most services *in vivo*, i. e., where the client is, rather than in an office or agency setting. Each morning, the staff meet at their community-based office to receive assignments, and then spend their working day going out into the community, to meet the client in his or her place of residence, neighbourhood, or site of work or leisure. Our data indicate that 78% of the time that our staff spend with clients takes place on their client's own territory; only 22% is in our office (Brekke & Test, 1987). Such assertive outreach prevents the drop-out of clients from contact, while providing services where the client uses them and eliminating the need for the client to transfer training from an agency setting to his/her natural environment.

The third critical aspect of how the team operates is that the services it provides are highly individualised. The great diversity of persons with severe mental illness and the fact that both the person and the disorder are constantly changing over time require that services be organised in this way (Strauss et al., 1985). In PACT, the treatment interventions are tailor-made for the current needs and preferences of each person, rather than assigning a client to a set of existing programmes. The content, amount, timing, and kinds of treatment, rehabilitation, and supports that are provided vary enormously between clients, as well as within the same client across time.

The treatment process begins with a thorough clinical and functional assessment, which results in the development of an individualised treatment plan in the following areas: (a) symptoms and psychological functioning; (b) social environmental supports; (c) activities of daily living, e. g., budgeting money, cooking, personal care; (d) vocational skills; (e) social and interpersonal skills, and (f) medical and general health. Some of the specific interventions that the team delivers are described below.

In the area of illness management, the core team provides medication, which is often delivered to clients at home. Staff have frequent one-to-one contacts with clients to help solve problems and provide an abundance of emotional support. Also, over time and within the context of a long-term relationship, staff attempt to educate the client about his/her illness, and sometimes help the client learn to self-manage symptoms. Staff also provide individualised psycho-education to family and community members such as landlords and employers. A team member is on call 24 hours per day to provide crisis intervention; brief admission to hospital is used when needed.

In the area of housing, staff help clients find rooms or apartments in the community, rather than using specialised residential settings. Clients appear to prefer the more informal settings, and support can be titrated there to the amount that is needed by the client at any given time. Staff spend a great deal of time doing outreach to where clients live, to help them meet their basic needs. This might involve teaching and assisting them with activities of daily living such as grocery shopping, money management, laundry upkeep, and use of transport. Staff also help clients to establish friendships and find satisfying leisure time activities. The role that staff play is one of "coach," both teaching clients how to do these things as well as providing them with "side by side" emotional support, when something new or difficult is attempted.

Employment plays a central role in PACT, and is the major means of facilitating a daily structure for clients. While in our previous studies we used sheltered workshops to a significant extent, it was often difficult to individualise this approach sufficiently and many of our clients found little meaning in this work. In our current programme, we use a "supported employment" model, in which we assist each client to secure and keep a real job in the community which matches the client's interests, skills, and current abilities. Some jobs are found by the client and PACT vocational staff person studying together the "Positions Available" section of the newspaper and making formal application for jobs that appear appropriate. Others are located by the staff person telephoning a variety of employers to enquire about potential work opportunities that might be appropriate for the client. Initially, most of these placements are part-time, and many involve minimal and subsidised pay. However, we provide clients with active skill teaching and/or support in such jobs; this involves working with both the client and the employer "on the spot," to help both learn means of coping and structuring the environment so that clients are able to work in spite of what are often continuing psychotic symptoms. Our goal is that each client be able to work at his/her optimal level; we anticipate that gradually and over the long run, this will include a number of clients working in the competitive job market for sustained periods of time.

In terms of vulnerability-stress theory, it can be seen that the PACT core services team provides clients with interventions to decrease their biological vulnerability; it helps them to learn skills and provides social supports to strengthen protective factors, as well as placing a major focus on helping clients to meet basic needs and secure supportive work and living environments, to weaken environmental stressors. While we are constantly trying to help clients decrease the severity of their symptoms and illness and to increase skills, an enormous emphasis is put on helping clients to find environments in which they can function optimally, despite their ongoing, often horrendous illnesses.

Staffing

The staffing of the PACT core team is critical to the success of the programme, since the team members must possess a wide range of aptitudes and professional skills. Clearly, the optimal team requires members who are capable of carrying out the variety of specialised tasks described above that clients require. Staff represent the various mental health professions – social work, psychiatric nursing, occupational therapy, psychology, rehabilitation counselling, and psychiatry. We suggest that, if possible, at least 75% of the staff of a PACT core team have master's or bachelor's degrees in mental health-related fields, and that no more than 25% of the total staff be of paraprofessional status. It is also important that the members of the PACT team in fact work as a team, rather than as a group of individual practitioners operating in the context of a case management programme and having primary responsibility only for their own case load. In the PACT model, all team members work with all clients, so that if a staff member is absent for whatever reason, clients can still find others with whom they have good working relationships. We have also found that having team members share responsibilities and create treatment plans together prevents the "burn out" often seen when only a single staff person is responsible for a caseload of clients.

Each team needs a clinical supervisor who is qualified in social work, nursing, rehabilitation counselling, or psychology, or who is a psychiatrist. This supervisor should have experience working with adults with serious mental illness, as well as a good understanding of the characteristics and problems of this client group, and of the principles and methods of PACT. The value of having a competent clinical supervisor cannot be overemphasised, but if the team supervisor is someone other than a psychiatrist, it is essential that a psychiatrist be part of the team, or provide routine and frequent psychiatric input.

Efficacy in the Short Run

Our initial major study, which took place in the 1970s, evaluated the use of PACT as an alternative to the mental hospital (Stein & Test, 1980). Subjects were an unselected group of diagnostically mixed clients (aged 18 to 62), who were seeking in-patient admission to the state mental hospital in Madison, and who had any diagnosis other than severe organic brain syndrome, mental retardation, or primary alcoholism. These clients were randomly assigned to either PACT or a control group. Control subjects received the usual treatment at the time, which was quite progressive: most were admitted to the hospital for a brief period of intensive inpatient treatment, and then were discharged to the aftercare system in Dane County, Wisconsin. Subjects assigned to the experimental condition (PACT) were usually not admitted, but instead returned to the community, where they were involved in the PACT model described above. In this study, the experimental subjects received the PACT treatment for a period of 14 months, and were then discharged to the existing community programmes in Dane County. All study subjects were followed-up and assessed by independent research analysts every four months, for a total of 28 months.

The treatment results were strikingly positive. During the 14 months that the experimental group was receiving the PACT model, relative to the control group they experienced a markedly reduced time in psychiatric institutions, greater independent living, and fewer symptoms. They also showed significant, though modest, advantages in the areas of work and social functioning: they had spent more time than the controls in sheltered, though not competitive, employment and reported having more trusted friends as well as belonging to more social groups.

These positive findings have now been replicated in a number of other controlled studies where adaptations of PACT have been used in a variety of settings, both in the United States and elsewhere (e. g., Hoult et al., 1983; Reynolds & Hoult, 1984; Bond et al., 1988, 1990; Morse et al., 1992; Muijen et al., 1992). Research is continuing to evaluate the usefulness of the PACT model for subgroups of clients by diagnosis and ethnic background (Taube et al., 1990).

An additional part of the evaluation in our initial study was a comprehensive economic benefit-cost analysis (Weisbrod et al., 1980). This revealed that the new model was economically feasible, with the overall costs and benefits of the PACT model and the usual (traditional) model of care being quite similar. Finally, a study of the relative social costs of PACT versus the traditional model demonstrated that the gains made by PACT clients were not at the expense of any additional burden to the family or community (Test & Stein, 1980).

It is important to ask, however, what happens when clients are discharged from comprehensive community care programmes such as PACT. Our initial study (Stein & Test, 1980) contained a 14-month follow-up period after discharge from PACT, and one of the most important findings was that many of the clients did not continue to do well then. Indeed, most of the positive effects of the PACT model relative to the control condition were lost by the end of the 14-month follow-up period.

A review of the literature reveals that similar results have been found with virtually all biological and psychosocial treatments studied to date – anti-psychotic medication, day treatment, family psycho-education, etc. (Test, 1981; Hogarty et al., 1991; Bellack & Mueser, 1993). Clients do well while they are receiving these special interventions and support, but there is a loss of the advantages relative to controls after discharge. It is not clear why this is the case, but the psychobiological deficits and vulnerability of schizophrenia are ongoing, and therefore many clients cannot survive without long-term biological and psychosocial protective factors. Thus, the ideal treatment programme for persons with schizophrenia may need to be not only comprehensive, but also long-term.

Efficacy in the Long Run

The major research question which is being examined by our current study (Test et al., 1985, 1991) concerns the impact of long-term, comprehensive care on young adults with schizophrenic disorders – whether or not the early positive effects of comprehensive community treatment programmes are sustained if treatment is ongoing, rather than time-limited. We are also investigating whether or not long-term community treatment and rehabilitation can enhance social and work functioning to a clinically significant degree. Most previous studies, including our own, have demonstrated only modest gains in these areas.

Subjects in the long-term study are 122 young adults, aged 18–30, with schizophrenic disorders who entered the study from either inpatient or out-patient treatment settings during an acute episode. They were randomly assigned to either the PACT model (60%) or to a control group (40%). We purposely allocated a greater proportion of subjects to the PACT condition so that we might have a large enough sample receiving this well defined treatment to investigate a variety of additional research interests. In this study, instead of being discharged, clients remain in their respective treatment conditions in an ongoing fashion for at least seven years; research assessments are done on all subjects by a team of independent evaluators, every six months.

Subjects assigned to the experimental PACT condition receive almost all of their services form the PACT core team, as described above. Thus there is continuity both of care and (collective) caregiver across this seven-year period, whereas subjects assigned to the control condition receive the existing treatment available to all persons in Dane County, Wisconsin. In the current study, this is an extremely stringent control condition since the Dane County system is now also a national model of good community care (Stein et al., 1992). The DANE system, which was heavily influenced by the earlier Stein and Test (1980) research, now operates on much the same philosophical basis as PACT. However, it is organised in a different way. Rather than emphasising one "core" team, which provides most services across functional areas and across time, the DANE system contains many exemplary components (e. g., a crisis service, psychosocial clubhouse, special living arrangements) which intervene at different times, depending on the individual client's needs at the time. Two years after the start of the long-term study, a Mobile Community Treatment team modelled after the PACT team was added to the DANE system to provide assertive outreach and care to clients who drop-out of treatment (Stein & Diamond, 1985). While we expect that clients in the DANE system will receive very good care, we anticipate that this will not be as intensive nor as continuous across time as PACT.

The sample ($n = 122$) in the long-term study can be described as young adults with schizophrenia or schizophrenia-related disorders of early onset and seemingly poor prognosis. Mean age at study entry was 23.11 years, and that at first mental health contact was 19.02. 67% of the subjects are male, and 94% were unmarried at time of entry. At the time of admission to the study, 73.8% were diagnosed as schizophrenic and 23% as schizo-affective by the Research Diagnostic Criteria (RDC); 3.3% were diagnosed schizotypal personality disorder (DSM-III). Eighty-one percent had previously been in hospital; indeed, the subjects in the sample had already experienced a mean of 3.35 admissions and had spent a mean accumulated duration in psychiatric inpatient settings of 64.95 days. A large percentage of the clients were also significant users of street drugs.

We reported some early findings from this study (Test et al., 1991) which are summarised here. These pertain to the functioning of all clients across their first two years in the study. Importantly, the clients in the PACT programme demonstrated a very sustained community tenure across this time period. For instance, during months 7–24, an 18-month period in which relapse might be expected, PACT clients spent a mean of only 5.24 days in psychiatric hospitals or skilled nursing homes, compared to a mean of 44.17 days for control (DANE) clients (p ≤ .001). Only 19.4% of the PACT versus 56.10% of the DANE clients spent any time in these settings during this period (p ≤ .001). Additionally, during this same period, PACT clients spent significantly more time than DANE clients residing in their own apartments.

These early findings from the long-term study replicate those of Stein and Test (1980), and are important for several reasons. Firstly, they extend the research on the efficacy of the PACT model to a group of clients not yet studied, i.e., young adults with schizophrenic disorders of poor prognosis. Secondly, the advantages of PACT are found even when this treatment model is compared to a very stringent control condition – the nationally known DANE county system. Thirdly, unlike our earlier study, in which most of the positive effects of PACT had dissipated by the end of two years, these advantages were sustained at the two-year point. We believe this is because, in the long-term study, the PACT treatment and support is continued across time, so that when the intervention is sustained, so is the effect.

Discussion

A growing body of research supports the effectiveness of the PACT model of community care for persons with schizophrenia and other severe mental illnesses. We now direct attention to a question that has significant implications for the more widespread implementation of this model or adaptations of it, namely, "What are the critical ingredients of the PACT model?" In other words, which of its multifaceted elements or features are responsible for its effectiveness? If the essential or active ingredients of this extensively researched model can be defined, developers of local community care systems can focus efforts on capturing these features as they design and necessarily mold programmes to fit their own settings and resources.

There is currently no research examining this "critical ingredients" question. However, what makes the PACT model effective may simply be that certain of its organisational and service delivery mechanisms optimise the probability that known effective treatments in fact *reach* clients. For instance, there is now wide agreement that the receipt of psychotropic medication and assistance in meeting basic needs such as housing, adequate food, health care, and some degree of social support will markedly reduce the rate of relapse and elevate quality of life for a substantial segment of persons with severe mental illnesses (e. g., Kane & Marder, 1993; Turner-Crowson, 1993). Thus these services are typically included in most community care systems. The critical or key difference between the PACT model and many others, however, is that in PACT responsibility is fixed with a designated team to make sure that clients actually receive these and other needed services. Furthermore, and importantly, the team that is charged with this responsibility is empowered with sufficient resources (e. g., high staff to client ratio) and flexibility (e. g., ability to individualise treatment and to work out of office) so that they are able to accomplish this mandate. Indeed, the team itself often provides many of the necessary services. Finally, this responsibility is fixed with the same team across time, which eliminates the need to transfer responsibility for the care to another provider, as a client progresses through periods of more pronounced illness or wellness.

The concept of "fixed point of responsibility" is not new to the field, and indeed this matter is now of central concern to most mental health system planners. Far too often, however, this most important aspect of an effective care system is vested in a single "case manager" or "care manager" or team which has neither the power, the resources, nor the flexibility to make sure that needed services are in fact provided. For instance, such a care manager is frequently responsible for assessment, treatment planning, linking, and monitoring, but he/she neither is a main provider of services, nor has much formal power over other providers, nor sufficient resources to fill in gaps in the existing system. Thus, despite heroic attempts, needed services may not reach clients due to factors such as stringent admission criteria of other providers, a client's difficulties in coming in to an agency to receive services, or the sheer lack of needed services in a given community. It is not surprising that controlled evaluations of this kind of generalised case management have yielded few indicators of effectiveness (e. g., Franklin et al., 1987). On the other hand, in the PACT model responsibility for seeing that clients receive the services they need is fixed with a well resourced team that can in fact provide many of the necessary services itself and can reach out into the community to assist the client on his/her territory when needed. The team can refer clients to other providers when this is optimal, but it never transfers responsibility for helping the client to meet his/her needs in all areas of life.

Because of its high staff to client ratio, questions about the cost of the PACT approach necessarily arise, along with speculation that this model might be effective simply because it appears to have greater resources than the treatments with which it has been compared. Our initial benefit-cost study (Weisbrod et al., 1980) suggested that overall the PACT model is not more costly than more traditional care; clearly, however, there is a great need for more economic studies of different approaches to community care. Meanwhile, it should be kept in mind that while the PACT team itself is well resourced, this team also provides comprehensive services itself, thereby eliminating the need for the administrative and clinical resources of some other agencies. Finally, while resources are certainly important for good care to occur, they are not themselves sufficient; they need to be organised and delivered in a way which assures that they reach their intended recipients.

If a well endowed and flexible fixed point of responsibility is the critical ingredient in PACT, system planners must consider what segment of persons with severe mental illnesses require or might benefit from a model with this feature. The most severely ill or disabled clients in a catchment area would logically be the most obvious beneficiaries of such an approach, for these persons are probably the least likely to be able to assume self responsibility for meeting their needs. Consideration might be given, however, to casting the net for receipt of a PACT type model more broadly than just to this most disabled group, since the episodic nature of many severe mental illnesses leads substantial numbers of better functioning clients to become severely disabled during segments of their lives. Through use of a PACT type model such severe (and costly) episodes can be prevented by the core team's "keeping their finger on the pulse" of the client through regular but infrequent contacts, and by modifying treatment or increasing supports if signs of prodromal symptoms begin to appear. Involvement of these better functioning clients in a PACT type approach need not be an expensive matter, for they do not need to be seen often during their more stable periods.

While the field is far from defining a cure for schizophrenia, research suggests that the provision of long-term, comprehensive community care can provide powerful assistance to people with this and other severe mental illnesses, so that they can experience sustained community tenure at a decent quality of life. The PACT model is one method of providing such care, but important questions remain about its critical ingredients and most appropriate target group. While we have speculated here about these issues, continuing rigorous research will help to facilitate a more widespread delivery of successful community care programmes in the most cost-effective manner.

Acknowledgements

The research reported here is a collaborative project between the University of Wisconsin-Madison and the Mendota Mental Health Institute of the State of Wisconsin Department of Health and Social Services. This research has been supported in part by the State of Wisconsin, and by grants #40886 and #4355 from the National Institute of Mental Health.

178

References

Allness, D. J., Knoedler, W. H. & Test, M. A. (1985) The dissemination and impact of a model program in process: 1972–1984. In *The Training in Community Living Model: A Decade of Experience* (eds L. I. Stein & M. A. Test), pp. 17–27. New Directions for Mental Health Services, No. 26. San Francisco: Jossey Bass.

Bellack, A. S. & Mueser, K. T. (1993) Psychosocial treatment for schizophrenia. *Schizophrenia Bulletin*, **19**, 317–336.

Bond, G. R., Miller, L. D., Krumweid, R. D. & Ward, R. S. (1988) Assertive case management in three CMHC's: A controlled study. *Hospital & Community Psychiatry*, **39**, 411–418.

Bond, G. R., Witheridge, T. F., Dincin, J. et al. (1990) Assertive community treatment for frequent users of psychiatric hospitals in a large city: A controlled study. *American Journal of Community Psychology*, **18**, 865–891.

Brekke, J. S. & Test, M. A. (1987) An empirical analysis of services delivered in a model community support program. *Psychosocial Rehabilitation Journal*, **10**, 51–61.

Ciompi, L. (1987) Toward a coherent multidimensional understanding and therapy of schizophrenia: Converging new concepts. In *Psychosocial Treatment of Schizophrenia: Multidimensional Concepts, Psychological, Family, and Self-Help Perspectives* (eds J. S. Strauss, W. Böker & H. D. Brenner), pp. 48–62. Toronto: Huber.

Franklin, J. S., Solovitz, B., Mason, M. et al. (1987) An evaluation of case management. *American Journal of Public Health*, **77**, 674–678.

Hogarty, G. E., Anderson, C. M., Reiss, D. J. et al. (1991) Family psychoeducation, social skills training, and maintenance chemotherapy in the aftercare treatment of schizophrenia: II. Two-year effects of a controlled study on relapse and adjustment. *Archives of General Psychiatry*, **48**, 340–347.

Hoult, J., Reynolds, I., Charbonneau-Powis, M. et al. (1983) Psychiatric hospital versus community treatment: The results of a randomized trial. *Australian & New Zealand Journal of Psychiatry*, **17**, 160–167.

Liberman, R. P. (1988) Coping with chronic mental disorders: A framework for hope. In *Psychiatric Rehabilitation of Chronic Mental Patients* (ed. R. P. Liberman), pp. 1–28. Washington, D.C.: American Psychiatric Press.

Kane, J. M. & Marder, S. R. (1993) Psychopharmacologic treatment of schizophrenia. *Schizophrenia Bulletin*, **19**, 287–302.

Marx, A. J., Test, M. A. & Stein, L. I. (1973) Extro-hospital management of severe mental illness. *Archives of General Psychiatry*, **29**, 505–511.

Morse, G. A., Calsyn, R. J., Allen, G. et al. (1992) Experimental comparison of the effects of three treatment programs for homeless mentally ill people. *Hospital & Community Psychiatry*, **43**, 1005–1010.

Muijen, M., Marks, I., Connolly, J. & Audini, B. (1992) Home based care and standard hospital care for patients with severe mental illness: a randomized controlled trial. *British Medical Journal*, **304**, 749–754.

Reynolds, I. & Hoult, J. E. (1984) The relatives of the mentally ill: A comparative trial of community-oriented and hospital-oriented psychiatric care. *Journal of Nervous & Mental Disease*, **172**, 480–489.

Stein, L. I. & Diamond, R. J. (1985) A program for difficult-to-treat patients. In *The Training in Community Living Model: A Decade of Experience* (eds L. I. Stein & M. A. Test), pp. 17–27. New Directions for Mental Health Services, no. 26. San Francisco: Jossey Bass.

Stein, L. I., Diamond, R. J. & Factor, R. M. (1992) A system approach to the care of persons with schizophrenia. In *Handbook of Schizophrenia*, Vol. 5 (eds M. I. Herz & J. P. Docherty). New York: Elsevier.

Stein, L. I. & Test, M. A. (1980) Alternative to mental hospital treatment. I. Conceptual model, treatment program, and clinical evaluation. *Archives of General Psychiatry*, **37**, 392–397.

Strauss, J. S., Hafez, H., Lieberman, P. & Harding, C. M. (1985) The course of psychiatric disorder. III. Longitudinal principles. *American Journal of Psychiatry*, **142**, 289–296.

Taube, C. A., Morlock, L., Burns, B. J. & Santos, A. B. (1990) New directions in research on assertive community treatment. *Hospital & Community Psychiatry*, **41**, 642–647.

Test, M. A. (1981) Effective treatment of the chronically mentally ill: What is necessary? *Journal of Social Issues*, **37**, 71–86.

Test, M. A. (1992) The training in community living model. In *Handbook of Psychiatric Rehabilitation* (ed. R. P. Liberman), pp. 153–170. New York: Macmillan.

Test, M. A. & Stein, L. I. (1980) Alternative to mental hospital treatment: III. Social cost. *Archives of General Psychiatry*, **37**, 1243–1247.

Test, M. A., Knoedler, W. H. & Allness, D. J. (1985) The long-term treatment of young schizophrenics in a community support program. In *The Training in Community Living Model: A Decade of Experience* (eds L. I. Stein & M. A. Test), pp. 17–27. New Directions for Mental Health Services, No. 26. San Francisco: Jossey Bass.

Test, M. A., Knoedler, W. H., Allness, D. J. et al. (1991) Long-term community care through an assertive continuous treatment team. In *Advances in Neuropsychiatry and Psychopharmacology. Vol. I: Schizophrenia Research* (eds C. A. Tamminga & S. C. Schulz), pp. 239–246. New York: Raven Press.

Torrey, E. F. (1986) Continuous treatment teams in the care of the chronically mentally ill. *Hospital & Community Psychiatry*, **37**, 1243–1247.

Turner-Crowson, J. (1993) *Reshaping Mental Health Services. Implications for Britain of US Experience*. King's Fund Institute, Research Report No. 16. London: King's Fund Institute.

Weisbrod, B. A., Test, M. A. & Stein, L. I. (1980) Alternative to mental hospital treatment: III. Economic benefit-cost analysis. *Archives of General Psychiatry*, **37**, 400–405.

Wing, J. K. (1987) Psychosocial factors affecting the long-term course of schizophrenia. In *Psychosocial Treatment of Schizophrenia* (eds J. S. Strauss, W. Böker & H. D. Brenner), pp. 13–29. Toronto: Huber.

The Implementation of Family Work in Everyday Practice

Daniel Hell

Summary

Over the past decade research studies have clearly demonstrated a good effect of family work on the prognosis of high-risk schizophrenic patients. But it is still not known how far relatives of schizophrenic patients are supported in everyday practice and which kind of relatives are particularly at risk to miss the support, information and help needed to develop coping strategies. In a representative study of 278 relatives in Switzerland there was a greater danger of lack of support and information for women than for men, although women carried the greater burden of caring and suffered more from impaired well-being than men. These general findings were significantly influenced by the psychiatric delivery systems used in different subgroups and by the models of schizophrenic illness adhered to. A sectorised system with an integrated organisation of in- and out-patient facilities and emphasis on a social psychiatric model satisfied demands of the studied relatives best.

The value of cooperation between mental health professionals and relatives of schizophrenic patients can no longer be questioned. A number of longitudinal studies have demonstrated that the prognosis of schizophrenic patients (with a high risk of relapse) can be improved, if their nearest relatives are supported systematically (Table 1). Tarrier (1990) has published a recent review of such intervention studies.

Though design of intervention programmes varies from study to study, three therapeutic elements are usually present in one form or another: information, coping with psycho-social problems, and emotional support. It cannot yet be said to what extent these three components and/or their interaction contribute to the success of a programme. It is likely that these intervention strategies will not only be effective with schizophrenics, but with certain categories of non-schizophrenic patients (Smyer & Birkel, 1989). The principles of these strategies might also be useful in non-family contexts such as psychiatric institutions or hostels, which have to deal with their clients' psychotic crises. Intensive support of families is present in all published intervention

181

Table 1. Family therapeutic intervention studies applying EE (EE = expressed emotion) (Source: Hell, 1988)

Author	Country	Sample	Results
Leff et al., 1982	GB	24 schizophrenics with initially "high-EE"-relatives	Within 9 months on neuroleptics: 9 % relapses with family therapy 50 % relapses with conventional treatment
Leff et al., 1995	GB	19 schizophrenics with initially "high-EE"-relatives	Within 24 months on neuroleptics: 20 % relapses with family therapy 78 % relapses with conventional treatment
Falloon et al., 1995	USA	36 schizophrenics from a home with "high-EE"-relatives or great stress	Within 24 months on neuroleptics: 11 % relapses with family therapy 83 % relapses with conventional treatment
Hogarty & Anderson, 1986	USA	88 schizophrenics with "high-EE"-relatives	Within 12 months on neuroleptics: 19 % relapses with only family therapy 36 % relapses with only conventional treatment 0 % relapses with combination of family therapy and social skills training

programmes, although different types of support may be more or less appropriate, depending on the types of patients.

Is it possible, though, to apply this significant research work to everyday psychiatric practice? Clinical work, both in in-patient and out-patient settings, is very different from that of specialised research teams. Patients and their relatives cannot be recruited using strict, uniform criteria. The time available for each patient is limited. Special tests like the Camberwell Family Interview and structured treatment programmes are difficult to use. The psychological implications are also different: in intervention studies, research requires the cooperation of relatives, and this may itself facilitate involved and empathic contact between staff and relatives, which helps to strengthen the self-confidence of the family in caring for the patient.

My Swiss research group has tried in the last few years to resolve the question how far research-based knowledge has been incorporated into everyday practice in the country. These studies were carried out by Germundson and Waldner (1990), and by Huber (1991). Following the work of Creer and Wing (1974), Hatfield (1983), and Holden and Lewine (1982), we have tried to measure the cooperation between mental health professionals and relatives via questionnaires.

To make the selection of the relatives more representative, various groups were selected, in contrast to earlier studies, in which only members of self-help organisations were included. In addition to all members of the Zurich Organisation of Relatives of Schizophrenics (VASK) all relatives of schizophrenic patients, who had made use of one hospital unit's (clinic A) information and group service and all relatives of patients admitted in a given year to another unit (clinic B) received a questionnaire.

Of a total of 445 relatives, 278 responded to the specially developed questionnaire, and 249 completed it without omitting any question (Fig. 1). The general willingness to cooperate in the study was further demonstrated by the fact that 63% of the responding relatives agreed to have a personal interview. The relatively high proportion of responses from a large and rather representative group as well as the additional information obtained from interviews suggest that the study should have been able to provide highly valid data. A detailed description of the methodology and the study groups has been published by Germundson and Waldner (1990). The study groups consist mainly of parents (65%) and spouses (20%) of schizophrenic patients who had been hospitalised several times and for prolonged periods of time (75% for more than six months).

Half of the patients were receiving disability benefits, while about half the relatives interviewed supported the patients financially as well as practically, such as by doing the laundry or, more rarely, other housework. However, many were not able to cope with the patient's illness: about 70% suffered from the change of family atmosphere, 80% said their mental well-being has

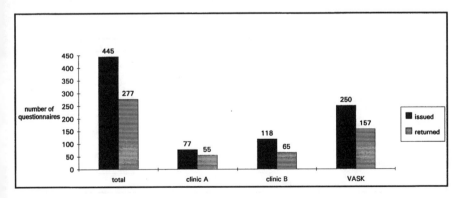

Figure 1. Methodology of the relatives' inquiry: Number of issued and returned questionnaires.

been negatively affected, and 50% worried about their physical capacity to cope with the situation.

The majority (55%) of relatives interviewed said that professionals were either not at all or only slightly interested in their point of view during the whole period of treatment (Fig. 2). The following comments to the questionnaire or interviews illustrate this: "Doctors mostly had no time," "They were only interested in the illness of my husband, not in the family and social context; our family was of no interest," "I missed help and support very much. I only got it when I cried, and then not very much."

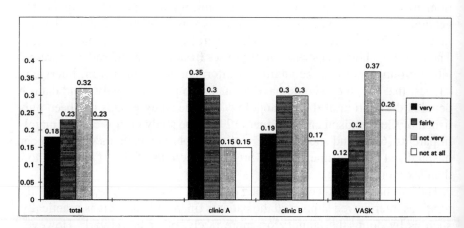

Figure 2. Responses to the question: "To what extent were the professionals interested in your point of view?"

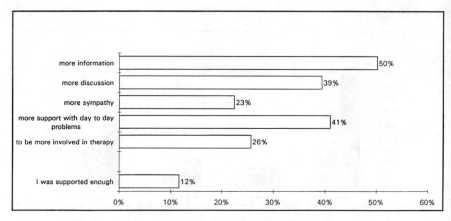

Figure 3. Responses to the question: "Was there any additional care you would have liked?"

Only every sixth relative of the total group felt really accepted by the mental health professionals. This finding, together with other comments, suggests how sensitively relatives of schizophrenic patients react to the non-supportive and unsympathetic behaviour of many mental health professionals, and how important the professionals' receptiveness is for them. This does not mean, though, that the relatives' desire for attention cannot be satisfied in everyday practice: as many as 35% of the relatives of patients of one unit (clinic A), who had received information and group services, felt very well supported and a further 30% felt fairly well supported. The relatives mainly wished for more information (50%), discussion (40%), and support in daily living (41%) (Fig. 3). These results indicate that relatives wish to be regarded less as participants in a therapeutic process than as partners by mental health professionals. Only 26% of the respondents asked for more therapeutic involvement, but more than half expected more information about the patient's illness.

Asked if they would appreciate knowing the diagnosis, only 1% answered negatively, whereas the overwhelming majority (90%) answered positively (Fig. 4); 20% of the respondents had never received any information about the diagnosis, and all of them would have liked some.

The relatives' comments suggested that they felt less stressed by information about the diagnosis of schizophrenia than by doctors' withholding the diagnosis or giving unclear and contradictory information. It is remarkable

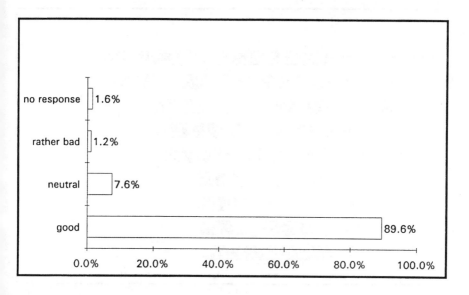

Figure 4. Responses to the question: "Is it (would it be) good to know the diagnosis?"

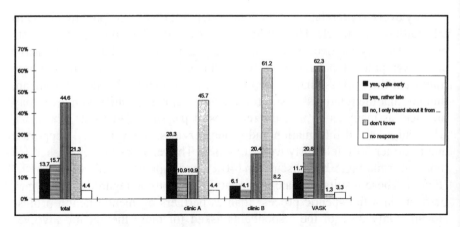

Figure 5. Responses to the question: "Were you told that there was a support group for relatives?"

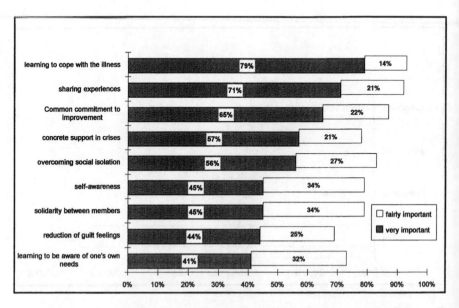

Figure 6. Responses to the question: "What is (was) important for you in a support group?"

186

that diagnostic information was not given more often when patients were hospitalised for longer periods.

Only 44% of the respondents said that the diagnosis had been explained to them, and only 14% had heard from doctors at an early stage about the existence of support groups for relatives (Fig. 5). A further 16% heard about such groups later on. The majority got information about the groups via the media or third parties, but not via mental health professionals; most relatives heard about VASK in the same way. Those who joined this organisation also benefit from its support groups: 80% of the members of VASK who were interviewed in this study took part in group sessions. The relatives who had had group experience rated the importance of support group meetings significantly higher than those who had not so far taken part in a group session (p < 0.001), so that they benefit more from group sessions than they had expected.

The principal potential benefits of joining a group were seen as learning to cope with the illness, exchanging experiences with others, and being able to exert more pressure on the health authorities (Fig. 6); 83% saw relatives' support groups as a mean of escaping social isolation. In this respect, there was an important difference between support groups led by a professional (professional dominance, Katschnig & Konieczna, 1989) and those organised as self-help groups (relative dominance). Self-help groups are more suited for forming new friendships than groups led by professionals: only 4% of the relatives who joined one professionally dominated group (clinic A) described other relatives as being helpful in their difficulties, in contrast to 37% of those who joined a self-help group. It is notable that the VASK strongly encourages private and informal relationships between its members.

Relatives Particularly at Risk

Two subgroups of the relatives responded to the questionnaire in a particular way: the members of VASK and the female relatives (some of whom belong to both groups). The relatives who joined a self-help organisation felt less supported by mental health professionals than others (p < 0.001), but at the same time, they felt more stressed by the illness (p < 0.001) and wanted more support in day-to-day problems (p < 0.001) and more discussions with professionals (p < 0.001). They rated support groups as more important for them (p < 0.01), especially in overcoming social isolation (p = 0.05) and as a way of working for improving mental health care (p < 0.001), than those who were not organised. They saw support groups primarily as a way out of isolation.

Table 2. The composition of the self-help organisation of schizophrenics' relatives (according to surveys).

Author (year, country)	Holden & Lewine (1982, USA)	Hatfield (1983, USA)	Germundson et al. (1990, Switzerland)
number of respondents (rate of questionnaires returned)	203 41%	198 50%	157 63%
of which: parents (in %)	87%	85%	75%
of which: women (in %)	74%	79%	74%
of which: relatives of male patients	71%	62%	69%

It is not possible to judge from the data whether the organised relatives felt freer to voice their dissatisfaction and to speak about the stress they felt than non-organised relatives – or whether conversely, it was their pre-existing higher level of stress and dissatisfaction itself that led to their joining a group.

The members of self-help organisations differed significantly in demographic and social terms from other relatives (Table 2), parents and women both being over-represented. In the whole sample, parents made up only half of the two clinic groups, and men made up about half the total.

Both this study and some in America (Hatfield, 1983; Holden & Lewine, 1982) indicate that mothers, in particular those from the middle and upper social classes are more involved in personal and mental health issues than other relatives. More mothers who are members of self-help groups live with an unmarried schizophrenic son than would be expected by chance. Because they are deeply involved in improving the therapeutic and social help available for their sick family members, such relatives may risk provoking a negative reaction in mental health professionals, if the latter fail to recognise that this group itself needs particular support and that its aims do not conflict with the needs of the patients themselves.

In general, there was a greater danger of lack of support for women than for men. Compared to men, women reported significantly more often that professionals were not very or not at all interested in their point of view ($p = 0.01$); that they received insufficient support from professionals ($p = 0.01$); and that psychiatric diagnosis was not explained to them ($p = 0.01$). Nevertheless, women reported more often than men that their well-being was seriously impaired by the schizophrenic illness in the family. These differences (Germundson & Waldner, 1990) might be explained by the fact that more women than men are members of the VASK. However, in the sub-group who were members of VASK, women felt less accepted and less informed by mental health professionals than men.

Discussion

The finding that female relatives, especially mothers and spouses, who carry the biggest burden, are most in danger of missing information, emotional support, and help in daily living was surprising. However, relatives who carry a heavy burden are often in a state of tension and anxiety, and so not able to communicate calmly (Parker et al., 1988), mental health professionals may feel themselves to be criticised, questioned, or overwhelmed, which can result in a vicious circle. The communication problems between helpers and help-seekers could be further aggravated because the relatives' greatest anxieties are about negative symptoms (such as inactivity, withdrawal or autistic behaviour), which are not visible. Therefore, these anxieties are more difficult to communicate than worries about positive symptoms or aggressive outbursts.

In addition, there are probably many transference problems connected with social role issues between men and women or with the childhood experiences of the mental health professionals. This raises the question: How can the strategies developed by researchers be incorporated into everyday psychiatry practice? Three factors seem to be important: (a) the structure of the delivery system; (b) the model of schizophrenic illness used; and (c) the kind of training mental health professionals receive.

The organisation of the psychiatric delivery system can either facilitate or hinder cooperation with relatives. For instance, the professionals' involvement and cooperation with relatives will be weakened, if there is a lack of continuity between out- and in-patient treatment so that integration of in- and out-patient facilities is a prerequisite of good cooperation between professionals and relatives. In the study discussed above, one unit (clinic A), which most nearly satisfied demands of the relatives, have an integrated organisation of in- and out-patient facilities. However, it is remarkable that 30% of the relatives, have an integrated organisation of in- and out-patient facilities. However, it is remarkable that 30% of the relatives using this clinic still felt inadequately accepted: individual cases showed that some of these relatives received no feedback in the early stages of the patients' treatment or had had previous conflict with the institution. An early initial contact between the mental health professionals and relatives seems to be important for their subsequent willingness to cooperate (MacCarthy et al., 1989).

In addition to the structure of the psychiatric delivery system, the dominant concept of illness might influence the degree of cooperation with relatives. Shepherd and Singh (1992) write: "When professionals have once begun to see schizophrenic patients more as persons who have to cope actively with the same kind of stress and burden as everybody and less as passive victims of an endogenous process, then it becomes more clear that the qualitative aspects of social support are so important." Adherence to either outdated sociological or family models of pathology, or narrow and rigid biological concepts which leave no room for psycho-social aspects can make the cooperation with relatives more difficult. In this context, it is of some interest that only 20% of the relatives themselves in this study think that their behaviour has no influence on the schizophrenic patients.

Cooperation with relatives can also be affected by the professionals' own training, in particular that in family work practice. In England, there are efforts to set up a national training network for family work with schizophrenia, which is aimed primarily at psychiatric nurses, though any psychiatric professional could benefit from the training. A practical guide (Kuipers et al., 1992) forms part of the training materials, which also include video-tapes and a manual. Such initiatives might bridge the gap between successful work done during research and everyday practice – a gap demonstrated in our study of the situation in Switzerland, which is probably no exception to that in many other countries.

References

Carpenter, W. T., Schooler, N. R., Wise, S. S. et al. (1988) Treatment, services and environmental factors. *Schizophrenia Bulletin*, **14** (3), 427–437.

Creer, C. & Wing, J. K. (1979) *Schizophrenia at Home*. Surbiton, England: National Schizophrenia Fellowship.

Germundson, S. & Waldner, P. (1990) *Die Angehörigen von schizophrenen Menschen*. Lizentiatsarbeit, Philosophische Fakultät Universität Zürich.

Hatfield, A. (1983) What families want of family therapists. In *Family Therapy in Schizophrenia* (ed. W. McFarlane), pp. 41–68. London: Guilford Press.

Hell, D. (1988) Angehörigenarbeit und Schizophrenieverlauf. *Nervenarzt*, **59**, 66–72.

Holden, D. F. & Lewine, R. (1982) How families evaluate mental health professionals, resources and effects of illness. *Schizophrenia Bulletin*, **8**, 626–633.

Huber, A. (1991) *Erfahrungen von Angehörigen Schizophreniekranker mit professionellen Helfern*. Doctoral thesis submittid at the MedicalSchool of the University of Zürich.

Katschnig, H. & Konieczna, T. (1989) Was ist in der Angehörigenarbeit wirksam? Eine Hypothese. In *Schizophrenie als systemische Störung. Die Bedeutung intermediärer Prozesse für Theorie und Therapie* (eds W. Böker & H. D. Brenner), pp. 315–328. Bern: Hans Huber.

Kuipers, L., Leff, J. & Lam, D. (1992) *Family Work for Schizophrenia*. London: The Royal College of Psychiatrists.

MacCarthy, B., Kuipers, L., Hurry, J. et al. (1989) Counselling the relatives of the long-term adult mentally ill, I. Evaluation of the impact on relatives and patients. *British Journal of Psychiatry*, **154**, 768–775.

Parker, G., Johnston, P. & Hayward, L. (1988) Parental "Expressed Emotion" as a predictor of schizophrenic relapse. *Archives of General Psychiatry*, **45**, 806–813.

Shepherd, G. & Singh, K. (1992) Zur praktischen Bedeutung des EE-Konzeptes für die Rehabilitation. *Psychiatrische Praxis*, **19**, 72–75.

Smyder, M. A. & Birkel, R. C. (1989) Interventions with families of the chronically mentally ill elderly. In *The Chronically Mentally Ill Elderly* (ed. E. Lipert). Washington DC: US Government Printing Office.

Tarrier, N. (1990) The family management of schizophrenia. In *Reconstructing Schizophrenia* (ed. R. P. Bentall), pp. 254–282. London: Routledge.

Focus on the Concept of Illness and on Coping Aimed at Episode Prevention

Early Pharmacotherapeutic Intervention in Relapse Prevention: Fundamentals, Indication and Management

Wolfgang Gaebel

Summary

Neuroleptic maintenance medication is clearly effective for relapse prevention in schizo-phrenia. However, besides benefits for the majority of patients, there are also failures and/or risks for some patients (e. g., tardive dyskinesia). Since the risk-benefit ratio is often difficult to predict in the individual case, this has stimulated the search for modifications and alternatives to maintenance treatment. In particular, neuroleptic low-dose treatment strategies compare favourably with standard-dose treatment concerning relapse prevention and side effects. Alternatively, based on prodromal symptoms preceding a relapse early intervention, intermittent neuroleptic treatment strategies have been developed. However, recent controlled two-year studies have not confirmed this strategy to be as effective as maintenance treatment in preventing relapse. Therefore, for the majority of patients inter-mittent treatment cannot be recommended.

The efficacy of long-term treatment in schizophrenia has been empirically proven (Davis et al., 1980). The main target of treatment is the prevention of relapse, which can be attained in approximately 70% of patients treated according to standard methods. Thus,the monthly rate of 10% of spontaneous relapse (with placebo) can be reduced to 3% with neuroleptics (Davis, 1985). Although the risk of spontaneous relapse decreases over the course of time, there still remains a significant placebo-verum difference (Hogarty & Ulrich, 1977), providing a strong reason for long-term neuroleptic treatment according to defined criteria (Kissling, 1991). As shown by more detailed analyses, including patients treated with placebo, relapse is not prevented by the suppression of symptoms, but rather the time of their re-occurrence is delayed (Hogarty et al., 1973), though the mechanism of prevention has not yet been clarified. There are transitions to symptom-suppression treatment, whereby neuroleptics are used for the permanent control of symptoms and a reduction or discontinuation of medication leads to their immediate exacerbation.

195

Whereas the long-term prognosis for schizophrenic patients has been improved markedly by long-term neuroleptic treatment, its application is restricted by several factors. Firstly, many patients do not profit from long-term treatment due to their limited degree of compliance, this proportion being estimated at up to 50% for outpatients (Johnson, 1984). Secondly, tardive dyskinesia must be expected to occur in up to about 15% (Gaebel, 1993 a). Finally, an average of 20–30% of the patients are non-responders or only partial responders, while with placebo an approximately similar percentage does not experience any relapse (Hogarty et al., 1974). Though an individual risk-benefit assessment is needed to assess the indication for long-term prophylaxis, few reliable criteria are available to do this.

Two modifications of standard neuroleptic treatment have been investigated as possible alternatives. Low dose long-term treatment – as long as it is not reduced below a certain minimum dosage – has been shown to be equivalent to standard treatment with respect to its prophylactic efficacy, along with a lower incidence of side-effects (Schooler, 1991). This is now widely accepted as an alternative to standard treatment, though in individual cases it may prove to be unsuitable. A second alternative is intermittent treatment with early neuroleptic intervention, which will be discussed below.

Early Pharmacological Intervention

Clinical Aspects

In general, psychotic decompensation does not develop abruptly, but rather stepwise via the intermediate stages of cognitive perceptive loss of control, depressive retreat, affective emotional disinhibition, and prepsychotic thought process over the course of several days (Conrad, 1958; Donlon & Blacker, 1973; Docherty et al., 1978). Based on retrospective reports of patients and relatives, Herz & Melville (1980) found that psychotic relapses are frequently preceded by non-specific prodromal symptoms, such as sleep disturbance, nervousness, and restlessness, as well as depressive mood. The treatment rationale of early neuroleptic intervention was based on the idea that a full-blown psychotic relapse can be prevented at the time of onset of prodromal symptoms by neuroleptic intervention. It was also assumed that with this procedure, the neuroleptics can possibly be discontinued completely during the remitted, psychosis-free intervals and only be readministered if prodromal symptoms re-occur. This treatment strategy has been described as "early intervention, time-limited, targeted pharmacotherapy" (Carpenter &

196

Heinrichs, 1983). Assuming, on the one hand, that longer lasting stability is attainable without neuroleptics and on the other hand, an incipient relapse may be recognised and prevented in time, this alternative promises a temporary exemption from medication and thus a lower life-time exposure to neuroleptics, which might be very important in relation to side-effects.

In fact, this procedure corresponds to what is often practised by the patients themselves under naturalistic conditions: if they feel better following a psychotic decompensation, they often discontinue medication. This is either due to a lack of insight into the necessity for treatment or to side-effects; they may start treatment again, either on their own or on medical advice, in anticipation of a recurrence of illness. This rather unsystematic method can be made use of as a targeted application of drugs, the appropriate therapeutic setting.

Pilot studies confirmed the general feasibility of this treatment strategy, with mainly positive results (Herz et al., 1982; Carpenter et al., 1982; Carpenter & Heinrichs, 1983), and these initial results were then tested under controlled conditions.

Results of Controlled Studies

The main results of controlled two-year studies on early neuroleptic intervention (Carpenter et al., 1987; Jolley et al., 1989, 1990; Carpenter et al., 1990; Herz et al., 1991) are shown in Table 1.

These demonstrate that early neuroleptic intervention treatment produces poorer results in terms of its relapse-preventing efficacy, compared to standard long-term neuroleptic treatment. Jolley et al. (1990) reported significant differences in the relapse rates between long-term medication and early intervention therapy (12% vs. 50%), and Carpenter et al. (1990) reported a significantly higher rate of decompensation per patient (2.8 episodes vs. 4.2). However, Carpenter et al. (1987) found an insignificantly higher rate of relapses – 52% vs. 45%, as did Herz et al. (1991) – 30% vs. 16%. Whereas the social adaptation of the patients was not significantly different under either treatment strategy, the drop-out rates under early neuroleptic intervention were significantly increased in all studies (Carpenter et al., 1990: 51%; Jolley et al., 1990: 56%; Herz et al., 1991: 62%). These results indicate that intermittent neuroleptic treatment is applicable for only a small portion of patients. Finally, all studies demonstrated that while the total neuroleptic dosage under intermittent treatment was lower, the rate of side-effects was not different between the two therapeutic strategies (Jolley et al., 1990; Herz et al., 1991). Quite similar results were found in a recent study by Schooler et al. (1993).

197

Table 1. Two-year results of controlled studies on intermittent neuroleptic, long-term treatment in schizophrenia.

Authors	Diagnosis	Design (n)	Dropout n (%)	Relapse n (%)	Rehosp. n (%)	Social Adapt.	Dose	Side-effects
Carpenter et al., 1987	RDC	random. open cont.(21)	9 (43)	9 (45)	9 (45)	LFS	720	?
				ns	ns	ns	c*	
		targ.(21)	7 (33)	11 (52)	11 (52)		196	
Carpenter et al., 1990	RDC	random. open cont.(59)	11 (19)	2.8	21 (36)	LFS	1.8	?
			**	a*	(*)	**	d**	
		targ.(57)	29 (51)	4.2	30 (53)		1.2	
Herz et al., 1991	RDC/ SADS-L	random. db.plac. maint.(51)	14 (27)	8 (16)	8 (16)	PAS	290	AIMS
			**	ns	ns	ns	c**	ns
		interm. (50)	31 (62)	15 (30)	12 (24)		150	
Jolley et al., 1990	DSM-III	random. db.plac. contr.(27)	9 (39)	3 (12)	2	SAS	1971	EPS / AIMS
			*	**	b(*)	ns	e**	*/ns
		interm.(27)	15 (56)	12 (50)	8		689	

LFS: Level of Functioning Scale
EPS: Extrapyramidal Symptom Scale
SAS: Social Adjustment Scale
PAS: Problem Appraisal Scale
AIMS: Abnormal Involuntary Movement Scale

random.: randomised
cont.: continuous
contr.: controls
db.plac.: double-blind placebo

targ.: targeted
interm.: intermittent
a: decompensations/patient
b: number of admissions
c: mg CPZ equivalents/die

d: mean dose scaling (0–4)
e: neuroleptic total dose (mg haloperidol equivalents)

(*) < .10; * < .05; ** < .01

These results show that the neuroleptic intervention does not prevent relapses to the same extent as long-term neuroleptic treatment.

Up to now it remains unclear why this should be so. The rationale of this treatment strategy is based on the assumption that prodromal symptoms represent valid predictors of relapse, and that in the case of their re-occurrence, reinstitution of neuroleptic treatment may prevent a relapse. However, none of the above-mentioned studies investigated explicitly and prospectively whether or not prodromal symptoms are actually valid predictors of relapse. This fundamental aspect of early intervention was examined though in a German multi-centre study (the ANI study) of long-term intermittent neuroleptic treatment (Pietzcker et al., 1983, 1986; Pietzcker, 1985), supported by the *Bundesministerium für Forschung und Technologie* (BMFT) and carried out at the Psychiatric Departments of the University Hospitals of Berlin, Düsseldorf, Göttingen, and Munich. Altogether, 364 patients who met the specified inclusion criteria were included: 159 (= 44%) of these classified according to ICD-9 and RDC with diagnoses of schizophrenic or schizo-affective psychoses, completed the two-year treatment and observation period. Following a three-months' post-discharge stabilisation phase, the patients were randomly assigned to three treatment strategies and then compared in an open study design.

The three strategies were:

1) *Long-Term Neuroleptic Treatment*
   In this standard treatment strategy, patients were stabilised on a minimal neuroleptic maintenance dosage (100 mg CPZ).

2) *Neuroleptic Early Intervention*
   In this strategy, medication was gradually withdrawn, and was not reinstituted before prodromal symptoms occurred.

3) *Neuroleptic Crisis Intervention*
   In this group also, the medication was discontinued step by step and resumed only on the occurrence of a relapse (crisis), as defined according to psychopathological criteria.

At the beginning of the study, prodromal symptoms were recorded retrospectively for previous relapses by using a modified list of prodromal symptoms (Herz et al., 1980), and were rated again at each therapeutic contact. Table 2 shows the frequency of the six non-specific prodromal symptoms.

Though the occurrence of prodromal symptoms was investigated in all three treatment groups, it was of therapeutic relevance only in the early in-

Table 2. Lifetime prevalence of the most common prodromal symptoms (ANI-study; N = 364). Pietzcker et al., 1993.

Prodromal symptoms	Frequency (%)
Trouble sleeping	83
Restlessness	81
Trouble concentrating	77
Tense and nervous	76
Loss of interest	59
Depression	51

Table 3. Relapse and rehospitalisation rates under intermittent and maintenance neuroleptic long-term treatment of schizophrenic patients (ANI-study; N = 364). Pietzcker et al., 1993.

	Maintenance treatment (N = 122)	Early intervention (N = 127)	Crisis intervention (N = 115)	H* p	(df)
Relapse rate (≥1)	28 (23%)	62 (49%)	72 (63%)	41.6 0.000	(2)
Rehosp. rate (≥1)	29 (24%)	47 (37%)	49 (43%)	9.3 0.009	(2)

* Kruskal-Wallis one-way analysis of variance

tervention group. How far prodromal symptoms, without intermediate neuroleptic intervention, actually predict the occurrence of a relapse, was to be investigated by means of the crisis intervention strategy. Treatment course and outcome were recorded by a number of acknowledged rating scales. The main criteria for the evaluation of therapy were: the rate of relapse and readmission, social adaptation, subjective well-being, total neuroleptic dosage, and side-effects.

In the main, the results of this study are in accordance with those mentioned above: the drop-out rates in the two intermittent therapeutic strategies (early intervention 60%, crisis intervention 67%) were significantly higher than with long-term treatment (43%). This must be attributed to the fact that in patients under intermittent treatment, neuroleptic medication could not be discontinued without an exacerbation of symptoms, so that these subjects had to be removed from the study. These were mainly patients who already showed a poorer level of remission and were receiving higher neuroleptic doses at the beginning of the study. The three treatment strategies differed significantly in terms of their relapse and rehospitalisation rates (Tab. 3).

Table 4. Statistical values (%) of the predictive qualities of prodromal symptoms (ANI-study). Gaebel et al., 1993.

	Maintenance treatment	Crisis intervention	Early intervention
Sensitivity	7.7	10.3	14.4
Specificity	90.3	93.0	70.4
Positive predictive value	21.4	42.9	15.3
Negative predictive value	73.9	67.0	69.0

Though early intervention – as opposed to crisis intervention – prevents relapses to some extent, it still furnishes poorer results than long-term medication.

Gaebel et al. (1993) found that there was no significant relationship between prodromal symptoms and relapse, in particular the predictive validity of prodromal symptoms could not be established in the crisis intervention group. Table 4 lists the corresponding statistical characteristics.

Whereas the comparably high specificity values indicate that non-occurrence (no relapse) along with absence of prodromal symptoms can be predicted fairly well (few false positive predictions), the very low sensitivity values indicate that the occurrence of relapse is not predicted adequately (many false negative predictions). As the low positive predictive value shows, the prodromal symptoms are ambiguous in their predictive quality; in practical terms this means that the occurrence of prodromes can be taken as a potential warning sign which should initiate early intervention. Accordingly, the early intervention strategy was set up with which the base rate of detected prodromes was strikingly high, possibly due to a rater bias. This because the treatment was open and hence the therapists' awareness for monitoring prodromes in early intervention was higher due to their allowance to treat patients in case of prodromes.

Findings with little predictive validity were also reported by Marder et al. (1991) and Johnston-Cronk et al. (1993). The nosologically non-specific prodromal symptoms that were used (Fava & Kellner, 1991) are not of predictive value, especially if the inclusion is neglected of psychotic prodromal symptoms, e. g., hallucinations, which must themselves be considered indicators of relapse. An alternative explanation could be that the mean frequency of contact – at least once every 2–4 weeks – was too little to record all prodromes occurring in between. This assumption is supported by data showing that the success of prodrome-based relapse prediction was higher with shorter intervals of time (Gaebel et al., 1993). Another aspect that might have been relevant is that the study was carried out in the normal outpatient setting of the university centres without any special psychosocial or educational intervention, although the patients were questioned extensively on the occurrence of prodromal symptoms in previous psychotic exacerbations, and enlightened on their potential prognostic value. On the other hand, all the previous studies mentioned had produced similar unsatisfactory results, independent of the intensity of the psychosocial programme that was offered. One task of future research will be the identification of objective markers of episodes, which will allow the earliest, subclinical beginning of an exacerbation of illness to be detected more precisely and in time for preventive action (cf. Birchwood et al., 1992).

These results make clear that a strategy whose rationale of therapy has been based on only unsatisfactorily verified empirical premises cannot be fully efficacious. Yet it is still not clear why in spite of this, early intervention treatment did produce better results than crisis intervention. One possible explanation is that the strategy of treatment in case of doubt has assimilated early intervention to become a kind of low-dose, long-term intervention. As with the previous studies, no differences were found in terms of psychosocial adaptation, subjective well-being, or side-effects between the individual therapeutic regimes. Only the cumulative neuroleptic dosage was significantly lower with intermittent treatment procedures, being the lowest in the early intervention group.

Psychopharmacological and Neurobiological Aspects

How far can our knowledge of psychopharmacological mechanisms of action and their time-course support a neuroleptic early intervention policy? On the one hand, we know that the development of a neuroleptic steady-state plasma level will take between several days to a few weeks. On the other hand, it can be shown by PET technology that with clinical doses of neuroleptics, a saturation of between 65–85% of the dopamine-D_2 receptors occurs in the striatum and probably in other dopaminergic pathways (Sedvall et al., 1986; Farde et al., 1988). If this was the therapeutically decisive mechanism of action, a fast clinical response could be anticipated, but this is not the case. Although clinical onset of action, defined by early psychopathological improvement, can be established within hours to days, and represents one of the most reliable predictors of response (Gaebel, 1993 b), full clinical efficacy develops as a rule only after weeks or months. The underlying mechanisms of this type of therapeutic latency effects are believed to be feedback-directed adaptive processes in the presynaptic neurones which lead over days or weeks to a reduction of activity (blockage of depolarisation), especially in the nigrostriatal and mesolimbic pathways, together with increased inhibitory activities in the mesocortical tracts (Pickar, 1988). The probable reason for this regional differentiation is that only in the former pathways can autoreceptors be found. Both mechanisms together lead to a reduction of activity in the mesolimbic dopaminergic pathways, which is considered to be of therapeutic relevance. Possibly adaptation processes in the glutaminergic system also play a role (Freed, 1988).

A further argument against a simple correlation between receptor blocking and clinical efficacy goes back to the observation that the extent of the blocking seems to be critical for response or non-response (Wolkin, 1990). Responders and non-responders do not differ as to the extent of receptor blockade – a finding which effectively supports previous observations that no differences in plasma levels are present. Thus, therapeutically relevant adaptive mechanisms in the postsynaptic signal transduction systems must be presumed to exist, influencing protein phosphorylation via second- and third-messenger systems and leading to alterations in gene expression (Hyman & Nestler, 1993). This is a possibly differential process in responders and non-responders respectively. These processes – described as the plasticity of neuronal systems under neuroleptic therapy – require some time. The same is true for the reverse process, on withdrawal of drugs, as can be seen from the latencies of three to six months prior to a psychotic relapse, even though the neuroleptics release the receptor within a few days after discontinuation (Wolkin, 1990).

Doubts therefore arise as to the neurobiological fundamentals of early intervention with neuroleptics. Even if one succeeded in recognising and treating a psychotic relapse at an early stage, the published data indicate that it probably takes from some weeks to several months until a new adaptive balance is established of the molecular level. Clinically effective intermittent treatment would only be possible in patients responding relatively fast to the onset of treatment, but reacting to withdrawal only with delay. The results of the ANI study demonstrate that almost one-third of the patients do not satisfy this criterion: 27.7% of those randomly assigned to the interval strategy either could not be discontinued at all within six months or could not be maintained without medication for more than four weeks. Irrespective of this, however, the question remains unanswered how far such repeated interventions in the molecular regulatory dynamics of the neuronal systems could lead to irreversible changes along with impaired therapeutic response in the long run. Such an unfavourable correlation has been suspected, at least in relation to the occurrence of tardive dyskinesia (Jeste et al., 1979). Also, within the conception of the vulnerability-stress model, intermittent neuroleptic treatment leads to a repeated shifting of the balance between vulnerability and protective factors. This must constitute a form of stress, not only in neurobiological, but also in psychological and social terms, as revealed by the results of Herz et al. (1991), which showed a greater family burden from those schizophrenics receiving intermittent treatment.

Indication for Early Neuroleptic Intervention

What is, then, the indication for early neuroleptic intervention? At first, only patients with a prognostically favourable, periodically remitting course, observed in only 20% of clinical populations with long-term follow-up (Huber et al., 1979), should be considered. As a rule, these are also the patients with favourable prognostic characteristics. The early intervention strategy is thus suitable for patients who remit spontaneously, respond completely to neuroleptics, and do not merely show a suppression of symptoms, while fundamental contra-indications are chronic persisting positive symptoms, as well as an unstable course with neuroleptics. Chiles et al. (1989) found that these exclusion criteria were fulfilled in 62% of an unselected sample. However, they also defined additional exclusion criteria: an acute conflict or stress situation or a recent (3–6 months) relapse, which led to hospital admission and after which complete stabilisation had not yet been reached. In addition to these absolute contra-indications, the authors defined relative contra-indications as lack of cooperation (33%) and endangering the self or others (16%), as well as management contra-indications, e. g., lack of relatives or living too far from the hospital. In the end, only 13% of the initial sample remained, for whom intermittent treatment with early intervention would have been indicated. From these data, it is clear that this must be a highly selective treatment strategy whose prophylactic efficacy has not yet been satisfactorily ascertained. Nevertheless, it is beyond question that individual patients do profit from this strategy.

Methods of Early Neuroleptic Intervention

The clinical studies referred to above were carried out with different intensities of psychosocial supporting measures and varying frequencies of contacts. Nevertheless, the results are remarkably similar, although the interpretation of the findings varies, depending on the initial position of the researchers. If the decision in the individual case, based upon the aforementioned criteria, is for intermittent treatment, both the general and individual prodromal symptoms must be discussed with the patient and relatives in detail, so that these become the basis of the therapeutic programme for all concerned. In this way, the threshold of anxious expectation is lowered, reducing any feeling of insecurity, which in turn may be stress-inducing. Models of disease and treatment are therefore essential to the context of treatment, along with psychosocial management. A high frequency of professional contacts with the patient (one per week, more often in case of an acute crisis) is mandatory, with the additional offer of a crisis management available round the clock, including week-ends. In general, this will be provided by the medical emergency service of the hospital, which has to be trained accordingly. However, for the patient this must mean a higher threshold of approach, when the familiar team is not available.

Withdrawal of medication should only take place over several weeks, and if an exacerbation of illness occurs, this strategy is not continued further. If the withdrawal is successful, the phase of observation then begins, with continuous monitoring for prodromal symptoms. In the case of their occurrence, a decision will have to be made for the individual patient whether these are actually early signs of a relapse, or a harmless indisposition. In case of doubt, one can decide to be on the safe side and start early treatment. Many patients who have gained sufficient experience in the course of their disease do this on their own. New medication will be, as a rule, with the same neuroleptic drug and at least the same dosage with which the patient had been stabilised prior to withdrawal. Since all previous side effects may occur again to their full extent, precautions must be taken accordingly. If stabilisation takes place without the occurrence of a psychotic relapse, then the same monitoring procedure will be started once more.

This procedure requires a high degree of continuity and reliability for all concerned. Even if this cannot be achieved, a few individual cases show that the method can be advantageous for those who – without a trial of withdrawal – would have been exposed to long-term neuroleptic treatment, which they do not in fact need. For the majority of the patients, however, this procedure remains an unjustifiable risk.

Conclusions

Thus, low-dose, long-term neuroleptic treatment still represents the most effective and biologically supported method of relapse prevention, which also has more favourable results with respect to all other target criteria, compared with intermittent treatment methods. Yet the question why early neuroleptic intervention produces poorer results has not been clarified. Further studies will have to scrutinise the time factor and the correlation between prodromal symptoms and psychotic relapse, with respect to neurobiological indicators. Undoubtedly, it will also be necessary in the future to search for more effective and safer therapeutic alternatives, in order to minimise the risks of long-term medication. For the present, the conclusion must be that early neuroleptic intervention is not suitable for the majority of patients, and only under certain conditions for individual cases.

References

Birchwood, M., MacMillan, J. F. & Smith, J. (1992) Early intervention. In *Innovations in the Psychological Management of Schizophrenia* (eds M. Birchwood & N. Tarrier), pp. 114–145. Chichester: Wiley.

Carpenter, W. T., Stephens, J. H., Rey, A. C. et al. (1982) Early intervention vs. continuous pharmacotherapy of schizophrenia. *Psychopharmacology Bulletin*, **18**, 21–23.

Carpenter, W. T. & Heinrichs, D. W. (1983) Early intervention, time-limited, targeted pharmacotherapy for schizophrenia. *Schizophrenia Bulletin*, **9**, 533–542.

Carpenter, W. T., Heinrichs, D. W. & Hanlon, T. E. (1987) A comparative trial of pharmacologic strategies in schizophrenia. *American Journal of Psychiatry*, **144**, 1466–1470.

Carpenter, W. T., Hanlon, T. E., Heinrichs, D. W. et al. (1990) Continuous versus targeted medication in schizophrenic outpatients: Outcome results. *American Journal of Psychiatry*, **147**, 1138–1148.

Chiles, J. A., Sterchi, D., Hyde, T. & Herz, M. I. (1989) Intermittent medication for schizophrenic outpatients: Who is eligible? *Schizophrenia Bulletin*, **15**, 117–121.

Conrad, K. (1958) *Die beginnende Schizophrenie*. Stuttgart: Georg Thieme.

Davis, J. M. (1985) Maintenance therapy and the natural course of schizophrenia. *Journal of Clinical Psychiatry*, **11**, 18–21.

Davis, J. M., Schaffer, C. B., Killian, G. A. et al. (1980) Important issues in the drug treatment of schizophrenia. *Schizophrenia Bulletin*, **6**, 70–87.

Docherty, J. P., Van Kammen, D. P., Siris, S.G. et al. (1978) Stages of onset of schizophrenic psychoses. *American Journal of Psychiatry*, **135**, 420–426.

Donlon, P. T. & Blacker, K. H. (1973) Stages of schizophrenic decompensation and reintegration. *Journal of Nervous & Mental Disorder*, **157**, 200–209.

Farde, L., Wiesel, F. A., Halldin, C. et al. (1988). Central D_2-dopamine receptor occupancy in schizophrenic patients treated with antipsychotic drugs. *Archives of General Psychiatry*, **45**, 71–76.

Fava, G. A. & Kellner, R. (1991) Prodromal symptoms in affective disorders. *American Journal of Psychiatry*, **148**, 823–830.

Freed, W. J. (1988) The therapeutic latency of neuroleptic drugs and nonspecific postjunctional supersensitivity. *Schizophrenia Bulletin*, **14**, 269–277.

Gaebel, W., Frick, U., Köpcke, W. et al. (1993 a) Tardive Dyskinesien unter Neuroleptika-Behandlung. *Deutsches Ärzteblatt*, **90**, 1041–1046.

Gaebel, W. (1993 b) Die prädiktorische Bedeutung einer Neuroleptika-Testdosis. In *Therapieresistenz unter Neuroleptikabehandlung* (ed. H. J. Möller), pp. 13–23. Wien: Springer-Verlag.

Gaebel, W. (1993) Early neuroleptic intervention in schizophrenia: Are prodromal symptoms valid predictors of relapse. *British Journal of Psychiatry*, **163** (suppl. 21), 8–12.

Herz, M. I. & Melville, Ch. (1980) Relapse in schizophrenia. *American Journal of Psychiatry*, **137**, 801–805.

Herz, M. I., Szymanski, H. V. & Simon, J. C. (1982) Intermittent medication for stable schizophrenic outpatients: an alternative to maintenance medication. *American Journal of Psychiatry*, **139**, 918–922.

Herz, M. I., Glazer, W. M., Mostert, M. A. et al. (1991) Intermittent vs maintenance medication in schizophrenia. Two-year results. *Archives of General Psychiatry*, **48**, 333–339.

Hogarty, G. E. & Goldberg, S. C. (1973) Collaborative Study Group. Drug and sociotherapy in the aftercare of schizophrenic patients. *Archives of General Psychiatry*, **28**, 54–64.

Hogarty, G. E., Goldberg, S. C., Schooler, N. R. et al. (1974) Drug and sociotherapy in the aftercare of schizophrenic patients. Two year relapse rates. *Archives of General Psychiatry*, **31**, 603–608.

Hogarty, G. E. & Ulrich, F. F. (1977) Temporal effects of drug and placebo in delaying relapse in schizophrenia. *Archives of General Psychiatry*, **36**, 585–590.

Huber, G., Gross, G. & Schüttler, R. (1979) *Schizophrenie: Eine Verlaufs- und sozialpsychiatrische Langzeitstudie*. Berlin: Springer-Verlag.

Hyman, S. E. & Nestler, E. J. (1993) *The Molecular Foundations of Psychiatry*. Washington. APA.

Jeste, D. V., Potkin, S. G., Sinha, S. et al. (1979) Tardive dyskinesia – reversible and persistent. *Archives of General Psychiatry*, **36**, 585–590.

Johnson, D. (1984) Observations on the use of long-acting depot neuroleptic injections in the maintenance therapy of schizophrenia. *Journal of Clinical Psychiatry*, **45**, 13–21.

Johnston-Cronk, K., Marder, S. R., Wirshing, W. C. et al. (1993) Prediction of schizophrenic relapse using prodromal symptoms. *Schizophrenia Research*, **9**, 259.

Jolley, A. G., Hirsch, S. R., McRink, A. et al. (1989) Trial of brief intermittent neuroleptic prophylaxis for selected schizophrenic outpatients: clinical outcome at one year. *British Medical Journal*, **298**, 985–990.

Jolley, A. G., Hirsch, S. R., Morrison, E. et al. (1990) Trial of brief intermittent neuroleptic prophylaxis for selected schizophrenic outpatients: clinical and social outcome at two years. *British Medical Journal*, **301**, 837–842.

Kissling, W. (Ed.) (1991) *Guidelines for Neuroleptic Relapse Prevention in Schizophrenia*. Berlin: Springer-Verlag.

Marder, S. R., Mintz, J., Van Putten, T. et al. (1991) Early prediction of relapse in schizophrenia: an application of Receiver Operating Characteristics (ROC) methods. *Psychopharmacology Bulletin*, **27**, 79–82.

Pickar, D. (1988) Perspectives on a time-dependent model of neuroleptic action. *Schizophrenia Bulletin*, **14**, 255–268.

Pietzcker, A. (1985) A German multicenter study on the long-term treatment of schizophrenic outpatients. *Pharmacopsychiatry*, **18**, 333–338.

Pietzcker, A., Gaebel, W., Köpcke, W. et al. (1986) A German multicenter study on the neuroleptic long-term treatment of schizophrenic patients. Preliminary report. *Pharmacopsychiatry*, **19**, 161–166.

Pietzcker, A., Gaebel, W., Köpcke, W. et al. (1993) Intermittent versus maintenance neuroleptic long-term treatment in schizophrenia: Two-year results of a German multicenter study. *Journal of Psychiatric Research*, **27**, 321–339.

Schooler, N. R. (1991) Maintenance medication for schizophrenia: strategies for dose reduction. *Schizophrenia Bulletin*, **17**, 311–324.

Schooler, N. R., Keith, S. J., Severe, J. B. et al. (1993) Treatment strategies in schizophrenia: effects of dosage reduction and family management on outcome. *Schizophrenia Research*, **9**, 260.

Sedvall, G., Farde, L., Persson, A. et al. (1986) Imaging of neurotransmitter receptors in the living human brain. *Archives of General Psychiatry*, **43**, 995–1005.

Wolkin, A. (1990) Positron Emission Tomography in the study of neuroleptic response. In *The Neuroleptic-Nonresponsive Patient: Characterization and Treatment* (eds B. Angrist & S. C. Schulz), pp 37–49. Washington: APA.

Coping-Orientated Therapy with Schizophrenic Patients: General Guidelines, Starting Points and Issues of Evaluation

Karl Heinz Wiedl

Summary

An approach for developing coping-orientated therapy is presented, which is based on three distinct conceptual foundations: Empirical results of coping research, knowledge concerning specific functional impairments in schizophrenic patients, and theoretical arguments derived from the transactional model of coping. Within the latter issue, the concepts of a "functional concept if disease" and a "functional concept of self," including expectations of self efficacy, are of paramount importance. Next, a programme is described for working with groups of schizophrenic patients, where cognitive and behavioural competence related to the three conceptual bases are developed by systematic application of different techniques of intervention. An illustration is given, describing a programme conducted in clinical practice and comprising about 50 sessions. For guiding the implementation of the programme and for testing its efficacy, different approaches of evaluation are proposed: Process evaluation using naturalistic data, evaluation of general effectivity at different levels (knowledge, behaviour, subjective concepts, attributions, quality of life) and estimation of differential effects with regard to the problem of differential indication.

The present paper deals with the transposition of results from basic research on coping with disease and various problems of daily living to therapeutic action. From the standpoint of philosophy of science, this is a controversial issue, which becomes even more complicated when empirical knowledge is insufficient (Wiedl, 1994). At the same time, and due to the importance of the concept of coping within the framework of modern aetiopathogenetic theories of schizophrenia (Liberman, 1986; Yank et al., 1993), there is a strong demand for methods of coping-orientated intervention, which are applicable and effective in clinical practice (for examples see Wiedl, 1991; Borst, 1992; Stark, 1992).

The levels and contents of coping theory and research which provide a basis for a systematic development of coping-orientated therapy will be discussed below as well as research findings on schizophrenia which may also be helpful in designing the therapeutic setting. How this approach can be put into practice will be illustrated with the help of a treatment concept which has been developed clinically. Due to the current state of knowledge (for a more comprehensive review and discussion see Wiedl, 1994; Wiedl & Schöttner, 1989), this paper is restricted to general guidelines on coping-orientated therapy, which have to be transformed into concrete therapeutic action (see Saupe et al., 1991).

Guidelines and Starting Points

The transformation of basic research into therapeutic concepts takes place within a social-normative framework, where the scientific community defines the approaches that should be considered (Perrez, 1989). As I have proposed elsewhere (Wiedl, 1993, 1994), the basic concepts of coping chosen to be translated into therapeutic action should meet the following criteria: their theoretical underpinnings should be relevant to prevalent models of mental disorder and health; their parameters should be basically treatable within the current framework of therapy or rehabilitation; their conceptual formulation and degree of complexity should permit empirical evaluation.

The model of coping proposed by Lazarus et al. (see Lazarus & Launier, 1978), which focuses on the perceptions, appraisals, emotions, and behaviour generated in the face of stressful events and on the interactions between these units, seems to meet these criteria. The issue of which therapeutic contents can be derived from the theoretical foundations of this transactional model of coping will be examined here. This focus is necessary, since empirical results from coping research have not proved to be sufficient for the development of coping-orientated therapy (see above; Wiedl, 1994). Yet however inconclusive these findings might be, they are helpful in delineating areas to be considered in therapy. A third principle guiding the development of therapy stems from research on specific impairments in schizophrenic patients; it can be assumed that these also have detrimental effects on the process of therapy. This raises the question as to the settings or procedures which may be helpful in minimising such harmful effects. Table 1 presents these general guidelines for the conceptualisation of coping-orientated therapy.

Table 1. Empirical and conceptual bases of coping-orientated therapy for schizophrenic patients.

Basis	Starting Points	Examples of Salient Concepts
	Multiple stress (related to disease, environment and self)	– Encomposing concept of illness – Daily Hassles – Stressful life events
	Appraisals; Relation of appraisals to actions	– Validity of perceptions/appraisals – Rule-conformity in coping
Results form research on coping with schizophrenia	Sociability of coping	– Social support, social comparison; – Environmental intervention
	Coping resources	– Cognitive abilities – Orientation variables (e. g., sense of coherence)
	Effects of course of disease on coping (vicious circles)	– Concept of disease; health beliefs; – Orientation in life
	Effects of psycho-pathology on coping (coping breakdown)	– Coping breakdown – Apparent futility of coping
Salie nt components of coping theory	Higher-order regulation of coping subject-object differentiation	– Functional concept of disease (i. e., vulnerability-stress-coping- competence model; comprehensibility; demystification) – Functional concept of self (i. e., efficacy-expectations; locus of control)
Results from research on disturbances that may affect participation in therapy	Cognitive impairments (attention, memory, concept-formation, etc.)	– Compensation directed at the process of therapy – e. g., visualisation, mnemonics – e. g., adequacy of social settings for therapy
	Social impairments (social overstimulation, social skills, etc.	

Basic Assumptions on Coping with Stress and Illness

Two implicit yet basic assumptions of the transactional model of coping seem to be useful guiding principles for the conceptualisation of coping-orientated therapy. First, coping is a complex process of transaction between person and environment. An examination of the particular variables involved in this process may be informative for scientific purposes and helpful in certain clinical cases (see Wiedl & Schöttner, 1989 a,b; Schaub, 1993). However, coping requires integrating components which, in the face of variations of behavioural parameters due to aspects of the situation, time, or state of the person, still retain a certain degree of constancy; these can thus be used to predict adaptational outcome or the development of generalisable coping resources. Folkman and Lazarus (1980) proposed focusing on the level of *general* opinions and attitudes for this purpose. Results from schizophrenia research support this approach, i. e., there is a definite relationship between insight into psychosis and recognition of being ill using different criterion, and outcome measures (Lange, 1981; see also McGlashan & Carpenter, 1981; Linden, 1982; Linden et al., 1988). Also central to the transactional coping model is the assumption that coping is a process of dealing with subjectively relevant situations or events, characterised by appraisals which are directed at demands ("primary appraisal") or one's own options of action ("secondary appraisal"). However, while the object of coping is explicitly conceptualised in terms of stressful states or events, neither the subject of coping nor its relation to the object are explained within the model. The implicit assumption underlying this concept of appraisal is that a subject is capable of placing him/herself at a distance to stressful situations which constitute the object of coping. Although this assumption seems to be self-evident, as far as external demands are concerned, it has implications for coping with psychosis. It means that – apart from certain things (see Wiedl & Schöttner, 1991) – inner experiences and subjectively experienced changes (e. g., symptoms, physical or psychological states or resources) must be transferred "outside," and defined as objects to be dealt with. The concept of subject-object-distinction can be used as a basis for conceiving therapeutic approaches. Based on an expanded version of Linden's concept of disease in schizophrenia (Linden et al., 1988), this subject-object distinction generated by the person receiving treatment should be conceptualised with the help of two constructs: the "functional concept of disease" and the "functional concept of self."

Consistent with Süllwold and Herrlich's use of the term (1990), the functional concept of "disease" refers to the range of cognitions (opinions, knowledge, appraisals, linguistic codings, anticipations, models of explanation, etc.), which can help schizophrenic patients understand their affliction, and equip them to deal with it effectively. Its distinctive features include "comprehensibility" (see Antonovsky, 1979) and related concepts (i. e., demystification), as well as a focus on the dynamic aspects of psychopathology and outcome in schizophrenia. These properties are well described in the vulnerability-stress-coping-competence model of schizophrenia (Zubin & Spring, 1977; Liberman, 1986). Rules as to which kind of behaviour is helpful in dealing with certain demands specific to schizophrenia (i. e., prevention of relapse) can be derived from this model. These cognitions constitute the field which requires explanation and elaboration in therapy.

We define the functional concept of self as the cognitions about the self (perceived subjective attitudes) and relations of the self to the environment (objective/attitudes), which facilitate dealing with the external world. Fruitful ideas concerning the nature of these can be found in the work of Strauss (1989), which focuses on the role of the self in coping with schizophrenia. Of great importance is Bandura's theory of self-efficacy, which conceptualises outcome expectancies, efficacy expectancies, and expectancies of futility (1978). The latter aspect is of particular relevance, since poor coping efficacy due to absent or depleted personal or social resources (e. g., loss of continuity in housing or work) may often occur in schizophrenic patients. Working with realistic expectations of futility is thus an important supplement to the development of expectancies of efficacy. A more detailed elaboration of this theory and its possible impact on coping-orientated therapy is given elsewhere (Wiedl, 1994). Figure 1 gives an illustration of our basic concepts.

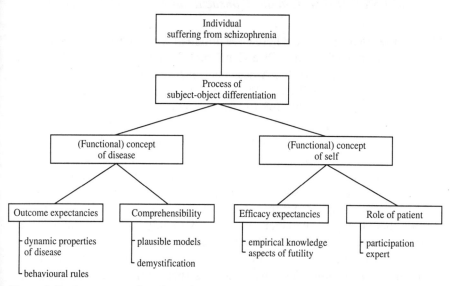

Figure 1. Basic concepts of coping-orientated therapy.

213

The initial question to be considered is which measures or techniques can be used to bring about a subject-object distinction: there is a need for those which externalise and make internal reactions or processes, knowledge and experience tangible. The "Metaplan Technique" (see below) may be helpful for this purpose, as well as creative techniques at different levels. Also, verbal coding of relevant aspects of the persons' subjective experience ("labelling," Süllwold & Herrlich, 1990) seems to be most important; further suggestions are described elsewhere (Wiedl, 1993, 1994). For a functional concept of disease, it is important to elaborate with the patient those features of psychosis which are accessible to change. Also, descriptions and explanations require clarification, and this helps to deal with psychosis both at a cognitive and an emotional level (Süllwold & Herrlich, 1990). According to Bandura (1978), the following aspects play a vital role in the development of a functional concept of self in the process of therapy: reactivating existing coping skills and acquiring new ones; systematically encouraging and reinforcing active participation and collaboration in patients; and proceeding according to the principles described in the concept of self-organised learning, which focus on goal-setting, selection of methods, feedback process, etc. (see Greif, Finger & Jerusel, 1993). Further descriptions are given elsewhere (Wiedl, 1993, 1994).

Empirical Studies Based on the Transactional Model of Coping

Most of the results presented here were obtained with the help of two methods developed in our laboratory: The Osnabrück Inventory of Stress & Coping (OBBI) and the Diary for the Assessment of Stress & Coping, including an interview (TEBBI; see Wiedl, 1992 a,b). The results can be summarised as follows (Wiedl, 1993; 1994 for a more detailed presentation): Although nearly all the subjects reported severe distress in different areas of life, that related to the symptoms of schizophrenia was considered to be the most distressing. This implies that coping-orientated therapy should help patients to deal with multiple life stresses and disease-related problems, rather than enhancing general problem-solving skills. It should also focus on the perception and appraisal of stress, the transposition of these cognitions to action, and on the fact that coping is characterised by an extremely poor social functioning in persons with schizophrenia. Since the beneficial effects of social support, social comparison, etc. will be impeded, we can infer a reduction in the effectiveness of coping. The implication is that coping-orientated therapy should include working in groups.

214

When working with coping behaviour in general, the direct relationship between coping processes, symptoms, and the intra-episodic course of the illness should be taken into consideration. This may imply that the ability to make use of one's personal and social resources may either be completely or partially diminished in the short run. Hence, a further goal of coping-orientated therapy is to acquire sensitivity and candour concerning one's limitations in coping competence (i. e., futility due to such factors as cognitive disorders, dysfunctional states of autonomous arousal, etc.). Finally, experiences related to the long-term course of the disease have detrimental effects on coping. The magnitude of the dysfunctional impacts on processes of appraisal and causal attribution, as well as on the coping strategies endorsed, are probably related to the duration of the disease and frequency of hospital admission. Analysing the patient's life from the perspective of the habitual strategies of adaptation that are mobilised and of an effort to make them more functional, should thus constitute an important field of therapeutic work.

Modification or Compensation?

Cognitive disturbances, especially those pertaining to attention and the working memory (Rund & Landrø, 1990) which are related to schizophrenia, may hinder patients' participation in therapy, and thus have a detrimental effect on outcome (for an example see Mueser et al., 1990). The concept of intervention should therefore be broadened to include differentiation between modification and compensation (see Wiedl, 1984, 1985; Carlson & Wiedl, 1992).

Modification is directed at changing functions or structures permanently, and thus corresponds to our notion of therapy or skill training. Compensation brings about changes that rely on the presence of help that is "prosthetic" or "catalytic" by nature (Wiedl, 1985). Thus, compensatory changes are adequate, yet durable only for the span of intervention. A good example of a compensatory measure is the "Metaplan-Technique," which has become popular both in adult education and in company training programmes. The material consists of flash cards designed by the patients themselves, depicting cognitive items which are considered to be relevant topics. These items can be kept present in the working memory, classified, reclassified, supplemented, etc. One of its advantages lies in the guidance of processes of finding, structuring, and problem-solving (see Bataillard, 1984). Further techniques which may also be useful in supporting memory functions and focusing attention include visualisation, signal cards, etc.

Apart from the cognitive domain, schizophrenic patients often show evidence of impairments in social functions (e. g., research on expressed emotion, Olbrich, 1983; Stark & Buchkremer, 1992). De Vries and Delespaul (1989) showed that there is a relationship between the degree of stress experienced by schizophrenic patients and the number of persons present. This finding highlights the risk involved in group therapy – a measure otherwise indicated to enhance sociability in relation to coping. This problem may be counteracted by dividing a group of six to eight persons into smaller groups of two to three to work on a prescribed task, or breaking a problem down into smaller component parts.

A Coping-Orientated Programme for Groups of Schizophrenic Patients

General Features

The programme presented here was developed on the conceptual basis described above, and has been utilised in clinical practice in recent years (see Wiedl, 1991). The term "programme" does not imply a highly structured sequence of single methods and techniques, but rather the consequent application of the principles outlined above. It consists of both individual and group therapy, and was originally developed for remitted or partially remitted in- and out-patients of a rehabilitation clinic. It is currently being implemented in a rehabilitation unit (Weig & Wiedl, 1995), operated in keeping with the treatment philosophy presented above. Training is conducted in groups of six to eight patients, meeting one hour a week for about a year.

Group therapy begins with an intensive planning phase, which enables participants to perceive themselves as taking an active role in therapy consistent with both the concept of self-organised learning and the functional concept of self. Methods of Metaplan (Bataillard, 1984, see above) lend transparency and structure to this process, and enable the therapists to point out the relevant steps systematically, and to reinforce the participants' contributions. The activities engaged in include generating, collecting, and classifying questions, evaluating and ranking ideas, making decisions, etc. Each step is recorded, so as to provide a mnemonic and a frame of reference for ongoing work (compensation for impairments of memory and attention, see above). These procedures require the use of such visual aids and equipment as posters, flip-charts, adjusting mechanisms, etc. After establishing the goals to be pursued, the targeted topics are worked on and terminated by regular feedback sessions, used as an instrument to ensure ongoing participation and responsibility in the group members. Group sessions are systematically recorded, resulting in a therapy manual which is

Table 2. Example of coping-orientated group therapy.

Session	Topics	Methods
2	Planning of goals, content, organisation	Metaplan
4	Mental disease: concepts, symptoms, different forms, diagnoses	Pair interviews, metaplan
6	Etiology: subjective models, vulnerability-stress-coping-model, implication for prognosis and treatment	Self-assessment inventories (causes of schizophrenia, basic disturbances, FBF), metaplan,, pair interviews
2	Communication on mental disease and treatment	Role-plays
2	Feedback, evaluation of work-plan	"Flashlight"; inventory; discussion
6	Early symptoms: identification, obstacles to action, agenda for crises	Inventory, pair interview, role-play (confidential person); checklist
2	Feedback, evaluation of work plan	"Flashlight," inventory, discussion
2	Stressful events (I): Identification, ranking	Flash cards, pair interview, metaplan
6	Stressful events (II): Behavioural training (i. e., "feeling lonely")	Problem analysis, discussion,, role-plays
3	Stressful events (III): Personal styles of coping (disease and problems in daily life)	Coping inventory; small-group discussion
2	Feedback, problems with ongoing vulnerability, evaluation of work plan	"Flashlight" inventory; planning techniques
4	Medication	Pair interviews, metaplan, interview with expert
1	Feedback, evaluation of work-plan	"Flashlight," inventory
5	Stressful events (IV): work problems	Pair interview, role-play (including video-feedback)
1	Feedback	"Flashlight," inventory
3	Planning future activities	Planning-techniques; discussion with invited persons (service facilities)

written by and for those who have actually worked with the therapy programme. At the end of every session, group members are asked to note the problem areas, which warrant further consideration in individual therapy. From the beginning, the principle of sociability in coping is given explicit consideration in group work. A useful procedure is working in small groups who are instructed in a way that enhances sociability, e. g., interviewing a confederate about his typical early symptoms of illness, sharing symptoms with the group. Furthermore, role playing can be used to teach and practice the competencies which are needed for sociable coping e. g., talking with relatives about issues of schizophrenia; asking adequate questions to clarify a stressful job situation. Generally, the development of and adherence to social norms and behavioural rules are given ongoing consideration, i. e., respecting others' privacy, explicitly saying when one does not want to talk about a certain issue. The advantages of sociability in coping are considered and reinforced by the therapists.

Encouraging active participation in planning and decision-making might result in patients omitting or avoiding important issues in therapy (prevention of relapse, medication, etc.), even though this fear has not been confirmed in clinical practice. On the contrary, the problem area "causes of the disease" is always designated for discussion. In elaborating this topic, the heuristic value of the vulnerability-stress-coping-competency model can be used to discuss the issues of early symptom management, stress management, and medication management. Our "open" approach does not exclude the use of highly structured modules, such as those developed by Liberman et al. (see 1990). Instead, the inclusion of a treatment method which is consistent with the concept of self-organised learning might be indicated. Table 2 gives an illustration of the topics that were elaborated in one of our groups.

Outline of the Programme

After the end of the planning phase, "mental disease" was the first topic to be considered. First, concepts of the disease (see above: "functional concept of disease") were collected and discussed using Metaplan-Techniques and – when necessary – were amplified so as to correspond to the basic ideas of the vulnerability-stress-coping-competence model. For individual clarification and anchoring of the concept of vulnerability, the Frankfurter Beschwerde Fragebogen (The Frankfurt Questionnaire of Complaints, Süllwold, 1986) or an abridged version of this instrument (Schöttner et al., 1988) can be used. In addition, Süllwold and Herrlich (1990) have provided therapeutic methods for subsequent work with the patient's experience of vulnerability. Next, from the vulnerability-stress-coping-competence model, differentiations were attained that were helpful in structuring a second topic, i.e., prevention and treatment, that the patients had agreed on in the planning phase. This topic is divided into various problem areas, including management of early symptoms, stress or straining demands; adaptation to ongoing vulnerability, and the issue of how vulnerability can be compensated for by medical treatment or even be reduced with the help of long-term psychotherapy.

In the module on "early symptoms," the principles outlined above were likewise applied so as to generate a "crisis checklist" specifying typical prodromal signs ("warning signs"), persons to contact, ways of relating to these significant others, and adequate ways of behaving in case of emergency. An important issue was why most patients suffer from relapses even though about 70–80% can identify and treat prodromal features (see Thurm & Häfner, 1987). Consequently, conditions which might prevent adequate monitoring of early symptoms in any individual case were elaborated. It became clear that shame and fear concerning the consequences of relapse were the critical issues, and that these feelings, rather than the identification of early symptoms, prevent an adequate reaction.

In the next module – "dealing with stress" – the procedures described above were first supplemented by self-assessment inventories, which are derived from empirical studies on distressing events described by schizophrenic persons (e.g., Angermeyer & Klusmann, 1988). After generating lists of the situations experienced as stressful, situations were selected for role-play. The method used was taken from the programme developed by Feldhege and Krauthan (1979); video-recording and feedback proved to be helpful. The next step involved the assessment and elucidation of the issue of personal coping style and its functional or dysfunctional effects with the help of the abridged version of the Stress-Inventory developed by Janke et al. (1985, Stress-Verarbeitungs-Fragebogen). In some cases, this issue was also followed up in individual therapy.

The next module – "medication problems" – which is part of a larger topic on ongoing vulnerability, involves three steps: In the preparatory phase, questions were collected and ordered with the help of pair interviews, brain storming, metaplan-techniques, etc. Then, an expert (doctor) was invited to answer and discuss these questions with the group. Finally, knowledge and experience acquired from these two steps was specified, expanded, and discussed in the group.

On special request, the module concerning stress was expanded to include the problem of dealing with stress at work. Based on the analysis of real-life problems and the use of role plays, reducing stress by means of clear and unambiguous communication is practised. Group therapy ends with a discussion on how to continue therapy on a private basis. Also, the issue of ongoing vulnerability was considered, whereby the goal was to stimulate motivation for psychotherapy.

A Strategy of Evaluation

Introduction of innovative treatment methods which lack an adequate empirical foundation requires an explicit link between the fields of basic research and methodology, empirical research, application, and evaluation (see Wiedl, 1994). Different levels of analysis are proposed for the evaluation of our approach. First, the efficacy of the approach has to be evaluated with regard to its goals. Since these goals were derived from the transactional model of coping, basic parameters of this model should be used to define criteria of evaluation. A second point results from the fact that schizophrenia is a disorder with a wide range of clinical features, impairments, aetiology, developmental influences, and effects of previous treatment. The assessment of differential efficacy and indications is thus necessary. Finally, a third guideline is derived from the global context which surrounds the implementation of the approach: the approach is new and thus needs procedural guidance and modification. It is part of a complex treatment setting, involving overlapping forms of treatment, which interact with each other. This therapeutic approach is applied to persons who – by definition – suffer from a specific vulnerability to life stress, in particular social stress, and thus show a certain risk of decompensation. This risk has to be accounted for when assessing the risk of relapse. Evaluation must therefore be directed to the process of intervention.

Process Evaluation

Targets of analysis include participation in group activities, results of group work, and attempts at transferring the gains of therapy to daily life. Assessment of these issues requires systematically recording the information which has been disseminated in the course of group work, thereby preventing further stress for the patients and reducing the risk of reduced validity due to reactive measurement. The latter may occur when repeated application of additional assessment causes effects in the patients, which tend to be confounded with the specific effects intended by the therapeutic approach.

An initial source of information of this kind is the feedback-rounds ("flashlights"), which are regularly conducted after termination of a module and used for procedural regulation. Further information can be derived from some

220

Table 3. Process-evaluation using naturalistic data.

Goals	Method	Time
Procedural steering	"Flashlight" rounds Analysis of metaplan-documentation	End of thematic units After application (continuously)
Coordination with other therapy measures	Memory cards for individual problems	Every session
Control of relapse risk	Memory cards (s.a.) Rating of strain Assessment instruments used in group works,	After application (continuously)

of the techniques of self-assessment (inventories, scales) mentioned above and from the metaplan-technique itself. Since the latter method is aimed at guiding procedural sequencing by documenting its different steps, it also lends itself to process evaluation, i. e., when discrete steps of work are recorded separately (i. e., using video or photographs). Problems due to group processes can also be assessed, when patients make a note of the issues which they want to follow up with their individual therapist (see above). This card is kept by the individual therapist and can thus (with the permission of the patients) also be used for documentation and coordination. Whether the course of work in the group has any impact on coping with the strains of daily living can be assessed by repeated administration of the OBBI (abridged and specified form), or with the help of TEBBI. Table 3 summarises the methods described and gives further information on procedural sequencing.

Evaluation of General Efficacy

As suggested above, efficacy should be evaluated using variables that can be defined on the basis of the transactional model of coping. Table 4 lists variables which are relevant in this regard.

According to this model, effective coping as well as subject-object differentiation presumes sufficient knowledge of the object of coping. This kind of knowledge can be assessed either with the help of scales developed by Pitschel-Walz et al. (1993), or with modified and expanded versions of these scales. Central to the model are the assumptions on a functional concept of self or functional concept of the disease. Methods for assessment do not exist, and thus have yet to be developed. The question also needs to be considered

221

Table 4. Evaluation of general efficacy.

Levels of Assessment	Concepts and Methods
Knowledge	General knowledge about disease (e. g., Pitschel-Walz et al., 1993) Individual knowledge about disease (e. g., early symptoms as experienced, typical strains)
Subjective concepts	Functional Concept of Disease (to be developed; also scales devised by Linden et al., 1988) Functional Concept of Self (to be developed; also: efficacy expectations, Krampen (1981); Sense of Coherence, Hölzl & Reiter (1992)
Attributions	Mental Health Locus of Control Scale (Hill & Bale, 1980) Kontrollüberzeugung von Krankheit und Gesundheit (KKG, Lohaus & Schmitt, 1989)
Operative concept of self/disease	Version of the Osnabrück Inventory of Strains & Coping (OBBI, in prep.; see Schöttner et al., 1988)
Special Insight	Rating according to Schaub (1993)
Coping in real-life situations	Osnabrück Inventory of Strains & Coping (OBBI, Schöttner et al., 1988) and Diary for the Assessment of Strains & Coping (TEBBI, Wiedl & Rauh, 1994)
Effects at global level	Quality of Life; Subjective well-being (e. g., Lehman, 1983; Lauer, 1993)

whether measures of perceived self-efficacy (Krampen, 1981) or "sense of coherence" (Antonovsky, 1979; see Hölzl & Reiter, 1992 for methodological issues) have a shared variance with the functional concept of self. Internal versus external locus of control with regard to stress related to a mental disease also seems to pertain to the assessment of these constructs (see Hill & Bale, 1980; for further discussion see Wiedl, 1994). The subjective concepts just mentioned are usually assessed in inventories, and thus probably indicate cognitive representations and general orientations. Apart from this, the activation of these concepts in concrete problem situations is of interest, since translation of concepts into action often seems to be impaired in schizophrenic patients (Wiedl et al., 1992). Thus, assessment of operative concepts (i. e., Operative Concept of Self, Operative Concept of Disease) is also needed. Special scales are currently being developed in our laboratory based on the OBBI and TEBBI. Likewise, insight into illness can be assessed at a behavioural level with the help of a scale devised by Schaub (1993).

Coping-orientated therapy should bring about changes in coping, which we prefer to assess at a behavioural level, as defined by the transactional theory. These instruments (OBBI, TEBBI, see above) are described elsewhere in more detail (Wiedl, 1992 a,b; Wiedl & Schaub, 1994).

In accordance with its transactional definition, coping cannot be assumed to *always* lead to solutions. However, it does make it possible for stress to be "tolerated, minimised, reduced" (Lazarus & Launier, 1978). Parameters of effectivity derived from models of problem-solving do not fit this definition. In accordance with Filipp and Klauer (1991), we propose including quality of life and subjective well-being to improve the assessment of coping effectivity. A scale which is usable with people suffering from schizophrenia was developed by Lehmann (1983; see also Lauer, 1993).

Perception and appraisals of stress, coping, and coping outcomes are parameters central to the transactional approach. Consequently, these parameters should not only be assessed in the "coper," but in significant others i. e., all the persons, relatives, professionals, spouses, who are involved in the process of coping with the manifold strains that are related to schizophrenia. Inclusion of key persons may contribute to a greater understanding of the effects of therapy on the one hand, while factors which influence the effects of coping-orientated therapy may be uncovered on the other (e. g., different subjective criteria or adaptive coping; Wiedl & Schöttner, 1989 b).

Differential Efficacy and Indications

Prevalent levels of analysis and methods of assessment in clinical research are listed in Table 4. An exception is the level of health beliefs, which integrates concepts dealing with appraisals and specific cognitions. This approach is compatible with the transactional model of coping. Also, it has proved useful in different areas of health psychology (see Basler, 1992). For instance, substantial group differences were found in the development of readiness to carry out health-related behaviour and maintain it even in case of relapse. Weinstein (1988) proposed a stage-model of preventive behaviour ("precaution adoption process"), distinguishing five stages of processing threatening information concerning illness or health, and vulnerability. Only at the final stage are cognitions conducive to preventive behaviour. Assessment of this kind of cognition and their mediating effects on coping-orientated therapy should contribute to the clarification of differential effects. Adequate instruments for diagnosis have yet to be developed, however.

A further problem in the evaluation of differential efficacy is related to the effect of therapy, which covaries with the following factors: awareness of risks, availability of coping resources, and attrition of resources due to clinical symptoms and cognitive dysfunctions. The differential assessment of the effects of therapy calls for the use of a wide range of levels and methods of

Table 5. Measures of differential effects.

Levels of Assessment	Concepts/Methods
Psychotherapy	Usual methods (PSE 10, PPHS, BPRS, SANS, SAPS, Prognostic Scales, etc.)
Clinical documentation	Diagnosis, course, duration of disease; frequency and length of hospitalisation; family situation (e. g., PPHS, GAF)
Markers of vulnerability	Experimental or psychometric methods (e. g., SAT, CPT)
Instrumental cognitive abilities	Intelligence, memory, attention and concentration (usual tests)
Self-concept	Frankfurt Self-Concept Scales (FSK)
Health beliefs	To be developed (e. g., according to Weinstein, 1988)

analysis, as described in Table 5. Identification of idiosyncratic changes must be determined using single-case analysis, based on adequate psychometric algorithms, rather than analysis at the group level (Wiedl & Schöttke, 1993). Only then it will be possible to give adequate answers to questions concerning the differential indications for coping-orientated therapy.

Conclusion

Psychotherapy for schizophrenic persons takes place within a context of daily life marked by persistent and recurring stress, and the apparent futility of coping. In line with our concept of intervention, which incorporates the aspects of modification and compensation, coping-orientated therapy should be supplemented by compensatory measures depending on the patient's vulnerability to life stress and the futility of his/her coping efforts, which in turn are related to therapy or to autochthonous development. This is in line with recent conclusions on the treatment implications of vulnerability concepts, which involve the dynamic integration of modifying and supportive measures (Yank et al., 1993).

References

Angermeyer, M. C. & Klusmann, D. (1988) The causes of functional psychoses as seen by patients and their relatives. *European Archives of Psychiatry & Neurological Sciences*, **238**, 47–54.

Bandura, A. (1977) Self-efficacy: Toward an unifying theory of behavioral change. *Psychological Review*, **84**, 191–215.

Basler, H.-D. (1992) Verhaltenstherapie in der Gesundheitsberatung. In *Verhaltenstherapie. Ihre Entwicklung – ihr Menschenbild* (eds H. Lieb & R. Lutz). Göttingen: Verlag für Angewandte Psychologie.

Bataillard, V. (1984) *Pinwand-Moderationstechnik*. Zürich: Organisator AG.

Borst, U. (1992) *Schizophrenie innerhalb und ausserhalb der Klinik: Krankheitskonzept, Bewältigungsstrategien und Lebenszufriedenheit*. Lecture given at the 1992 GFTS Conference. Münsterlingen: Psychiatrische Klinik (unpublished manuscript).

Carlson, J. S. & Wiedl, K. H. (1992) The Dynamic Assessment of Intelligence. In Interactive Assessment Series: Disorders of Human Learning, Behavior, and Communication (eds H. C. Haywood & D. Tzuriel). New York: Springer-Verlag.

DeVries, M. W. & Delespaul, P. A. E. G. (1989) Time, context, and subjective experiences in schizophrenia. *Schizophrenia Bulletin*, **15**, 233–244.

Feldhege, F. & Krauthan, G. (1979) *Verhaltenstrainingsprogramm zum Aufbau sozialer Kompetenz*. Berlin: Springer-Verlag.

Filipp, S. H. & Klauer, T. (1991) Subjective well-being in the face of critical life events: The case of successful copers. In *The Social Psychology of Subjective Well-Being* (eds F. Strack, M. Argyle & N. Schwarz). Oxford: Pergamon.

Folkman, S. & Lazarus, R. S. (1980) An analysis of coping in a middle-aged community sample. *Journal of Health & Social Behavior*, **21**, 219–239.

Greif, S., Finger, A. & Jerusel, S. (1993) *Praxis des selbstorganisierten Lernens*. Köln: Bund Verlag.

Hill, D. J. & Bale, R. M. (1980) Development of the mental health locus of control and mental health locus of origin scales. *Journal of Personality Assessment*, **44**, 148–156.

Hölzl, M. & Reiter, L. (1992) Kohärenzerleben, Stressverarbeitung und Partnerschaft. *System Familie*, **5**, 121–123.

Janke, W., Erdmann, G. & Kallus, W. (1985) *Der Stressverarbeitungsfragebogen (SVF) nach Janke/Erdmann/Boucsein*. Göttingen: Hogrefe.

Krampen, G. (1981) *ICP-Fragebogen zu Kontrollüberzeugungen* (German version of the IPC-Scales by K. Levenson). Göttingen: Hogrefe.

Lange, H. U. (1981) Anpassungsstrategien, Bewältigungsreaktionen und Selbstheilversuche bei Schizophrenen. *Fortschritte in der Neurologie & Psychiatrie*, **49**, 275–285.

Lauer, G. (1993) Ergebnisse der Lebensqualitätforschung bei chronisch psychisch Kranken. *Psychiatrische Praxis*, **20**, 88–90.

Lazarus, R. S. & Launier, R. (1978) Stress-related transactions between person and environment. In *Perspectives in Interactional Psychology* (eds L. Pervin & M. Lewis). New York: Plenum Press.

Lehman, A. (1983) A quality of life interview for the chronically mentally ill. *Evaluation & Program Planning*, **11**, 51–62.

Liberman, R. P. (1986) Coping and competence as protective factors in the vulnerability-stress model of schizophrenia. In *Treatment of Schizophrenia: Family Assessment and Intervention* (eds M. J. Goldstein, I. Hand & K. Hahlweg). Berlin: Springer-Verlag.

Liberman, R. P., Mueser, K. T., Wallace, C. J. et al. (1990) Training skills in the psychiatrically disabled: Learning coping and competence. In *Schizophrenia: Concepts, Vulnerability and Intervention* (eds E. R. Straube & K. Hahlweg). Berlin: Springer-Verlag.

Linden, M. (1982) Die Veränderung von Krankheitsmodellen und Compliance bei schizophrenen Patienten. In *Psychotherapie in der Psychiatrie* (eds H. Helmchen, M. Linden & U. Rüger). Berlin: Springer-Verlag.

Linden, M., Nather, J. & Wilms, H. U. (1988) Zur Definition, Bedeutung und Messung der Krankheitskonzepte von Patienten. Die Krankheitskonzeptskala (KK-Skala) für schizophrene Patienten. *Fortschritte in Neurologie & Psychiatrie*, **56**, 35–43.

Lohaus, A. & Schmitt, G. (1989) Kontrollüberzeugungen zur Krankheit und Gesundheit. *Diagnostica*, **35**, 59–72.

McGlashan, T. H. & Carpenter, W. T. (1981) Does attitude towards psychosis relate to outcome? *American Journal of Psychiatry*, **138**, 797–800.

Mueser, K. T., Bellack, A. S., Douglas, N. S. et al. (1991) Prediction of social skill acquisition in schizophrenic and major affective disorder patients from memory and symptomatology. *Psychiatry Research*, **37**, 281–296.

Olbrich, R. (1983) Expressed Emotion (EE) und die Auslösung schizophrener Episoden: eine Literaturübersicht. *Nervenarzt*, **54**, 113–121.

Perrez, M. (1989) Psychotherapeutic methods between scientific foundation and everyday knowledge. *New Ideas in Psychology*, **7**, 133–145.

Pitschel-Walz, G., Boerner, R., Mayer, C. et al. (1993) Informationszentrierte Patientengruppen bei schizophrenen Psychosen: Einfluss auf Krankheitskonzept und Wissensstand der Patienten – Ergebnisse der PIP-Studie. *Verhaltenstherapie*, **3**, A40-A41.

Rund, B. R. & Landrø, N. I. (1990) Information processing: A new model for understanding cognitive disturbances in psychiatric patients. *Acta Psychiatrica Scandinavica*, **81**, 305–316.

Saupe, R., Englert, J. S., Gebhardt, R. et al. (1991) Schizophrenie und Coping: Bisherige Befunde und verhaltenstherapeutische Überlegungen. *Verhaltenstherapie*, **1**, 130–138.

Schaub, A. (1993) *Formen der Auseinandersetzung bei schizophrener Erkrankung*. Frankfurt: Peter Lang.

Schöttner, B., Wiedl, K. H. & Schramer, K. W. (1988) *Osnabrücker Belastungs- und Bewältigungsinventar* (OBBI) (hektograph. Manuskript). Osnabrück: Universitäts.

Stark, F. M. (1992) Strukturierte Information über Vulnerabilität und Belastungsmanagement für schizophrene Patienten. *Verhaltenstherapie*, **2**, 40–47.

Stark, F. M. & Buchkremer, G. (1992) Die Therapeut/Patient-Beziehung in der Therapie schizophrener Patienten: Beurteilung durch Patienten und Therapeuten. *Zeitschrift für klinische Psychologie*, **21**, 133–155.

Strauss, J. S. (1989) Subjective experiences of schizophrenia: Toward a new dynamic psychiatry – II. *Schizophrenia Bulletin*, **15**, 179–187.

Süllwold, L. & Herrlich, J. (1990) *Psychologische Behandlung schizophren Erkrankter*. Stuttgart: Kohlhammer.

Thurm, T. & Häfner, H. (1987) Perceived vulnerability, relapse risk and coping in schizophrenia – An explorative study. *European Archives of Psychiatry & Neurological Sciences*, **237**, 46–63.

Weig, W. & Wiedl, K. H. (1995) Die Rehabilitationseinrichtung für psychisch Kranke und Behinderte (RPK) – Erste Erfahrungen mit einem Modell. Krankenhauspsychiatrie (in press).

Weinstein, N. D. (1988) The precaution adoption process. *Health Psychology*, 7, 355–386.

Wiedl, K. H. (1984) Lerntests: nur Forschungsmittel und Forschungsgegenstand? *Zeitschrift für Entwicklungspsychologie & Pädagogische Psychologie*, 16, 245–281.

Wiedl, K. H. (1985) Theoretische und empirische Beiträge zum Ansatz des dynamischen Testens in der Intelligenzdiagnostik. In *Psychologie und komplexe Lebenswirklichkeit* (eds W. F. Kugemann, S. Preiser & K. A. Schneewind), pp. 167–184. Göttingen: Hogrefe.

Wiedl, K. H. (1991) *Krankheitsbewältigung bei Schizophrenen: Zur Umsetzung des Coping-Modells in verhaltenstherapeutische Massnahmen*. Lecture given at the Berner Psychotherapiewochen, November 1991. Osnabrück: Fachbereich VIII, Universität (unpublished manuscript).

Wiedl, K. H. (1992 a) Assessment of coping with schizophrenia: Stressors, appraisals and coping behaviour. *British Journal of Psychiatry*, 161 (Suppl. 18), 114–122.

Wiedl, K. H. (1992 b) Zur Einschätzung der Bewältigung einer schizophrenen Erkrankung: Belastungen, Bewertungen und Bewältigungsverhalten. In *Verlaufsprozesse schizophrener Erkrankungen. Dynamische Wechselwirkungen relevanter Faktoren* (eds H. D. Brenner & W. Böker), pp. 245–261. Bern: Huber.

Wiedl, K. H. (1993) Therapeutische Ansätze bei schizophrenen Patienten auf der Grundlage des Bewältigungsparadigmas. *Schizophrenie. Beiträge zu Forschung, Therapie & psychosozialem Management*, 8.

Wiedl, K. H. (1994) Bewältigungsorientierte Therapie bei Schizophrenen. *Zeitschrift für Klinische Psychologie, Psychopathologie & Psychotherapie*, (42) 2, 89–117.

Wiedl, K. H. & Rauh, D.-A. (1994) Ein halbstrukturiertes Tagebuch als Zugang zur Belastungsbewältigung schizophrener Patienten. In *Krankheitsverarbeitung* (eds Heim & M. Perrez), pp. 13–29. Göttingen: Hogrefe.

Wiedl, K. H. & Schöttke, H. (1993) *Dynamic Assessment of Selective Attention in Schizophrenic Subjects: The Analysis of Intraindividual Variability of Performance* (Research Report Nr. 90). Osnabrück: Universität.

Wiedl, K. H. & Schöttner, B. (1989 a) Die Bewältigung von Schizophrenia (I): Theoretische Perspektiven und empirische Befunde. *Zeitschrift für Klinische Psychologie, Psychopathologie & Psychotherapie*, 37, 176–193.

Wiedl, K. H. & Schöttner, B. (1989 b) Die Bewältigung einer schizophrenen Erkrankung (II): Weiterführende Forschungsansätze. *Zeitschrift für Klinische Psychologie, Psychopathologie & Psychotherapie*, 37, 317–340.

Wiedl, K. H. & Schöttner, B. (1989 c) Krankheitsbezogene Belastungen und deren Bewältigung bei Schizophrenen (Research Report Nr. 68). Osnabrück: Universität.

Yank, G. R., Bentley, K. J. & Hargrove, D. S. (1993) The vulnerability-stress model of schizophrenia: Advances in psychological treatment. *American Journal of Orthopsychiatry*, 63, 55–69.

227

Developing a Group Format Coping-Orientated Treatment Programme for Schizophrenic Patients

Annette Schaub, Karl Andres, Hans Dieter Brenner and Gudrun Donzel

Summary

This article outlines the theoretical and empirical background of coping-orientated therapy and gives an overview of different types of treatment programmes. A coping-orientated treatment programme was developed for groups of schizophrenic patients, providing information about the illness and treatment interventions on the basis of the vulnerability-stress-coping-competence model. It aims at improving coping with illness-related burden or daily stressors, as well as developing a lifestyle that supports health and quality of life. Whereas former treatment approaches tried to avoid emotionally stressful situations and illness-related or private topics in group therapy with schizophrenics, the integration of these elements may lead to a better transfer to real life situations. Two pilot studies were conducted to evaluate the clinical feasibility of this programme. The development of coping-orientated treatment programmes both from a theoretical point of view and on the basis of coping research is considered especially promising and could enable patients to be more socially integrated and to live more independently.

Pharmacological treatment is the mainstay of the management of schizophrenia today, but accumulating evidence supports the role of psychosocial interventions as an important component in comprehensive treatment programmes (Brenner et al., 1992; Bellack & Mueser, 1993). During the last decade, the therapy and rehabilitation of schizophrenic patients has changed considerably due to social skills training programmes (Bellack et al., 1984; Liberman et al., 1986, 1990) and cognitive treatment programmes (Brenner et al., 1990; Perris, 1992; Tarrier et al., 1993 a,b), which have achieved modest changes in social functioning, social skills, cognitive functioning, coping, and/or prevention of relapses. The Integrated Psychological Treatment Programme (Brenner et al., 1980, 1990, 1994; Roder et al., 1992), based on a hierarchically organised model in which the emphasis gradually shifts from training cognitive processes to social skills, has enjoyed wide dissemination, mainly in German-speaking countries, but also in the United States and Japan. Its current modifications emphasise coping with maladaptive emotions on the one hand (Hodel & Brenner, 1995), and improving social skills in specific domains of psychosocial functioning i. e., job maintenance, living situation, and leisure time (Roder & Brenner, in prep.) on the other.

Although the influence of life events and stressors (e. g., family communication styles) on the course of schizophrenia (Bebbington et al., 1993; Norman & Malla, 1993) has been repeatedly shown, only a few psychosocial interventions have focused specifically on improving the patient's competence to cope with these stressors. Recently, treatment approaches have emerged that endeavour to provide schizophrenic patients both with information about their illness and coping strategies to deal more effectively with stressors (Liberman, 1988; Süllwold & Herrlich, 1992; Wiedl, 1994). The vulnerability-stress-model of schizophrenia (Zubin & Spring, 1977) and its modifications (Liberman, 1986; Nuechterlein, 1987; Nuechterlein et al., 1992), which highlight the interaction between biological vulnerability, stressors, and protective factors such as coping strategies, have played an important role in the development of these psychosocial programmes. In the light of our present knowledge schizophrenia can at best be understood as a developmental, systemic disorder (cf. Brenner et al., 1992); according to this viewpoint, genetically determined or early acquired variations in cerebral structure and/or physiology underlie differences in perceptual and cognitive functioning, i. e., information processing. These individual differences in turn interact with environmental influences to transform the inherent biological predispositions into clinical symptoms. Thus, the onset and course of the illness can be substantially affected by environmental events, psychosocial interventions, and coping strategies.

Coping Research in Schizophrenia

Modern coping research, focusing on active coping behaviour, has a long tradition in clinical psychology and somatic medicine, but has only recently received attention in the field of psychiatry (Böker & Brenner, 1983). The transactional concept of coping devised by Lazarus and his group (Lazarus & Launier, 1978; Lazarus, 1991) has gained prominence in this field of research. This concept posits that coping is the result of a dynamic relationship between person and environment, which means that both are involved in a reciprocal exchange that proceeds in time and is mediated by cognitive appraisal processes. Coping is defined as, "the person's cognitive and behavioural efforts to manage (reduce, minimise, master, tolerate) the internal and external demands of the person-environment transaction that is appraised as taxing or exceeding the person's resources" (Lazarus, 1991, p. 112).

Despite former pessimistic opinions, a wide range of active problem-centred coping reactions in patients with schizophrenia are recorded in more recent literature. Research indicates that most patients employ active coping strategies to deal with their symptoms or problems, even though it may be unclear which effects these efforts have. The symptoms and demands that have to be coped with in schizophrenia depend on the stage of the illness (i. e., prodromal episodes, acute exacerbation, remission, residual phase) and its ensuing consequences. In the first place, patients try to cope with the symptoms and impairments that are typical of prodromal episodes (Cohen & Berk, 1985; Thurm & Häfner, 1987); a high proportion of patients and their relatives are aware of early warning signs that are predominantly non-psychotic (Herz & Melville, 1980; McCandless-Glimscher et al., 1986; Birchwood et al., 1989; Häfner et al., 1993). Awareness of early warning signs can prevent further deterioration and even rehospitalisation, if patients are then able and willing to cooperate with mental health professionals (Herz et al., 1989; Heinrichs et al., 1985). Many patients suffer from "basic symptoms" i. e., subjectively experienced discrete symptomatic phenomena which diminish their functioning and which either fluctuate or are fairly prolonged (Süllwold, 1986). Significant correlations have been found between these discrete self-perceived phenomena and problem-orientated coping reactions (Süllwold, 1977; Böker et al., 1984; Brenner et al., 1985). Schizophrenic patients also try to cope with chronic psychotic symptoms, such as hearing voices, by using cognitive, behavioural, sensory, or physiological coping strategies (Falloon & Talbot, 1981; Breier & Strauss, 1983; Carr & Katsikis, 1987; Tarrier, 1987). The respective coping reactions are very heterogeneous and seem to have no explicit relationship to clinical or sociodemographical variables. Only Wiedl (1992) found a relationship between high levels of negative symptoms in schizophrenia and emotion-orientated, less cognitive ways of coping. In addition to studies which focus on coping with symptoms, other research has examined how patients cope with other stresses associated with the illness (Thurm & Häfner, 1987; Wiedl, 1992; Schaub, 1993). These have shown that the majority employ active coping strategies in respect to both psychosocial functioning and independent living.

The effectiveness of coping strategies is usually evaluated according to the course of the illness, but aspects of social integration (e. g., community tenure) and personal well-being have also been examined. These are different criteria for evaluation, however, no studies are available that look at possible covariations. In addition, effectiveness can be judged from points of view of

230

the patient, the social environment, and the mental health professional (Heim, 1988). Some studies refer to differences in this area (Englert et al., 1994), and such problems in defining the effectiveness of coping strategies should be kept in mind when considering the respective results. A coping style marked by integration rather than sealing-over was found to be correlated with good outcome and a more flexible and variable attitude towards illness (Soskis & Bowers, 1969; McGlashan et al., 1975). Specific coping strategies, e. g., changing one's expectancies in respect to life goals, and keeping up a positive morale as well as compliance, were found to be the most important coping variables correlated negatively with relapse (Schaub, 1994). The prognostic power of classical predictors could probably be increased if coping strategies were added (Brenner et al., in prep.).

Illness-Management Programmes in Schizophrenia

Encouraged both by current aetiopathogenetic theories of schizophrenia and by the results of coping research that have provided evidence that schizophrenic patients actively try to cope with their illness, different coping-orientated treatment approaches have recently been developed. These can be divided into three different types: First, primarily psychoeducational-orientated programmes that provide information about the illness; second, programmes that focus on teaching strategies to cope with early warning signs or chronic symptoms (Tab. 1 a); and third, comprehensive programmes that deal with the disease and various problems of living related to it (Tab. 1 b). In spite of differences concerning the treatment goals, the time-frame, the format (single vs. group), and the structure (highly structured vs. flexible), these programmes are all based on the vulnerability-stress-model and employ behavioural learning principles. They all include psychoeducational elements providing information about the illness, and the patient is seen as an active partner in the treatment process.

Primarily psychoeducational-orientated programmes on a short-term basis involve teaching patients about symptoms, causes of the illness, the treatment of acute and chronic symptoms, and prevention of relapse. They have been found to increase knowledge about psychosis, to improve compliance and tendency to a reduction in relapses, compared to standard treatment was also found (e. g., Brücher, 1992; Stark, 1992; Bäuml et al., 1993, 1994). Treatments focusing on early warning signs were based on the hypothesis that schizophrenic patients might become more effective in preventing relapse by perceiving and coping with early warning signs prior to relapse (Herz et al., 1982, 1989; Herz, 1984). These treatments are often combined with low dose or intermittent neu-

231

Table 1 a. Primarily psychoeducational and symptom management programmes.

Title	Treatment goal	Methods	Format	Time frame	Results
Primarily psychoeducational programmes (Bäuml, 1993; Brücher, 1992; Stark, 1992)	Information about symptoms, treatment, prevention of relapse	Lessons, handouts	Group	4–8 sessions once a week	Increase in knowledge, compliance and tendency to a reduction in relapses ($n = 21$) compared to control group ($n = 22$) (Bäuml et al., 1993)*
Early warning signs programmes (Herz et al., 1989, 1994)	Information about early warning signs, prevention of relapse	Lessons, Early Warning Signs Questionnaire	Group	Unclear	Insight in early warning signs can prevent rehospitalisation (Herz et al., 1989)
Symptom Management Module (Liberman, 1988 a)	Coping with early warning signs, chronic symptoms. Avoidance of drug and alcohol.	Information, video modeling, role-play, problem solving	Group	Twice weekly sessions for 6 months	Gains in knowledge about psychosis and skills that were taught ($n = 20$), compared to occupational therapy ($n = 21$) (Eckman et al., 1992)*
Coping strategy enhancement (Tarrier et al., 1993 a,b)	Training of more effective strategies in coping with chronic symptoms	Behavioural analysis of situations in which psychotic symptoms occur. Identifying potentially usable coping strategies and in-vivo training.	Individual	Twice weekly sessions for 5 weeks	Significant increases in the number of positive coping strategies and in their efficacy; trend to higher reduction in psychotic symptoms in the coping group ($n = 15$) compared to problem-solving group ($n = 12$) (Tarrier et al., 1993 a,b)*

Table 1 b. Coping-orientated treatment programmes.

Title	Treatment goal	Methods	Format	Time frame	Results
Cognitive approach to auditory hallucinations (Chadwick & Birchwood, 1994)	Restructuring beliefs about chronic symptoms	Engagement, education, rapport, disputing and testing beliefs empirically	Individual	About 13 – 18 sessions spaced over 3 to 6 months	Large and stable reductions in beliefs about voices; reduced distress, increased adaptive behaviour, a fall in voice activity (Chadwick & Birchwood, 1994)
Individual focused therapy (Süllwold & Herrlich, 1990, 1992)	Teaching a functional concept of the illness, awareness of prodromes, stress-management	Psychoeducation, behavioural principles, cognitive restructuring	Individual	On average 20 sessions (up to 99)	Increase in compliance, insight into illness, decrease of psychopathology, only 30% relapse at two-year follow-up
Coping oriented treatment programme (Wiedl, 1994)	Teaching a functional concept of the illness, awareness of prodromes, stress-management	Psychoeducation, behavioural principles, cognitive restructuring "metaplan-analysis", questionnaires	Group	Weekly sessions in one year	No outcome data available
Individual psychotherapy of schizophrenia (Hogarty et al., 1995)	Increasing foresight through the accurate appraisal of emotional states	Phase specific psycho-education and behavior therapy	Individual/ Group	Weekly sessions in one year, greater spacing in subsequent two years	Statistically significant and frequently an incremental gain over time in personal and social adjustment in the first two years

roleptic medication. A cognitive-orientated treatment programme, i. e., problem solving on possible predictors of relapse showed a lower relapse rate compared to action-orientated as well as standard treatment programmes (Buchkremer & Fiedler, 1987). Patients treated with the medication management and symptom management modules developed by Liberman (1988 a,b), compared with occupational therapy, showed a significant increase in knowledge about psychosis and in the skills that were taught (Eckman et al., 1992). Studies with a modified version of the symptom management module showed a decrease of external locus of control and an increase of internal locus of control (Behrendt, 1993; Schaub et al., 1994), whereas mere follow-up studies indicate that perceived self-control is a stable marker over time (Lasar & Loose, 1994). Both Tarrier et al. (1993 a,b) and Chadwick and Birchwood (1994) demonstrated that schizophrenic patients can be taught more effective coping skills in dealing with chronic symptoms. Their beliefs about these symptoms can be restructured leading to reduction in the severity and frequency of psychotic symptoms.

Comprehensive coping-orientated treatment programmes deal with the disease and various problems of living related to it. By providing a "functional concept of the illness," they focus on a better understanding of the symptoms, on its interplay with stressful situations, and on beneficial coping strategies (e. g., Süllwold & Herrlich, 1990, 1992; Wiedl, 1994). Such a concept refers to plausible models of the illness (e. g., diatheses-stress model) and outcome expectancies that demystify the illness and encourage the patient to develop adequate efficacy expectancies based on empirical knowledge. However, coping with daily stressors plays an important role in these programmes too. Süllwold and Herrlich's (1990) individual behaviour-orientated treatment format teaches the recognition of conditions that provoke psychotic disturbances as well as dealing with stressors more effectively. Providing schizophrenic patients with a "functional concept of their illness" proved to be an essential element of therapy, as patients become aware of symptoms and behavioural deviances that they exhibit, and thereby gain insight into their illness and treatment strategies. In a study with 40 schizophrenic patients, Süllwold and Herrlich (1990) found an increase in insight into the illness and compliance after treatment, and the rehospitalisation rate was only 30% at two year follow-up. However, the absence of a control group limits the conclusions that can be drawn from this study. Wiedl (1994) developed a group format coping-orientated treatment approach for groups that includes psychoeducation, stress-management, social skills training, and cognitive restructuring. It refers to different areas of living, but has still to be evaluated. Hogarty et al. (1995) developed an individual psychotherapy of schizophrenia that, by means of graduated, internal coping strategies, aims at a growing awareness of personal vulnerability, including the "internal cues" of affect dysregulation.

A Coping-Orientated Treatment Programme for Groups

Even though some current therapeutic approaches try to improve patients' ability to identify situations which precipitate the onset of psychotic phenomena, as well as their coping competence in dealing with the illness and daily stressors, there is no demonstrated short-term group format available for coping with early warning signs, chronic symptoms, daily stressors, and building up rewarding activities. Therefore, this study was implemented to pursue that goal. The development of our treatment programme was strongly influenced by our own research on coping in schizophrenia (Böker & Brenner, 1983; Schaub, 1993, 1994; Brenner et al., in prep.) as well as by elements of already existing treatment approaches (Schaub & Möller, 1990; Süllwold & Herrlich, 1990, 1992; Wiedl, 1994). However, in contrast to both Süllwold & Herrlich's and Wiedl's approach, this programme is more short-term (with an approximate duration of three months) and more structured, but still encourages the patient to be an active participant. Whereas former treatment approaches tried to avoid emotionally stressful situations and illness-related or private topics in group therapy with schizophrenics, this programme focuses on those topics, as the integration of such elements may lead to a better transfer to real-life situations. According to Lazarus (1991), therapy should address the lack of skills for handling adaptational demands and the emotional distress resulting from faulty appraisal and coping processes, as well as dysfunctional emotions due to a lack of meaning and commitment in life.

The programme is devised as a group format, to be used in conjunction with the standard treatment offered to patients in institutional settings, to encourage widespread dissemination and use by mental health services. It should be provided in the context of a comprehensive treatment approach that includes short-term psychoeducational family therapy (e. g., providing families with information about schizophrenia, how to cope with family crises and how to contribute to the prevention of relapse) and case management. This coping-orientated treatment programme consists of three subprogrammes: First, providing information about the illness and treatment interventions on the basis of the vulnerability-stress-coping-competence model (Liberman, 1986, Nuechterlein, 1987); second, stress management to improve coping with symptoms and everyday stressors in different areas of living; and third, developing a lifestyle that supports health and quality of life (e. g., organisation of leisure time). It includes psychoeducational elements (e. g., written material) and employs behavioural learning principles (e. g., role play, cognitive restructuring, problem-solving). Table 2 gives a description of the coping-orientated treatment programme.

235

Table 2. Description of the coping-orientated treatment programme.

Education about the illness and therapeutic interventions on the basis of the vulnerability-stress-model
    Providing information about schizophrenia
    Providing information about therapeutic interventions
    Identifying, monitoring and coping with early warning signs of relapse

Coping with stressors
    Identifying stressful situations related to psychopathology, psychosocial functioning and independent living
    Recognising signs of stress, i.e., psychophysiological, cognitive and emotional aspects
    Stress management: problem solving, social competence training and relaxation training

Improving quality of life
    Identifying pleasant situations
    Learning to engage in pleasant activities

The first subprogramme "education about the illness and therapeutic interventions on the basis of the vulnerability-stress model": After a short introduction for the patients concerned with their needs and expectations as well as the contents of the therapy, this starts with education about the illness and therapeutic interventions on the basis of the vulnerability-stress-coping-competence model (Liberman, 1986). This model provides the basis for a "functional concept of the disease," i.e., illness-related cognitions that enable the patient to understand his or her illness and to realise how he or she can possibly influence its manifestations (Süllwold & Herrlich, 1992). The interaction between vulnerability, stressors, deterioration in well-being, and relapse are highlighted. Patients are told that psychotic symptoms can be explained as coping-breakdown in a stressful situation, "basic symptoms" (e.g., slipping of thoughts) as reactions to overload due to overstimulation. The patients are encouraged to talk about their concept of illness including possible causes of onset and relapse, their symptoms, and how they cope with them. The patients and the therapist engage collaboratively in devising a definition of schizophrenia which is focused both on the patients' subjective concept of illness and on information provided by the therapist. The therapist and the patients try to integrate these issues into the vulnerability-stress model so that the patients' illness concepts become less idiosyncratic and more orientated to psychiatric concepts. The patients are informed about neuroleptics, their effects and side-effects, as well as about behavioural psychotherapy, e.g., family

236

therapy and social skills training. The "functional concept of schizophrenia" enables the patients to recognise how the various forms of therapy are related to their symptoms e. g., how the use of neuroleptics influences biological liability to stress.

Another important goal of this first subprogramme is that patients learn to identify early warning signs of relapse that are common in chronic mental illness, by administering the Early Signs Questionnaire (Herz & Melville, 1980). They monitor the severity and frequency of these signals throughout the time of treatment and are encouraged to continue doing this further. Former psychotic episodes, situations which precipitated the onset of psychotic symptoms, and warning signs are analysed, and plans worked out for warning signs to be dealt with more effectively in order to avoid full relapse.

The second subprogramme "coping with stressors" aims at learning to recognise stressors and to cope with them more effectively. The patients learn to identify for themselves stressful situations, their personal stress symptoms and the coping activities that could help them reduce emotional distress. They are asked to describe stressful situations and to classify them. A possible system of classification includes illness (e. g., problems at work due to poor concentration or persistent positive symptoms), psychosocial functioning (e. g., structuring daytime, problems making friends, keeping a job), and self-perception (e. g., dealing with feelings of inferiority due to mental illness). Building up a hierarchy of these stressors illustrates the individual amount of burden for each patient in the various areas of stress, as well as the degree of stress for the group itself. Stress is defined as "specific external and/or internal demands that are appraised as taxing or exceeding the resources of the person" (Lazarus & Folkman, 1984, p. 141) and which requires a person to adapt or modify their behaviour.

According to Lazarus (1991), emotional distress cannot be separated from cognition, motivation, adaptation, and physiological activity. Emotions include different variables and processes: the eliciting environmental and internal conditions that produce a person-environment relationship, the mediating process of appraisal of that relationship, the coping process, as well as the response itself. Therefore, the patients are asked to analyse stressful situations according to a scheme that includes the psychophysiological, cognitive, and emotional changes that take place, as well as coping reactions and the consequences on the situation. The situations described by the patients are discussed in the group and different ideas on how to deal with this situation are elicited, evaluated and the patients role-play the solution they think the best. Emphasis is put on improving social skills and coping strategies, but identifying and changing maladaptive cognitions are also important elements. Relaxation exercises, such as the progressive muscle relaxation devised by Jacobson, are also taught. In subsequent sessions, the patients are asked for feedback on the strategies they elaborated; they continue to identify and monitor stressful situations, so that they become more aware of stressors and their ways of dealing with them.

The third subprogramme "improving quality of life" aims at developing a life style which promotes health and well-being. The patient's concept of self should not be defined exclusively in terms of vulnerability to schizophrenia, but should also be based on a conception of their individuality and on the remaining possibilities in life. Analogous to analysing stressors, the patients are encouraged to identify pleasant situations so that they become aware in which situations they are feeling well. They are encouraged to engage in activities they find enjoyable, e. g., developing interests and organisation of leisure time, and to plan their leisure time according to their ideas and give feedback about their activities.

Pilot studies of the coping-orientated treatment programme

Method

Rationale and design

To evaluate the clinical feasibility of this treatment programme, two uncontrolled pilot studies were undertaken with 14 schizophrenic patients. Training took place twice a week for 1.5 hours, with 24 sessions, and lasting 2.5 months on average. The treatment programme administered in the first pilot study (cf. Schaub & Möller, 1990) did not include all the psychoeducational elements described above, some of which were added in the second. The absence of a control group and the small sample size limit the conclusions that can be drawn. However, due to the importance of the concept of coping within the framework of current theories about factors influencing the course of schizophrenia (Liberman, 1986; Nuechterlein et al., 1992), there is a strong need for clinically validated treatments that enhance psychological coping. In addition, this endeavour is supported by the empirical results of coping research, although there are still some unresolved issues, especially the effectiveness of different coping strategies. The development of appropriate treatment programmes should therefore be linked to the elaboration of adequate evaluation strategies. In such a situation, nevertheless, even results from small pilot studies demonstrating the feasibility of this treatment programme can be considered worthwhile.

To assess the effectiveness of this approach, different perspectives (the views of the patients, family, health caregivers) and levels of functioning have to be taken into account. Both improving the awareness of basic symptoms and warning signs as well as increasing knowledge about psychosis, insight into the illness, and compliance with treatment are important goals. In terms of personality variables, an improved self-concept, increase in self-efficacy, and better social competence should result. A hypothesis which was investigated in the second pilot study concerns the role of information processing as a basic condition to benefit from the programme. As research on rate-limiting factors documents, a certain level of cognitive functioning, memory, and "learning potential" (i. e., ability to improve functioning after a certain training was applied) are considered to be important prerequisites for this kind of therapy (Mueser et al., 1991; Kern et al., 1993). Habitual forms of coping with stressful demands as a trait marker will probably be more difficult to change, in contrast to the subjective appraisal of illness-related, individual, and environmental stressors, with its respective coping behaviour. It was hypothesised that if patients succeed in coping with stressors more effectively, they do not have to withdraw from cognitively or socio-emotionally challenging situations so often. Long-term effects should refer to a better course of the illness (e. g., lower relapse rate), better social adjustment, and improved quality of life.

Patient Sample

The first pilot study included six chronic schizophrenic or schizoaffective in-patients (according to ICD-10), mean age: 30.33 years (SD = 5.24), mean duration of illness: 7.42 years (SD = 5.70), mean number of hospital admissions: 2.17 (SD = 1.17). The second study comprised eight chronic schizophrenic in-patients with mainly paranoid symptoms (according to ICD-10). Their mean age was 33.71 years (SD = 9.21), mean duration of illness 10.86 years (SD = 9.86), mean number of admissions 3.71 (SD = 2.21), and mean level of intelligence IQ 97.29 (SD = 9.43). One patient had to be excluded because of a psychotic relapse towards the end of treatment. All were treated with psychotropic medication, mainly antipsychotics. They had experienced a recent symptom exacerbation (within the past three months) and were identified for treatment during inpatient psychiatric care because of enduring high levels of psychopathology and behavioural disturbance.

Measures

Before and after, psychopathology was assessed with semi-structured interviews using the Brief Psychiatric Rating Scale (BPRS; Overall & Gorham, 1962) and the Scale for the Assessment of Negative Symptoms (SANS; Andreasen, 1981). The Stress Coping Questionnaire (SCQ; Janke et al., 1985) was administered to identify the coping strategies generally used. The Frankfurt Self-Concept Scale (FSCN; Deusinger, 1986) was used to assess relevant aspects of the self-concept and the Frankfurt Complaint Questionnaire (FCQ; Süllwold, 1986) to rate basic symptoms, i.e., the subjectively experienced deficits of schizophrenic patients. In the first study, additionally, psychosocial functioning was assessed by the Global Assessment Scale (GAS; Endicott et al. 1986) and cognitive functioning by the Repeated Psychological Measurement Test (RPM; Fahrenberg et al., 1977). In the second study, knowledge about the illness was assessed by the Knowledge Test about Psychosis in a modified version (Bäuml et al., 1993) while compliance and insight into the illness were rated on a five-point scale (Schaub, 1993). To assess changes in generalised expectancies, illness concepts, actual coping behaviour, and quality of life, the following questionnaires were employed: Locus of Control & Self-Perceived Competence Questionnaire (LCSCQ; Krampen, 1991), Illness Concept Scale (ICS; Linden et al., 1988), Osnabrück Stress & Coping Inventory (OSCI; Schöttner et al., 1988), and Social Interview Schedule (SIS; Hecht et al., 1987). Cognitive functioning was assessed before treatment by the abridged Wechsler Intelligence Test (WIP; Dahl, 1986), Verbal Learning & Memory Test (VLMT; Helmstedter & Durwen, 1990), and Wisconsin Card Sorting Test (WCST, Heaton 1981). The latter instrument was applied in a dynamic version (Wiedl & Schöttke, 1993), i.e., a first trial with few instructions, a second trial with extensive instructions, and a third trial without further information. The difference between the performance on the first and the third trial can be considered as a measure of the learning potential.

Results

Analyses were conducted to evaluate the changes in clinical variables throughout the study. Table 3 shows the results of Wilcoxon-Signed-Rank-Tests comparing pre- and postscores of the first pilot study. Patients improved on most dimensions of psychopathology as measured with the BPRS and on overall functioning as measured with the GAS. There was a tendency to ex-

240

Table 3. Comparison of scores before and after treatment for psychopathology, psychosocial functioning and coping behaviour in Pilot study I (Wilcoxon-Signed-Rank Test).

Variable	Pretreatment mean	s.d.	Posttreatment mean	s.d.	Z-value	P
BPRS	40.17	8.89	28.33	5.43	–2.201	.0277
Anxiety/						
depression	11.33	4.23	8.33	1.75	–1.753	.0796
Anergia	9.50	4.32	7.00	2.19	–2.023	.0431
Thought disorder	8.00	3.16	4.17	0.41	–2.023	.0431
Activity	5.50	1.38	4.67	1.75	–0.730	.4652
Hostility	5.83	1.72	3.83	0.75	–2.023	.0431
SANS	9.33	4.32	3.83	1.94	–2.201	.0277
GAS	43.50	11.22	56.83	9.33	–2.201	.0277
FCQ	27.33	15.07	21.33	18.50	–1.826	.0679
Overstimulation	3.00	2.28	2.17	2.14	–2.023	.0431
Self-						
assertiveness	45.33	18.22	49.83	17.81	–2.023	.0431
SCQ						
Social						
withdrawal	57.33	8.82	46.83	13.35	–2.201	.0277
Self-pity	55.50	6.38	46.33	12.11	–2.023	.0431

perience less basic disorders, as assessed by the FCQ, at the end of training . The subscale "overstimulation" of this questionnaire showed a significant decrease, as well as passive coping behaviour such as "social withdrawal" and "self-pity," as assessed by the SCQ. The means of the coping strategies before treatment were within the normal range, except for "flight." The value of this coping strategy had decreased remarkably after treatment, though without statistical significance. According to the results of the FSCN, there was a significant change in self-confidence, related to self-assertiveness in social situations. Cognitive functioning (Repeated Measurement Tests) did not change significantly after training.

Because there was no control group, another statistical technique was used to investigate the treatment effects, which – in comparison to other studies – permits their evaluation to some extent. The difference of the means of before and after treatment scores was related to the deviation of the prescore. The resulting quotient describes the "effect size" of the treatment in a given variable (Smith et al., 1980; Grawe et al., 1990 a,b). Figure 1 shows the "effect sizes" of Pilot study I. The "effect size (es)" were high for the total score of the BPRS (es = 1.133), the subscores "thought disorder" (es = 1.212) and

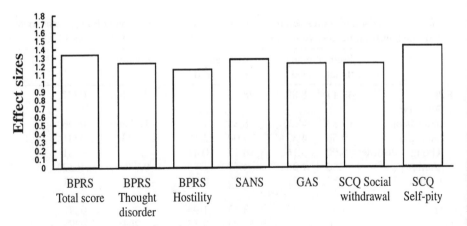

Effect sizes

BPRS Total score | BPRS Thought disorder | BPRS Hostility | SANS | GAS | SCQ Social withdrawal | SCQ Self-pity

Figure 1. "Effect sizes" of pilot study I.

"hostility" (es = 1.161), the SANS (es = 1.273), the GAS (es = 1.188) and the coping strategies "social withdrawal" (es = 1.189) and "self-pity" (es = 1.436). These "effect sizes" are comparable with those found in studies with well-established cognitive behavioural therapy (Grawe et al., 1994). The "effect sizes" of the other significant variables are below 0.80, which is regarded as a critical marker for treatment effects (Grawe et al., 1990a).

Table 4 shows the results comparing scores of Pilot study II before and after treatment by means of Wilcoxon-Signed-Rank Tests. The patients improved on psychopathological variables, on knowledge about psychosis, on compliance, and on insight into the illness, there was no change in subjectively experienced basic symptoms, i. e., non-clinically manifest impairments in psychological functioning. As far as illness concepts (ICS), generalised expectancies (LCSCQ) and coping strategies (either habitual or related to specific situations) (SCQ; OSCI) are concerned, there were no statistically significant changes. However, there was a tendency to engage in fewer passive coping strategies (e. g., "minimising") and fewer worries concerning a sudden onset of illness. The means of the coping strategies before treatment were within the normal range, except for "fulfilment of needs by substitution" and "taking drugs," the latter being still above-average at the second assessment. However, the total number of stressors with a focus on illness (e. g., knowing that relapse can occur, feelings of anxiety, poor concentration, slipping of thoughts), questions concerning the way of living (e. g., purpose of life) and problems concerning side-effects of medication (e. g., loss of energy and motility, weight problems) did not change during treatment. At both assessments, problem-focused coping was more frequent than non-problemfo-

Table 4. Comparison of scores before and after treatment for psychopathology, knowledge about psychosis, compliance, and coping behaviour in Pilot study II (Wilcoxon-Signed-Rank Test).

Variable	Pretreatment mean	s. d.	Posttreatment mean	s. d.	Z-value	P
BPRS	47.43	10.39	33.14	8.93	−2.367	.0180
Anxiety/depression	12.86	3.29	9.71	2.43	−1.437	.1508
Anergia	12.71	2.75	7.86	3.80	−2.366	.0180
Thought disorder	9.71	6.16	6.57	4.83	−2.023	.0431
Activity	6.85	1.68	4.00	1.53	−2.367	.0180
Hostility	6.14	2.91	4.43	2.15	−2.201	.0277
Knowledge about psychosis	31.29	12.04	39.86	7.73	−2.367	.0180
Insight into the illness	2.71	0.76	3.29	0.76	−1.826	.0679
Compliance	2.43	0.78	3.43	0.53	−2.201	.0277
Minimising (SCQ)	46.00	12.10	43.00	8.33	−1.753	.0796
Worries about sudden onset of illness	7.75	0.96	5.75	2.06	−1.887	.0592

cused coping. In regard to quality of life (SIS) there was an increase in reported satisfaction with leisure-time activities as well as with social contacts, the latter being the most impaired at the first assessment related to the given situation. Patients who showed a high amount of correct responses on the WCST tended to improve more on the BPRS total score than patients who had a poor performance (Pearson correlation r = .63, p = 0.091). Patients with a higher level of cognitive functioning at the beginning benefited from coping-orientated therapy more than patients with less cognitive functioning.

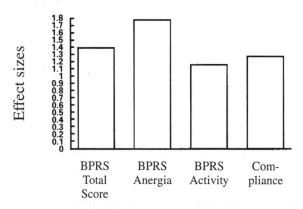

Figure 2. "Effect sizes" of pilot study II.

243

The "effect sizes" in this study were high for the total score of the BPRS (es = 1.374) too and its subscores "anergia" (es = 1.765) and "activity" (es = 1.704), as well as for compliance (es = 1.270). The "effect sizes" of the other significant variables were below 0.80. At follow-up, three months later, all but one patient were still stabilised. There were no significant changes, compared with immediately after, even though the patients were now managing to live outside the hospital.

Discussion

Current theories about schizophrenia and coping research call for coping-orientated therapy in schizophrenia aimed at improving coping with illness-related and daily stressors and minimising the risk of relapse. The pilot studies reported here demonstrated the clinical feasibility of a coping-orientated treatment programme on a group basis. All patients but one attended more than 80% of the sessions. One patient dropped-out, as he stopped taking neuroleptics close to the end of treatment. When it is considered that the patients had a high and stable level of psychopathology, the clinical effects of decrease in psychopathology and increase in psychosocial functioning, knowledge about psychosis, and compliance with treatment seem to be very encouraging. However, no definite conclusions can be drawn, because there were no control groups. Ongoing research on larger samples, with random assignment to control or treatment group, funded by the National Swiss Fund for a duration of three years, will further examine the clinical effectiveness of this treatment programme.

There was a tendency for schizophrenic patients to have experienced fewer basic disorders as well as a higher quality of life, after this treatment. To assess quality of life seems to be an important aspect of the evaluation of the effectiveness of treatment programmes. However, there were differences between the patients' description of given situations (e. g., having no job) and their level of satisfaction. Coping strategies and level of self-confidence changed in the first group, but not in the second, which may be due to the higher level of chronicity in the second sample. Even though the coping-specific instruments showed no overall differences at the end of training, the patients themselves reported changes which they found helpful. One patient who complained about body sensations at the beginning of group therapy, then unrelated to any stressful situation, found that these were his physical indicators in situations when he felt uneasy, because he was confronted with demands he thought he could not fulfil. Another patient learned to monitor his warning signs more seriously, and to reduce stress when these occurred. Not many changes were expected in habitual coping strategies, as these have proved to be quite stable over time in schizophrenia (Brenner et al., in prep.). Neither the subjective appraisal of the disease, individual and environmental stressors, respective coping behaviour changed over time. However, little is known about the adequateness of different coping strategies: the characteristics of stressful situations have to be taken into account in assessing the effectiveness of coping. According to Perrez and Matathia (1994), active coping behaviour is most appropriate in situations that seem to be controllable, whereas if they are appraised as uncontrollable, accepting them as they are seems to be a more effective strategy.

Because of the different psychosocial interventions that are available, future research should focus on identifying patients' characteristics which best predict treatment outcome with different programmes. The results of this study support the hypothesis that good learning potential, assessed by a dynamic version of the WCST, is a helpful basis for a good treatment outcome. Patients with a concept of the illness like the diathesis-stress model seem especially inclined to benefit from this therapy (Süllwold & Herrlich, 1992), but even those with a lack of or limited insight into the severity of the illness, an exclusively biological concept of the illness, and no or only limited awareness of stressful situations could take advantage from this kind of therapy, by being confronted with a different perspective.

Coping-orientated programmes could be implemented in an inpatient setting, in a day clinic, or on an outpatient basis. Booster sessions that are scheduled before and during high-risk periods (e. g., 3–5 months after discharge) should be available for the patients and their families, as these could be moderately successful in both maintaining treatment-induced behaviour change (Whisman, 1990) and in preventing relapse after longer intensive treatment programmes (Test, 1991). The patients' practitioners should also be asked to focus on warning signs. Both patients' coping and behavioural deficits as well as their strengths to achieve their goals, should also be integrated in an individualised rehabilitation plan that is followed through by the patient and staff. The role of case managers and the individual therapist should provide opportunities for patients to talk about more personal topics that could not be dealt with in group therapy. From this point of view, a comprehensive treatment programme based on individual as well as group sessions seems to be a promising direction.

Acknowledgements

The development of the treatment programme and its first evaluation was supported by Sandoz-Stiftung zur Förderung der medizinisch-biologischen Wissenschaften, the Ciba-Geigy-Jubiläums-Stiftung, and the Helmut Horten Stiftung.

References

Andreasen, N. C. (1981) *Scale for the Assessment of Negative Symptoms (SANS)*. Iowa City: University of Iowa.

Bäuml, J., Kissling, W., Buttner, P. et al. *(1993) Informationszentrierte Patienten- und Angehörigengruppen zur Complianceverbesserung bei schizophrenen Psychosen. Erste Ergebnisse der Münchner PIP-Studie.* Paper presented at the IVth Kongress der Deutschen Gesellschaft für Verhaltensmedizin und Verhaltensmodifikation (25.3.–27.3. 1993).

Bäuml, J., Kissling, W. & Pitschel-Walz, G. (1994) *Psychoeducational groups for schizophrenic patients and their relatives – Influence on compliance and coping during the long term treatment with neuroleptics.* Paper presented at the International Congress on Clinical Psychopathology in Timisoara. May 1994.

Bebbington, P., Wilkins, S., Jones, P. et al. (1993) Life events and psychosis. Initial results from the Camberwell Collaborative Psychosis Study. *British Journal of Psychiatry*, **162**, 72–79.

Behrendt, B. (in press) *Das Symptom-Management-Modul als Standardbehandlung in einem tagesklinischen Setting.* (ed A. STARK) Mitteilungen der Deutschen Gesellschaft für Verhaltenstherapie (DGVT). Tübingen.

Bellack, A., Turner, S. M., Hersen, M. et al. (1984) An examination of the efficacy of social skills training for chronic schizophrenic patients. *Hospital & Community Psychiatry*, **35**, 1023–1028.

Bellack, A. & Mueser, K. T. (1993) Psychosocial treatment for schizophrenia. *Schizophrenia Bulletin*, **19**, 317–336.

Birchwood, M., Smith, J., MacMillan, F. et al. (1989) Predicting relapse in schizophrenia: The development and implementation of an early signs monitoring system using patients and families as observers. *Psychological Medicine*, **19**, 649–656.

Böker, W. & Brenner, H. D. (1983) Selbstheilungsversuche Schizophrener: Psychopathologische Befunde und Folgerungen für Forschung und Therapie. *Nervenarzt*, **54**, 578–589.

Böker, W., Brenner, H. D. & Gerstner, G. et al. (1984) Self-healing strategies among schizophrenics: Attempt at compensation for basic disorders. *Acta Psychiatria Scandinavica*, **69**, 373–378.

Breier, A. & Strauss, J. S. (1983) Self-control in psychotic disorders. *Archives of General Psychiatry*, **40**, 1141–1145.

Brenner, H. D., Stramke, W. G., Mewes, F. et al. (1980) Erfahrungen mit einem speziellen Therapieprogramm zum Training kognitiver Fähigkeiten in der Rehabilitation chronisch schizophrener Patienten. *Nervenarzt*, **51**, 106–112.

Brenner, H. D., Böker, W., Andres, K. et al. (1985) Efforts at compensation with regard to basic disorders among schizophrenics. In *Primary Health Care in the Making* (eds U. Laaser, R. Senault & H. Viefhues), pp. 267–273. Berlin: Springer-Verlag.

Brenner, H. D., Kraemer, S., Hermanutz, M. et al. (1990) Cognitive treatment in schizophrenia. In *Schizophrenia. Concepts, Vulnerability & Intervention* (eds E. R. Straube & K. Hahlweg), pp. 161–191. Berlin: Springer-Verlag.

Brenner, H. D., Hodel, B., Genner, R. et al. (1992) Biological and cognitive vulnerability factors in schizophrenia: Implications for treatment. *British Journal of Psychiatry*, **161** (suppl. 18), 154–163.

Brenner, H. D., Roder, V., Hodel, B. et al. (1994) *Integrated Psychological Therapy for Schizophrenic Patients*. Toronto: Hogrefe & Huber.

Brenner, H. D., Böker, W., &, Schaub, A. (in prep.) *The role of coping in the course of schizophenia: Results of a prospective study and implications for a newly devised coping orientated treatment programme*. International Congress on Clinical Psychopathology in Timisoara, Rumania, May 12–15, 1994.

Brücher, K. (1992) Ein individualisiertes psychoedukatives Therapiekonzept in der stationären Behandlung Schizophrener – Modelle und eigene Erfahrungen. *Psychiatrische Praxis*, **19**, 59–65.

Buchkremer, G. & Fiedler, P. (1987) Kognitive versus handlungsorientierte Therapie. *Nervenarzt*, **58**, 481–488.

Carr, V., & Katsikis, M. (1987) Illness behavior and schizophrenia. *Psychiatric Medicine*, **5**, 163–170.

Chadwick, P. & Birchwood, M. (1994) The omnipotence of voices. A cognitive approach to auditory hallucinations. *British Journal of Psychiatry*, **164**, 190–201.

Cohen, C. J. & Berk, L. A. (1985) Personal coping style of schizophrenic outpatients. *Hospital & Community Psychiatry*, **36**, 407–410.

Dahl, G. (1986) *Reduzierter Wechsler-Intelligenztest (WIP)*. 2nd revised and expanded edition. Bern: Testzentrale der Schweizer Psychologen, Hans Huber.

Deusinger, I. M. (1986) *Die Frankfurter Selbstkonzeptskalen (FSKN)*. Göttingen: Hogrefe.

Eckman, T. A., Wirshing, W. C., Marder, S. R. et al. (1992) Technology for training schizophrenics in illness self-management: A controlled trial. *American Journal of Psychiatry*, **149**, 1549–1555.

Endicott, J., Spitzer, R. L., Fleiss, J. L. et al. (1986) The Global Assessment Scale. Procedure for measuring overall severity of psychiatric disturbances. *Archives of General Psychiatry*, **33**, 766–771.

Englert, J. D., Gebhardt, R., Kliefoth, M. (1994) *Coping and psychopathology in the course of schizophrenia: The Berlin Coping Study*. International Congress on Clinical Psychopathology in Timisoara, Rumania, May 12–15.

Fahrenberg, J., Kuhn, M., Kulick, B. et al. (1977) Repeated Pschological Measurement Test: Methodenentwicklung für psychologische Zeitreihenstudien. *Diagnostica*, **23**, 15–36.

Falloon, I. R. H. & Talbot, R. E. (1981) Persistent auditory hallucinations: coping mechanisms and implications for management. *Psychological Medicine*, **11**, 329–339.

Grawe, K., Bernauer, F. & Donati, R. (1990 a) Psychotherapien im Vergleich: Haben wirklich alle einen Preis verdient? *Psychotherapie & Medizinische Psychologie*, **40**, 102–114.

Grawe, K., Caspar, F. & Ambühl, H. (1990b) Die Berner Therapievergleichsstudie: Wirkungsvergleich und differentielle Indikation. *Zeitschrift für Klinische Psychologie,* **19**, 338–361.

Grawe, K., Donati, R . & Bernauer, F. (1994) *Psychotherapie im Wandel: Von der Konfession zur Profession.* Göttingen: Hogrefe. Verlag für Psychologie.

Häfner, H., Maurer, K., Löffler, W.,et al. (1993) The influence of age and sex on the onset and early course of schizophrenia. *British Journal of Psychiatry,* **162**, 80–86.

Heaton, R. K. (1981) *A Manual for the Wisconsin Card Sorting Test.* Odessa, FL: Psychological Assessment Resources.

Hecht, H., Faltermaier, A. & Wittchen, H.-U. (1987) *Social Interview Schedule (SIS).* Materialien zur Klinischen Psychologie und Psychotherapie. Regensburg: Roderer.

Heim, E., (1988) Coping und Adaptivität: Gibt es geeignetes oder ungeeignetes Coping? *Psychotherapie & Medizinische Psychologie,* **38**, 8–18.

Heinrichs, D. W., Cohen, B. P. & Carpenter, W. T. (1985) Early insight and the management of schizophrenic decompensation. *Journal of Nervous & Mental Disease,* **173**, 133–138.

Helmstedter, C. & Durwen, H. F. (1990) VLMT: Verbaler Lern- und Mekfähigkeitstest. *Schweizer Archiv für Neurologie & Psychiatrie,* **141**, 21–30.

Herz, M. I. (1984) Recognizing and preventing relapse in patients with schizophrenia. *Hospital & Community Psychiatry,* **35**, 344–349.

Herz, M. I. & Melville, C. (1980) Relapse in schizophrenia. *American Journal of Psychiatry,* **137**, 801–805.

Herz, M. I., Szymanski, H. V. & Simon, J. C. (1982) Intermittant medication for stable schizophrenic outpatients: An alternative to maintenance medication. *American Journal of Psychiatry,* **139**, 918–922.

Herz, M. I., Glazer, W., Mirya, M. et al. (1989) Treating prodromal episodes to prevent relapse in schizophrenia. *British Journal of Psychiatry,* **155** (suppl. 5), 123–127.

Hogarty, G. E., Kornblith, S. J., Greenwald, D. et al. (1995) Personal Therapy: A disorder-relevant psychotherapy for schizophrenia. *Schizophrenia Bulletin,* **21**, 379–393.

Janke, W., Erdman, G. & Kallus, W. (1985) *Streßverarbeitungsfragebogen.* Göttingen: Hogrefe.

Kern, R. S., Green, M. F. & Satz, P. (1992) Neuropsychological predictors of skills training for chronic psychiatric patients. *Psychiatry Research,* **43**, 223–230.

Krampen, G. (1991) *Fragebogen zu Kompetenz- und Kontrollüberzeugungen.* Göttingen: Hogrefe.

Lasar, M. & Loose, R. (1994) Kontrollüberzeugungen bei chronischer Schizophrenie. *Nervenarzt,* **65**, 464–469.

Lazarus, R. S. (1991) *Emotion and Adaptation.* New York: Oxford University Press.

Lazarus, R. S. & Launier, R. (1978) Stress-related transactions between person and environment. In *Perspectives in Interactional Psychology* (eds L. Pervin & M. Lewis). New York: Plenum Press.

Lazarus, R. S. & Folkman, S. (1984) *Stress, Appraisal and Coping.* New York: Springer-Verlag.

Liberman, R. P. (1986) Coping and competence as protective factors in the vulnerability-stress model of schizophrenia. In *Treatment of Schizophrenia: Family Assessment and Intervention* (eds M.J. Goldstein, I. Hand & K. Hahlweg), pp. 210–215. Berlin: Springer-Verlag.

Liberman, R. P. (1988 a) *Social & Independent Living Skills. The Symptom Management Module. Trainer's Manual and Patient's Handbook.* Los Angeles: Clinical Research Center for Schizophrenia & Psychiatric Rehabilitation.

Liberman, R. P.(1988 b) *Social & Independent Living Skills. The Medication Management Module. Trainer's Manual and Patient's Handbook.* Los Angeles: Clinical Research Center for Schizophrenia and Psychiatric Rehabilitation.

Liberman, R. P., Mueser, K. T. & Wallace, C. J. (1986) Social skills training for schizophrenic individuals at risk for relapse. *American Journal of Psychiatry,* **143,** 523–526.

Liberman, R. P., Mueser, K. T. & Wallace, C. J. et al. (1990) Training skills in the psychiatrically disabled: Learning, coping, and competence. In *Schizophrenia. Concepts, Vulnerability, and Intervention* (eds E. R. Straube & K. Hahlweg), pp 193–216. Berlin: Springer-Verlag.

Linden, M., Nather, J. & Wilms, H. U. (1988) Zur Definition, Bedeutung und Messung der Krankheitskonzepte von Patienten. Die Krankheitskonzeptskala (KK-Skala) für Schizophrene Patienten. *Fortschritte der Neurologie & Psychiatrie,* **56,** 34–43.

McCandless-Glinscher, L., McKnight, S., Hamera, E. et al. (1986) Use of symptoms by schizophrenics to monitor and regulate their illness. *Hospital & Community Psychiatry,* **37,** 929–933.

McEvoy, J. P., Freter, S., Everett, G. et al. (1989) Insight and the clinical outcome of schizophrenic patient. *Journal of Nervous & Mental Disease,* **177,** 48–51.

McGlashan, T. H., Levy, S. T. & Carpenter, W. T. (1975) Integration and sealing-over. *Archives of General Psychiatry,* **32,** 1269–1272.

Mueser, K. T., Bellack, A. S., Douglas, M. S. et al. (1991) Predictions of social skill acquisition in schizophrenic and major affective disorder patients from memory and symptomatology. *Psychiatry Research,* **37,** 281–296.

Norman, R. M. & Malla, A. K. (1993) Stressful life events and schizophrenia. I. A review of the research. *British Journal of Psychiatry,* **162,** 161–166.

Nuechterlein, K. H. (1987) Vulnerability models for schizophrenia: state of the art. In *Search for the Causes of Schizophrenia* (eds H. Häfner, W.F. Gattaz & W. Janzarik), pp. 297–316. Berlin: Springer-Verlag.

Nuechterlein, K. H., Dawson, M. E., Gitlin, M. et al. (1992) Developmental processes in schizophrenic disorders: longitudinal studies of vulnerability and stress. *Schizophrenia Bulletin,* **18,** 387–425.

Overall, J. E. & Gorham, D. R. (1962) The Brief Psychiatric Rating Scale. *Psychological Reports,* **10,** 799–812.

Perrez, M. & Matathia, R. (1994) *Differentielle Effekte des Bewältigungsverhaltens und seelische Gesundheit.* Unpublished manuscript.

Perris, C. (1992) A cognitve-behavioral treatment program for patients with a schizophrenic disorder. *New Directions for Mental Health Services,* **53,** 21–32.

Roder, V., Brenner, H. D., Kienzle, N. et al. (1992) *Integriertes Psychologisches Therapieprogramm für schizophrene Patienten (IPT).* 2en expanded edition. München, Weinheim: Psychologie Verlags Union.

Roder, V., Jenull, B. & Brenner, H. D. (in prep.) Behaviour therapy with schizophrenic patients: residential, vocational and recreational rehabilitation.

Schaub, A. (1993) *Formen der Auseinandersetzung bei schizophrener Erkrankung.* Frankfurt am Main: Peter Lang.

Schaub, A. (1994) Relapse and coping behavior in schizophrenia. *Schizophrenia Research*, **11** (2), 188.

Schaub, A., Behrendt, B. & Brenner, H. D. (1994) The influence of the German version of the Symptom Management Module on perceived self-control in schizophrenia. *Proceedings for the 28th Annual Association for Advancement of Behavior Therapy (AABT) Convention*, p. 282., San Diego CA, November 10–13, 1994.

Schaub, A. & Möller, H. J. (1990) *Training kognitiver und sozialer Defizite bei schizophrenen Patienten*. Paper presented at the Conference DGPN, September 26–28, 1990, Bonn. Zentralblatt Neurologie & Psychiatrie (eds O. Hallen & G. Huber), **255**, 277. Heidelberg: Springer-Verlag.

Schöttner, B., Wiedl, K. H. & Schramer, K. H. (1988) *Vorläufiges Manual zum Osnabrücker Belastungs- und Bewältigungsinventar (OBBI)*. Osnabrück: Universität.

Smith, M. L., Glass, G. V. & Miller, T. I. (1980) *The Benefits of Psychotherapy*. Baltimore: John Hopkins University Press.

Soskis, D. A. & Bowers, M. B. (1969) The schizophrenic experience – A follow-up study of attitude and posthospital adjustment. *Journal of Nervous & Mental Disease*, **149**, 443–449.

Stark, F. M. (1992) Strukturierte Information über Vulnerabilität und Belastungsmanagement für schizophrene Patienten. *Verhaltenstherapie*, **2**, 40–47.

Süllwold, L. (1977) *Symptome schizophrener Erkrankungen. Uncharakteristische Basisstörungen*. Monographs on the entire field of psychiatry. Vol. 13. Berlin: Springer-Verlag.

Süllwold, L. (1986) Die Selbstwahrnehmung defizitärer Störungen: Psychologische Aspekte des Basisstörungskonzeptes. In *Schizophrene Basisstörungen* (eds L. Süllwold & H. Huber), pp. 1–38. Heidelberg: Springer-Verlag.

Süllwold, L. & Herrlich, J. (1990) *Psychologische Behandlung schizophren Erkrankter*. Stuttgart: Kohlhammer.

Süllwold, L. & Herrlich, J. (1992) Providing schizophrenic patients with a concept of illness. An essential element of therapy. *British Journal of Psychiatry*, **161** (suppl. 18), 129–132.

Tarrier, N. (1987) An investigation of residual psychotic sypmtoms in discharged schizophrenic patients. *British Journal of Clinical Psychology*, **26**, 141–143.

Tarrier, N., Beckett, R., Harwood, S. et al. (1993 a) A trial of two cognitive behavioral methods of treating drug-resistant residual psychotic symptoms in schizophrenic patients. I. Outcome. *British Journal of Psychiatry*, **162**, 524–532.

Tarrier, N., Sharpe, L., Beckett, R. et al. (1993 b) A trial of two cognitive behavioral methods of treating drug-resistant residual psychotic symptoms in schizophrenic patients. II. Treatment-specific changes in coping and problem-solving skills. *Social Psychiatry & Psychiatric Epidemiology*, **28**, 5–10.

Test, M. A. (1991) Training in community living. In *Handbook of Psychiatric Rehabilitation* (ed. R.P. Liberman). Elmsford, NY: Pergamon.

Thurm, I. & Häfner, H. (1987) Perceived vulnerability, relapse risk and coping in schizophrenia. *European Archives of Psychiatry & Neurological Sciences*, **237**, 46–53 .

Whisman, M. A. (1990) The efficacy of booster maintenance sessions in behavior therapy: Review and methodological critique. *Clinical Psychology Review*, **10**, 155–170.

Wiedl, K. H. (1992) Assessment of coping with schizophrenia. Stressors, appraisals and coping behaviour. *British Journal of Psychiatry*, **161**, (suppl. 18), 114–122.

Wiedl, K. H. (1994) Bewältigungsorientierte Therapie bei Schizophrenen. *Zeitschrift für Klinische Psychologie, Psychopathologie & Psychotherapie*, **42**, 89–117.

Wiedl, K. H. & Schöttke, H. (1993) *Dynamic Assessment of Selective Attention in Schizophrenic Subjects: The Analysis of Intraindividual Variability of Performance.* Research report, No. 90. Osnabrück: Universität.

Zubin, J. & Spring, B. (1977) Vulnerability – A new view of schizophrenia. *Journal of Abnormal Psychology*, **86**, 103–126.

Processes of Healing and the Nature of Schizophrenia

John S. Strauss

Summary

The mental health field has made important efforts to tear away from past traditions that depended excessively on anecdote and theory with little appreciation for the nature of proof. But in these efforts we have gone to the opposite extreme, underestimating how much ours must be a human science attending to the need to be both human and scientific. Studies of people with schizophrenia who have improved suggest that understanding improvement and illness processes requires an effort to incorporate the principles of other sciences together with principles about the nature of human experience that have been suggested by the arts. Principles in other sciences, for example, attention to reliable measurement, sampling, and data analysis, are well known. In the mental health field, equally important may be the principles for understanding human experience such as attention to the details of experience, not just to gross phenomena that can be reliably measured and to the subjective experience of the observer as well as the objective description of the patient. This report describes such principles for understanding human experience and data indicating why they are essential to understanding schizophrenia and improvement.

Almost a century ago, Kraepelin and then Bleuler stated that the essential core of dementia praecox, or schizophrenia, was the person's loss of will, the disintegration of the personality. Though I believe they were right, we have lost track of exactly what that might imply. Even Kraepelin and Bleuler, questing after theory and limited to particular patient populations, were not able to follow adequately the path that can be traced by careful involvement with the wide range of patients with schizophrenia, including those who improve. Following this path, however, leads us away from what we have come to consider to be the scientific method and into consideration of variables and processes which are extremely difficult to deal with when using its traditional approaches. The problems of psychiatry require that we struggle with these issues rather than avoid them, that we consider again and again two basic questions: 1) On what variables and processes should we focus? 2) And then, but only then, how should we deal with these variables and processes scientifically?

In our efforts to understand human functioning, including schizophrenia and its healing processes, a dominant tendency has been to simple explanations – oral deprivation, abnormal dopamine metabolism, social labelling. In all such efforts at crystallising, we have lost much of the essence of what we are trying to understand – the essence first suggested by Kraepelin and Bleuler. It is not that any of these interpretations is necessarily incorrect or worthless, merely that they are only pieces of a larger puzzle, rather than the puzzle itself. In their considerations, they leave out totally the core of the human experience, of the personality, the subtleties of feeling, of intuition, of meaning, of sense of the world, of who one is, was, and wants to become. And the answers we have tried also leave out an understanding of the disruption and the improvement in these core experiences. Yet how are we to proceed towards developing a more adequate human science that does not exclude prematurely these masses of complex data, towards a better understanding of the essence of schizophrenia and of the healing process?

To include these features as potentially important parts of our science, we need to start again at the key points made by Kraepelin and Bleuler. What does "disintegration of the personality" mean, and how is its reversal reflected in the healing process? We must start again by observing and describing those processes. And since we are dealing with human beings, the phenomena of human experience form the base of all our inquiry, whether that inquiry be biological, psychological, or social. We must therefore deal with how one collects information from humans – a process in which the Heisenberg principle is probably even more important than it was in physics, a process in which our interaction with the phenomenon we are studying profoundly affects what we will see and what we will exclude.

Crucial to our approach for human science are several methods and considerations which are as paradoxical as they are obvious. These may seem unscientific, but are central to a science which includes human experience, its richness, its depth, and its complexity. Because of these concerns, when conducting research interviews with people with schizophrenia with a special focus on people who are improving or have improved, to learn more about these processes I have tried progressively to listen more and more openly. Only towards the end of the interviews were certain basic traditional, measurement-type data collected on levels of functioning, symptomatology, and demographics. These studies of improvement have involved a wide range of individuals with the DSM-III-R diagnosis of schizophrenia, age 18–70; located geographically in various sites including South Carolina, Connecticut, Maine, Ohio, California, and Canada; homeless, living in institutions, living with families, living alone; both persons in their first inpatient admission with schizophrenia and others who have been in hospital for the larger part of 40 years or more; people treated with traditional medication, with clozapine, with rehabilitation programmes, or receiving no treatment at all. My interviews were conducted often as part of larger studies, carried out with various collaborators mentioned in the acknowledgement.

Data have been collected from 43 people with schizophrenia who have improved significantly during the course of their illness. For those subjects on whom I conducted two or more sequential interviews (N = 28), "significant improvement" signifies a gain of at least 15 points on the Global Assessment Scale (Endicott et al, 1976), but many of these subjects had scale increases of 30 points or more. For those subjects (e. g., members of mental health consumer groups) on whom I conducted only one follow-up interview, "significant improvement" indicates that since being admitted for schizophrenia, they were at least living out of the hospital and their symptoms had improved markedly. On the other hand, some of these subjects were asymptomatic, living independently and working – some in high-level, full-time jobs.

Beyond the formal interviews with these persons, I tried to listen to the current and past experiences they described, and their hopes for the future. Beyond reviewing their records and talking to family members and staff, other encounters have also influenced how I talk to these patients. All these experiences have affected my view on learning about human phenomena and on the methods that might be most useful in that pursuit. On this basis, there are four principles which I regard as particularly central.

Firstly, in an acting class in which I participated, the teacher helped us in many ways to "find the person" that we were portraying. One of the crucial interventions he made was asking the question, "Who is this person?" But how does one characterise a person, grasp who that person is? From the perspective of the apprentice actor, this task must be felt rather than intellectualised; it is a task probably never fully accomplished, but only approximated. But this can be done. In thinking about the patients with whom we work and whom we study, the principle I suggest from this experience is that we must attempt to get some sense of a gestalt of that person, of who that person is, and what is his/her world. Although such an effort is the antithesis of most of our current attempts at diagnostic labelling, it seems to me to be an effort that cannot be neglected in developing our human science, as well as in understanding schizophrenia and the healing process.

Secondly, "the life is in the details." A creative writing teacher of mine repeats this basic rule again and again (Strauss, 1994). As with the tiny dot of a flying bird in the Turner oil painting – an image that powerfully augments the massiveness of the clouds and the unstoppable power of the crashing waves. Or the detail of the little turn of a piano phrase, briefly recasting the melody towards the end of the slow movement in Brahms' First Piano Con-

254

certo. Or the detail of the warm hug the schizophrenic woman with "chronically flat affect" gives me at the end of the research interview. This message also appears to conflict with many efforts at labelling, at bringing together under one rubric a wealth of data and information. Yet, if we are to develop a science that does not lose the life of the people with whom we are working, we cannot ignore this principle.

Thirdly, including ourselves in our understanding and description of patients (Strauss, in press). This again goes against most of the tenets of established science, but I would propose that "objectivity," in the sense of treating ourselves as nameless, personality-less beings and focusing entirely on the patient in fact interferes with our practising an adequate human science. In a group of mental health professionals writing about patients, we have noted repeatedly that whenever we try to be impersonal and objective about our descriptions, we lose the meaningful description of the patient. As important as it might be, for some purposes, to describe a person as a "35-year-old, white, single male with a ten-year history of paranoid schizophrenia" loses key characteristics of the person we are describing.

Fourthly, and also in conflict with the traditions of non-human sciences, is the principle also emphasised by writing and acting teachers, "show, don't tell." Similarly, in understanding people with schizophrenia, the more we talk about them rather than showing by description, often using a first-person perspective, what their experience is like, the more we seem to lose the essence of who they are and of that experience.

In attempting to follow these principles, we begin to notice data that have probably been there all the time, but are often not considered or even elicited in research efforts. Some data are extremely difficult to place within traditional scientific frameworks, but they appear to be important, even crucial, to understanding the phenomena we are pursuing.

It is strange that people with schizophrenia who are improving or have improved often talk as though they have read Kraepelin and Bleuler, or that these authors have talked to them. "I had to pull myself together," "I had to find myself," "I had to learn how to control myself," "I had to learn how to get along with the voices." This is the re-integration of the self, and such a process of re-integration, as reported by patients, appears to have many components. A 48-year-old woman with schizophrenia, who had had 18 admissions since the age of 20, said in a research interview, "Well, I don't think it's just the medication. You have to accept yourself, and you gotta, um, have a thought about getting out of there and doing something." (This was the patient who hugged me at the end of our research interview.)

But should we believe such reports? People with mental disorders have been known to distort descriptions of their experiences and to err about causal

255

attributions – just as professionals have. The sheer frequency of such reports – if we listen for them – in our own interviews and in public presentations by people with schizophrenia, are powerful reasons not to ignore them. Once again, there is an uncanny connection between such reports and the pioneering theorists Kraepelin and Bleuler.

What is the nature of the process which undergoes this disintegration and, in instances of healing, re-integration? I have noticed a first clue primarily in persons with paranoid schizophrenia, perhaps because they are more verbal, or perhaps because the process is limited to them. This suggests that the disintegration occurs around a particularly important theme in a person's life. What this theme is varies, but its presence is reported over and over again by people in our research interviews. One young man, Dan, had paranoid schizophrenia; he came from a tightly-knit family with a minority background and limited education. His goal in life was to be successful and to move away from his family, but at each effort to accomplish that goal, the voices would become worse, making it impossible for him to continue his career or his university studies. Following such efforts, he would be readmitted to hospital, then return home, and take a menial job. As time went on, he discovered that ignoring the voices or trying to shout them down just made them worse. To exist with them he had to take them seriously, consider them, and even at times negotiate with them. As Tyson has suggested (Unpublished M.D. thesis), for Dan these voices appeared to represent "voices from the past," the past being his close connections with his family or origin; the theme was how to live with them and still become autonomous.

Another patient in our follow-up study is Ian, a 68-year-old man who has had paranoid schizophrenia since his late teens; most of his life has been spent in psychiatric hospitals. In his teens, Ian wanted to be a poet, but was told by his family that this was not practical career and that he would have to do something else. It was around this time of career choice and family disagreement that he first became psychotic. It was not until about 30 years later at a time when he finally decided to give up trying to be a poet, that the symptoms diminished enough for him to spend a great deal of time out of hospital, with only infrequent psychotic relapses.

Yet a third patient in our study, Mary, became psychotic for the first time when in her mid-teens, she attempted to free herself from her "mother's apron strings." About 12 years later, the psychosis began to remit considerably, apparently after Mary was able to move out and slowly become more established with her boyfriend, living in an apartment with him.

Although it may be coincidence that these people's apparent life themes and the sense of who they are and where they belong in the world interact with their schizophrenia, the existence of these themes and its connection with the rise and fall of symptomatology is reported very commonly by people who have improved. "Pulling oneself together" usually involves the sense of finding who one is, bringing together conflicting goals and values, or resolving them in some way, whether in the happier ways reflected by Dan and Mary, or by giving up as did Ian.

The second extremely common process described by people with schizophrenia who are improving is the role of relationships. In a great many of our interviews, people who have improved attribute a major contribution to their improvement again and again to someone who cared – sometimes a clinician, but often a family member or friend. There is an old belief that people with schizophrenia *don't* relate to others. This belief is almost as strong as the one that they never improve. I personally have conducted research interviews with over 300 people with various kinds of mental disorders as well as "normal controls." The only person who ever hugged me after an interview was, as mentioned above, a woman in a state hospital who appeared at the beginning to have totally flat affect. She had been in the state hospital for the last 18 months in this, her most recent admission. Besides questions about her past and current situation, I asked her about some of her hopes; suddenly, she began to smile and said if she got better she might reconnect with her husband and her children whom she had not seen for many years. Her smile during these exchanges was brief but very bright. As I got up to leave and was packing up my tape recorder, Gladyce approached me to say goodbye, shook my hand, and suddenly hugged me warmly. Being in a state hospital and having all the stigmata of chronic schizophrenia, she probably did not often have the opportunity to talk about her hopes.

In the *Symposium*, Plato has Aristophanes describe the original state of people as having four arms and four legs and being composite beings. Apparently, because they became too conceited, the powers-that-be split them in half, and according to Aristophanes we have spent the rest of our existence trying to find our other half. People with schizophrenia who improve, and even many who don't, speak repeatedly about the crucial role of other people in their lives. As one patient told me "Dr. Strauss, having mental illness is very lonely." For some, it is almost as though some people with schizophrenia took a particular approach to overcome that horrible fate that Virgil describes in *The Aeneid* (1983 translation) for men about to die during a storm at sea, "never again to hear a voice that called them" (page 11). People with schizophrenia often manufacture their own voices to call them.

At this point I would like to respond to some of my own voices rising in criticism.

John 2: "But these are just anecdotal reports."

John 1: "I know, but I hear them again and again from so many people in so many different settings."

J2: "But I never hear them. People tell me about their hallucinations or delusions or about how good they are, or that they don't have any mental illness, but they never talk about the things you mention."

J1: "I think that's because, as with many of us, you've been trained only to look for certain things and to see people with mental disorders in particular contexts. Just as no one will ever discover insight learning from only watching animals (or humans) in a box, where all they can do is press a bar to get a pellet, so it is unlikely that you will ever hear about these themes and these feelings if you restrict your patient contacts to the usual settings and the usual kinds of interrogations. For me, some of the most valuable and surprising contexts I have had have been at conferences where people with schizophrenia are acting as consumer advocates or as consultants. In settings like that, I see things that I never would have imagined could be true, it's a little like going outside at night, and only after you've become dark adapted you see all those stars. And these things that people with schizophrenia talk about when given the opportunity have made me change a lot of my ideas that I held firmly for many years. But I would like to talk a bit more about the nature of our science a little later."

J2: "Well, then I have another major criticism – that you're just going back to all the old psychodynamic stuff."

J1: "I worry about that too, but I don't think it's true. The metapsychology of psychoanalytic theory may or may not be accurate, but it's very speculative, built on a very limited data base collected in a very narrow range of ways. What we need is not so much complex theory, but much more information – a greatly expanded way of dealing with people with schizophrenia in a research paradigm that does not reduce their activity by limiting it to responses on questionnaires or particular kinds of tests. By trying to be scientific in this particular way, we have in fact been terribly unscientific, through failing to become familiar with the huge range of the phenomena that exist in the experiences of people with schizophrenia. Our limitations in this regard become particularly apparent when we start talking more fully with people who are improving or have improved; this is partly because they are more verbal and partly because they have a wider perspective on their past experiences, just as any of us would."

258

J2: "But all you're really doing is bringing up that age-old argument again, whether we should focus on the individual or the group, an idiopathic focus or a nomothetic one. And worse, you want to destroy our hard-won scientific tradition."

J1: "No, that's not really right. My point is that to make psychiatry a human science, we need to take the next step beyond that dichotomy. Psychoanalysis focused almost exclusively and in-depth on the individual (as we interpreted him or her), with almost no attention to measurement or rules of evidence. With descriptive/biological psychiatry, we have focused on these aspects which are indeed crucial. Now, we have to demand of ourselves that we move towards bringing careful description not just to superficial characteristics of people with schizophrenia – things like delusions and hallucinations that are relatively easy to conceptualise and measure – but also to the whole range of the data, of their experiences. We must no longer exclude the richness and depth which is the reality in things like the sense of self, and of relationships."

Where does this lead us for research and treatment and for educating mental health professionals? As skulls x-rays are to the PET scan for understanding organic processes, I think some of our standard psychiatric or psychological descriptions of patients are to the potential depth and richness of experiences that these people have.

"This is a 35-year-old, white, single male with a history of paranoid schizophrenia admitted now for recurrence of auditory hallucinations" is an important but grossly inadequate representation of the experience of that person. Plato and Virgil, amongst others, have tried to tell us something about the nature of human beings; we need to explore how such art can become a part of our science, rather than continuing to separate it off.

Advances in medication and rehabilitation, as important as they are, must be accompanied by another aspect of treating a human condition, the interpersonal one. In a day when being with a person with schizophrenia in the sense of "just" listening, of talking with him/her, of trying to understand "Who is this person?" is less and less frequently the experience of clinicians in practice or in training, we are losing another source of information (and of treatment) which is as crucial as a PET scan (although incredibly cheaper). It is worth repeating that to understand human experience, at least three things which people in the arts have to teach us are crucial: the life is in the details; "show don't tell," and experiences of a person in depth almost always include the writer's or the actor's own experience. Paradoxically, to reflect human experience by only being "objective," actually distorts and diminishes the accuracy of description.

But then, what becomes of measurement, of the reliability and replicability of judgements that are so central to science? I do not know. Most likely, we will have to define science, at least human science, more broadly than we do currently. Consistently distorting or ignoring huge masses of data in order to meet a particular conception of science cannot, in a broader sense, be "scientific"; whether we like it or not, human data include the depth and richness that are part of the human experience.

Just as learning about the nature of human experience requires special attention and attitudes by the human scientist, so does interpersonal treatment. "Listening," "being there" for the patient, "caring" are all too often thrown off by the supervisor, the treater, the writer about treatment, as "of course, you need to listen to (take seriously, care about) the patient." But reports by those who have received treatment testify to how crucial – and how rare – it is to find someone, especially a doctor, who "took me seriously."

Listening, taking seriously, caring about – and getting better at those things – is probably a life's work that may be approximated but rarely achieved – as our spouses and children, to say nothing of our patients, may readily testify. For both treatment and research, moving in these directions will require creativity in how we think about science and the human context, but this can probably be accomplished, or at least approximated. The PET scan was not built in a day, or cheaply either. Kraepelin and Bleuler were probably right about the disintegration of the personality in schizophrenia, but we have so much more to learn about what that really means, and about how that process gets reversed.

Acknowledgements

This report was supported in part by an NIMH Research Scientist Award #MH00340, an Established Investigator Award from the National Alliance for Research on Schizophrenia and Depression, and a grant from the Supreme Council of the Scottish Rite. The author wishes to express his gratitude to groups and individuals who have contributed so much to this work: Connecticut Valley Hospital, Connecticut Mental Health Center, Connecticut Department of Mental Health, West Haven Veterans Administration Medical Center, Paula Goering, PhD, Donald Wasylenki, MD, Kay McCrary, EdD, Charles Goldman, MD, Karen Kangas, PhD, Herbert Meltzer, MD, Courtenay M. Harding, PhD, Jaak Rakfeldt, PhD, Paul Lieberman, MD, Hisham Hafez, MD, and Larry Davidson, PhD. This work was funded in part by NIMH Grant #MH00340 and grants from the National Alliance for Research on Schizophrenia and Depression (NARSAD) and the Scottish Schizophrenia Research Programme.

260

References

Endicott, J., Spitzer, R. L., Fleiss, J. L. et al., (1988) The Global Assessment Scale: A procedure for measuring overall severity of psychiatric disturbance. *Archives of General Psychiatry*, **33**, 766–771.

Strauss, J. (1994) The person with schizophrenia as a person: II. Approaches to the subjective and complex. *British Journal of Psychiatry*, **164**, 103–107.

Tyson, A. (1989) *The Interaction between Developmental Striving and the Course of Mental Disorder*. Unpublished MD Thesis, Yale University.

Virgil, P. (1983) *The Aeneid* (trans. R. Fitzgerald). New York: Random House.

The Humanity of the Schizophrenic Patient

Gerald J. Sarwer-Foner

Summary

The association areas of the brain, particularly the temporal and parietal lobes, combined with the frontal lobes for the purposes of planning and control, help to form the human symbols which create the Psyche. The symbols for these images and all the emotions linked to them are treated by the brain as living matter. In schizophrenia, the patient has a fragmented or poorly formed concept of self, which these symbols reflect and evoke; this leads to the pathological ego-defences with which the patient attempts to cope. The "I" and "Me" symbols in the Psyche are treated as living matter by the brain, adding to their significance. Inhibition of neuronal networking and possible interference with dendritic formation may occur as a result, producing impoverished, improperly "wired," or tortuously linked brain and Psyche.

Schizophrenia is specifically a human disease (Benedetti, 1987), and its most significant clinical manifestations are in relationship to how people express their humanity (Sarwer-Foner, 1979, 1983, 1986, 1993; Wynne et al., 1978). That is to say – how they form symbols of themselves and of other human beings in their Psyche and how they respond to these (Benedetti, 1987; Ciompi, 1988; Fromm-Reichmann, 1950; Hafner et al., 1987; Hill, 1957; McGlashan, 1983; Sechehaye, 1951; Wright, 1952). There is no complete animal model of this disease at present, even though recent experimental work has made some advances in this direction (Carlsson & Dancon, 1993; McKinney & Moran, 1981). Patients with schizophrenia have a very variable body image, resulting in a conflictive and defective sense of self (the "I," the "Me"). They develop pathological ego defences in attempts to preserve and protect their damaged sense of "Me," and "I," and to maintain some semblance of worth and self-esteem. As a human disease, schizophrenia presents with difficulties in channelling basic biological energies and drives into forming an adequate concept of self.

Difficulties in Childhood

The schizophrenic patient's intrapsychic conflicts often present in childhood with difficulties in adaptive problem-solving; they effect the forming of a body image and a concept of self that worsen in later life. Symptoms often show themselves, as such patients attempt ordinary progressive (developmental) achievements, but they also appear as these patients attempt to regress, in the face of severe anxiety-causing conflicts, including those which result from falling back onto earlier steps in childhood development. In such patients, there is already an inadequate and split sense of what becomes, the "Me" in the Psyche; in the symbols that represent their evolving sense of personal identity. This produces further problems in the efforts which are made as an adolescent or a young adult to grow into someone with a relatively intact sense of adult personal identity.

Patients with schizophrenia therefore have more difficulties than the non-schizophrenic in dealing with or using the representations (symbols) in their Psyche that illustrate their own completeness, or competence to feel worthy and adequate as a person. They have difficulty using patterns of social skills that represent personal completeness or competence in a particular society, for achieving those socially and culturally determined levels which are needed to establish in their own minds a secure place for themselves and a sense of personal worth.

Association Areas of the Brain and Symbols in the Psyche

It is the association areas of the brain, particularly the parietal and temporal lobes, that form and store the symbols that form much of the Psyche. These form the multiple symbolic systems in the Psyche which combine, and are used with the frontal lobe's functions for planning and for control. Many symbolic systems are formed, some dealing largely with imaginative and playful imagery i. e., not real external or internal objects. Particularly in responding to sensorial stimuli, the brain makes important distinctions, treating symbols of the "I" and "Me" or representational images closely related to the Self as living flesh; this means the entire person in all its forms, thoughts, and feelings. The brain thus treats, and equates, those symbols as being the same as the real physical body and its full complement of thoughts, emotions, decisions, and actions. On the other hand, different symbols are recognised as non-self representations.

The Psyche becomes a survival organ, in directing the brain in relationship to the needs of the "I," and the "Me." In schizophrenic patients, the developmental processes which normally lead to a solid sense of "Me" and "Self," including a sense of identity for gender after adolescence, are impeded. This process may become fragmented or stopped at different stages. Thus, the Self symbols represent the skewed sense of inadequacy, of only partial completeness, and therefore of deficiency (Benedetti, 1987; Fromm-Reichmann, 1950; McGlashan, 1983).

Ego Defences in these Processes

The patient's ego-defences try to preserve or create a better personal sense of adequacy than exists in reality, since the severe anxiety and emotional pain related to these feelings of inadequacy are difficult to bear. Paradoxically, though, schizophrenic patients often show good reality-testing about which contacts can bring them to the limits of their own mental discomfort at closeness to another human being. Attraction, any form of sexuality, or aggression, can all be quasi-intolerable to the individual patient. They defend themselves against the affects that this can provoke in them and, often in an extreme way, against the possibility of being thus stimulated.

Possible Defensive Inhibition of Synaptic and Dendritic Connections

It is possible that for ego defensive purposes (i. e., the patient's attempts to limit his/her own psychic pain), the schizophrenic patient may inhibit both the furthering of neuronal formation and the growth of synaptic connections, particularly in adolescents and young adults. There may also be a disuse atrophy of certain association patterns (Andreason et al., 1990; Roberts & Bruton, 1990), which is also largely ego-defensive.

Even when the organic association circuits seem anatomically intact (Berman & Weinberger, 1986; Andreason et al., 1990; Bogerts, 1993; Gur & Pearlson, 1993) schizophrenic patients probably use individually selective ego-defensive inhibition to minimise anything which will bring into their consciousness, associations, motor impulses, and drives that are currently intolerable for them. These include envy, possessiveness, longing to be valued, intolerable sexuality, and aggression. Avoiding their entry into consciousness produces the same inhibition of the subject's awareness of them, as would the absence of the neuronal circuits that convey this information.

Pre-existing Brain Damage and Severity of Schizophrenia

Through these mechanisms, it seems likely that patients with pre-existing brain damage who then develop schizophrenia would tend to have a more severe and chronic form of the disease (Buchanan et al., 1991; Cleghorn et al., 1991; Bogerts, 1993). Similarly, patients whose schizophrenia began very early in life, and therefore existed in major areas of their life and personality for a very long time, may form a more severe and chronic group of patients (Hafner, 1987). However, some of these may show relatively intact, and in some cases remarkably developed capacities in limited areas.

Fortunately, there are schizophrenic patients without pre-existing brain damage in whom such processes seem clinically less invasive and more limited. These may show a greater degree of ego-defensive inhibition of intact neuronal systems, thus forming a group with better capacity to relate to both external and internal objects, and thus with a better prognosis.

The Frontal Lobes for Planning and Control

Very likely, the functions of the frontal lobes (Cleghorn et al., 1987; Berman et al., 1988; Bogerts, 1993), which link to the parietal and temporal lobes for planning needs and control purposes, can also be inhibited by the actions of the symbols for an inadequate sense of "I" and "Me" in the Psyche in the association areas. Here, they would no doubt be linked with symbols expressing difficulties in self-confidence and self-esteem, resulting in a skewed and incompetent sense of self. These conflicts in the psyche could well inhibit both the formation of new dendritic connections and the actions of existing ones. This in turn would result in interference with temporal, parietal, and frontal lobe networking (Ingvar & Franzen, 1974; Cleghorn et al., 1987, 1991; Buchanan et al., 1991; Kishimato et al., 1987; Berman et al., 1988). The circuiting (Kovelman & Scheibel, 1984; Berman & Weinberger, 1986; Andreason et al., 1990; Bogerts, 1993; Gur, 1993) of existing dendritic connections could also be ego-defensively inhibited, either by being diverted to more torturous routes, or by a more indirectly torturous formation of such dendrites.

265

Thus, it is speculated that the laying down of associations of very painful affects, linked to symbols representing an inadequate "Me," "I," and "Self," leads to ego-defensive and (hypothetical) neuronal-inhibiting processes. The result would be a distorted, impoverished (Risberg et al., 1975; Weinberger et al., 1986, 1987, 1989, 1993; Roberts & Bruton, 1990; Zipursky et al., 1990; Sharif et al., 1993), improperly wired brain, together with a poorly formed and impoverished Psyche. As mentioned above, schizophrenic patients with pre-existing brain damage – early or later (traumatic, biochemical, endocrinological, etc.) – experience a further limitation of their ability to form a proper sense of self.

The consequences hypothesised here seem more likely to account for the absence of brain cell and neuronal fibre mass (Zipursky et al., 1990), seen in the brains of some schizophrenic patients (Weinberger et al., 1986, 1987, 1989, 1993; Andreason, 1990; Roberts & Bruton, 1990; Buchanan et al., 1991; Cleghorn et al., 1991; Zipursky et al., 1991; Bogerts, 1993; Gur & Pearlson, 1993; Sharif et al., 1993) than such hypothesised factors as viral, retro-viral, cytomegalic, or other infections (Crow, 1984; Kirch, 1993) or seasonal effects.

Thus inhibition, in the formation of an adequate sense of "Me" correlates with identity crises and poor symbolic formation, accompanied by delays in or the absence of neuronal development, and in poor dendritic connections, producing an "incomplete wiring." This compromises functioning. The result is a reciprocal relationship between a poorly formed Psyche, which defensively inhibits the free use of the neuronal and dendritic association area systems. This provides an impoverished neuronal network, giving its user a further impoverished Psyche. *Fruste* forms of such disorders are more easily reversible over time, but the early development of massive inhibitory processes would be harder to remedy.

Schizophrenia as a Way of Life

Among schizophrenic patients, one is more likely to find a poorer sense of self, low-self-esteem, and lack of sureness about who and what the person is then among those with non-schizophrenic psychiatric disorders (Sechehaye, 1951; McGlashan, 1983; Ciompi, 1988). In the reality of their lives, there has often been an absence of truly significant people. In sub-acute and chronic schizophrenia, the characterological patterns (Hill, 1957; Sarwer-Foner, 1984) and major ego defensive structures (Fromm-Reichmann, 1950; Sechehaye, 1951; Sarwer-Foner, 1961; Benedetti, 1987; Ciompi, 1988) are incor-

266

porated in relationship to the illness. Here, they function to make the patient's individual pathological ego defences the "normal," instantly responsive, "way I am as an adult" (Hill, 1957; Sarwer-Foner, 1984). This becomes, "the schizophrenic way of life" (Hill, 1957), in which the entire character structure and ego defences largely support the disease, rather than any strivings for health. Therapeutic efforts then have to cope with these chronic, psychotic, character defences (Hill, 1957; Sarwer-Foner, 1984). The use of these personality defences often helps to prolong the duration of the psychotic episode and sometimes of the entire illness. The patient is concerned about minimising his/her individual psychic pain and tests reality reasonably well about what causes this pain – about which characterological tendencies, attitudes, and habit patterns in those around them might lead to intrusions, creating emotions which, consciously or unconsciously, are frightening. These intrusions include the patient's fear of the other's capacity for human warmth and outgoingness, as well as other penetrating contacts with his/her Psyche. They would demand responses too uncomfortable for the patient with stimulation of his/her poorly tolerated needs for closeness, love, aggression, hate, and aspects of their own sexuality. Lack of self-mastery, the sense of not belonging, low self-esteem, and not being a well loved "Me," is part of the poor tolerance for this sort of stimulation.

It is the ego defensive, inhibiting, avoidance of the emotional sense of the inadequate "Me," the "I," the "Self" which limits attempts to successfully engage in such activities, if the patient feels he/she is a shattered, inadequate, fragment. It is the emotional pain the patient feels around this, the anxiety (Wright, 1952), self-blaming, fault-finding, frustration, anger, rage, fury, sense of helpless inadequacy and of non-belonging that lead to multiple avoidance on the one hand (including profound regression) and massive use of inhibition and characterological ego-defences on the other. Lewis Hill (1957) spoke of "Schizophrenia as a way of life," in alluding to these defences in the chronic schizophrenic patient.

Brain Imaging, Metabolic, and Blood Flow Studies

Weinberger (1986, 1987, 1989, 1993; Berman & Weinberger, 1986), working with brain imaging (Cleghorn, 1987, 1991; Andreason et al., 1990; Zipursky et al., 1990; Zipursky et al., 1991; Gur, 1993; Sharif et al., 1993), metabolic (Wiesel et al., 1987; Berman et al., 1988; Buchanan et al., 1991) and blood techniques (Ingvar, 1974; Risberg et al., 1975; Kishimato et al., 1987), as well as radioactive glucose and other measures of energy use, has investigated some of the biological mechanisms in the brain that can show hypofunction in schizophrenic patients. These physiological findings are of importance in understanding the schizophrenic patient's inability to participate fully in areas that have been painful, and which provoke anxiety and avoidance. These patients' attempts to avoid, minimise, contain, or if necessary destroy what they fear may also lead to inhibiting the free use of the association and motor areas of the brain and their systems. This in turn may progress to inhibiting neuronal growth and development as well as dendritic formation, thus inhibiting the larger networking of brain cells.

It is possible that the schizophrenic patient unconsciously fears developing maximal anxiety, which could occur if he/she attempts to master with an inadequate "I" or "Me" tasks such as, "Where do I work, can I hold a job, who can stimulate me sexually, who do I marry, relate to, am I seen as competent, do I see myself to be worthy?" Inhibiting potentially painful associations over a span of many years may lead to an actual impoverishment of the capacity to mobilise the frontal lobes for planning and control, as well as similar effects on the affective association areas of the temporal and parietal lobes. The patient often succeeds in avoiding this emotional pain, but at a very great price.

In current diagnostic usage, the diagnosis of schizophrenia is increasingly being reserved for only the most severe patients with poorer prognoses (Sarwer-Foner, 1983, 1986). Cases that recover, particularly if they recover quickly, receive a diagnosis other than schizophrenia. This is different from the general usage of 20 or 30 years ago in North America, when Bleulerian and Meyerian concepts were more commonly in vogue.

Therapeutic Consequences

It follows from what has been presented above that therapy should be directed to establishing a proper sense of personal identity, with a good intrapsychic "I," "Me," and "Self" in each patient with schizophrenia. All treatment would have to share this goal, regardless of what other aspects of clinical symptomatology might be targeted. For patients who retain the ability to relate to external objects, and who present with acute psychotic episodes followed by a relative return to normality, having some therapeutic "success" means less illness and fewer episodes. However, for those who relate poorly to external objects, and have a chronic course with exacerbations of acute psychosis, "success" would mean strengthening their ability to relate, both internally and

externally, and would increase the individual's sense of being a more integrated person, as well as reducing the number and/or severity of episodes.

Psychopharmacology (Sarwer-Foner, 1960; Sarwer-Foner & Kerenyi,
1960; Seeman, 1987; Alphs, 1993; Poirier, 1993) has to be skillfully used and
integrated with supportive, reality-testing psychotherapy (Sarwer-Foner &
Ogle, 1955, 1956; Sarwer-Foner, 1960, 1989). In addition, ego-supportive,
uncovering psychotherapy is a specialised technique which could be useful
for perhaps 25–40% of schizophrenic patients.

Atypical Neuroleptics

The atypical neuroleptics (Alphs, 1993; Poirier, 1993) have already allowed
about 20% of patients suffering from severe chronic schizophrenia to improve
remarkably, while others demonstrate improvements of a lesser order. At the
same time, intensive, supportive, reality-testing and social skill-forming psychotherapy is needed as part of the rehabilitative efforts. Psychiatrists need
to be specifically trained for these procedures, with a good knowledge of both
psychotherapy and pharmacotherapy. Properly planned, funded, and staffed
facilities are needed for this type of work, including allied health professionals and social agency facilities – sheltered workshops, group homes, shared
apartments, etc. Ideally, every schizophrenic patient should be studied individually, with attempted understanding of the patient's human conflicts, in-
capacity, and level of self-esteem.

The patient should know which psychiatrist is responsible for his care, and
should be able to relate to this person throughout the different levels of treatment and rehabilitation. It is possible that the roughly 25% of long-term patients who seem to mature late in life (Daum et al., 1977) may be those who
can relate to others, even in the early acute phase of the illness.

Ego-supportive, uncovering, psychoanalytically-oriented therapy of long-
term schizophrenic patients is a difficult and exacting task. McGlashan
(1983) has shown that 25% of such patients did well with such intensive psychotherapy, and this is a significant achievement for such a difficult group of
patients, even though it can never be the therapy of the mass.

Reductions in Funding

In a practical sense, these needs demand time, money, and personnel. In the
mid-1990s, government policies in a number of countries are directed towards rapid solutions ("quick fixes"), whether or not these in fact exist. Train-

ing large groups of professional staff to a high standard is not seen as an urgent necessity. Sometimes, the availability of personnel and resources is reduced in another way, by transferring them from a medical aegis into social agencies for rehabilitative programmes, many of which are non-medical. These are often described as placing patients into the community. However, when done in isolation from the range of medical facilities needed for the detection, treatment, and rehabilitation of schizophrenia, it is not at all as good a way of handling the individual patient as a system integrated over its entire range.

Despite this, the humanity of the schizophrenic patient manifests itself for all who wish to see. As always, individual professionals learn form their patients, and newcomers learn their own versions of the same old truths. The humanity of the patient forces these verities into therapy.

References

Alphs, L. (1993) *On New Psychotropic Agents for Schizophrenia Available or Being Researched in the U.S.A.* Plenary Session on Schizophrenia, 9th World Congress of Psychiatry, Rio de Janerio, June 11.

Andreason, N. C., Ehrhardt, J. C., Swayze, V. et al. (1990) Magnetic resonance imaging of the brain in schizophrenia: The pathophysiologic significance of structural abnormalities. *Archives of General Psychiatry*, **47**, 35–44.

Benedetti, G. (1987) *Psychotherapy of Schizophrenia*. New York: New York University Press.

Berman, K. F., Illowsky, B. P. & Weinberger, D. R. (1988) Cerebral blood flow studies in schizophrenia. In *Handbook of Schizophrenia*, Vol. I (eds H. A. Nasrallah & D. R. Weinberger). Amsterdam: Elsevier.

Berman, K. F., Illowsky, B. P. & Weinberger, D. R. (1988) Physiological dysfunction of dorsolateral prefrontal cortex in schizophrenia: IV. *Archives of General Psychiatry*, **45**, 609–622.

Bogerts, B. (1993) Recent advances in the neuropathology of schizophrenia. *Schizophrenia Bulletin*, **19**, 431–445.

Buchanan, R. W., Breier, A., Kirkpatrick, A. et al. (1991) The deficit syndrome: Functional and structural characteristics. *Schizophrenia Research*, **4**, 400–401.

Carlsson, A. & Dancon, J. M. (1993) *Animal Models of Schizophrenia*. Presented at Symposium, Animal Models of Schizophrenia, 9th World Congress of Psychiatry, Rio de Janerio, June 11.

Ciompi, L. (1988) *The Psyche and Schizophrenia: The Bond between Affect and Logic.* Cambridge, MA: Harvard University Press.

Cleghorn, J. M., Garnett, E. S., Nahmias, C. et al. (1987) Increased frontal and reduced parietal glucose metabolism in acute untreated schizophrenia. *Psychiatry Research*, **28**, 119–133.

Cleghorn, J. M., Zipursky, R. B. & List, S. J. (1991) Structural and functional brain imaging in schizophrenia. *Journal of Psychiatry & Neuroscience*, **16** (2), 53–74.

Crow, T. J. (1984) A re-evaluation of the viral hypothesis: Is psychosis the result of retroviral integration at a site close to the cerebral dominance gene? *British Journal of Psychiatry*, **145**, 243–253.

Daum, C. M., Brooks, G. W. & Albee, G. W. (1977) Twenty-year follow-up of 253 schizophrenic patients originally selected for chronic disability: Pilot study. *Psychiatric Journal of the University of Ottawa*, **2**, 129.

Fromm-Reichmann, F. (1950) *Principles of Intensive Psychotherapy*. Chicago: University of Chicago Press.

Gur, R. E. & Pearlson, G. D. (1993) Neuroimaging in schizophrenia research. *Schizophrenia Bulletin*, **19**, 337–354.

Hafner, H., Gattaz, W. F. & Janzarik, W. (Eds.) (1987) *Search for the Causes of Schizophrenia*. Berlin: Springer-Verlag.

Hill, L. B. (1957) The nature of extramural schizophrenia. In *Schizophrenia in Psychoanalytic Office Practice* (ed. A. H. Rifkin), pp. 3–9. New York: Grune-Stratton.

Ingvar, D. H. & Franzen, G. (1974) Abnormalities of cerebral blood flow distribution in patients with chronic schizophrenia. *Acta Psychiatrica Scandinavica*, **50**, 425.

Kirch, D. G. (1993) Infection and autoimmunity as etiologic factors in schizophrenia: A review and reappraisal. *Schizophrenia Bulletin*, **19**, 355–370.

Kishimato, H., Kuwahara, H., Ohnos, O. et al. (1987) Three subtypes of chronic schizophrenia identified using 11C-glucose positron emission tomography. *Psychiatry Research*, **21**, 285–292.

Kovelman, J. A. & Scheibel, A. B. (1984) A neurohistological correlate of schizophrenia. *Biological Psychiatry*, **19**, 1601–1621.

McGlashan, T. H. (1983) Intensive individual psychotherapy of schizophrenia: A review of techniques. *Archives of General Psychiatry*, **40**, 909–920.

McKinney, W. T. & Moran, E. C. (1981) Animal models of schizophrenia. *American Journal of Psychiatry*, **138**, 478–483.

Poirier, M. (1993) *On New Psychotropic Agents for Schizophrenia Available or Being Researched in Europe*. Presented at Plenary Session on Schizophrenia, 9th World Congress of Psychiatry. Rio de Janerio, June 11.

Risberg, J., Ali, Z. et al. (1975) Regional cerebral blood flow by 133 xenon inhalation. *Stroke*, **6**, 142.

Roberts, G. W. & Bruton, C. J. (1990) Notes from the graveyard: Neuropathology and schizophrenia. *Neuropathology & Applied Neurobiology*, **16**, 3–16.

Sarwer-Foner, G. J. & Ogle, W. (1955) The use of reserpine in open psychiatric settings. *Canadian Medical Association Journal*, **73**, 187.

Sarwer-Foner, G. J. & Ogle, W. (1956) Psychosis and enhanced anxiety produced by reserpine and chlorpromazine. *Canadian Medical Association Journal*, **74**, 526.

Sarwer-Foner, G. J. (1960) *The Dynamics of Psychiatric Drug Therapy*. Springfield, IL: C.C. Thomas.

Sarwer-Foner, G. J. & Kerenyi, A. B. (1961) Accumulated experience with transference and countertransference aspects of the psychotropic drugs 1953–1960. In *Neuropsychopharmacology*, Vol. 2 (ed. E. Rothlin) New York: Elsevier.

Sarwer-Foner, G. J. (1979) On social paranoia: the psychotic fear of the stranger and that which is alien. Dr. Karl Stern Memorial Lecture. *Psychiatric Journal of the University of Ottawa*, **4**, 9–21.

Sarwer-Foner, G. J. (1983) The Simon Bolivar Lecture. American Psychiatric Association. Some thoughts on the current status of the schizophrenic group of illnesses, treatment, research and social aspects. *Psychiatric Journal of the University of Ottawa*, **8**, 1–16.

Sarwer-Foner, G. J. (1984) The basic concepts of character in character neurosis and character disorders. In *Character Pathology: Theory & Treatment* (ed. M. R. Zales), pp. 5–22. American College of Psychiatrists. New York: Brunner Mazel.

Sarwer-Foner, G. J. (1986) Some aspects of current treatment, research and social problems in schizophrenia. In *Handbook of Studies in Schizophrenia*, Part 2 (eds G. Burrows, T. Norman & G. Rubinstein), pp. 275–289. New York: Elsevier.

Sarwer-Foner, G. J. (1989) Psychodynamic action of psychopharmacologic drugs and the target symptom versus the anti-psychotic approach to psychopharmacologic therapy: Thirty years later. *Psychiatric Journal of the University of Ottawa*, **14**, 268–278.

Sechehaye, M. A. (1951) *Symbolic Realization*. New York: International University Press.

Sechehaye, M. A. (1951) *Autobiography of a Schizophrenic Girl*. New York: Grune & Stratton.

Seeman, P. (1987) Dopamine receptors and the dopamine hypothesis of schizophrenia. *Synapse*, **1**, 133–152.

Sharif, Z., Gewirtz, G. & Iqbal, N. (1993) Brain imagery in schizophrenia: A review. *Psychiatric Annals*, **23**, 123–134.

Weinberger, D. R., Berman, K. F. & Zec, R. F. (1986) Physiologic dysfunction of dorsolateral prefrontal cortex in schizophrenia I: Regional cerebral blood flow evidence. *Archives of General Psychiatry*, **43**, 114–124.

Weinberger, D. R. (1987) Implications of normal brain development for the pathogenesis of schizophrenia. *Archives of General Psychiatry*, **44**, 660–669.

Weinberger, D. R. & Berman, K. F. (1989) Speculation on the meaning of metabolic hypofrontality in schizophrenia. *Schizophrenia Bulletin*, **14**, 157–168.

Weinberger, D. R. (1993) *Dopamine and Schizophrenia: A View from the Cortex*. Special Lecture, 9th World Congress of Psychiatry. Rio de Janerio, June 8.

Wiesel, F. A., Wik, G., Sjögren, I. et al. (1987) Regional brain glucose metabolism in drug free schizophrenic patients and clinical correlates. *Acta Psychiatrica Scandinavica*, **76**, 628–641.

Wright, D. G. (1952) Discussion of Dr. Fromm-Reichmann's paper "Some Aspects of Psychoanalytic Psychotherapy with Schizophrenics." In *Psychotherapy with Schizophrenics* (eds E. B. Brody & F. C. Redlich), pp. 121–129. New York: International University Press.

Wynne, L. C., Cromwell, R. L. & Matthysse, S. (1978) *The Nature of Schizophrenia*. New York: J. Wiley & Sons.

Zipursky, R. B., Lim, K. O. & Pfefferbaum, A. (1990) Evidence for diffuse grey matter abnormalities in schizophrenia. Presented at annual meeting of Society of Neuroscience, St. Louis, Missouri, *Abstracts*, **16**, 139.

Zipursky, R. B., Lim, K. O. & Pfefferbaum, A. (1991) Brain size in schizophrenia. *Archives of General Psychiatry*, **48**, 179–180.

Author Index

Abraham, R. 35,
Abuzzahab, F.S. 67
Aebi, E. 32ff., 38
Ahlers, C. 12
Alford, G.S. 94
Allness, D.J. 167ff.
Alphs, L. 269
Ambühl, B. 28
Andersen, K. 66
Anderson, L.T. 58
Anderson, S.W. 82
Andreasen, N.C. 33, 64, 240
Andreason, N.C. 264
Andres, K. 123, 228ff.
Angermeyer, M.C. 219
Angst, J. 68
Anton, R.F. 56
APA, 137
Arora, R.C. 52
Asarnow, R.F. 87
Asberg, M. 102

Babloyantz, A. 18
Bandelow, B. 64
Bandura, A. 213, 214
Barnes, T.R. 64
Basler, H.-D. 223
Bataillard, V. 215ff.
Bateson, G. 23
Bäuml, J. 231, 240
Bebbington, P. 229
Beck, A.T. 95, 98
Behrendt, B. 234
Bellack, A.S. 81, 84, 118, 120, 122, 130,
    137ff., 168, 174, 228
Benedetti, G. 262, 264, 266
Benton, M.R. 138
Berenbaum, H. 118, 120

Bergé, P. 39
Bergold, J.B. 12
Berman, K.F. 81, 264ff.
Bersani, G. 53
Birchwood, M. 202, 230
Bischof, N. 34
Bleich, A. 52
Bleuler, E. 129
Bogerts, B. 264ff.
Böker, W. 3ff., 8, 10, 28, 33, 229ff., 235
Bond, G.R. 173
Borison, R.L. 51ff., 55ff.
Borst, U. 209
Böse, R. 3
Bowen, L. 80, 113
Bowers, M.B. 23
Bowlby, J. 97, 98
Box, G.E.P. 38,
Bozormenyi, Z. 52
Braff., D.L. 81, 118
Breier, A. 230
Brekke, J.S. 170
Brenner, H.D. 3ff., 5, 10, 81, 94, 106,
    109, 118ff., 121, 122, 129, 130, 228ff.,
    230, 235, 245
Briggs, J.F. 18
Brown, G.L. 58
Brücher, K. 231
Brunner, E.J. 9
Buchanan, R.W. 265
Buchanon, R. 81
Buchkremer, G. 94, 234
Bunge, M. 33

Campbell, M. 58
Carlson, J.S. 215
Carlsson, A. 262
Carpenter, M.D. 196, 197

Carpenter, W.T. Jr. 64ff 71
Carr, V. 230
Chadwick, P.D.J. 94, 234
Chambon, O 95
Chiles, J.A. 204
Chouinard, G. 54ff., 67, 71
Ciompi, L. 5, 6, 9, 12, 18ff., 22ff., 25, 32, 35, 38, 97, 167, 262, 266
Claghorn, J. 68
Claus, A. 56
Cleghorn, J.M. 265
Cohen, C.J. 230
Cole, J.O. 65
Conrad, K. 23, 196
Cornblatt, B.A. 118
Corrigan, P.W. 80, 90, 113, 118, 130
Cramer, F. 18
Creer, C. 182
Crow, T.J. 65, 266
Cutting, J. 120

Dahl, G. 240
Daum, C.M. 269
Davidson, L. 163
Davis, J.M. 195
DeCuyper, H.J.A. 55
Degn, H. 18
De Leon, J. 66, 67
Deusinger, I.M. 240
Diamond, B.I. 51ff.
Doane, J.A. 150
Docherty, J.P. 196
Donlon, P.T. 196
Donzel, G. 228ff.
Dougherty, F.E. 120
Dworkin, R.H. 118

Eckman, T.A. 234
Eckmann, J. 41
Edwards, J.G. 67
Eison, M.S. 57
Elting, D. 106ff.
Emrich, H. 28, 44
Endicott, J. 240, 254
Englert, J.D. 231

Fahrenberg, J. 124, 240
Falloon, I.R.H. 121, 129, 230
Farde, L. 202
Fava, G.A. 201
Feinberg, I. 120
Feldhege, F. 219
Filipp, S.H. 223
Foerster, H. 9
Fowler, D. 94ff.
Franke, P. 87
Franklin, J.S. 177
Freed, W.J. 203
Fromm-Reichmann, F. 262, 264, 266
Fukuda, M. 81

Gaebel, W. 64, 66, 195ff., 202
Gallant, D.M. 67
Gelders, Y.G. 56, 68
Gerlach, J. 53
Germundson, S. 182ff., 189
Gessler, S. 120
Gibbons, R.D. 64
Gjerde, P.F. 118ff.
Glass, L. 33,
Gleick, J. 18
Goldberg, S.C. 65
Goldberg, T.E. 81ff.
Goldstein, M.J. 147ff.
Gould, R.J. 66
Grant, S. 55
Grassberger, P. 27
Grawe, K. 126, 241ff.
Green, M.F. 79ff., 115
Greene, R.J. 94
Gur, R.E. 264ff.

Haas, S. 67
Häfner, H. 32, 230, 262
Haken, H. 18, 20, 34
Halford, W.K. 138
Hartman, L.M. 94
Hashimoto, T. 52,
Hatfield, A. 182, 188
Heaton, R.K. 140, 240
Hecht, H. 240
an der Heiden, U. 5, 19, 34

Heim, E. 231
Heimberg, C. 144
Heimberg, D. 118, 120
Heinrich, K. 55
Heinrichs, D.W. 230
Hell, D. 181ff.
Hellman, S.G. 79ff.
Helmchen, W.F. 64
Helmstedter, C. 240
Hemsley, D.R. 118ff.
Hermanutz, M. 94
Hersen, M. 138
Herz, M.I. 196ff., 199, 204, 230ff., 237
Hill, D.J. 222
Hill, L.B. 262, 266ff.
Hodel-Wainschtein, B. 10, 118ff., 229
Hoffman, R.E. 24, 64
Hogarty, G.E. 11, 174, 195ff., 234
Holden, D.F. 182, 188
Hole, R.W. 94
Hölzl, M. 222
Holzman, P.S. 130
Honigfeld, G. 124
Hoult, J. 173
Hfyberg, O.J. 55ff.
Huber, A. 182
Huber, G. 204
Huberman, B.A.24
Hyman, S.E. 203
Huang, M.-L. 53

Ingvar, D.H. 265
Itil, T.M. 52

Jackson, H.J. 118
Janke, W. 219, 240
Janssen, P.A.J. 53
Jaspers, K. 158
Jeste, D.V. 204
Johnson, D.A.W. 196
Johnson, W.G. 94
Johnston-Cronk, K. 201
Jolley, A.G. 197
Jones, D.L. 53

Kaehler, W.M. 130

Kahn, R.S. 52, 53
Kameshima, S. 167ff.
Kane, J.M. 52, 57, 67, 176
Käsermann, M.L. 120
Kavanagh, D.J. 147
Kay, S.R. 54, 64ff., 112
Kern, R.S. 79ff., 130, 239
King, R. 24
Kingdon, D.G. 95
Kirch, D.G. 266
Kishimoto, H. 265
Kissling, W. 195
Kline, J.S. 120
Knoedler, W.H. 167ff.
Knorr-Cetina, K. 8
Kolivakis, T. 66
Konen, A. 122
Korsgaard, S. 53
Koukkou-Lehmann, M. 5, 7, 26
Kovelman, J.A. 265
Kraemer, S. 81, 94, 121, 129
Krampen, G. 222, 240
Kriz, J. 19
Kruse, P. 46
Krystal, J.H. 52
Kupper, Z. 26, 27

Lam, D.H. 148
Lang, P.J. 118
Lange, H.U. 212
Lasar, M. 234
Lauer, G. 223
Laux, G. 67
Lazarus, R.S. 210, 212, 223, 229ff., 235,
    237
Lecrubier, Y. 67
Lehmann, A. 223
Leysen, J.E. 53
Liberman, R.P. 10, 121ff., 129, 138, 209,
    213, 218, 228ff., 234ff., 238
Linden, M. 212, 240
Lorenz, K. 20
Ludewig, K. 12f
Luhmann, N. 8, 12
Lukoff., D. 150
Lundh, L.G. 96

275

MacCarthy, B. 190
Mackey, M.C. 5, 28
Mager, T. 63ff.
Maier, W. 64
Malm, U. 67
Mandal, M.K. 120
Mandelbrot B.B. 18, 22
Mannens, G. 53
Marder, S.R. 68, 201
Marx, A.J. 169
Maturana, H.R 7, 9 12
Maurer, K. 45
Mayer-Kress, G. 46
McCandless-Glinscher, L. 230
McElroy, S.L. 56
McGlashan, T.H. 94, 212, 231, 262, 264, 266
McKinney, W.T. 262
Meichenbaum, D. 94, 121, 129
Meltzer, H.Y. 52, 57, 64ff., 67ff.
Merlo, M.C.G. 9
Mertens, C. 55
Meyers, A. 94
Miklowitz, D.J. 149ff.
Milner, B. 81
Milton, F. 94
Modai, I. 52
Möller, H.-J. 63ff., 66, 68
Morse, G.A. 173
Morrison, R.L. 118, 138
Mueser, K.T. 81, 113, 138ff., 215, 239
Muijen, M. 173
Müller, H. 63ff.
Müller-Spahn, F. 67
Muzekari, L.H. 120

Nicolis, G. 33
Niemegeers, C.J. 68
Norman, R.M. 229
Novic, J. 120
Nuechterlein, K.H. 5, 87, 89, 118, 147ff., 235, 238
Nyback, H. 52

Olbrich, R. 81, 94, 216
Overall, J.E. 240

Paul, G.L. 109
Parker, G. 189
Penick, E.C. 11
Penn, D.L. 87, 106ff., 115
Perrez, M. 210, 245
Perris, C. 10, 94ff., 228
Peter, K. 94
Petit, M. 67
Pickar, D. 203
Pietzcker, A. 199
Pinder, R.M. 66
Pitschel-Walz, G. 221
Pogue-Geile, M.F. 87
Poirier, M. 269
Pitman, R.K., 120
Pribram, K.H. 119
Prigogine, I. 18
Prosser, E.S. 64

Rapp, P.E. 22
Reed, D. 106ff.
Reiter, L. 3, 7ff.
Retzer, A. 160, 162
Reynolds, G.P. 52
Reynolds, 173
Risberg, J. 266
Roberts, G.W. 264, 266
Roder, V. 121, 123, 228ff.
Ropohl, G. 3
Rosen, R., 39
Rosenfarb, I. 147ff.
Rösler, M. 64
Rössler, O. 35
Rounds, L. 167ff.
Rundt, B.R. 215
Russel, J.A. 120

Safran, J.D. 97
Sandner, M. 122
Sarwer-Foner, G.J. 262ff.
Saupe, R. 210
Scarone, S. 87
Schain, R.J. 58
Scharfetter, C. 45
Schaub, A. 212, 222, 228ff., 234ff., 238, 240

Scheflen, A.E. 4, 23
Scheier, C. 32ff.
Schiepek, G. 5, 6, 25ff., 33, 46
Schmid, G.B. 6, 19, 35
Schneider, H. 120
Schooler, N.R. 55, 196ff.
Schöttner, B. 240
Schuster, H.G. 18
Scott, R.D. 158
Sechehaye, M.A. 262, 266
Sedval, G. 202
Seeman, P. 269
Senn Burke, S. 167ff.
Sharif, Z. 266
Shaw, R.S. 18
Shepherd, G. 190
Simon, F.B. 26,160
Smith, M. 126ff., 241
Smyer, M.A. 181
Sommers, A.A. 64
Soskis, D.a. 231
Spaulding, W.D. 94, 106ff.
Stark, F.M. 209, 216, 231
Steck, H. 24
Stein, L.I. 173ff.
Steiner, E. 12
Steitz, A. 35, 39
Stierlin, H. 158ff.
Stramke, W.G. 94
Strauss, J.S. 32, 45, 64, 141, 170, 213, 252ff.
Sugihara, G. 39, 42
Süllwold, L. 10, 124, 212, 214, 218, 229ff., 234ff., 240, 245
Summerfelt, A.T. 84, 90, 115
Svestka, J. 55

Takens, F. 39
Tarrier, N. 181, 228, 230, 234
Taube, C.A. 173
Terryberry-Spohr, L. 109
Test, M.A. 167ff., 245
Theiler, J. 41
Thomas, R. 26
Thoms, R. 18

Thurm, J. 219, 230
Tong, H. 38
Toomey, R. 113
Torrey, E.F. 169
Tschacher, W. 8ff., 28, 32ff., 41, 44
Turner-Crowson, J. 176

Vanden-Bussche, E. 53
van der Does, A.J.W. 140
Vaughn, C. 148ff.
Virgil, P. 257

Waddington, J.L. 64
Walker, E. 120
Watts, F.N. 94
Weber, G. 162
Weig, W. 216
Weinberger, D.R. 81, 266
Weinstein, M. 223
Weisbrod, B.A. 173, 177
Weizäcker von, V. 9
Welter-Enderlin, R. 4
Wendel, H.J. 8
Whisman, M.A. 245
Whitaker, P.M. 52
White, M. 164
Wiedl, K.H. 209ff., 213ff., 220, 224, 229ff., 234ff., 240
Wiesel, F.A. 272
Wilkinson, L. 42
Willi, J. 10
Wing, J.K. 23, 64, 140, 167
Wolf, A. 42
Wolkin, A. 203
Woo, S.M. 147ff.
Wood, P.L. 52
Wright, D.G. 262, 267
Wynne, L.C. 262

Yank, G.R. 209, 224

Zehnder, D. 130
Zinner, H.J. 64
Zipursky, R.B. 266
Zubin, J. 87, 96, 213, 229

Subject Index

aetiology 106
affect
  benign 142
  logic 28, 38
  negative 142
  neutral 142
  perception 143
affective style (AS) 150ff.
affect-logical systems 12
agents
  antipsychotic 53, 63
  serotonergic 56
  parkinsonian 55
agonist, direct 52
allopoietic 8
ambivalence 164
antagonist, serotonin-dopamine 58
anti
  cholinergics 65
  cholinergic side-effects 57
  dopaminergic 52
  psychotic 53
  serotonergic 56
anxiety 141ff.
approach
  chaos-theoretical 18ff.
  contingency-management-based 108
  coping-orientated treatment 231
  cross-sectional research 45
  molar 94
  molecular 94
attractor 20, 22, 24, 34, 46
  Lorenz 21
  point 21
  Rössler 21
autopoiesis 8, 10ff., 13
autopoietic systems 7
avoidance 141

Bénard instability 19
benefit-cost analysis 173
bifurcation 5, 20, 24, 34
bio-psycho-social treatment 168
butterfly effect 20, 24

chaos 13, 32, 46
  control 46
  deterministic 20, 22
  theoretical approach 18ff.
  theory 3, 19, 22ff., 28, 107
chaotic
  deterministic systems 42
  states 24
clozapine 52, 56, 67
cluster analysis 42
COGLAB (computerised
  cognitive/neuropsychosocial test
  battery) 108ff., 111ff.
cognition 9
cognitive
  changes 106ff.
  deficits 79, 94
  disortions 98, 119
  functioning 108, 112ff.
  impairment 106, 140
  indicators 90
  processes 8
  remediation 79ff.
  therapy 79, 94, 102
collaborative empirism 98
competence 5
  social 137
complex systems 18ff., 33, 46
compliance 51, 234
computer
  models 6
  simulation 6, 26

community
  care 167ff.
  treatment 167ff., 175
concepts of
  aetiological 4
  aetiopathogenic 4
  expressed emotion 129
  illness 10, 11, 234
  self 10, 262
  systemic 3ff.
consensuality 8ff., 13
constructivism radical 7ff.
coping 5, 209ff.
  -orientated 11
    programme 216, 238ff.
  intervention 209
    therapy 209ff.
    treatment 228ff.
  illness 212
  model of 210
  research 209, 229
  strategies 230
  stress 212
  stressors
  symptoms 235
  theory 209
  course of
  illness 32ff., 168
  psychotic 42
  rehabilitation 106ff.
cost-benefit analysis 173
cues 120
cybernetically related 4
cybernetics 13, 33
  first-order 5, 12
  second-order 13

D_2-
  blockade 52
  blocker 52
  receptors 202
deficits
  cognitive 79, 94
  social skills 137ff.
deterministic
  chaos 20, 33

factors 5
  chaotic courses 42
determinism
  recursive 8
  structural 3, 8ff., 11
disorder, dynamic 32
disability
  long-term 5
  social 137
dissipative structures 6, 19, 23, 28
dissociation
  diachronous 160ff.
  synchronous 160ff.
dopaminergic activity 52
dopamine
  D_2-receptor 202
  hypothesis 52
  receptor 51ff.
dosage 55, 69, 196
drop-out 200
dynamic(s) 35
  chaotic 37
  classification of 32ff.
  disease 28, 33ff., 44, 46
  disorders 32, 45
  illness 5
  non-linear 18
  psycho 35
  systems 34
dysfunctional self-schema 97

early
  intervention 195ff.
  warning signs 230ff.
ego-defences 262, 264
effect(s)
  direct and indirect drug 68
  sizes 242ff.
  therapeutic latency 203
efficacy 55, 63, 71, 221ff.
  long run 174
  long-term treatment 195ff.
  relapse-preventing 197
  short run 173
emotional
  appraisal 120

information-processing 120
management training 118ff., 122ff.,
  129ff.
processing 118ff., 121
responsiveness 120
employment 171
evaluation of emotional management
  training 123ff.
excommunication 158ff.
expressed emotion (EE) 129
  high 147, 148
expulsion 159
externalisation 164

facilities, outpatient 189
family
  psychoeducational 148
  treatment 147ff.
  work 181ff.
  training network for 190
feasibility 79ff., 90
  clinical 238
  general 197
feedback 22, 24
  negative 5
  positive 5
fluctuation 5, 6, 20
forecasting algorithm 38ff.
functional
  brain state 7
  concept of illness 10ff., 212, 234
  model 7
  self 10, 11
functioning
  cognitive 108, 112ff.
  macro- and microsocial 107, 112ff.
  levels of 10
  social 137

generalisation 80ff., 90, 141
  downward 81
  upward 81
group format
  coping-orientated treatment
    programme 228

healing, process of 252ff.
homeostasis 3, 5, 8, 13, 35
5-HT$_2$ blockade 52
housing 171
humanity 262ff.

illness
  course of 32
  dynamic 5
  management programme 231
  onset of 5
  psychotic 32
indicators, cognitive 90
information processing 9
  disorders 119
  emotional 120
  training 81
integrative
  psychobiological model 7
  treatment 94ff.
interaction, recursive 8
intermittent treatment 200ff.
inter-relatedness 3
intervention 121
  crisis 199
  early pharmacotherapeutic 195ff.
  early neuroleptic 197ff., 203
  recursive 10
IPT (Integrated Psychological Therapy)
  118ff., 228
isolation, social 187

life
  sense of 266
  style 235
long-term
  disability 5
  low dose treatment 196
  treatment 195ff.
Lyapunov exponents 41ff.

markers of episodes 202
medication
  antipsychotic 51ff.
  discontinuation of 195
  reduction of 195

withdrawl of 205
methods of metaplan 216
models
  biosystemic 106
  computer 6
  coping 210, 214
  developmental 106
  disorder 106
  functional 7
  multi-dimensional 5
  integrative psychobiological 7
  psycho-socio-biological 22, 106
  synergetics 6
  systemic 106
  vulnerability-stress 26
molar and molecular approach 94, 95

negative
  feedback 5
  symptoms 51ff., 55, 63ff., 68, 71, 72
neuroleptic(s) 63ff.
  atypical 269
  crisis intervention 199
  early intervention 199
  long-term treatment 199
  treatment 195ff., 199
non-linear 19, 44
  forecasting algorithm 39
  dynamics 18ff.
  time courses 44
non-linearity 32ff.
nonverbal indicators 154

PACT (Programme of Assertive Community Treatment) 167ff.
parkinsonism 57
  syndrome 64
partnership 10
paths of psychoses 32ff.
perception 9, 142
  affect 143
pervasiveness 10
pharmacotherapy 196
placebo 54ff., 65, 195
positive
  feedback 5

symptoms 51ff., 55, 71ff.
predictors of response 202
prevention of relapse 195ff.
processes
  cognitive 8
  healing 252ff.
  interactive 97
  negative feedback 5
  psychotic 32
  self-organisational 5
  structurally organised 3
  transactional 147ff.
prodromal symptoms 196, 199, 201
Programme of Assertive Community
  Treatment (PACT) 167ff.
  coping-orientated 216
  group format coping-orientated
    treatment 228ff.
  illness-management 231
  longitudinal intervention 167
  psychoeducational-orientated 231
  treatment 238
psychopathology, sub-clinical 154ff.
psychosocial
  aspects 190
  interventions 228
  treatment 167
psycho-socio-biological model 22

quality of life 235, 238

recursive
  interactions 8
  intervention 10
  structural coupling 9
rehabilitation 9, 107, 174
  course of 106ff.
  programme 107ff.
relapse 5, 195, 201
  prevention 195ff.
  risk of 244
relatives support groups 187
remediation
  cognitive 79ff.
remission 5
research

cross-sectional approach 45
clinical 51
experience 51
response predictor 202
risk
factor 147ff.
of relapse 244
relatives at 187
Risperidone 51ff., 55ff., 63, 68

schema-focused integrative treatment 94ff.
secure-base 98
self
concept of
esteem 262, 264
help groups 187
instruction 94, 121
organisation 8ff., 13, 19, 33
organisation processes 5
schema 97
sense of 266
serotonergic
anti 56ff.
dysfunction 57
serotonin 52, 56, 58
dopamin antagonist 58
side-effects 196
autonomic 57ff.
anticholinergic 57
cardiovascular 58
extrapyramidal 51, 55, 69
social
competence 137
disability 137
functioning 137
impairments 137
isolation 187
perception 142ff.
problem-solving 140
postmorbid adjustment 5
skills deficits 137ff.
skills training 144, 156
supports 171
systems 12
Soteria Berne 27ff., 38
Span of Apprehesion Test (Span) 87ff.

staffing 172
stress(ful) 5
coping with 212
events 210
management 121, 235
stressors 335ff.
coping with 237
daily 244
illness-related 244
structural
coupling 8, 9
determinism 3, 7ff.
structures dissipative 6, 19, 23
support
groups for relatives 187
social 171
symbols 263
symptoms
basic 230
coping with 235
deficits 65
negative 51ff., 55, 58, 63ff., 66, 68,
71ff., 137
positive 51ff., 55, 58, 68, 71ff.
prodromal 196, 199, 201
synergetics 13
models of 6
systemic 46
concepts 3ff., 13
therapy 6, 158ff.
thinking 13
systems
affect-logical 12
autopoietic 7
chaotic-deterministic 42
complex 18ff., 46
concepts 5
dynamical 32, 34
information processing 9
self-organising 46
theory 4, 7

team, core-services 169
theory
bio-psycho-social 5
chaos 3, 19, 22ff., 24

social systems 12
systems 3, 32
therapeutic
  partnership 8
  relationship 98
  splitting 164
therapy
  cognitive 79, 94
  coping-orientated 209ff.
  family 6
  implications for 3
  pharmaco- 196
  psychoeducational family 148
  relaxation 123
  research 3ff.
  systemic 6, 158ff.
time series analysis 36, 32, 38
training
  emotional management 118ff 122ff.,
    129ff.
  family social skills 156
  indirect 129
  network for family work 190

programmes 9
  self-instructional 94, 121
  social skills 137ff., 144
treatment
  bio-psycho-social 168
  community 167ff.
  continuous 169
  family 147ff.
  group format coping-orientated 228ff.
  long-term 195
  neuroleptic 195
  programme 238
  psychosocial 167
  schema-focused integrative 94ff., 96
  standard 196

vulnerability 5, 96, 106
  biological 171
  indicators 87
  theory 171

WCST (Wisconsin Card Sorting Test)
  81ff., 84ff., 140